PROBLEMS AND INTERVENTIONS IN LITERACY DEVELOPMENT

# NEUROPSYCHOLOGY AND COGNITION

## VOLUME 15

*Series Editor:*

R. Malatesha Joshi, *Oklahoma State University, U.S.A.*

*Advisory Board:*

Alfonso Caramazza, *Harvard University, U.S.A.*
George Hynd, *University of Georgia, U.S.A.*
C.K. Leong, *University of Saskatchewan, Canada*
John Marshall, *University of Oxford, U.K.*
Gabriele Miceli, *Università Cattolica Del Sacro Cuore, Italy*
Loraine Obler, *City University of New York, U.S.A.*
Sandra Witelson, *McMaster University, Canada*


The purpose of the Neuropsychology and Cognition series is to bring out volumes that promote understanding in topics relating brain and behavior. It is intended for use by both clinicians and research scientists in the fields of neuropsychology, cognitive psychology, psycholinguistics, speech and hearing, as well as education. Examples of topics to be covered in the series would relate to memory, language acquisition and breakdown, reading, attention, developing and aging brain. By addressing the theoretical, empirical, and applied aspects of brain-behavior relationships, this series will try to present the information in the fields of neuropsychology and cognition in a coherent manner.

*The titles published in this series are listed at the end of this volume.*

# PROBLEMS AND INTERVENTIONS IN LITERACY DEVELOPMENT

Edited by

P. REITSMA

*Free University Amsterdam, The Netherlands*

and

L. VERHOEVEN

*University of Nijmegen, The Netherlands*

KLUWER ACADEMIC PUBLISHERS
DORDRECHT / BOSTON / LONDON

A C.I.P. Catalogue record for this book is available from the Library of Congress.

ISBN 0-7923-5557-1

Published by Kluwer Academic Publishers,
P.O. Box 17, 3300 AA Dordrecht, The Netherlands.

Sold and distributed in North, Central and South America
by Kluwer Academic Publishers,
101 Philip Drive, Norwell, MA 02061, U.S.A.

In all other countries, sold and distributed
by Kluwer Academic Publishers,
P.O. Box 322, 3300 AH Dordrecht, The Netherlands.

*Printed on acid-free paper*

All Rights Reserved
©1998 Kluwer Academic Publishers
No part of the material protected by this copyright notice may be reproduced or
utilized in any form or by any means, electronic or mechanical,
including photocopying, recording or by any information storage and
retrieval system, without written permission from the copyright owner

Printed in the Netherlands.

# TABLE OF CONTENTS

Preface vii
List of Contributors ix

## Introduction

Problems in literacy acquisition and interventions
  *Pieter Reitsma and Ludo Verhoeven* 3

### Part 1: Literacy development

Two basic questions about reading and learning to read
  *Charles A. Perfetti* 15
General and specific abilities as predictors of reading achievement
  *Peter de Jong and Aryan van der Leij* 49
Preschool oral language competence and literacy development
  *Bente Hagtvet* 63
Phonemically aware in a hop, skip, and a jump
  *Ralph Wesseling and Pieter Reitsma* 81
The Simple View of Reading: A developmental perspective
  *Janwillem Bast and Pieter Reitsma* 95

### Part 2: Problems in literacy development

Language processing and schooling in European Portugese
  *Inês Gomez and São Luís Castro* 113
Reading-listening discrepancy definitions of dyslexia
  *Carsten Elbro* 129
Phonological skills and literacy acquisition in German
  *Heinz Mayringer, Heinz Wimmer, and Karin Landerl* 147
Methods to establish subtypes of developmental dyslexia
  *Nathalie Genard, Philippe Mousty, Alain Content,*
  *Jesus Alegria, Jacqueline Leybaert, and José Morais* 163
Problems in text comprehension: Current perspectives and
  recent research
  *Jane Oakhill and Kate Cain* 177

Reading comprehension problems in second language learners
*Mienke Droop and Ludo Verhoeven* — 193

## Part 3: Training metalinguistic awareness

Fostering metalinguistic awareness during storybook reading
*Leena Laurinen* — 211

Training of phonological awareness and letter knowledge in children-at-risk
*Ellen Roth and Wolfgang Schneider* — 225

Training of phonological awareness vs inductive reasoning in kindergarten
*Petra Kuespert and Wolfgang Schneider* — 241

The effects of a Flash Card training program on normal and poor readers' phonological decoding skills
*Hanneke Wentink, Inge Drent, Wim van Bon, and Robert Schreuder* — 257

Teaching morphological awareness to dyslexic students
*Elisabeth Arnbak and Carsten Elbro* — 277

## Part 4: Interventions at the word level and beyond

Reading disabilities and cognitive competence
*Aryan van der Leij* — 293

The ecology of spelling instruction: Effective training in first grade
*Martin van Leerdam, Anna Bosman, and Guy van Orden* — 307

Effects of reading and spelling practices on reading skill
*Monique Coenen, Wim van Bon, and Robert Schreuder* — 321

Promoting reading skills in a computer-based training program
*Elisa Poskiparta, Marja Vauras, and Pekka Niemi* — 335

Helping students become constructively responsive readers
*Peter Afflerbach* — 349

Author Index — 363

Subject Index — 371

# PREFACE

From August 19-23 1996 an international expert meeting on problems and interventions in literacy development took place in Amsterdam. The meeting was organized by Pieter Reitsma (Paedologisch Instituut – Vrije Universiteit Amsterdam) and Ludo Verhoeven (University of Nijmegen), and funded by the Dutch National Science Foundation. Various experts in the field of literacy problems from 12 countries attended the meeting while presenting a paper based on current perspectives and recent research. A selection of the papers being presented is now integrated into a single academic reference, after being edited and updated. The editors wish to thank all contributors to this volume for redrafting their original papers.

The present volume aims to integrate recent research in field of literacy problems and interventions into a single academic reference. The volume will capture the state of the art in the rapidly expanding field of literacy problems and interventions. The target group of readers of this volume includes researchers and graduate students in language and literacy development. Moreover, the book is of interest for practitioners working in the field of literacy problems.

Pieter Reitsma and Ludo Verhoeven

# LIST OF CONTRIBUTORS

Peter Afflerbach – University of Maryland, 2304C Benjamin Building, College Park MD 20742, USA
Jesus Alegria – Université Libre de Bruxelles, LAPSE CP 191, Avenue F. Roosevelt 50, B-1050 Bruxelles, Belgium
Elisabeth Arnbak – Department of General & Applied Linguistics, Njalsgade 80, DK-2300 Copenhagen, Denmark
Janwillem Bast – Paedologisch Instituut–VU Amsterdam, Postbus 303, 1115 ZG Duivendrecht, The Netherlands.
Wim van Bon – Department of Special Education KUN, Postbus 9104, 6500 HE Nijmegen, The Netherlands
Anna Bosman - Department of Special Education KUN, Postbus 9104, 6500 HE Nijmegen, The Netherlands
São Luís Castro – Faculdade de Psicologia e de Ciências da Educação, Universidade do Porto, Rua do Campo Alegre 1055, P-4150 Porto, Portugal
Kate Cain – Department of Experimental Psychology - University of Sussex, Biology Building, Brighton BN1 9QG, United Kingdom
Monique Coenen – Department of Special Education KUN, Postbus 9104, 6500 HE Nijmegen, The Netherlands
Alain Content – Université Libre de Bruxelles, LAPSE CP 191, Ave F. Roosevelt 50, B-1050 Bruxelles, Belgium
Inge Drent – Department of Special Education KUN, Postbus 9104, 6500 HE Nijmegen, The Netherlands
Mienke Droop – Department of Special Education KUN, Postbus 9104, 6500 HE Nijmegen, The Netherlands
Carsten Elbro – Department of General & Applied Linguistics, Njalsgade 80, DK-2300 Copenhagen, Denmark
Nathalie Genard – Université Libre de Bruxelles, LAPSE CP 191, Avenue F. Roosevelt 50, B-1050 Bruxelles, Belgium
Inês Gomez – Faculdade de Psicologia e de Ciências da Educação, Universidade do Porto, Rua do Campo Alegre 1055, P-4150 Porto, Portugal
Bente Hagtvet – Department of Special Education - University of Oslo, Boks 1170, Blindern, Oslo 3, Norway
Peter de Jong – Department of Education - Vrije Universiteit, Van der Boechorststraat 1, 1081 BT Amsterdam, The Netherlands
Petra Kuespert – Institut für Psychologie, Universität Würzburg, Wittelsbacherplatz 1, 97074 Würzburg, Germany

# LIST OF CONTRIBUTORS

Karin Landerl – Institut für Psychologie, Universität Salzburg, Hellbrunnerstrasse 34, A-5020 Salzbrug, Austria
Leena Laurinen – Nissilanpiha I C , Fin - 04250 KERAVA, Finland
Martin van Leerdam – Department of Psychology, University of Amsterdam, Roeterstraat 15, 1018 WB Amsterdam, The Netherlands
Aryan van der Leij – Department of Education–Vrije Universiteit, Van der Boechorststraat 1, 1081 BT Amsterdam, The Netherlands
Jacqueline Leybaert – Université Libre de Bruxelles, LAPSE CP 191, Avenue F. Roosevelt 50, B-1050 Bruxelles, Belgium
Heinz Mayringer – Institut für Psychologie, Universität Salzburg, Hellbrunnerstrasse 34, A-5020 Salzburg, Austria
José Morais – Université Libre de Bruxelles, LAPSE CP 191, Avenue F. Roosevelt 50, B-1050 Bruxelles, Belgium
Philippe Mousty – Université Libre de Bruxelles, LAPSE CP 191, Avenue F. Roosevelt 50, B-1050 Bruxelles, Belgium
Pekka Niemi –Abo Akademi, Department of Psychology, Nunneg 5, FIN-20500 Turku, Finland
Jane Oakhill – Department of Experimental Psychology - University of Sussex, Biology Building, Brighton BN1 9QG, United Kingdom
Guy van Orden – Cognitive Systems Group, Department of Psychology, Arizona State University, USA
Charles A Perfetti – LRDC - University of Pittsburgh, 3939 O'Hara Street, Pittsburgh PA 15260, USA
Elisa Poskiparta – Center for Learning Research, Lemminkäisenkatu 1h-18b, 20520 Turku, Finland
Pieter Reitsma – Paedologisch Instituut–Vrije Universiteit Amsterdam, Postbus 303, 1115 ZG Duivendrecht, The Netherlands.
Ellen Roth – Kinder- und Jugendpsychiatrie, Füchsleinstr. 15, 97080 Würzburg, Germany
Wolfgang Schneider – Institut für Psychologie, Universität Würzburg, Wittelsbacherplatz 1, 97074 Würzburg, Germany
Robert Schreuder – Department of Special Education KUN, Postbus 9104, 6500 HE Nijmegen, The Netherlands
Marja Vauras – Center for Learning Research, University of Turku, Turku FIN 20014, Finland
Ludo Verhoeven – Department of Special Education KUN, Postbus 9104, 6500 HE Nijmegen, The Netherlands
Hanneke Wentink – Department of Special Education KUN, Postbus 9104, 6500 HE Nijmegen, The Netherlands
Ralph Wesseling – Paedologisch Instituut–Vrije Universiteit, Postbus 303, 1115 ZG Duivendrecht, The Netherlands.
Heinz Wimmer – Institut für Psychologie, Universität Salzburg, Hellbrunnerstrasse 34, A-5020 Salzburg, Austria

# INTRODUCTION

PIETER REITSMA AND LUDO VERHOEVEN

# PROBLEMS IN LITERACY ACQUISITION AND INTERVENTIONS

Literacy acquisition involves learning how language is encoded in a writing system and learning the orthographic rules that relate graphic units to linguistic units. In learning to read the child must learn to decode language forms from written forms. In learning to spell the learning task is the encoding of linguistic forms into written forms. In varying theoretical perspectives, such as Dual Route and Parallel Distributed Processing, word recognition is considered as the critical component of the reading process. For the process of reading, syntactic parsing and background knowledge can be seen as other important components saturating central processes of global interpretation, inference tracking, and comprehension monitoring (see e.g., Balota, Flores D'Arcais, & Rayner, 1990). Acquisition of literacy, however, is not a natural developmental process, and specific home, cultural, and schooling conditions are required. But even when these conditions are accommodated, some children still have serious and sometimes unexpected problems in attaining fluent literacy skills. Why?

## PROBLEMS IN LITERACY ACQUISITION

First of all, literacy problems can be associated with the cognitive capacity of learners. In past research, much emphasis has been placed on definitional issues with regard to dyslexia and on the methodology of testing multifactor theories of dyslexia. An important issue with regard to definitions has been the merit of exclusionary criteria, i.e., dyslexia as a 'surprising' impairment in reading and spelling development that cannot be attributed to obvious causes (neurological damage, sensory handicaps, low IQ, etc.). However, many causes have proven to be less obvious than expected (see e.g., Elbro, this volume, for a discussion of IQ as an exclusionary criterion). Another approach is to hypothesize dyslexia as a 'syndrome'. In line with this proposal cognitive-developmental models have been introduced, synthesizing language and cognitive development, and defining a dyslexic person as potentially having multiple deficits that may change over time. In recent years, however, many researchers have focused on the interaction of development of literacy and phonological skills (e.g., Bryant, MacLean, Bradley, & Crossland, 1990; Cataldo & Ellis, 1988; Holligan & Johnston, 1991). There is now convincing evidence that phonological skills, such as rhyming and analysis of words into syllables can develop in the absence of literacy instruction. However, the analysis of words into smaller phonetic segments appears to require the experience of (alphabetic) reading instruction.

Much research evidence is available to suggest that many problems in acquiring literacy skills are related to a phonological deficit (Blachman, 1997). It is hypothesized that high quality phonological representations are mentally present in normal children, but not in the phenotypically dyslexic child. In order to test such hypotheses there is an urgent need for prospective studies in which the development of children born with significant risk for dyslexia and a matched control group are followed. In order to be successful such longitudinal studies should start soon after birth and continue until age 10, since dyslexia cannot reliably be diagnosed before age 10. An early attempt of a prospective study in the field of dyslexia research is the work of Gjessing and Karlsen (1989). They presented a comprehensive description of a ten-year longitudinal study of dyslexic children in the city of Bergen (Norway). With regard to the issue of the phonological deficit hypothesis important studies recently appear. For example, Elbro, Borstrøm and Petersen (1998) made an attempt to predict dyslexia from phonological processing abilities of kindergartners. Children from dyslexic parents were followed in a longitudinal study from kindergarten through to second grade. The results showed that the quality of phonological representations in the child's mental lexicon can be seen as the essential determinant of the development of both phonemic awareness and phonological recoding in reading. In Finland a prospective longitudinal study involving 80 children born with a genetic risk for dyslexia and a matched control group of equal size has recently started (see Lyytinen, Ahonen, Leiwo, & Gilger, 1994). The first data in this project showed that the phonological deficit of impaired readers is phonetic in origin. The children at risk for dyslexia had difficulties in discriminating speech sounds that are phonetically quite similar but phonologically contrastive.

In addition to characteristics of the child, literacy problems can also be related to children's social and economic background. Recent research on the home environments of young children has revealed significant limitations in some children's preschool exposure to functional reading and writing materials and activities. Also, limitations in experiences with print and the decontextualized forms of talk often associated with children's storybooks, shared or interactive book reading may well be a disadvantage to children's preparedness for formal instruction once they begin school. Wells (1990) has shown that a match between linguistic experience in children's home and the linguistic demands in the classroom is essential for academic progress.

He found that the degree of experience with literate practices in the home had a positive influence on the understanding of the functions and the mechanisms of literacy. In a longitudinal study by Snow, Barnes, Chandler, Goodman, and Hemphill (1991) on the literacy development of lower socio-economic children it was shown that different home factors predict various literacy skills. The most powerful predictors of children's word recognition and vocabulary development were the literacy environment of the home, the mother's education and the mother's expectations for the child. Variables relating to the emotional organizational dimensions of the family strongly predicted the children's writing skills. Reading comprehension was related to a wide range of home variables. Finally, frequent contacts between parents and teachers regarding academic matters turned out to be related with improved schoolwork and progress in reading.

One of the defining characteristics of serious problems in literacy acquisition is the persistence of problems. The responsiveness to treatment seems to be an important consideration in the diagnosis of dyslexia. Despite favourable circumstances, regular instruction at school, or even appropriate remediation, some children seem to be "resistant" to treatment. But, of course, the question then is what constitutes appropriate treatment?

## INTERVENTIONS

In recent research projects on the learning and teaching of literacy in industrialized societies the interrelationship of various language modes has been acknowledged. Detailed analyses of literacy environments highlighted the importance of early encounters with print in the home (e.g., Snow et al., 1991; Weinberger, Hannon, & Nutbrown, 1990). A number of programs have demonstrated positive influences on young children's literacy socialization by focussing on home environments as part of their early intervention efforts (e.g., McCormick & Mason, 1986; Rubert, 1994; Valdez-Menchacha & Whitehurst, 1992). Thus, it seems that conditions that strengthen the relevance and purpose of literacy for learners are quite important for the development of literacy. The development of a broad literacy curriculum in which language experiences are highly emphasized is therefore often promoted (Clay, 1991). Though in many publications a language experience approach to literacy acquisition is promoted, it is generally accepted that a naturalistic model which relies exclusively on exposure and immersion does not fully justify the complex task of learning to read and write. Iversen and Tunmer (1993), for example, found that the addition of explicit code instruction is a significant and beneficial component in such programs. Accumulated research evidence indicates that, especially in a more advanced stage, children need sequentially structured activities that are mediated by a teacher, by skilled peers, or with assistance of a well-designed computer program in order to acquire automaticity in (de)coding and appropriate strategies for reading and writing (Adams, 1990; Oakhill & Garnham, 1988; Rayner & Pollatsek, 1989; Reitsma & Wesseling, 1998; Verhoeven, 1996).

An important question is how the remediation of dyslexia can be dealt with. Dyslexic children turn out to be subject to verbal naming difficulties which cannot be accounted for by generally low levels of vocabulary knowledge, but rather by difficulties with the lexical-phonological representation of spoken words they know (Snowling & Hulme, 1989; Elbro, 1995). Given the fact that an important core of the dyslexic problem can be seen as a phonological processing deficit, it can be expected that the age level of 3–4 years is an extremely important stage in the emergence of precursors of later reading development. Several studies provided evidence that a training program for kindergartners, consisting of metalinguistic games and exercises, affects the development of metalinguistic skills (see Lundberg, Frost & Peterson, 1988; Lundberg, 1994). Subsequent literacy interventions have a lot of common ground (McGuinness, 1997; Olson & Wise, 1992; Reitsma & Wesseling, 1998; Snowling, 1996). The primary focus is on the phoneme as the basic unit for teaching the writing system. In a more advanced stage syllables, morphemes, and spelling units can be additional units of focus. Along with an analysis of the writing system, there is a need for comprehensive training in phoneme awareness, phoneme segmentation and blending (Hatcher, Hulme & Ellis, 1994).

Also, there is empirical evidence of positive findings of programs that specifically focus on the acquisition of word recognition at the single word level (cf. Lovett, Borden, DeLuca, Lacerenza, Benson, & Brackstone, 1994). Furthermore, positive effects were shown for the use of speech feedback. For moderately disabled readers speech feedback was most successful if segmentation is at the onset-rime boundary, while for severely retarded readers feedback of larger units was more effective (Elbro, Rasmussen, & Spelling, 1996; Olson & Wise, 1992; Van Daal & Reitsma, 1993; Wise, Olson, & Treiman, 1990). By keeping track of the child's cognitive development the complexity of the code breaking activities can be managed through carefully sequenced lessons. Much time should be allotted to automatization of the decoding process (Nicholson & Fawcett, 1990). In general, increasing the length and complexity of the interventions can have a positive influence on reducing the number of children resistant to treatment. But the agenda for future research should include the specification of characteristics of children that make good progress in intervention studies and of those that are the most difficult to remediate.

## THE PRESENT VOLUME

The present volume aims to integrate recent research in the field of literacy problems and interventions into a single academic reference. Given the fact that the topic of literacy problems has gained so much attention in past and ongoing research the volume will capture the state of the art in this rapidly expanding field. The focus of the entire volume will be both on processes at the intra-word level and at the text level.

The volume further consists of four parts. Part 1 goes into the course of literacy development. Charles Perfetti opens this section by addressing two questions. "What does it mean to read a word?" and "What does it mean to learn a word?" In addressing these questions he makes an attempt to delineate the universal properties of reading and learning to read and to specify the constraints imposed by writing systems and orthographies. In the next chapter, Peter de Jong and Aryan van der Leij report on a longitudinal study on the effects of phonological skills in kindergarten on word decoding at the end of the first grade. Specificity of the phonological effects was further examined by contrasting the effects of phonological skills on word decoding to their effect on reading comprehension. Children from various ethnic groups were included in their study. In the following chapter, Bente Hagtvet reports on an empirical study focusing on the relation between preschool oral language abilities and later written language development. The relative contribution of phonological, syntactic and semantic abilities at age 6 to reading difficulties at ages 8 and 9 were examined. Moreover, a comparison was made between the linguistic precursors of early reading and later poor readers. In the subsequent chapter, Ralph Wesseling and Pieter Reitsma report on a study in which changes in phonological sensitivity in Dutch children at kindergarten and grade 1 were monitored. Three phonological tasks were administered: phoneme blending, phoneme segmentation, and phoneme deletion. Their results strongly suggest that schooling and especially formal instruction in reading is a major influence on the development of phonological skills. In the final chapter of Part 2, Janwillem Bast and Pieter Reitsma test the simple view of reading, claiming that only two components, word recognition and language comprehension, are necessary for reading success. In a longitudinal study they contrasted the product of decoding and listening comprehension with an additive model. Moreover, the effect of developmental aspects were included in their model. Although decoding and listening comprehension were found to be important predictors of reading comprehension, they could not be seen as the only reading components.

Part 2 focuses on the causes of literacy problems. Inês Gomes and São Luís Castro open this part with a chapter on the diagnosis of language processing and schooling in European Portuguese. They observed language and literacy data in children and adults, and found that schooling affects low level components of language processing. Higher level abilities, such as sentence repetition and pointing span tasks were not directly related to schooling. In the next chapter, Carsten Elbro goes into reading-listening discrepancy definitions of dyslexia. He compared decoding abilities and receptive vocabulary of adults with and without a history of difficulties in learning to read and found that listening comprehension does not appear to improve the validity of a dyslexia definition based upon poor phonological recoding. Heinz Mayringer, Karin Landerl and Heinz Wimmer report in the next chapter, on the relationship between (relatively easy) phonological skills and literacy development in German. They found low correlations between phonological measures and criterion variables. Phonological predictors explained only a minor proportion of reading and spelling variance. In the following chapter, Nathalie Genard, Philippe Mousty, Alain Content, Jesus Alegria, Jacqueline Leybaert, and José Morais make an attempt to find methods to establish subtypes of developmental dyslexia. They found evidence for a relatively pure form of dyslexia with impaired pseudoword reading along with normal irregular word reading performance. However, most dyslexics were impaired on both measures. Moreover, a relatively small proportion of phonological dyslexics was reported on, which might be associated with the greater transparency of French orthography in comparison with English. In the subsequent chapter, Jane Oakhill and Kate Cain examine current perspectives on problems in text comprehension. They review research carried out on inference skills, ability to understand story grammar, and monitoring comprehension problems. They also consider possible underlying causes of comprehension difficulties with a focus on working memory. In the final chapter of this part, Mienke Droop and Ludo Verhoeven focus on reading comprehension problems in second language learners. They investigate differences in reading comprehension between Dutch children and minority children learning to read in their second language. An attempt is made to uncover the relation between children's linguistic knowledge and their reading comprehension development. It was found that lexical knowledge, and to a lesser degree morpho-syntactic knowledge, were stronger determinants of second language reading as compared with first language reading.

In Part 3 the training of metalinguistic awareness is dealt with. In the opening chapter of this part, Leena Laurinen explores the impact of storybook reading on the development of metalinguistic awareness. Using a longitudinal design, the storybook reading interaction of three Finnish children in private day-care was described and subsequently evaluated. In the next chapter, Ellen Roth and Wolfgang Schneider report on the effects of a training of phonological awareness and letter knowledge of children at risk in kindergarten on later literacy acquisition. They found maximum training effects by using a combined intervention program emphasizing the integration of phonological awareness and letter-sound correspondences. In the following chapter, Petra Kuespert and Wolfgang Schneider compare the effects of training phonological awareness and training inductive reasoning in kindergarten on later literacy development. They found significant training effects for phonological awareness and subsequent reading and writing. Similar effects could not be demonstrated by the inductive reasoning program. In the next chapter, Hanneke Wentink, Inge Drent, Wim van Bon and Rob Schreuder evaluate the effects of a flash-card, computer-based training program on normal and poor readers' phonological decoding skills. The children were trained in reading aloud multisyllabic pseudowords. The results showed that the normal readers improved in decoding speed during the training, while decoding speed in the poor readers remained unchanged. Grapheme and syllable effects in the orthographic structures were evidenced in both groups. In the final chapter of Part 3, Elisabeth Arnbak and Carsten Elbro report on the effects of training morphological awareness in dyslexic students. Moreover, the effects of morphological awareness on reading and spelling complex words and on reading comprehension were examined. A small, but positive training effect was found on one of the three morphological awareness measures. There was no gain in word decoding and a minor gain in reading comprehension on the part of the experimental training group.

Part 4 discusses possible interventions for children with literacy problems at the word level and beyond. In the opening chapter, Aryan van der Leij reviews research on reading disabilities in relation to children's cognitive competence. He criticizes the exclusionary definition of dyslexia, allowing for a specific cause with no involvement of general factors. Data are presented to test the hypothesis that the reading deficit of students of varying intellectual abilities is highly comparable. In addition, Martin van Leerdam, Anna Bosman and Guy van Orden review what contributes to effective spelling instruction. They describe an empirical study illustrating different outcomes of several instruction methods. Visual dictation appears to be the most effective training. It includes practicing the whole word from memory, with immediate feedback and kinematics supporting the learning process. The results are discussed in the light of dynamic systems theory. In the following chapter, Monique Coenen, Wim van Bon and Rob Schreuder discuss the effect of reading and spelling practice on reading skill. In an empirical study it is examined whether training in phonological encoding improves phonological decoding skill. The results showed that spelling practice increased the naming speed of practiced words as much as reading practice did. The accuracy results suggested that lexical representations that are constructed during reading are more useful for reading than representations that are constructed during spelling. In the prefinal chapter, Elisa Poskiparta, Marja Vauras, and Pekka Niemi compare the effects of a computer-based program using synthetic speech feedback with traditional word recognition training. The computer-based program turned out to have beneficial effects on children's word recognition and word spelling skills. However, the two teaching methods were equally ineffective in promoting reading comprehension. In the final chapter, Peter Afflerbach presents a conceptual framework in order to help students to become constructively responsive readers. The engagement perspective is followed viewing readers as knowledgeable, motivated, strategic, and socially interactive. Constructively responsive readers understand the varied purposes of reading, negotiate the construction of meaning in relation to the social setting, collaborate with classmates in literate work, and appreciate the uses of teamwork.

## REFERENCES

Adams, M. J. (1990). *Beginning to read: Thinking and learning about print.* Cambridge, MA: MIT Press.
Balota, D. A., Flores D'Arcais, G. B., & Rayner, K. (Eds). (1990). *Comprehension processes in reading.* Hillsdale, NJ: Erlbaum.
Blachman, B. A. (Ed.). (1997). *Foundations of reading acquisition and dyslexia.* Mahwah, NJ.: Erlbaum.
Bryant, P. E., MacLean, M., Bradley, L. L., & Crossland, J. (1990). Rhyme and alliteration, phoneme detection, and learning to read. *Developmental Psychology, 26,* 429–438.
Cataldo, S., & Ellis, N. (1988). Interactions in the development of spelling. *Journal of Research in Reading, 11,* 86–109.
Clay, M. M. (1991). *Becoming literate: The construction of inner control.* Portsmouth, NH: Heinemann.
Elbro, C. (1995). Early linguistic abilities and reading development. *Reading and Writing, 8,* 257–276.
Elbro, C., Borstrøm, I., & Petersen, D. K. (1998). Predicting dyslexia from kindergarten. The importance of distinctness of phonological representations of lexical items. *Reading Research Quarterly, 33,* 36–60.

Elbro, C., Rasmussen, I., & Spelling, B. (1996). Teaching reading to disabled readers with language disorders: A controlled evaluation of synthetic speech feedback. *Scandinavian Journal of Psychology, 37*, 140-155.

Gjessing, H., & Karlsen, B. (1989). *A longitudinal study of dyslexia.* New York: Springer Verlag.

Hatcher, P. J., Hulme, C., & Ellis, A. W. (1994). Ameliorating early reading failure by integrating the teaching of reading and phonological skills: the phonological linkage hypothesis. *Child Development, 65*, 41-57.

Holligan, C., & Johnston, R. S. (1991). Spelling errors and phonemic segmentation ability: The nature of the relationship. *Journal of Research in Reading, 14*, 21-32.

Iversen, S., & Tunmer, W. E. (1993). Phonological processing skills and the Reading Recovery program. *Journal of Educational Psychology, 85*, 112-126.

Lovett, M. W., Borden, S. L., DeLuca, T., Lacerenza, L., Benson, N. J., & Brackstone, D. (1994). Treating the core deficits of developmental dyslexia. *Developmental Psychology, 30*, 805-822.

Lundberg, I. (1994). Reading difficulties can be predicted and prevented. A Scandinavian perspective on phonological awareness and reading. In C. Hulme & M. Snowling (Eds.), *Reading development and dyslexia* (pp. 180-199). London: Whurr.

Lundberg, I., Frost, J., & Petersen, O. P. (1988). Effects of an extensive program for stimulating phonological awareness in preschool children. *Reading Research Quarterly, 23*, 263-284.

Lyytinen, H., Ahonen, T., Leiwo, M., & Gilger, J. (1994). In search for the precursors of dyslexia. *NMI-Bulletin, 2*, 12-19.

McCormick, C., & Mason, J. (1986). Intervention procedures for increasing preschool children's interest in and knowledge about reading. In W. Teale & E. Sulzby (Eds.), *Emergent literacy: writing and reading* (pp. 90-115). Norwood, NJ.: Ablex Publishers.

McGuinness, D. (1997). *Why our children can't read.* New York: Free Press.

Nicholson, R. I., & Fawcett, A. J. (1990). Automaticity: A new framework for dyslexia research? *Cognition, 35*, 159-182.

Oakhill, J. V., & Garnham, A. (1988). *Becoming a skilled reader.* Oxford: Basil Blackwell.

Olson, R. K., & Wise, B. W. (1992). Reading on the computer with orthographic and speech feedback. *Reading and Writing, 4*, 107-144.

Perfetti, C. A. (1985). *Reading ability.* Oxford: University Press.

Rayner, K., & Pollatsek, A. (1989). *The psychology of reading.* Englewood Cliffs, NJ: Prentice Hall.

Reitsma, P., & Wesseling, R. (1998). The effect of computer-assisted training of blending skills in kindergarten children. *Scientific Studies of Reading, 2*, 301-320.

Rubert, H. (1994). The impact of a parent involvement program designed to support a first-grade reading intervention program. In C. K. Kinzer & D. J. Leu (Eds.), *Multidimensional Aspects of Literacy Research, Theory and Practice* (pp. 230-239). Chicago: NRC.

Snow, C. E., Barnes, W., Chandler, J., Goodman, I., & Hemphill, L. (1991). *Unfulfilled expectations: Home and school influences on literacy.* Boston: Harvard University Press.

Snowling, M. J. (1996). Annotation: Contemporary approaches to the teaching of reading. *Journal of Child Psychology, 37*, 139-148.

Snowling, M. J. & Hulme, C. (1989). A longitudinal case study of developmental phonological dyslexia. *Cognitive Neuropsychology, 6,* 379–401.

Valdez-Menchacha, M., & Whitehurst, G. (1992). Accelerating language development through picture-book reading: A systematic extension to Mexican day-care. *Developmental Psychology, 28,* 1106–1114.

Van Daal, V. H. P., & Reitsma, P. (1993). The use of speech feedback by normal and disabled readers in computer-based reading practice. *Reading and Writing, 5,* 243–259.

Verhoeven, L. (1996). Language in education. In F. Coulmas (Ed.), *Handbook of Sociolinguistics* (pp. 389–404). London: Basil Blackwell.

Weinberger, J., Hannon, P., & Nutbrown, C. (1990). *Ways of working with parents to promote early literacy development.* University of Sheffield: Educational Research Centre.

Wells, G. (1990). Talk about text: Where literacy is learned and taught. *Curriculum Inquiry, 20,* 369–405.

Wise, B. W., Olson, R. K., & Treiman, R. (1990). Sub-syllabic units as aids in beginning readers' word learning: onset-rime versus post-vowel segmentation. *Journal of Experimental Child Psychology, 49,* 1–19.

# PART 1

# LITERACY DEVELOPMENT

CHARLES A. PERFETTI

# TWO BASIC QUESTIONS ABOUT READING AND LEARNING TO READ

I address two seductively simple questions. The first is "What does it mean to read a word?" This simple identification question is a scientific one about which research has had much to say. But it remains a tricky question with multiple answers, and the answer chosen provides a path of theoretical and methodological sequelae.

My second question is "What does it mean to learn to read?" Unlike the first question, one senses that this question may have nonscientific as well as scientific components. It certainly has evoked a wide range of answers. In the United States, for example, many reading educators take a very broad view of reading that includes a range of literacy activities and begins with comprehension. The decision to define learning to read in this way or that way is usually associated with some broader purpose and often seems to be a compromise between the narrowest and the broadest possibilities.

In addressing both questions, some attention to the nature of writing systems and orthographies is required. Reading (and spelling) occur in the context of a specific language, writing system, orthography, and script. I take as the overall goal of a theory of reading and learning to read to delineate the universal properties of reading and to specify the constraints imposed by writing systems and orthographies. In what follows I discuss the two simple questions about reading, in order, from this perspective.

## TO READ A WORD IS TO IDENTIFY IT

Research on word reading has advanced over the last 10 years, fueled partly by theoretical debates, especially the merits of Dual Route (Besner, in press; 1990; Coltheart, Curtis, Atkins, & Haller, 1993; Paap & Noel, 1991) vs. PDP models (Plaut, McClelland, Seidenberg, & Patterson, 1996; Seidenberg & McClelland, 1989) in accounting for word and nonword reading. Also, a recent model places linguistic representations in a more central position (Berent & Perfetti, 1995), independent of the architecture of cognition issues. These models provide highly general frameworks that accommodate writing system differences, without directly addressing them. Although the research base for these models was based on English, more recent work has extended to other languages and orthographies, including several alphabetically encoded European languages (e.g., Dutch, French,

German, Italian, and Serbo-Croatian), Hebrew (Frost, 1995; Frost, Katz, & Bentin, 1987; Shimron, 1993), Persian (Baluch & Besner, 1991), Japanese (Wydell et al, 1993; Flores D'Arcais, Saito, & Kawakami, 1995; Leong & Tamaoka, 1995) and Korean (Simpson & Kang, 1994). Our studies in Chinese, along with those of others (e.g., Leck, Weekes, & Chen, 1995; Tan & Peng, 1991; Zhang, Feng, & He, 1994) have produced data on the writing system that provides maximal contrast with alphabetic systems.

*Writing systems and reading*

Writing systems vary in how they represent the languages they encode, and several views have emerged on how this matters for reading. The *Universal Direct Access Hypothesis* (Baluch & Besner, 1991) is that word reading occurs by a visual route in all writing systems and orthographies, with phonology used only when required by individual reader and word characteristics (Baluch & Besner, 1991; Sebastian-Galles, 1991; Tabossi & Laghi, 1992). The *Orthographic Depth Hypothesis* is that the use of phonology is determined by properties of the orthography (Frost, 1994; Frost et al., 1987). The *Universal Phonological Principle (UPP)* states that encounters with printed words activate multiple levels of phonology in all writing systems, which control only the details of activation (Perfetti, Zhang, & Berent, 1992; Perfetti & Zhang, 1995b). The Orthographic Depth Hypothesis and the Universal Direct Access Hypothesis contrast in how writing systems constrain reading, but they both seem to predict that reading Chinese can be a graphic form-to-meaning process, in which phonology is by-passed.

The UPP, while generally compatible with the Orthographic Depth Hypothesis, emphasizes a different aspect: The partial dependency of writing systems on spoken language, even when they have a semantic-morphological component (DeFrancis, 1989; Mattingly, 1992), and a human preference for speech coding suggest that reading is a phonology plus meaning process in all writing systems. This leads to the important and very basic hypothesis that reading a word universally brings about the retrieval of phonological and semantic constituents in specific relation to an orthographic constituent.

*The constituency principle*

According to the Constituency Principle, regardless of whether phonology intervenes (mediates) between visual form and meaning, it is an essential *constituent* of identification (Perfetti & Zhang, 1995b; Perfetti & Tan, 1998). This Constituency Principle assumes that interconnected lexical components--graphic form, phonological form, and meaning--are made available during word reading. The word representation system ordinarily provides these components in strongly interconnected form. An acquisition corollary to this principle is that reading skill develops from poorly interconnected to highly interconnected lexical components (Ehri, 1980; Perfetti, 1992).

The central claim is that word identification consists in making available a familiar phonological form connected to an orthographic form. If this claim seems tepid, compare it with the more standard view of lexical "access", which usually refers to access of meanings as the defining event of word recognition. To suggest that a phonological output is a defining part of the event of word reading is to place meaning access in a secondary role instead of the primary role, reversing the usual priority. In the "lexical access" approach to reading, meaning is primary and the processing question is whether or under what conditions nonsemantic information might be involved. Thus we have the classic question of whether lexical access is mediated by phonology or whether phonological information is activated "post-lexically" or not at all.

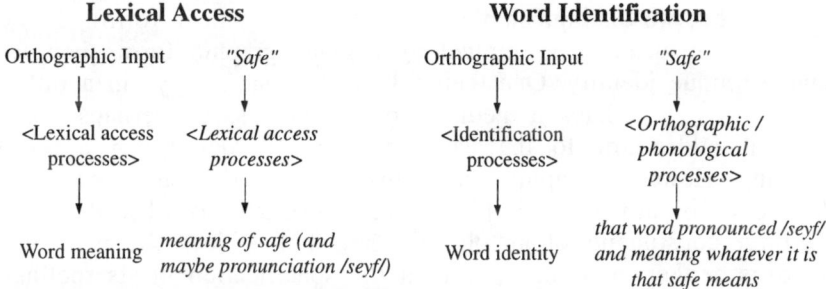

Fig. 1. Two views of word reading. Lexical Access assumes the input of a letter string is "looked" up in a lexicon, giving access to meanings. Phonological outputs may or may not be generated also. In Word Identification, a printed letter string retrieves a specific phonological word form, accompanied by semantic and syntactic possibilities. Based on Perfetti & Zhang (1995b).

Thinking of word reading not as lexical access but as word identification leads to a different perspective, as shown in Figure 1. Whereas lexical access asks what happens in order to gain "access" to a word's dictionary "entry", word identification asks what happens in order to identify a word. What is different are the presupposition and the entailments of posing one problem rather than the other. The lexical access problem entails an account of processes that produce some minimal contact with a word (a word's "location" in some accounts) in a lexicon; it presupposes a concept of access and asks what influences it. For example, is access mediated by phonology? Does access produce meaning?

The word identification problem entails an account of processes that produce identification, which must include a phonological representation of a printed word; it presupposes a concept of identification and asks what brings it about. Certainly, as in the access question, one can ask whether phonology mediates identification. But because identification itself requires an identified object, the object itself requires specification. And it turns out to be impossible to provide an object description of a word in the absence of specifying its phonology.[1]

Consider a description of an identified object sufficient to differentiate it from among all other objects. Surely identification of a word must be at least that. If so, then the identified object, in the case of a word, must be something like the object such that it has graphic form $x$, phonological form $y$, and range of meanings, $z$. The graphic form alone is not enough (compare *record* (re'-cord vs re-cord') or *wind* (/waynd/ vs /wInd/); the graphic form has to associate with something else; the pre-theoretical choice for this something else in reading research seems to be meaning. We can certainly discriminate the two *winds* or the two *records* on the basis of their meanings (to complicate things a bit, we distinguish the latter by grammatical form). If we know which meaning is implied by a given graphic form, then we have a unique identity. One then asks about phonology, in a rather casual way, as perhaps a mediator of the process or perhaps some optional addendum to the basic process of identifying a word meaning. However, graphic form plus meaning does not work as a description of an identified object; it can work only as a list of two of the three constituents of an object. The whole object--the perceived word--is neither more nor less than the specification of its spelling, phonology, and meaning.

To see the role of all three constituents, imagine that the perceived object is not a word but a person. One sees a vaguely familiar person (the graphic form) and retrieves its meaning (the guy that waits tables at the cafe). In this situation, one gets meaning from visual form--there is no name (phonological form) to associate with the person. Such a case is "person access", roughly analogous to lexical access: Some meaningful response to a perceptual object, without any phonology. In fact, phonology may be "post-access", if the waiter's name comes to us later. But this is a very impoverished identification; it can not distinguish this object from something that is similar visually and in meaning (another waiter). Reading can be like this, of course, as

---

[1] When models of word naming (e.g. Besner & Smith, 1992) focus on "phonological" output, they would seem to become models of explicit identification.

when one sees a word in a foreign language or a very long unpronounceable name that can be used only to remind the reader of some meaning or association.

With the addition of a name, identification is more complete and it leads to functionality that is lacking in its absence. There is full specification of a perceived object: In the case of a person, the object perceived is the person having the appearance $x$, the name $y$, and associated meaning $z$. The perceiver can generate a description of the object that is identifying, i.e., picks out $\{x,y,z\}$ from all other persons. And, given $x$ *and* $y$, one can retrieve $z$ uniquely; in the absence of $x$, $y$ alone may or may not allow $z$, depending on the number of x-like persons known to the perceiver, etc. Similarly, given $x$ and $z$, $y$ can be retrieved, and given $z$ and $y$, $x$ can be retrieved. It is important in the person-identification example, which turns out to be an imperfect analogy to word identification, to notice that there is no inherent privilege to any one of the three identification constituents. Any two can allow generation of the third, and any one can allow generation of the other two (just when there is no ambiguity), given only that the perceive represents all three constituents. Similarly, ambiguity resolution can be provided equally, in principle, by any one of the constituents given the other two.

In the case of identifying a word, the Constituency Principle--that there are three constituents of the identified object that define its identification--holds in roughly the same manner. Ordinarily, the identification of words in ordinary reading brings together all three constituents--graphic form, phonological form, and meaning. An exception noted above, the use of a foreign word or a truly unfamiliar word to "stand for something" (i.e., to acquire a kind of meaning in a particular context, as when a reader of Tolstoy's *Anna Karenina* takes the word *Scherbatsky* not as a phonological name, but as a form that "stands for" Kitty.) Notice, however, that because such reading is to identify a word as $\{y,z\}$ it is an incomplete identification and can not be used to generate a description of the identified word. Similarly, a case of unknown meaning $\{x,y\}$ is an incomplete identification. However, the case of missing-meaning identification appears to support more functional reading than does the case of missing-name. The name (or the graphic form-phonological form pair) can be used to search memory further for some meaning, whereas from the meaning alone, there is little chance of searching successfully for a name in anything like the real time frame of reading; tip-of-the-tongue states can be unsuccessful. Furthermore, a phonological form can be stored in a temporary memory during reading, giving context an opportunity to provide help in inferring meaning. Context will not ordinarily help infer a name.

The argument, thus, is that the central word reading event is not lexical access but identification, the recovery of a specific phonological object having certain linguistic and meaning properties. To identify a word such as *safe* is to be able to name it. Actual naming is not synonymous with identification, but the potential to provide a phonologically-specified name is the heart of identification. Identifying a word gives its referential and linguistic possibilities. A more general claim is implied from this perspective: Word identification, the recovery of a phonological object and its associated nonphonological constituents is the fundamental obligatory process of reading. Perfetti & Zhang (1995b) referred to this process as a Universal Phonological Reflex.

*The asymmetry between form and meaning in word identification*

Although I have suggested an analogy between person and word identification in order to develop a common constituency framework for identification, it turns out that there is an interesting difference between the two. There is no obvious basis for assuming that, in person identification, any one of the three constituents is privileged over any other. A name, for example, has no special privilege in identification, except where visual appearances are so similar (twins) or meanings are so similar (all persons in the set are the same "type"). And because so many people can have the same name, the name's value is truly relational--in relation to appearance and meaning. In word identification, at least in real reading, things seem to be different. In word identification, there is an asymmetry among the constituents of identification. In particular, the pairing of forms $\{x,y\}$, the graphic and the phonological forms, is relatively deterministic; the pairing of the graphic form and meaning $\{x,z\}$ is relatively less deterministic.

The phonological form of a printed word is well specified; the meaning of a printed word form is not. Whereas phonological forms associate fairly predictably with written word forms (at the lexical level), word meanings do not. Instead, meanings can be reasonably considered as ranges of values that are filled in by contexts. In effect, *form-form* mappings are nearly one-to-one, whereas *form-meaning* relations are one-to-many.

Consider the English word *safe*, referred to in Figure 1. This word has a range of dictionary meanings: Noun. A place to keep valuables. Adjective 1. The feeling or state of being free from harm. Adjective 2. Baseball: Judged to have reached base ahead of an attempted putout. Because these three meanings appear to be related in some way, there might be some economy of semantic organization that serves a reader, compared with word forms that are fully polysemous with unrelated meanings (e.g., *lean* as "not fat" and as "lean against"). However, for a word that appears to have a single meaning with extended referential possibilities, such as *safe,* there is not a single reliable semantic value that is a good candidate for a context-free meaning retrieval. "The safe in the wall", "safe streets", and "safe at home" all invite slightly different interpretations.

What kind of lexical process "extracts" just the right kind of meaning from a word? The literature on word disambiguation has grown large trying to answer this question, oscillating between a view that selective access of word meaning is impossible and a view that allows at least dominant meanings of ambiguous words to be preselected by a context. (See Simpson, 1994 for review of this research.) Evidence in this research usually depends on primed lexical decisions to single words that are associates of one or the other meaning of the ambiguous word. Such associations do not constitute the meaning of a word in any deep sense, and in fact are assumed to deactivate rapidly in the interest of real sentence comprehension. But it is these associations that are detected within a few milliseconds of the exposure of a word in these priming experiments. So for *safe*, for example, associates such as "money", "jewels", "and sound", "out", "slide", etc. might be bouncing around, either selectively or all at once.

This glut of meaning associates stands in strong contrast to the single phonological form connected to *safe*. The phonological object /seyf/ isn't just an "associate" of *safe*, it is its identity. And it is its unique identity. (Only a very few words in English have split identities, e.g., *wind*, *lead*, and none present the range of identities implied by associative accounts of meaning activation.) This phonological identity is the most reliable thing a word can have. Meaning is not reliably associated with an isolated word. Reading processes take advantage of this reliable identification process rather than merely accepting the vagaries of meaning. Phonological form thus becomes the foundation for whatever meaning gets dragged along. In earlier work on this problem, I referred to this function of phonology as "reference securing" (Perfetti & McCutchen, 1982). If a reader has the phonological form as part of the representation of a word, than he or she has secured the reference that helps constrain interpretation as more text becomes available.

Semantics is both logically and psychologically secondary to phonology. If we cast this in terms of how representations might serve processing, phonological form, but not meaning, can be bound to orthographic form. Not only is *safe* bound to /seyf/, but *afe* is bound to /eyf/, *s* to /s/, and *f* to /f/. Only the vowels behave as context-dependent variables, and most contexts are deterministic even for vowels. There is nothing close to this degree of determinism for meaning.

*The generality of the constituency and asymmetry principles*

Is this account of form-meaning relations specific to English or to alphabetic writing systems? No. If we turn to Chinese, the picture changes only in the details. The writing system does not provide information at the level of the phoneme. But at the syllable and word levels, Chinese is more deterministic. For most single character words, especially the most common ones, the pronunciation of a character is fixed. One interesting difference does emerge in Chinese, however. A reader encountering a low frequency word might be able to figure out a likely meaning of the word, using a combination of context and the semantic component of the character, without being able to identify the word. At the same time, however, he or she has a good chance of inferring the pronunciation, because the validity of the phonetic component of a compound increases with decreasing frequency (Perfetti, Zhang, et al., 1992). Unless the reader actually recognizes the retrieved phonological word form in this situation, what happens is not word identification but "decoding". Again, however, both of these processes are available to the reader of English to some extent. The real difference is one of degree. The reader of an alphabetic system can do better at recovering the phonological form, less well at recovering the semantic category of the word. But even the reader of Chinese cannot readily obtain a precise meaning from a single character in isolation. This asymmetry between form and meaning suggests that phonological form will be a constituent of word identification in both writing systems.

The psychological status of the form-form form-meaning asymmetry has in fact been demonstrated in a weak form in Chinese by Tan, Hoosain, and Peng (1995) and by Perfetti and Tan (1998). In a masking paradigm, in which a word is presented at around or just below the identification threshold and followed by a masking word bearing some relation to the form or meaning of the word, Tan, et al. (1995) showed that semantic effects depended on the mask having high frequency and precise meaning. When it did, it facilitated target identification within 60 ms, but when the mask's meaning was vague, it did not facilitate identification. Perfetti and Tan (1998) carried out primed naming experiments in which readers named Chinese characters following primes of three types, corresponding to the three constituents of a word's identity: Graphemic (Characters with visual similarity to the target), Phonological (Characters with the same syllable-name as the target, Semantic (character with meanings similar to the target). They found that the facilitative effect of a semantic prime depended on its meaning precision: When the meaning of the prime was relatively precise, it facilitated naming within 85 ms; when its meaning was vague, its facilitation was delayed until 115 ms.

The question of what constitutes "vague" and "precise" meaning is important in specifying the meaning information available in a word, but is beyond the present purpose. Suffice it to say that the availability of specific semantic information is highly variable, and that it makes sense to speak of a range of context-dependent meaning potentials rather than a fixed meaning when referring to a word in isolation. Thus the studies of Tan, et al. and Perfetti and Tan demonstrate that the semantic processing of a word during identification depends on the relative precision of meanings associated with the isolated character. Thus, form-meaning relations are variable and relatively indeterminate (i.e., relative to form-form relations).

By contrast, studies have shown a stronger connection between graphic and phonological form in Chinese. Thus Tan, et al. (1995) found that when a mask had the same phonological form as the word to be identified, identification was facilitated at 60 ms. And Perfetti and Tan (1998) found that naming was facilitated by a homophone prime within 57 ms of prime exposure, compared with 85 ms required for a semantic prime effect. Thus, phonological form precedes meaning in becoming functional in these situations. In a different paradigm, Perfetti and Zhang (1995a) presented subjects with pairs of characters for a judgment of meaning similarity. When the two characters shared pronunciation rather than meaning, they found a phonological interference effect in decision times and errors. This result demonstrates that phonology could not be suppressed even in a task requiring meaning judgments. In further experiments examining the time course of phonological interference (in meaning judgment) and semantic interference (in phonological judgment), Perfetti and Zhang (1995a) found phonological effects to be earlier. Although there are problems in interpreting time course results across different tasks, even with the same materials, it is safe to say that there are no results in either Perfetti and Zhang, (1995a) or Perfetti and Tan (1998) to suggest that semantics has any privilege in Chinese word identification. Indeed, the differences observed suggest the opposite ordering, with phonology available first, then semantics. Such an ordering makes little sense for the view of Chinese reading that sees it as a script-to-meaning process. However, it is quite explainable within the constituency framework, supplemented by the asymmetry principle. Phonology is privileged because it is reliably mapped at the whole word level, whereas meaning is not. The identification process is served very well by the rapid availability of phonological information.

The research in alphabetic reading has been pre-occupied with the question of whether phonology is pre-lexical. There is substantial evidence for early (pre-lexical) and automatic phonology, especially from brief exposure paradigms, which are arguably more sensitive to the narrow window in which phonological information is activated (Berent & Perfetti, 1995). The alternatives to an early and automatic phonology are usually conceived as either optional pre-lexical or an unspecified post-lexical (again optional) phonology. It is ironic that the fundamental role of phonology in identification that I am suggesting here has been relatively ignored in alphabetic writing systems. Because the intriguing question seems to have been whether phonology is assembled during word reading in order to access a word, the critical question of whether identification of words requires phonology seems to have been ignored or relegated to questions of task demands. Thus it is often assumed that phonology is required for naming but not for lexical decision. To the extent that lexical decisions were taken to reflect the "access" process, then phonology might not be important (even though many lexical decision results do show phonological effects). But the Chinese results ought to bring this into question. In Chinese, the results can be summarized as demonstrating powerful phonological effects at the word-syllable level, whether or not there are effects at the sub-word (character component) level, as suggested in naming paradigms (e.g., Fang, Hong, & Tzeng, 1986). There is no reason to think that an alphabetic system would somehow be different, avoiding phonology at the word level, at the same time that it allows it a the subword (letter-phoneme) level. On the contrary, phonology in reading English or German or Italian, regardless of differences in the transparency of their orthographies must require the identification of phonological word forms as the defining event of word reading. That phonology can be generated prior to the retrieval of meaning constituents in an alphabetic system simply amplifies the role of phonology.

## Phonological "mediation" vs phonological constituency

An interesting implication of the Constituency Principle is that the role of phonology is not simply mediation, i.e., that it is *used* for something else --"lexical access". Whereas most accounts assume phonology is often nonmediational, merely an optional "post-lexical" process, constituency implies a hypothetical "moment" of identification that includes a reference to phonological form as well as meaning. Thus phonology is neither mediational nor optional. Identification is the retrieval of a phonological form in relation to both graphic form and semantic information.

Identification, to state the basic argument in another way, can be conceived as a relational description of information sources, e.g., the lexical object such that it is spelled D-O-G, has the phonological form /dawg/, and means whatever it is that "dog" means. A cognitive moment of identification suggests a short lived integration of constituents--a simultaneous availability of graphemic, phonological, and semantic information. These constituents accumulate in overlapping time courses, beginning with graphic information. Even so, a phonological word form may be available prior to the complete specification of a graphemic representation (Lukatela & Turvey, 1994; Perfetti, Bell & Delaney, 1988; Van Orden, 1987). In a non-alphabetic writing system, the situation may prove to be slightly different. Chinese has graphic-phonological relationships defined over the syllable-lexical levels rather than the grapheme-phoneme level. The basic phonological constituent of Chinese word identification, accordingly, will differ in its form and perhaps in its processing synchrony. But both English and Chinese have phonological constituents in word identification. And both can be said to show mediation in a particular sense: Phonology brings together the graphic form and the meaning associated with both graphic and phonological form. In this view, we might get rid of "mediation" altogether, because it implies a sequential and instrumental process of phonological "recoding" and then lexical "look up". Instead, a more apt term might be phonological "binding", in that the three constituents of a word get joined in an identification moment. Alternatively, we can begin to understand mediation in the way proposed by Van Orden and Goldinger, which nicely captures the rapid and transient nature of word components within a dynamic systems framework[2].

Given this extended argument about what word identification is, it becomes of practical and theoretical importance to link the argument to the problem of learning to read. What is learning to read?

---

[2] Van Orden and Goldinger (1994) have argued for a sense of mediation that is compatible with the Constituency Principle. In their dynamic systems approach to this issue, phonological and visual information interact in recurrent subsymbolic networks to produce word recognition. In such a model "mediation" is the critical role phonological connections play in the network's achievement of self-consistency. Although the full implications of a dynamic systems approach are beyond my purpose, its treatment of mediation captures an important aspect of how phonology functions in skilled word recognition. On the self-consistency view, phonological connections can function in any writing system.

## LEARNING TO READ IS THE MASTERY OF A WRITING SYSTEM AND AN ORTHOGRAPHY

The title of this section is an approximate answer to the question of what it means to learn to read, although it needs some critical elaboration. Notice that it differs from some of the broadly encompassing definitions of reading that focus on comprehension and even a wide range of literacy uses. Each definition can be defended on some practical, logical, or programmatic grounds and each has its own set of entailments that affect the framing of scientific and educational issues. To some extent, the wide range of definitions arises from a tendency to conflate the various purposes of reading with the need for definition. Thus, reading is a means of acquiring information of all sorts (from bus schedules to recipes), a means of cultural participation (literature, broadly conceived), and a source of life-long learning; broad definitions of reading echo these purposes. In most of its purposes, reading has as an intermediate goal, gaining meaning from print. (But note that a significant if proportionally modest amount of reading activity, e.g., some poetry, puns, humor, and even ordinary reading of both fiction and nonfiction, entails a goal of *form* as much as *meaning*.) Definitions, however, strive to delineate not the purpose of some activity but rather its distinguishing features.[3] The distinguishing features of reading center on its conventionalized, graphic input and the conversion of that input into messages, especially language encoded messages. Its nondistinctive features, including comprehension, are equally important from a functional perspective, but these features are shared with a wide variety of other activities.

The most common construal of learning to read is learning to get meaning from print. Although a bit vague, this is actually a very serviceable definition, and I do not want to throw it out. But I would like to see whether the learning problem can be specified more clearly than getting meaning from print. Learning to read, whatever else it is, is *learning*. And what the reader learns is how his or her language is encoded in a *writing system* and its specific *orthography*.

To say a child learns a writing system is to say that he or she comes to know implicitly how that writing system works--the principles on which it is based. To learn an orthography is to learn the controlling details of a system's specific instantiation for a given language. These are two interrelated learning tasks, equally important for successful reading. A child born in Italy, Hungary, Russia, or Korea must learn the principles of an alphabetic writing system, although each learns a

---

[3] This conflation of purpose with distinguishing features seems to be avoided in other areas. As far as I know, no one has been tempted to define arithmetic as a system for keeping track of money.

different orthography (as well as a different script). In an alphabetic writing system, basic (meaningless) graphic units (letters) associate with basic (meaningless) speech units (phonemes). An Iranian, Egyptian, or Israeli child learns a modified alphabetic system in which consonants are more reliably represented than vowels. And child born in China or Taiwan will learn a system usually referred to as a "logographic" system, in which graphic units are assumed to associate primarily with morphemes. However, because the graphic units also associate with syllables to some extent, Chinese may be better described as *morphosyllabic* (DeFrancis, 1989 ) or even *morphophonological*. A Japanese child learns a primary syllabary system (Kana) in which graphic units correspond to syllables and a second system corresponding to the Chinese system (Kanji).

How does the child discover the principles of writing system design and the orthographic details that he or she has to master? It would be convenient if a child had the same biological advantage for reading that he or she has for primary (spoken) language. A large component of prior implicit knowledge about the possible forms of language appears to guide the language acquisition process. The forms that spoken language can take may be guided by evolved structures, whether specific to language or shared with other cognitive systems, that have tuned the design of possible language. These design features, in some tractable sense, are biologically provided to the child and assist the task of acquiring a first spoken language (Pinker, 1984). Thus, language acquisition is rapid for the first few years of life regardless of the particular language. Opportunities to learn are very important as well, but they build on a biological foundation.

In contrast to the biological foundation of language, writing systems result from human invention and are culturally transmitted across generations. At first glance, there is little in the child's native language endowment to provide any constraints on the learning of the writing system--no design system that corresponds to that for primary language. However, a more careful examination suggests one important constraint: Writing systems are based partly on speech.

*Writing systems and languages*

Reading is the decoding of language forms *from* written forms and spelling is the encoding of linguistic forms *into* written forms. The linguistic units--phonological strings, morphemes, and words--are provided by the spoken language. The writing units are provided by the writing system and its inventory of graphic devices. Figure 2 illustrates the general form of the relationship between languages and writing systems.

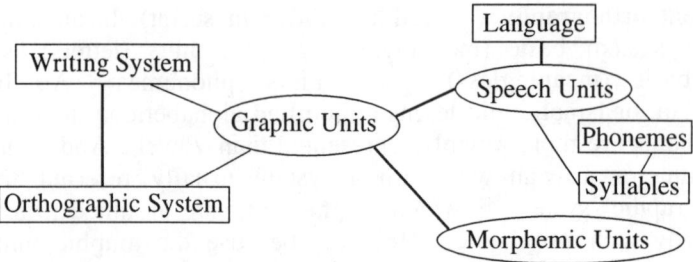

Fig. 2. The relationships between writing systems and languages and spelling and reading. Both reading and spelling processes use a lexical representation that contains orthographic (O) and phonological (Ph) constituents. Both spelling and reading use both sets of constituents and both have a verification stage. Based on Perfetti (1997).

The linkages between the units of the two systems define the essential meaning of reading and writing. Both require that graphic units be connected to linguistic units.

Unlike the linguistic system, which is assumed to be systematic, multi-layered, and abstract, writing is often treated as unsystematic, strictly linear, and highly conventional. Spellings are often said to be "arbitrary" or at best "conventionalized", enforced by appeal to authority. More important, however, is the fact that spelling and reading both reflect the general principles of a writing system--the writing system design--and the specific orthography that embodies the general design plus its distinctive orthographic features.

In Figure 2, there is a distinction between writing system and orthography that is often ignored in psychological treatments of reading and spelling. Generally speaking, the writing system dictates the level at which general linguistic constraints are imposed on writing, whereas the orthography dictates the specific details of these constraints. Accordingly, writing systems can be said to be logographic, syllabic, and alphabetic, depending on the smallest linguistic unit encoded in the basic writing unit. Orthographies within writing systems show minor but significant variation concerning the rules that relate graphic units to linguistic units. Thus, written Chinese (morphosyllabic), Japanese Kana (syllabic) and Italian (alphabetic) belong to different writing systems. But written English, Italian, and French, all alphabetic systems, can be said to have different orthographies.

*Alphabetic writing systems*

The story of alphabetic writing systems is well known, and my treatment here is not a recounting, but a reminder. The Phoenician-Greek invention of the alphabetic principle appears to have been a unique cultural achievement, one that followed far behind the use of visual symbols for objects and meanings (Gelb, 1952). As Gleitman and Rozin (1977) observed, an idea so slow in coming to the species might not spring easily to the mind of a child. Fortunately, although difficult to discover, the alphabetic principle is quite learnable. The basic idea of reading instruction in an alphabetic system is that children can be taught the alphabetic principle, either directly or indirectly.

The alphabetic principle is simple: The elementary unit in the writing system corresponds to a meaningless speech segment. It is the meaninglessness of both the writing unit and the speech unit that is at the heart of the alphabetic principle. This is what allows the tremendous productivity of an alphabetic writing system--its limitless representation of the words of a language from its small inventory of graphic symbols.

The obstacles to learning the alphabetic principle are also well known. Children have only dim awareness of the phonological structure of their language prior to schooling. Because phonemes are abstractions over highly variable acoustic events, their status as discrete speech segments that exist outside of ordinary word perception is beyond routine perception. Children perceive speech and recognize words, but there is nothing in that ability that makes visible the composition of the speech in terms of phoneme constituents. Furthermore, the child's pre-school use of language is communicative and contextualized, seldom directing attention to spoken word forms.

Overcoming these obstacles requires gaining knowledge of phonemes as abstract speech segments. Some phonemic awareness is required for children to be successful in reading in an alphabetic writing system (Bradley & Bryant, 1983; Mann, 1991; Tunmer, Herriman & Nesdale, 1988; Vellutino & Scanlon, 1991). In addition, evidence suggests that phonemic awareness develops as a consequence of reading instruction in an alphabetic system (Morais, Bertelson, Cary, & Alegria, 1986; Perfetti et al, 1987) Thus, for learning to read in an alphabetic writing system, the relationship between awareness of phonology and progress in reading acquisition is reciprocal and mutually facilitative. Becoming literate and acquiring full appreciation of the phonological structure of written words are interlocking developments; it is probably a mistake to fix attention on phonological awareness as strictly as a prerequisite to reading instruction.

*The Chinese writing system*

From the morpho-syllabic Chinese, through the syllabic Japanese Kana, to the alphabetic Korean, Southeast Asian scripts span the full range of writing systems. The Chinese system provides the highest contrast with alphabetic systems.

Lacking components (e.g., letters) that represent sub-word speech units, a pure logography would be controlled by a morphological (meaning) principle. One would learn the meaning of each character without any reference to its phoneme constituents in speech. Such a writing system, in principle, is very different from both alphabetic and syllabaric systems. Each symbol would associate uniquely with a unit of meaning, a morpheme, and would be limited in productivity to families of morphemes.

Such a system would present a formidable learning task to a child, essentially one of associating each character with a meaning. Such economy as could be gained would come from symbols that have meaning relations in common. For example, the character referring to "sun" is used as part of the compound character that refers to "sunshine". (The character for "sun" is actually a radical, one of the 214 elementary morphemic units of the writing system that are used independently as words and as components of compounds). A reader who knows the character for "sun" may be able to infer that the compound character that contains "sun" has something to do with sun. But the reader will have to learn the rest of the compound and connect the whole specifically with "sunshine", rather than, say, "bright" or some other word that has the character for sun as a component.

The compound character "sunshine" also contains a second character, the word *qing*, meaning "green". In using the character for *qing* as part of the character for "sunshine", Chinese produces a phonetic compound: The word meaning "sunshine" is also *qing*. Only the tones differ between the word meaning "green" (*qing1*) and the word meaning "sunshine" (*qing2*). Compounds consisting of two single characters comprise a substantial portion of Chinese characters (82%, according to Zhou, 1978). However, the compound does not always work as in the *qing* example, where the phonetic component and the compound have segmentally identical pronunciations. In an attempt to estimate the extent to which phonetic components assist the pronunciation of compounds, Zhou (1978), based on combining two statistics, estimated that 39% of compounds contain a phonetic component that provides its pronunciation. This means that the odds of encountering an invalid phonetic component (i.e., an invalid cue to pronunciation) in a compound could be higher than the odds of encountering a valid phonetic component. Nevertheless, this phonological component for the Chinese writing system is of potential importance in reading and the mere existence of this phonological potential provides an important fact concerning writing systems.

Given that the composition of Chinese compounds combines a semantic and phonological component, the characterization of Chinese as a logography appears to be misleading (Boudberg, 1937;

DeFrancis, 1989). From its ancient origins as a system based on pictographic and then semantic symbols, Chinese writing, according to DeFrancis (1989), has evolved into a system dominated by symbols that carry both semantic and phonetic information: a morphophonological system rather than an exclusively morphological one. It may be, as DeFrancis (1989) argues, that all human writing systems have evolved toward some reliance on speech, even those whose origins are assumed to be strictly meaning-based.

Because Chinese includes meaning-based components, some researchers and educators have been led to suggest a correlated nonsequitur: that reading Chinese is strictly a visual-semantic process, one in which phonology plays no role. However, as I noted in the previous section, the evidence by now suggests a rather different view of reading Chinese. Rather than ignoring phonology in a direct script-to-meaning process, skilled Chinese readers appear to activate phonology as part of the reading process (Perfetti & Zhang, 1991, 1995b; Tan et al, 1995; Tan & Perfetti, 1997; Zhang & Perfetti, 1993).

What causes phonological processing to occur in a writing system that is supposed to be meaning-based? For one thing, as noted in the last section, the writing system is not exactly meaning-based, but rather rests on both meaning (morphology) and the syllabic structure of the language. But even if there were no phonological basis for the system, it does not follow that phonology is not a part of word identification. The Constituency Principle indeed says that reading words includes the phonological constituents of those words. On this account, as the reader identifies a character, the name of that character--the phonological word form associated with it--is retrieved just as its meaning is.

Phonological processes in reading are natural products of human cognition, and that is why they are universal. The adaptation that a reader might make to a writing system does not arise from the conscious selection of some strategy, but rather is a natural result of learning the writing system. As the writing system is learned, the phonological processes naturally accommodate the properties of the learned system. According to the UPP, all readers use phonological processes, if they are able. Speech is ontogenetically prior to print. All children learn a native language; not all children learn to read. Such considerations compel the conclusion that speech processes are privileged as a child begins to learn to read. Furthermore, skilled reading continues to make use of phonological information well beyond the time in which one might suppose that it could be discarded. The reason, again, is simple and fundamental. Human language processing and human memory systems are structured to rely on speech-based coding.

## LEARNING TO READ IN AN ALPHABETIC WRITING SYSTEM

In learning to read, children acquire implicit knowledge of how their writing system works. In learning an alphabetic writing system, this entails learning that letters, not only individually but as letter strings, correspond to speech segments. In principle, this learning might occur implicitly (through the extraction of print-speech correspondences in text) or explicitly (through direct instruction). However, some evidence suggests that children are not likely to infer the principles of correspondence on their own (Byrne, 1991). English presents a problem that is less important in other alphabetic writing systems, because it is a "deep" orthography (Frost, et al., 1987): Many letter patterns in English may associate with more than one pronunciation. Thus, in addition to learning the *alphabetic principle*--the principle that the writing system associates meaningless graphic units with meaningless speech units--, the child who learns to read English must learn the details of the orthography system that sometimes associates *ow* with /ow/ (as in *how*) and sometimes with /o/ (as in *tow*). Although the irregularity of English is widely lamented, it is useful to note that many of the "irregularities" turn out to be quite predictable, provided one takes into account more than a single letter.

Theories of leaning to read have generally framed acquisition as a series of stages (Chall, 1983; Ehri, 1980; 1987; 1991; Frith, 1985; Gough and Hillinger, 1980; Marsh et al, 1981). There are some important shared ideas among the theories, especially those of Ehri, Gough & Hillinger, and Frith. They note that the earliest stage of reading is characterized by a nonproductive attempt to learn associations between features of graphic forms (not complete orthographic word forms) and that there is a subsequent stage of full use of graphic-phonological decoding that brings on a truly productive capability in reading. Alternative theoretical accounts emphasize the incremental acquisition of lexical representations, rather than discrete stages (Perfetti, 1992; Share, 1995). These theories share a central role for phonological information, which provides the "glue" for lexical representations.

### *What fuels progress in reading?*

According to the Restricted Interactive Model of lexical representation (Perfetti, 1991, 1992), learning to read increases the number of orthographically addressable words and modifies individual word representations. What a child knows about words is represented by specified strings of letters, phonemes, and whole words in an interconnected network consistent with the kinds of representations proposed by McClelland and Rumelhart (1981). Thus, for a skilled reader, there is a representation of the word with its position-correct letters, the phonemic values of those letters, and the pronunciation of the word as a whole. The representations of words develop in two ways with increased reading competence. First, the representations increase in *specificity*: the number of position-correct specific letters in a lexical representation. The second quality modification involves *redundancy*: an increase in the number of redundant phonemic representations contained in a lexical entry. The redundancy idea rests on the assumption that word names (pronunciations) are part of the child's earliest lexical representations and that phonemes are added to this representation in connection to individual letters with learning. Thus, learning is a question of the child's acquisition of increased specificity and increased redundancy in lexical representations.

Together, increasing specificity and redundancy allow high quality word representations to be reliably activated by orthographic inputs. As individual words become fully specified and redundant, they move from a functional lexicon that allows reading, to the autonomous lexicon that allows efficient resource-cheap reading (Perfetti, 1992). It is the words in the autonomous lexicon that produce the kind of automatic phonological activation we see in highly skilled reading.

What enables these increasingly high quality words to be developed appears to center on phonological-orthographic representations. Although there may be a brief period during which some children attempt to "read" without real attention to a word's orthography (Gough & Hillinger, 1980; Gough & Juel, 1991), there is a rapid use of letters in concert with phonological values of their names (Ehri, 1991). Indeed, there must be if the child is to read productively—use the finite set of letter-phoneme correspondences to generate approximations to the reading of large numbers of words. Any strategy that limits learning to a set of associations between selected parts of printed words and spoken words (or meanings) is doomed to failure eventually.

Phonological awareness is a large part of what enables the child to move into a productive stage of reading in an alphabetic system. Early studies showed a strong association between a child's ability to perform segmentation tasks and the ability to read (Liberman, Shankweiler, Fischer, & Carter, 1974). Later studies suggested that such awareness could also be a consequence of learning to read, rather than only a prerequisite (Morais et al., 1986). Especially relevant for the alphabetic nonalphabetic comparisons, Read, Zhang, Nie, & Ding (1986) found that Chinese readers who had not learned pin yin (an alphabetic system for Chinese) did not show awareness of phonemes. Such research clearly shows that the functional relationship can go from reading to phonological awareness. Training studies, however, have clearly demonstrated that there is a direct relationship between phonological sensitivity and learning to read by showing gains in reading following training with phonological tasks (Ball & Blachman, 1991; Blachman, 1989; Bradley & Bryant , 1983, 1985; Byrne & Fielding-Barnsley, 1991, 1993; Cunningham, 1990; Hatcher, Hulme, & Ellis, 1994; Lie. 1991; Lundberg, Frost, & Petersen, 1988; Torgesen, Morgan, & Davis, 1992; Treiman & Baron, 1983; Williams, 1980). The relationship between the development of phonological awareness and learning to read is probably a reciprocal one, in which some sensitivity to phonological structures is necessary to make initial progress in learning to read, whereas reading itself supports further gains in phonological sensitivity that in turn support further gains in reading (Perfetti, Beck, Bell, & Hughes, 1987). This relationship implies what the training studies have found: that enhancing phonological awareness will improve reading.

Studies by Stuart and Coltheart (1988) and Stuart (1990) illustrate the importance of these early phonologically-based approaches to reading. The extent to which children made phonological errors in word reading early in the first grade predicted end of year reading achievement. Non phonological errors--including errors that shared letters but not in-position phonemes (e.g., "like" for *milk*) were associated with low end-of-year achievement. The point at which phonological errors became more common than non-phonological errors coincided with the child's attainment of functional phonological skill, measured by knowledge of at least half the alphabet and of success in at least some tests of phonological sensitivity. Stuart (1990) added to these results by finding that the level of a child's phonological sensitivity corresponded in some detail to the level of achievement in word reading.

Fully productive reading (the ability to read novel words) comes only from an increase in orthographic representations that include phonology--what Gough and Hillinger (1980) called the "cipher" stage. (And what Frith (1985) called "the alphabetic stage".) This requires attention to letter strings and the context-sensitive association of phoneme sequences to these letter strings. This is where phonological sensitivity should play its most important role. Children who have attained this level of reading can read pronounceable nonwords, and their errors in word reading show a high degree of phonological plausibility.

Progress in learning to read may be fueled by several factors. One, consistent with Gough and Hillinger (1980) is that children encounter more words than they can discriminate by selective association. For example, early in reading, a child can attend to the "m" in "mouse" to distinguish it from "cat" and "house". But as "moon" and "moose" are encountered the association cue that was sufficient for "reading" becomes insufficient. This problem then fuels progress in the child's attending to more orthographic information. This is a functional perspective on reading progress that needs to be supplemented by a cognitive mechanism perspective.

The main mechanism available to the child is phonological recoding. A model of how this mechanism works comes from Share (1995), who emphasized the "self-teaching" role of phonological recoding. What is important in this model is that children attempt to phonologically recode words. The result of each attempt is a feedback process that incrementally builds up the orthographic representation of specific words. The role of phonology, in effect, is on word-specific orthography. The letter-by-letter processing in sequential decoding may be the main factor in producing high quality word representations that incorporate letter constituents (Adams, 1990; Ehri, 1980; 1992; Venezky & Massaro, 1979). Several studies have observed that a few exposures to a word may be sufficient for the acquisition of word-specific orthographic information (Brooks, 1977; Manis, 1985; Reitsma, 1983), incrementing the *specificity* (exact letters) and *redundancy* (context-sensitive letter-phoneme mappings) of the child's printed word lexicon (Perfetti, 1992). Although other mechanisms might promote the acquisition of print-accessible lexical items, a careful analysis of all the possibilities concludes that phonological recoding is the most effective mechanism (Share & Stanovich, 1995).

Thus, increasing the size of the print lexicon is one of the main outcomes of a phonological mechanism. Share's (1995) self-teaching model, like the restricted-interactive acquisition model of Perfetti (1992), emphasizes the child's acquisition of individual word representations, rather than stages. This perspective asks "which words can a child read?" rather than "what stage is the child in?" The rapid build-up of the child's lexicon through reading promotes many words to a functional high frequency (familiarity) status. Texts that contain a high proportion of familiar words will be read well, and the occasional low-frequency word provides an opportunity for phonological self-teaching. The child will face many words of very low frequency over time. The phonological recoding mechanism thus represents a very powerful, indeed essential, mechanism throughout reading development, not merely for beginners. The later benefits of this mechanism may be illustrated by the finding that third-grade children skilled in reading quickly and accurately read a novel word that they have previously only heard; less skilled readers tend to reach the same level of word reading accuracy and fluency on these words only when they have previously actually seen the novel words (Hogaboam & Perfetti, 1978).

Additional progress in reading entails increases in fluency and automaticity. Gaining fluency in reading entails developing rapid and perhaps automatic word identification processes. The main mechanism for gains in automaticity is, in some form or another, practice at consistent input-output mappings (Schneider & Shiffrin, 1977). In reading, automaticity entails "practice" at word identification, frequent retrievals of word forms and meanings from print. On a word-based account of reading acquisition, automaticity is a characteristic of words, not readers. Words move from the functional lexicon to the autonomous lexicon in this perspective (Perfetti, 1992).

Experience not only builds automaticity, it appears to establish an important lexical-orthographic source of knowledge for reading (Stanovich & West, 1989). This lexical-orthographic skill is tapped by tasks that assess spelling knowledge, as opposed to tasks that tap mainly phonological knowledge, and is indexed by the amount of reading a person has done (Stanovich & West, 1989). The phonological and lexical-orthographic abilities are correlated, but each makes unique contributions to reading achievement. It is noteworthy that a similar duality is seen in studies of reading disabled children (Olson, Wise, Conners, & Rack, 1990). There are two complementary but overlapping kinds of knowledge that support the reading of words: One is grounded in knowledge of the phonological structure of spoken words and knowledge that orthographic units represent these structures. The other develops with reading experience (made possible by the first) with printed word forms.

In summary, learning to read in an alphabetic writing system requires not just phonological awareness, but a phonological mechanism that generates phonological word forms as part of word identification. The Constituency Principle, that word identification includes a phonological constituent, applies as soon as the child begins to treat the letters of a word as having speech associated with them. This is part of what it means to learn to read in an alphabetic writing system. What about a nonalphabetic system?

*Implications of learning to read in Chinese*

Before addressing the learning question directly, consider how a model of written Chinese compares with the model of representation for English. As in English, *specificity* and *redundancy* are important in characterizing a quality word representation. A Chinese word is identified to the extent that the reader has a precise representation of its specific components. Thus, a compound character is represented as a graphic object comprising two components, and a multi-character word as a string of characters with these components. The character composition process itself, the sequence of strokes, may also be a part of the word representation (Flores D'Arcais, Saito & Kawakami, 1995). The representation of the character itself must include the stroke composition that gives a character its unique identity. The character is linked to phonological as well as semantic information through connections to a spoken word lexicon and to a set of meaning features. (See Perfetti & Tan, 1998 for a description of a model representing this idea.)

A model of Chinese reading, like a model of alphabetic reading, requires graphic, phonological and semantic constituents to become active during word identification. Prior to the moment when all constituents are combined into a cognitive moment, there may be partial activation of relevant phonology from a phonetic component; there may be activation of irrelevant, misleading phonology, again from a phonetic component; and there may be activation of both relevant and irrelevant semantic information from a character component. There is, as in a restricted interactive model of the type we propose for English, the idea that multiple levels of activation occur, only some of which are decisive in the final product of identification.

Word identification, as I have argued, is not the access of meaning, but the retrieval of phonological form and the activation of meaning. Neither in English nor in Chinese does a reader ordinarily identify a word by accessing its meaning. Word identification has to entail the potential ability to name the word that is being accessed, and this requires consulting its phonological representation. This does not mean that Chinese reading is the same as English; there are important differences. Nor does it mean that Chinese reading is driven by phonology. It is driven by meaning, but phonology is a constituent. Whether phonological activation precedes or follows semantic activation is a detail, important for certain purposes. If reading a word is identifying it, then the word's pronunciation is part of what's identified, in Chinese as well as in English.

*Chinese schooling*

A Chinese child comes to acquire these kinds of representations through sustained, frequent, and effective practice. Children spend a lot of time reading and writing characters, both in school and out of school. Estimates suggest that Chinese children learn more than 600 characters each year over 6 years of schooling (Leong, 1973), an accumulation of 3600 characters, which is sufficient to read a newspaper. A second important feature of Chinese literacy instruction may be the closer connection between reading and writing. Instruction at first is focused more on reading than writing, as it is in most Western reading instruction. However, Chinese children, by the second half of the first year, are spending a lot of time writing characters. The approach to writing is systematic and the composition process itself, which is based on a strict spatial ordering of strokes, undoubtedly strengthens the lexical representations the child acquires. Chinese children acquire a lexical representation of very high quality because they both write the character and read it, the two activities mutually reinforcing each other.

In English, increases in reading skill reflect increases in the number and quality of word representation--specificity and redundancy. In Chinese, there is a corresponding increase in the number and quality of word representations. Clearly, specificity of representation is part of the picture--the precise representation of the character components, their connection with phonology, and their connection with appropriate meanings. Indeed, compared with the development of lexical representations in English, the young Chinese reader's functional lexicon may have a more fully specified lexical representation--one free of "variables," and containing mainly "constants" (Perfetti, 1992). Less clear in Chinese is whether there is a redundancy principle, similar to that in alphabetic systems, operating on the components of the characters. That is, does the child learn that the simple character for sheep (*yang*) provides the name for the compound character for ocean? Of course the child does learn that the first is a constituent of the second in some sense. Whether this is a piece of "redundant" information similar to that in our model of English reading is less clear. However, evidence from Chen, Lau, and Yung (1993), showing a strong link between second and third grade reading and knowledge of component character pronunciation, is consistent with this possibility.

Chinese children acquire their reading skill through a level of homework orders of magnitude greater than is seen in the United States. Stevenson and Lee's (1990) comparison of a cities in Taiwan and the United States showed greater achievement in reading for Chinese children. First grade children, according to parent interviews, spent seven times as much time on homework as did American first grade children. Interestingly, they spent less time being read to and came to school with less knowledge of reading. Of course, cross-cultural comparisons are misleading unless they are part of broader culturally-referenced study. Still, one does not have to abandon the idea of first-grader-as-child to imagine that homework is helpful to learning to read and write.

The teaching of reading in China appears to have undergone its share of pushes and pulls over the years. A major push came with the introduction of Pin Yin instruction. Pin Yin, literally "spell-sound", provides Romanized alphabetic spellings during initial reading instruction. Chinese children, in fact, learn to read with this alphabetic writing system before they learn characters. The child first gets Pin Yin instruction, then characters appear with Pin Yin, and finally the Pin Yin is taken away and the characters can be read. Pin Yin is most helpful for new words the child encounters, because it provides a pronunciation for an unfamiliar word.

The typical sequence of instruction is as follows: The child first learns a 26 letter alphabet along with some instruction in phonological awareness. The first 8 weeks of instruction present the child with simple and compound vowels (in isolation), followed by an introduction to simple syllables in a pattern that repeats syllable endings (e.g., *ba, ma, fa; ban, man, fan*). Instruction soon includes reading sentences written in Pin Yin. The goal is that after 8 weeks, the child should know Pin Yin very well. The success of this instruction suggests that 8 weeks is sufficient to learn to read in an alphabetic system.

Following mastery of pin yin, characters are introduced, written above pin yin, for the remainder of the first school year. Pin yin is removed gradually, first for familiar characters, later for all characters, except when they are first introduced. Over 43 days of instruction (only 20 days in the newest methods of instruction), the child learns 202 characters, on his way to 2,500 after the first two years (Zhang, 1993).

One current issue in teaching reading in China concerns the role of phonetic components. The fact that Chinese compounds can share phonetic components has led to different approaches concerning these components. The traditional way has been to largely ignore phonetic components and teach the characters in what is called a "distributed" method. In this method, the fact that two components happen to share the same pronunciation, e.g., "yang", would not cause them to be taught together. A move in the opposite direction, an experimental approach called the "concentrated" method, instead introduces compounds containing the same phonetic at the same time during instruction. Essentially, in the concentrated method, children learn families of characters that share the same phonetic component.

Clearly, this "concentrated" method reflects a belief that children can and should take advantage of phonological information in forming their lexical representations. Thus, connections among the lexical representations for the many words that have the phonetic component *yang* would be strengthened in learning, as would the many words sharing the pronunciation *mao*, etc. Such a procedure would highlight the usefulness of phonology in the reading system and perhaps make it a more important part of the representation system. On the other hand, the fact that the child will face more invalid components (those not giving the pronunciation of the whole character) than valid components (those giving the pronunciation of the whole character) may imply some caution in use of such a method.

The issue of concentrated versus distributed methods seems surprisingly similar to debates in America and Europe about the teaching of reading. At one level, it is a technical issue about how to order materials in a decoding based system. At another level, it may be approximately a contrast between "sight learning" and "code based learning", including some of the side issues typical of such debates. Thus, one of the criticisms of the concentrated method is that it relies too much on reading of characters out of context. Although this debate may sound familiar, it is very different in one important respect: The differences in these two Chinese methods are trivial compared with their shared commitment to pin yin instruction. Children in China learn the alphabetic principle through what must be considered direct decoding instruction. Obviously, the corresponding debate in the West about teaching reading lacks that fundamental consensus.

This digression into method is also relevant for instruction in an alphabetic system. Teaching every character as a unique association is a possibility in Chinese, whereas it is clearly counterproductive in English or in any alphabetic writing system. Thus, it is of interest that, in China, there is any movement in the other direction, i.e., to teach Chinese as a partly phonetically productive system, as the concentrated method does. This implies not only that there is a principle organizing the Chinese writing system other than meaning and morphology, but that this principle can be applied to instruction. The Chinese example adds irony to the resistance to the application of this phonological principle in countries with alphabetic writing systems. For such systems, in contrast to Chinese, its application is essential rather than merely convenient.

## CONCLUSIONS

Two basic interrelated questions have been addressed: What does it mean to read a word? What does it mean for a child to learn to read? There are other possible answers to these questions and, indeed, the literature on reading has often assumed quite different answers from those I have suggested here.

None of what I propose should be misconstrued as claiming that meaning is not important in word reading or that comprehension is not involved in learning to read. Quite the contrary: Meaning is fundamental as the means to comprehension, which is the overarching subgoal in reading.[4] However confusing the goal of something with its essence is not progress. On theoretical grounds, there is reason to conclude that phonological forms are not simply constituents of word identification, but that they are privileged constituents. They are more reliable than meaning as well specified constituents of a specific word identification event. Phonological forms do not exactly mediate the access of meaning; along with their associated orthographic form, they constitute the word to which one might assign some meaning.

As for learning to read, I have suggested that the question to ask is how a child comes to learn how his or her writing system and its orthography work--the principles and the details. Reading for meaning and reading motivating and interesting texts are important ways to implement the goal of learning a writing system. It is important not to be misunderstood on this point. There is nothing in this argument that implies a de-emphasis on meaning and comprehension in the development of teaching strategies. I assume that children from the beginning should have their natural interest in stories and other meaning laden texts converted to instructional advantage. However, it is at least equally important to see that a child learns to read in the long run only by acquiring the knowledge about how his or her writing system works--how it encodes the language. This has to be the center of attention in defining the goals--not the implementation-- of beginning reading instruction.

The case of Chinese is interesting for several reasons. First, superficial considerations of Chinese have promoted the misconception that writing systems not only can be completely meaning-based, but can be read by strictly visual-to-semantic processes. The consequences of this misleading analysis have been to reinforce a mistaken belief that English also could be read as a visual-to-semantic system. Based on recent evidence, it appears that not even Chinese is read in exactly this way.

Another implication from Chinese is what it takes to become good at reading. The differences in what Chinese parents and educators expect children to do and what American parents and educators expect children to do in the way of learning is profound. With comparable expectations and commitments to meeting them, it is hard to imagine that educators would still be debating the "best method" in the U.S and Europe. All details about teaching methods would be swamped by a massive increase in the amount of time children spent learning their writing system. Furthermore, an alphabetic system is significantly easier to learn than a non-alphabetic system, so an

---

[4] Comprehension is more properly a subgoal than a goal in reading. It is a means to some functional or aesthetic goal.

English speaking child has a big advantage. The writing system is productive: A handful of letters and phonemic elements combine to generate an indefinitely large set of words. The system is there to be acquired as a system, despite its irregularities.

Beyond these specific implications of Chinese for reading English, there is a more general suggestion about learning to read. If writing systems were based on associations between visual objects and meaning, then there would be a problem in learning. The learner would not be able to interpose knowledge of the structure of spoken language in between the visual objects and the meaning. In fact, it appears that there is no writing system in current use that is like that. Writing systems cannot be seen as fundamentally arbitrary in their design. Of course, they are quite variable in the mix of principles that underlie their design. But there are no systems of writing based only on meaning and not on speech, not even Chinese.

An important function is served by the speech-based feature of writing systems. It allows users of the writing system to take advantage of their pre-existing linguistic knowledge, especially their knowledge of speech. As the learner figures out how his or her writing system encodes his or her language, and begins to gain some functional control over the orthographic details, decoding written sentences into language becomes possible. With more and more reading, the orthographic details become increasingly internalized and highly skilled reading emerges.

## ACKNOWLEDGMENTS

Parts of the chapter are drawn from previously published material, especially Perfetti & Zhang (1995b, 1996). The research on which the paper draws was funded by the National Science Foundation (grant SBR 9293125) and the Learning Research and Development Center, University of Pittsburgh.

## REFERENCES

Adams, M. J. (1990). *Beginning to read: Thinking and learning about print.* Cambridge, MA: MIT Press.

Ball, E. W., & Blachman, B. A. (1991) Does phoneme awareness training in kindergarten make a difference in early word recognition and developmental spelling? *Reading Research Quarterly, 26,* 49–66.

Baluch, B., & Besner, D. (1991) Visual word recognition: Evidence for strategic control of lexical and nonlexical routines in oral reading. *Journal of Experimental Psychology: Learning, Memory, and Cognition, 17,* 644–652.

Berent, I., & Perfetti, C. A. (1995) A rose is a REEZ: The two-cycles model of phonology assembly in reading English. *Psychological Review, 102,* 146–184.

Besner, D. (in press). Basic processes in reading: Multiple routines in localist and connectionist models. To appear in P. A. McMullen & R. M. Klein (Eds.),

*Converging methods for understanding reading and dyslexia.* Cambridge, MA: MIT Press.
Besner, D. (1990). Does the reading system need a lexicon? In D. Balota, G. B. Flores d'Arcais, & K. Rayner (Eds.), *Comprehension processes in reading* (pp. 73-99). Hillsdale, NJ: Lawrence Erlbaum Associates.
Besner, D., & Smith, M. C. (1992). Basic processes in reading: Is the orthographic depth hypothesis sinking? In R. Frost, & L. Katz (Eds.), *Orthography, phonology, morphology, and meaning* (pp. 45-66). Amsterdam: North-Holland.
Blachman, B. A. (1989). Phonological awareness and word recognition: Assessment and intervention. In A. G. Kamhi & H. W Catts (Eds.), *Reading disabilities: A developmental language perspective* (pp. 133-158). Boston: College Hill Press (Little, Brown and Company).
Bradley, L. L., & Bryant, P. E. (1983). Categorizing sounds and learning to read - a causal connection. *Nature, 301,* 419-421.
Bradley, L. L., & Bryant, P. E. (1985). *Rhyme and reason in reading and spelling.* Ann Arbor, MI: University of Michigan Press.
Brady, S. A., & Shankweiler, D. P. (Eds.) (1991). *Phonological processes in literacy: A tribute to Isabelle Y. Liberman.* Hillsdale, NJ: Lawrence Erlbaum Associates.
Boudberg, P. A. (1937). Some proleptic remarks on the evolution of archaic Chinese. *Harvard Journal of Asiatic Studies, 2,* 329-372.
Brooks, L. (1977). Visual pattern in fluent word identification. In A. S. Reber & D. L. Scarborough (Eds.), *Toward a psychology of reading* (pp. 143-181). Hillsdale, NJ: Lawrence Erlbaum Associates.
Byrne, B., & Fielding-Barnsley, R. (1991). Evaluation of a program to teach phonemic awareness to young children. *Journal of Educational Psychology, 83,* 451-455.
Byrne, B., & Fielding-Barnsley, R. (1993). Evaluation of a program to teach phonemic awareness to young children: A 1-year follow-up. *Journal of Educational Psychology, 85,* 104-111.
Chall, J. S. (1983). *Learning to read: The great debate.* Updated ed. New York: McGraw-Hill.
Chen, M. J., Lau, L. L. & Yung, Y. F. (1993). Development of component skills in reading Chinese. *International Journal of Psychology, 28,* 481-507.
Coltheart, M. (1978). Lexical access in simple reading tasks. In G. Underwood (Ed.), *Strategies of information processing* (pp. 151-216). New York: Academic Press.
Coltheart, M., Curtis, B., Atkins, P., & Haller, M. (1993). Models of reading aloud: Dual-route and parallel-distributed-processing approaches. *Psychological Review, 100,* 589-608.
Cunningham, A. E. (1990). Explicit versus implicit instruction in phonemic awareness. *Journal of Experimental Child Psychology, 50,* 429-444.
DeFrancis, J. (1989). *Visible speech: The diverse oneness of writing systems.* Honolulu: University of Hawaii.
Ehri, L. C. (1980). The development in orthographic images. In U. Frith (Ed.). *Cognitive processes in spelling* (pp. 311-388). London: Academic Press.
Ehri, L. C. (1987). Learning to read and spell words. *Journal of Reading Behavior, 19,* 5-31.
Ehri, L. C. (1991). Learning to read and spell words. In L. Rieben & C.A. Perfetti (Eds.), *Learning to read: Basic research and its implications* (pp. 57-73). Hillsdale, NJ: Lawrence Erlbaum Associates.
Ehri, L. C. (1992). Reconceptualizing the development of sight word reading and its relationship to recoding. In P. B. Gough, L. C. Ehri, & R. Treiman (Eds.), *Reading acquisition* (pp. 107-144). Hillsdale, NJ: Lawrence Erlbaum Associates.

Fang, S. P., Hong, R. Y., & Tzeng, O. J. L. (1986). Consistency effects in the Chinese character and pseudo-character naming tests. In H. S. R. Kao & R. Hoosain (Eds.) *Linguistics, psychology and the Chinese language* (pp. 11–21). Hong Kong: University of Hong Kong Press.

Flores D'Arcais, G. B., Saito, H., & Kawakami, M. (1995). Phonological and semantic activation in reading Kanji characters. *Journal of Experimental Psychology: Learning, Memory, and Cognition, 21,* 34–42.

Frith, U. (1985). Beneath the surface of developmental dyslexia. In K. E. Patterson, J. C. Marshall, & M. Coltheart (Eds.), *Surface dyslexia: Neuropsychological and cognitive studies of phonological reading* (pp. 301–330). London: Lawrence Erlbaum Associates.

Frost, R. (1995). Phonological computation and missing vowels: Mapping lexical involvement in reading. *Journal of Experimental Psychology: Learning, Memory, and Cognition, 21,* 398–408.

Frost, R. (1994). Prelexical and postlexical strategies in reading: Evidence from a deep and a shallow orthography. *Journal of Experimental Psychology: Learning, Memory, and Cognition, 20,* 116–129.

Frost, R., Katz, L., & Bentin, S. (1987). Strategies for visual word recognition and orthographical depth: A multilingual comparison. *Journal of Experimental Psychology: Human Perception and Performance, 13,* 104–115.

Gelb, I. J. (1952). *A study of writing.* Chicago: University of Chicago Press.

Gough, P. B., & Hillinger, M. L. (1980). Learning to read: An unnatural act. *Bulletin of the Orton Society, 20,* 179–196.

Gough, P. B., & Juel, C. (1991). The first stages of word recognition. In L. Rieben & C.A. Perfetti (Eds.), *Learning to read: Basic research and its implications* (pp. 47–56). Hillsdale, NJ: Lawrence Erlbaum Associates.

Gleitman, L. R., & Rozin, P. (1977). The structure and acquisition of reading I: Relations between orthographies and the structure of language. In A. S. Reber & D. L. Scarborough (Eds.), *Toward a psychology of reading: The proceedings of the CUNY conferences* (pp. 1–54). Hillsdale, NJ: Erlbaum (Distributed by Wiley).

Hatcher, P. J., Hulme, C., & Ellis, A. W. (1994). Ameliorating early reading failure by integrating the teaching of reading and phonological skills: The phonological linkage hypothesis. *Child Development, 65,* 41–57.

Hogaboam, T. W., & Perfetti, C. A. (1978). Reading skill and the role of verbal experience in decoding. *Journal of Educational Psychology, 70,* 717–729.

Leck, K. J., Weekes, B. S., & Chen, M. J. (1995). Visual and phonological pathways to the lexicon. *Memory & Cognition, 23,* 468–476.

Leong, C. K. (1973). Reading in Chinese with reference to reading practices in Hong Kong. In J. Downing (Ed.), *Comparative reading: Cross-national studies of behavior and processes in reading and writing* (pp. 383–402). New York: Macmillan.

Leong, C. K., & Tamaoka, K. (1995). Use of phonological information in processing Kanji and Katakana by skilled and less skilled Japanese readers. *Reading and Writing: An Interdisciplinary Journal, 7,* 377–393.

Liberman, I. Y., Shankweiler, D. P., Fischer, F. W., & Carter, B. (1974). Explicit syllable and phoneme segmentation in the young child. *Journal of Experimental Child Psychology, 18,* 201–212.

Lie, A. (1991). Effects of a training program for stimulating skills in word analysis in first-grade children. *Reading Research Quarterly, 26,* 234–249.

Lukatela, G., & Turvey, M. T. (1994). Visual lexical access is initially phonological: 1. Evidence from associate priming by words, homophones, and pseudo-homophones. *Journal of Experimental Psychology: General, 123,* 107–128.

Lundberg, I., Frost, J., & Petersen, O. P. (1988). Effects of an extensive program for stimulating phonological awareness in preschool children. *Reading Research Quarterly, 23,* 263–284.

Manis, F. R. (1985). Acquisition of word identification skills in normal and disabled readers. *Journal of Educational Psychology, 77,* 78–90.

Mann, V. A. (1991). Phonological abilities: Effective predictors of future reading ability. In L. Rieben & C.A. Perfetti (Eds.), *Learning to read: Basic research and its implications* (pp. 121–133). Hillsdale, NJ: Lawrence Erlbaum Associates.

Marsh, G., Friedman, M., Welch, V., & Desberg, P. (1981). A cognitive-developmental theory of reading acquisition. In G. E. MacKinnon & T. G. Waller (Eds.), *Reading research: Advances in theory and practice, Vol 3* (pp. 199–221). San Diego: Academic Press.

Mattingly, I. G. (1992). Linguistic awareness and orthographic form. In R. Frost & L. Katz (Eds.), *Orthography, phonology, morphology, and meaning* (pp. 11–26). Amsterdam: North-Holland.

McClelland, J. L., & Rumelhart, D. E. (1981). Interactive activation model of context effects in letter perception: 1. Account of basic findings. *Psychological Review, 88,* 357–407.

Morais, J., Bertelson, P., Cary, L., & Alegria, J. (1986). Literacy training and speech segmentation. *Cognition, 24,* 45–64.

Olson, R. K., Wise, B. W., Conners, F., & Rack, J. (1990). Organization, heritability, and remediation of component word recognition skills in disabled readers. In T. H. Carr & B. A. Levy (Eds.), *Reading and its development: Component skills approaches* (pp. 261–322). New York: Academic Press.

Paap, K. R., & Noel, R. W. (1991). Dual-route models of print and sound: Still a good horse race. *Psychological Research, 53,* 13–24.

Perfetti, C. A. (1991). Representations and awareness in the acquisition of reading competence. In L. Rieben & C. A. Perfetti (Eds.), *Learning to read: Basic research and its implications* (pp. 33–44). Hillsdale, NJ: Lawrence Erlbaum.

Perfetti, C. A. (1992). The representation problem in reading acquisition. In P. B. Gough, L. C. Ehri, & R. Treiman (Eds.), *Reading acquisition* (pp. 145–174). Hillsdale, NJ: Lawrence Erlbaum.

Perfetti, C. A., Beck, I., Bell, L., & Hughes, C. (1987). Phonemic knowledge and learning to read are reciprocal: A longitudinal study of first grade children. *Merrill-Palmer Quarterly, 33,* 283–319.

Perfetti, C. A., Bell, L., & Delaney, S. (1988). Automatic phonetic activation in silent word reading: Evidence from backward masking. *Journal of Memory and Language, 27,* 59–70.

Perfetti, C. A., & McCutchen, D. (1982). Speech processes in reading. In N. Lass (Ed.), *Speech and language: Advances in basic research and practice* (pp. 237–269). New York: Academic Press.

Perfetti, C. A., & Tan, L. H. (1998). The time course of graphic, phonological, and semantic activation in Chinese character activation. *Journal of Experimental Psychology: Learning, Memory, and Cognition, 24,* 101–118.

Perfetti, C. A., & Zhang, S. (1991). Phonological processes in reading Chinese characters. *Journal of Experimental Psychology: Learning, Memory, and Cognition, 17,* 633–643.

Perfetti, C. A., & Zhang, S. (1995). Very early phonological activation in Chinese reading. *Journal of Experimental Psychology: Learning, Memory, and Cognition, 21,* 24–33.

Perfetti, C. A., & Zhang, S. (1995). The word identification reflex: A universal principle. In D. L. Medin (Ed.), *The psychology of learning and motivation, Vol*

32. New York: Academic Press.

Perfetti, C. A., & Zhang, S. (1996). What it means to learn to read. In M. F. Graves, B. M. Taylow, & P. Van den Broek (Eds.), *The first R: Children's right to read* (pp. 37-60). New York: Teachers College Press.

Perfetti, C. A., Zhang, S., & Berent, I. (1992). Reading in English and Chinese: Evidence for a "universal" phonological principle. In R. Frost & L. Katz (Eds.), *Orthography, phonology, morphology, and meaning* (pp. 227-248). Amsterdam: North-Holland.

Pinker, S. (1984). *Language learnability and language development.* Cambridge, MA: Harvard University Press.

Plaut, D. C., McClelland, J. L., Seidenberg, M. S., & Patterson, K. (1996). Understanding normal and impaired word reading: Computational principles in quasi-regular domains. *Psychological Review, 103,* 56–115.

Reitsma, P. (1983). Word-specific knowledge in beginning reading. *Journal of Research in Reading, 6,* 41–56.

Read, C., Zhang, Y., Nie, H., & Ding, B. (1986). The ability to manipulate speech sounds depends on knowing alphabetic reading. *Cognition, 24,* 31–44.

Sebastian-Galles, N. (1991). Reading by analogy in a shallow orthography. *Journal of Experimental Psychology: Human Perception and Performance, 17,* 471–477.

Seidenberg, M. S., & McClelland, J. L. (1989). A distributed, developmental model of word recognition and naming. *Psychological Review, 96,* 523–568.

Share, D. L. (1995). Phonological recoding and self-teaching: *sine qua non* of reading acquisition. *Cognition, 55,* 151–218.

Share, D. L., & Stanovich, K. E. (1995). Cognitive processes in early reading development: Accommodating individual differences into a model of acquisition. *Issues in Education, 1,* 1–57.

Shimron, J. (1993). The role of vowels in reading: A review of studies in English and Hebrew. *Psychological Bulletin, 114,* 52–67.

Schneider, W., & Shiffrin, R. M. (1977). Controlled and automatic human information processing: I. detection, search, and attention. *Psychological Review, 84,* 1–66.

Simpson, G. B. (1994). Context and the processing of ambiguous words. In M. A. Gernsbacher (Ed.), *Handbook of psycholinguistics* (pp. 359–374). San Diego: Academic Press.

Simpson, G. B., & Kang, H. (1994). The flexible use of phonological information in word recognition in Korean. *Journal of Memory and Language, 33,* 319–331.

Stevenson, H. W., & Lee, S.-Y. (1990). *Contexts of achievement: A study of American, Chinese, and Japanese children.* Chicago: University of Chicago Press.

Stanovich, K. E., & West, R. F. (1989). Exposure to print and orthographic processing. *Reading Research Quarterly, 24,* 402–433.

Stuart, M. (1990). Factors influencing word recognition in pre-reading children. *British Journal of Psychology, 81,* 135–146.

Stuart, M., & Coltheart, M. (1988). Does reading develop in a sequence of stages? *Cognition, 30,* 139–181.

Tabossi, P., & Laghi, L. (1992). Semantic priming in the pronunciation of words in two writing systems: Italian and English. *Memory & Cognition, 20,* 303–313.

Tan, L. H., Hoosain, R., & Peng, D.-L. (1995). Role of early presemantic phonological code in Chinese character identification. *Journal of Experimental Psychology: Learning, Memory, and Cognition, 21,* 43–54.

Tan, L. H., & Peng, D.-L. (1991). Visual recognition processes of Chinese characters. *Acta Psychologica Sinica, 3,* 272–278.

Tan, L. H., & Perfetti, C.A. (1997). Visual Chinese character recognition: Does phonological information mediate access to meaning? *Journal of Memory and Language, 37*, 41–57.
Torgesen, J. K., Morgan, S. T., & Davis, C. (1992). Effects of two types of phonological awareness training on word learning in kindergarten children. *Journal of Educational Psychology, 84*, 364–370.
Treiman, R., & Baron, J. (1983). Phonemic-analysis training helps children benefit from spelling-sound rules. *Memory & Cognition, 11*, 382–389.
Tunmer, W. E., Herriman, M. L., & Nesdale, A. R. (1988). Metalinguistic abilities and beginning reading. *Reading Research Quarterly, 23*, 134–158.
Van Orden, G. C. (1987). A ROWS is a ROSE: Spelling, sound, and reading. *Memory & Cognition, 15*, 181–198.
Van Orden, G. C., & Goldinger, S. D. (1994). The interdependence of form and function in cognitive systems explains perception of printed words. *Journal of Experimental Psychology: Human Perception and Performance, 20*, 1269–1291.
Vellutino, F. R., & Scanlon, D. M. (1991). The effects of instructional bias on word identification. In L. Rieben & C.A. Perfetti (Eds.), *Learning to read: Basic research and its implications* (pp. 189–203). Hillsdale, NJ: Lawrence Erlbaum Associates.
Venezky, R. L., & Massaro, D. W. (1979). The role of orthographic regularity in word recognition. In L. B. Resnick, & P. A. Weaver (Eds.) *Theories and practice in early reading, Vol 1* (pp. 85-107). Hillsdale, NJ: Lawrence Erlbaum Associates.
Williams, J. P. (1980). Teaching decoding with an emphasis on phoneme analysis and phoneme blending. *Journal of Educational Psychology, 72*, 1–15.
Wydell, T. N., Patterson, K. E., & Humphreys, G. W. (1993). Phonologically mediated access to meaning for Kanji: Is a *rows* still a *rose* in Japanese Kanji? *Journal of Experimental Psychology: Learning, Memory, and Cognition, 19*, 491–514.
Zhang, C. F. (1993). Introducing the method of direct reading into the teaching of concentrated literacy. *Chinese Language Construction, 3*, 24–26.
Zhang, S., & Perfetti, C.A. (1993). The tongue twister effect in reading Chinese. *Journal of Experimental Psychology: Learning, Memory, and Cognition, 19*, 1082–1093.
Zhang, W. T., Feng, L., & He, H. D. (1994). The activation of phonological and semantic information in Chinese character recognition. In H.-W. Chang, J.-T. Huang, C. -W Hue, & O. J. L. Tzeng (Eds.) *Language processing in Chinese* (pp. 185–198). Amsterdam: Elsevier.
Zhou, Y. G. (1978). To what degree are the "phonetics" of present-day Chinese characters still phonetic? *Zhongguo Yuwen, 146*, 172–177.

# GENERAL AND SPECIFIC ABILITIES AS PREDICTORS OF READING ACHIEVEMENT

A considerable amount of research has been devoted to the search for early and specific predictors of reading achievement, i.e., of word decoding and reading comprehension. Phonological abilities are believed to be a major determinant of the development of word decoding (Wagner & Torgesen, 1987) and are generally found to be better predictors than measures of vocabulary (Baddeley & Gathercole, 1992; Mann & Ditunno, 1990; Wagner, Torgesen, & Rashotte, 1994), In contrast, vocabulary seems to be a major determinant of reading comprehension (Anderson & Freebody, 1981; Bast, 1995, but see Schneider & Näslund, in press).

A number of longitudinal studies has been conducted to determine the specificity or causal nature of the relation between phonological processing abilities in kindergarten and the acquisition of word decoding (Baddeley & Gathercole, 1992; Bast, 1995; Mann & Ditunno, 1990; Perfetti, Beck, Bell, & Hughes, 1987; Vellutino & Scanlon, 1987; Wagner et al., 1994). Also, a few longitudinal studies have been concerned with the specific relation between vocabulary and reading comprehension (Bast, 1995; Schneider & Näslund, in press). The interpretation of the results of these studies is critically dependent on the application of a well-specified causal model. One source of misspecification concerns the omission of known plausible causes, which might account for the observed relationship between phonological abilities and reading achievement.

One obvious plausible cause is the autoregressive effect of reading acquisition (Wagner et al., 1994). The best predictor of reading achievement is the development of reading at an earlier age. Most of the studies mentioned before have not incorporated this effect. Of course, children in kindergarten are unable to read. But reading related skills, as letter knowledge, could have been used as an alternative (e.g., Schneider & Näslund, in press; Wagner et al., 1994). Other plausible alternative causes are likely to entail more general abilities than phonological skills. Recent analyses of the structure of ability tests tend to support a hierarchical model with specific abilities at the lowest level, broader abilities at an intermediate level, and one general ability at the highest level (e.g., Carroll, 1993; Gustafsson, 1984; Undheim & Gustafsson, 1987). In a hierarchical model the performance on a lower order ability is assumed to be partly dependent on higher order abilities. Consequently, a relation between a specific ability and reading achievement might be due to a more general ability, the specific ability at hand, or both. Thus, inclusion of more general abilities is needed to determine the specific contribution of phonological abilities to the acquisition of reading.

Ideally, a broad range of abilities should be selected so that the phonological abilities can be situated within an hierarchical model of human abilities. More pragmatically, one might argue that at least aspects of nonverbal and verbal abilities should be selected, because these abilities are close to the major higher order factors included in current models of human abilities.

TABLE 1
Correlations between kindergarten measures of Vocabulary (Voc), Nonverbal IQ (NV) or IQ and Word Decoding in Grade 1 or 2 from various longitudinal studies

| Study | N | Gr | TC | Correlations Voc | NV | IQ |
|---|---|---|---|---|---|---|
| Share et al. (1984) | 220 | 1 | O | .39 | - | - |
| Vellutino & Scanlon (1987) | 202 | 1 | O | .24 | - | .34 |
|  | 126 | 2 | O | .26 | - | .39 |
|  | 61 | 1 | O | .40 | .39 | - |
|  | 92 | 2 | O | .52 | .32 | - |
| Francis et al. (1989) | 220 | 2 | E | .47 | .48 | - |
| Mann & Ditunno (1990) | 31 | 1 | O | .44 | .51 | - |
|  | 39 | 1 | O | .33 | .39 | - |
| Bryant et al. (1990) | 64 | 2 | E | ? | - | .56 |
| Baddeley & Gathercole (1992) | ? | 1 | O | .37 | .42 | - |
|  | ? | 1 | O | .27 | .44 | - |
| Wagner et al. (1994) | 244 | 1 | E | .34 | - | - |
| Bast (1995) | 235 | 1 | O | .02 | .28 | - |
| Schneider & Näslund (in press) | 163 | 2 | O | ? | .27 | - |
|  | 163 | 2 | O | ? | .17 | - |

Note. N = Number of participants; Gr = Grade in which word decoding is measured; TC = Type of correlation (O = observed, E = estimated)

In Table 1 correlations are presented that have been reported between kindergarten measures of vocabulary, nonverbal abilities and overall IQ, and reading achievement at the end of Grade 1 or Grade 2. Only studies on word decoding are listed, because for reading comprehension hardly any longitudinal studies were available. The results suggest that all abilities are substantially correlated with word decoding. In most studies the correlation of word decoding with nonverbal abilities or IQ is equal or larger than its correlation with vocabulary. These results clearly suggest that in addition to verbal abilities, nonverbal abilities should also be incorporated in a longitudinal study on the specific predictors of word decoding.

Word decoding is often assumed to underlie reading comprehension in the early phases of learning to read. Predictors of word decoding are therefore likely to account for individual differences in reading comprehension as well. Bast (1995), however, reported results which suggest that already after one year of formal reading instruction early predictors of word decoding and reading comprehension can be differentiated. These results are in accordance with a general belief that the cognitive and environmental determinants of these aspects of reading differ (Leseman, 1993; Snow, 1991, 1993). Therefore, additional research on this issue seems to be worthwhile.

In this chapter we first report on a longitudinal study in which we investigated the effects of phonological skills in kindergarten on word decoding at the end of Grade 1. Three types of phonological skills were distinguished: 1) phonological awareness, 2) phonological coding in short term memory, and 3) retrieval of a phonological code from a long term store (cf. Wagner & Torgesen, 1987). To determine the specificity of the effects of these phonological abilities we included measures of both verbal and nonverbal abilities, and letter knowledge as a proxy variable for reading acquisition in kindergarten. Specificity was further examined by contrasting the effects of phonological skills on word decoding to their effects on reading comprehension. Finally, we included children from various ethnic groups in our study. Two of these groups are known to lag behind in vocabulary acquisition in comparison to their Dutch peers (De Jong, Klapwijk, & Van der Leij, 1995). If vocabulary affects the acquisition of word decoding large differences can be expected between these groups and their Dutch peers.

Wagner et al. (1994) found a large effect of phonological awareness in kindergarten on word decoding at the end of Grade 1. Other types of phonological skills did not exert an effect, after phonological awareness was controlled for. However, a major difference between our study and the study of Wagner et al. is, that they did not include a measure of nonverbal intelligence. The high relationship between phonological analysis and word decoding in their study might be due to a more general ability. Interestingly, in a previous study (Wagner, Torgesen, Laughon, Simmons, & Rashotte, 1993) a measure of general ability was included. In this cross-sectional study with children from kindergarten and Grade 2 similar phonological abilities were measured as in the study by Wagner et al. (1994). However, Wagner et al. (1993) did not report on the specific effects of the various phonological abilities on word decoding after general ability was taken into account. Therefore, next to the presentation of our own study, a supplementary analysis of the data of Wagner et al. (1993) is presented in order to gain further insight in the specificity of the relationship between phonological skills and early word decoding, and the possible effects of omitting nonverbal IQ.

## SPECIFIC PREDICTORS OF READING ACHIEVEMENT: NEW DATA

In this study we investigated the specific effects of phonological skills and vocabulary on word decoding and reading comprehension. Phonological skills and vocabulary were measured at the beginning of the second year in kindergarten. At this time also nonverbal intelligence and letter knowledge were tested. Word decoding and reading comprehension were measured at the end of Grade 1.

## Method

### Participants

Participants were 262 children from 28 elementary schools situated in or near the four major cities of the Netherlands. The children participated in a longitudinal study about school carriers (for a detailed description, see De Jong & Van der Leij, 1998). The children were from diverse ethnic origins: 175 children (62 boys and 113 girls) came from native Dutch families, 57 children (30 boys and 27 girls) were from Surinamese families and 30 children (15 boys and 15 girls) originated from Turkish families.

### Instruments

Nonverbal intelligence was measured by two tests:

*Block Design* (subtest of the Leidse Diagnostische Test; Schroots & Van Alphen de Veer, 1976). The test required the reconstruction of a printed pattern in red and white colours from wooden red and white triangles. The printed pattern remained visible. Testing stopped when a child failed on three consecutive items.

*Figural exclusion* (subtest of the RAKIT; Bleichrodt, Drenth, Zaal, & Resing, 1987). The child had to indicate within 30 seconds which one of four figures differs from the other three. The test was stopped when four consecutive items failed.

Two measures of vocabulary were included:

*Receptive Vocabulary* (subtest of Taaltoets voor Allochtone Kinderen; Verhoeven & Vermeer, 1986). Each item consisted of four pictures and a spoken word. The picture had to be chosen that best matches the spoken word. The administration of the test was stopped when the child failed six or more of the last eight items.

*Productive Vocabulary.* An easier test (Schoonen & Damhuis, 1992) and a more difficult test (a subtest of the TAK; Verhoeven & Vermeer, 1986) were administered. On both tests items required the production of a word that best described a given picture. The tests were administered to random groups and the scores were made equivalent.

Three domains of phonological skills were distinguished. Phonological awareness was measured by three sound categorization tasks. For phonological coding in short-term memory, for short denoted as verbal working memory, two span tests and a nonword repetition test were used. Finally, retrieval of a phonological code was measured by a rapid naming task.

*Sound Categorization.* Three sound-oddity detection tests were used, each with 10 items preceded by 2 practice items and presented on audiotape with a 1-s interword interval. Each item consisted of 3 words of 3 sounds, and was presented twice. On the first test, rhyme detection, the child had to indicate which of the three words did not rhyme with the other two. The second test required the identification of the word with a different first sound. On the third test the child had to identify the word which had a final sound that differed from the other two words.

*Word Span.* The test required the retention and reproduction of a sequence of two to five monosyllabic words that were presented on audiotape with a 1-s interword interval. After the presentation of a sequence of words a number of pictures was presented, always one more than the number of words presented. The child was asked to select the pictures in the same order as the words they had heard on the audiotape.

*Interference Span.* This test was similar to the word span test, but differed in three respects. Firstly, different words were used, Secondly, the interword interval was 3 seconds instead of one. Finally and more importantly, between the presentation of two words and after the last word of a sequence a simple figural exclusion item had to be executed. The number of words in a series increased from two to five.

*Nonword Repetition.* The test required the repetition of one to four syllable nonwords that were presented on audiotape (Gathercole, Willis, Baddeley, & Emslie, 1994). Each word was presented twice before a response was requested.

*Rapid Naming.* The test required the speeded naming of a series of pictures which represented five common objects. Following one card for practice, two test cards were presented. For each card the number of pictures named per second was scored.

Knowledge of the ten most frequently used letters in Dutch books for children (Staphorsius, Krom, & de Geus, 1987) was tested. Five of these letters were used to test for receptive letter knowledge. the other letters were included in the test for productive knowledge.

*Receptive knowledge of letters.* Five printed letters were presented on a card. The sounds of these letters were named. After each sound the child had to indicate the printed letter that matched this sound.

*Productive knowledge of letters.* Five printed letters were presented on a card and the child had to name each of these letters. Both the sound and the name of a letter were considered correct.

Reading achievement was measured by the following tests:

*Word Decoding.* A standardized decoding test (One Minute Test; Brus & Voeten, 1979) requires the speeded decoding of 116 single words of increasing difficulty, and has two parallel versions. The score is the number of words read correctly in one minute. Separate scores were taken for both versions.

*Reading Comprehension.* This test (Verhoeven, 1993) required the understanding of anaphora (e.g., where, what, and who). The test contained six stories of 29 to 57 words. Each story was followed by four multiple choice questions. Separate scores were computed for the odd and the even items.

## Procedure

All testing was done by trained test assistants. The interference span test and the nonword repetition test were administered to a subsample only. The other tests were made by the complete sample of participants.

## Analyses

*Missing data.* The data of this study were part of a larger longitudinal study, and most variables were measured on several occasions. Missing data could be replaced on the basis of the observations of the same variable on other occasions, assuming that at least two such observations were available. Except for reading achievement, this appeared always to be the case. Missing observations were imputed with regression analyses.

*Structural equation modeling.* Confirmatory factor analyses were conducted with the program EQS (Bentler, 1989). Model fit was evaluated with the $\chi^2$ statistic, the Non-normed Fit Index (NNFI) and the Comparative Fit Index (CFI; Bentler, 1989, 1990). We performed multiple group analyses (Bentler, 1989). One group consisted of 150 children who had completed all tests. The other group contained 112 children who did not complete the two tests mentioned before (see Procedure). Unlike stated otherwise, the parameter estimates in both groups were constrained to be equal.

Ethnicity was incorporated as a dummy variable in the analyses (Muthén, 1989). Observed and latent variables were regressed on these dummy variables and only significant coefficients were maintained in the model. Thus, mean differences between the ethnic groups on the variables were incorporated in the model. The intercorrelations among the variables were assumed to be equal across the three ethnic groups (Muthén, 1989).

## RESULTS

*Descriptive statistics and preliminary analyses*

Table 2 presents the means and standard deviations on the tests for the three ethnic groups. One-way analyses of variance to test for mean differences among the ethnic groups were performed and the resulting F-statistics are also displayed in the table.

TABLE 2
Means and standard deviations (between brackets) on the tests per ethnic group and F-value for the difference between the means

| Test | Max | Dutch | Surinamese | Turkish | F |
|---|---|---|---|---|---|
| *Nonverbal Intelligence* | | | | | |
| Block Design | 30 | 17.28 | 16.35 | 15.92 | 1.78 |
| | | (4.50) | (4.61) | (3.71) | |
| Exclusion | 30 | 18.93 | 18.77 | 18.01 | .46 |
| | | (4.93) | (4.97) | (4.35) | |
| *Vocabulary* | | | | | |
| Receptive Vocabulary | 98 | 52.60 | 44.75 | 24.29 | 45.07** |
| | | (16.34) | (13.21) | (12.48) | |
| Productive Vocabulary | 48 | 32.21 | 27.85 | 15.96 | 131.69** |
| | | (4.50) | (5.75) | (7.04) | |
| *Phonological Skills* | | | | | |
| Rapid Naming | – | 1.62 | 1.50 | 1.57 | 2.89 |
| | | (.33) | (.35) | (.39) | |
| Sound Categ. Rhyme | 10 | 5.82 | 4.87 | 4.88 | 6.81* |
| | | (1.85) | (2.19) | (2.04) | |
| First Sound Categ. | 10 | 4.18 | 3.99 | 3.61 | 1.90 |
| | | (1.60) | (1.26) | (1.52) | |
| Last Sound Categ. | 10 | 3.38 | 3.63 | 3.60 | 1.06 |
| | | (1.28) | (1.16) | (1.18) | |
| Word Span | 12 | 5.51 | 4.85 | 4.66 | 2.29 |
| | | (2.58) | (2.71) | (2.55) | |
| Interference Span [a] | 12 | 3.44 | 3.11 | 2.84 | 1.51 |
| | | (1.73) | (1.59) | (1.25) | |
| Nonword Repet. [a] | 48 | 25.75 | 25.00 | 25.52 | .18 |
| | | (6.19) | (6.56) | (6.36) | |
| *Knowledge of Letters* | | | | | |
| Passive Knowledge | 5 | 2.08 | 1.43 | 1.58 | 4.22* |
| | | (1.65) | (1.43) | (1.53) | |
| Active Knowledge | 5 | 1.33 | .55 | .95 | 4.11* |
| | | (1.55) | (.83) | (1.34) | |
| *Reading Achievement* | | | | | |
| Word Decoding | 232 | 43.23 | 39.92 | 41.40 | .63 |
| | | (25.00) | (21.38) | (23.82) | |
| Reading Compr. | 24 | 14.40 | 14.45 | 12.18 | 1.79 |
| | | (6.45) | (5.24) | (5.35) | |

[a] Test was administered to a subgroup only; * $p < .05$. ** $p < .01$.

Two results reported in Table 2 are noteworthy. Firstly, the mean scores on two sound categorization tests (first sound and last sound) were hardly above chance. These tests appeared too difficult at this age and were dropped. Secondly, the differences among the groups are not uniform. Especially the similar performance on the tests for reading achievement in combination with the huge differences among the groups in vocabulary supports the contention that vocabulary is hardly important in the early phases of reading acquisition.

*Separation of general and specific predictors*

Before we pursued the best predictors of reading achievement, we examined the hypothesized structure of the predictors. We specified a five factor model, in which the remaining indicator of phonological awareness, sound categorization, was supposed to reflect working memory (cf. Wagner et al., 1993, for a similar approach). The five factors were formed by 1) two tests for nonverbal intelligence, 2) two tests for vocabulary, 3) two versions of the Rapid Naming test, 4) the tests for verbal working memory and the test for sound categorization (rhyme), and 5) two tests for letter knowledge. Ethnicity, with two dummy variables (Surinamese or not, and Turkish origin or not), was incorporated in the model. After the deletion of one outlier, the model appeared to have a good fit, $\chi^2$ (142,N=261) = 147.19, p=.37 (NNFI=1.00; CFI=1.00).

Next, a General Specific-model (GS-model), which consists of a set of factors that differ in degree of generality (Gustafsson & Balke, 1993), was specified. The model has one general factor on which all tests can load, and a number of specific factors, orthogonal to the general factor on which only certain tests are free to load. The present GS-model consisted of one general factor and the five factors mentioned above. The factors were considered as independent. To ensure model fit two fixed factor loadings had to be freed. This model appeared to fit the data, $\chi^2$ (141, N=261) = 134.48, p=.64 (NNFI= 1.00; CFI=1.00). Inspection of the parameter estimates, however, revealed that the variance of the verbal working memory factor was not significant, and was therefore dropped. The model with one general factor and four specific factors did also have a good fit, $\chi^2$ (145,N=261) = 142.09, p=.55 (NNFI=1.00; CFI=1.00). Finally, a significant improvement of the model was obtained when both tests for letter knowledge were accepted to load on the Vocabulary factor, $\Delta \chi^2$ (2,N=261)= 7.09, p< .05.

The parameter estimates of the final GS-model are displayed in Table 3. The tests for nonverbal intelligence and verbal working memory had their major loadings on the General Factor (GF). This factor described the major part of the systematic variation on these tests, ranging from 26% for Exclusion to 44% for Interference Span. Block Design and Exclusion had additional loadings on a nonverbal intelligence factor, but these loadings were too small to be of interest. The tests for vocabulary, rapid naming and letter knowledge had their largest loading on their specific factor. These factors, therefore, might have an effect on reading achievement that is independent from the effect of GF.

TABLE 3
Standardized factor loadings of the tests on the general factor and on the specific factors

| Tests | GF | NV | VO | RN | LK |
|---|---|---|---|---|---|
| Block Design | .57 | .32 | | | |
| Exclusion | .51 | .30 | | | |
| Receptive Vocabulary | .46 | | .69 | | |
| Productive Vocabulary | .31 | | .69 | | |
| Rapid Naming 1 | .39 | | .14 | .72 | |
| Rapid Naming 2 | .32 | | | .72 | |
| Sound Categorization | .58 | | | | |
| Word Span | .65 | | | | |
| Interference Span | .66 | | | | |
| Nonword Repetition | .65 | | | | |
| Passive Letter K. | .43 | | .13 | | .65 |
| Active Letter K. | .51 | | .18 | | .71 |

*Note.* GF = General Factor; NV = Nonverbal Intelligence; VO = Vocabulary; RN = Rapid Naming; LK = Letter Knowledge.

## Prediction of reading achievement

The next step was to extend the GS-model with extra factors for word decoding and reading comprehension. Word decoding was indicated by both versions of the single word reading test. The factor reading comprehension was formed by the scores for the odd and the even items of the test, respectively. Then, we regressed the factors for word decoding and reading comprehension on the latent predictors. Note here that the latent predictor variables are independent. Thus, problems of multicollinearity will not occur.

TABLE 4
Standardized regression coefficients and percentages of explained variance ($R^2$) for the prediction of Word Decoding and Reading Comprehension

| Achievement | Predictor | | | | | |
| | GF | NV | VO | RN | LK | $R^2$ |
|---|---|---|---|---|---|---|
| Word Decoding | .53 | - | - | .16 | .17 | .33 |
| Reading Comprehension | .71 | - | - | - | - | .50 |

*Note.* GF = General Factor; NV = Nonverbal Intelligence; VO = Vocabulary; RN = Rapid Naming; LK = Letter Knowledge.

The $\chi^2$ statistic of the extended GS-model proved to be acceptable, $\chi^2$ (255, N=258) = 296.88, p=.04 (NNFI=.98; CFI=.98). The standardized regression coefficients between the predictors and the factors for reading achievement are presented in Table 4. For Word Decoding about one third of the variance ($R^2$) could be described by the predictors, mainly by GF. Of the other factors only Rapid Naming and Letter Knowledge described additional variance. The only significant predictor of Reading Comprehension was the general factor, accounting for about 50% of the variance.

## SUPPLEMENTARY ANALYSIS OF WAGNER ET AL. (1993)

Wagner et al. (1993) investigated the structure of phonological abilities in children from kindergarten and Grade 2 and the relations of these abilities with general abilities and word decoding. They administered tasks that were assumed to reflect a range of phonological abilities and tasks that were selected to reflect general abilities and word decoding. Conducting confirmatory analyses they found four phonological factors in kindergarten and five in Grade 2. The main difference was that in kindergarten phonological analysis and working memory could not be separated. Note that in the present study, we also could not find a separate factor for phonological awareness. The phonological factors both groups had in common were synthesis, isolated naming and serial naming. In addition to the phonological factors, Wagner et al. distinguished a factor for general ability and for word decoding.

To examine general and specific effects of the phonological factors on word decoding, we conducted fixed order regression analyses in which the general ability factor was always entered first. In the next step each phonological factor was entered. The regression analyses for the kindergarten sample were based on the factor intercorrelations reported in Table 7 (Wagner et al., 1993, p. 97). Regression analyses of the Grade 2 sample were based on the factor intercorrelations in Table 8 (Wagner et al., 1993, p. 99).

In Table 5 the results of the regression analyses for the Wagner et al. (1993) study are presented. For the children in kindergarten the results are similar to the results of our own study. The Analysis/ Working Memory factor did hardly add extra variance in the prediction of word recognition after General Ability was accounted for. Naming, both isolated and serial, did however have an extra effect after entering General Ability. In Grade 2 the influence of the phonological factors was much larger. Especially, Analysis had an extra influence on word decoding after General Ability was controlled for.

TABLE 5
Supplementary analysis of Wagner et al. (1993):
Results of stepwise regression analyses for the prediction of word decoding

| Steps | Ability | Incremental $R^2$ | |
| --- | --- | --- | --- |
| | | Kindergarten | Grade 2 |
| 1. | General Ability | 28.8** | 30.6** |
| 2. | Analysis/Working Memory | 2.2+ | |
| | Analysis | | 10.2** |
| | Synthesis | 2.6+ | 4.3* |
| | Working Memory | | 0.3 |
| | Naming-Isolated | 3.9* | 1.0 |
| | Naming-Serial | 6.2** | 3.3* |

*Note.* Kindergarten $N = 95$, Grade 2 $N = 89$. $^+ p < .10$. $^* p < .05$. $^{**} p < .01$.

## GENERAL DISCUSSION

The main purpose of the present chapter was to examine the specific contributions of kindergarten children's' phonological abilities to early reading acquisition, i.e., word decoding. Specificity was considered in two ways. One was to determine the relationship between phonological abilities and word decoding, when other plausible causes of word decoding, as the autoregressive effect and general abilities, were taken into account. Another way was to consider whether the effects of phonological abilities were limited to word decoding or generalized to other types of reading achievement such as reading comprehension. To pursue the specific contributions of phonological abilities we conducted a longitudinal study and presented a supplementary analysis on the data of Wagner et al. (1993).

Our main finding is that general abilities in kindergarten best predict the differences in early reading acquisition. In our longitudinal study we found that the general factor was the most important predictor of both word decoding and reading comprehension at the end of Grade 1. For word decoding letter knowledge and rapid naming appeared to have small additional effects. With respect to word decoding highly similar results were revealed by the supplementary analysis of the Wagner et al. (1993) study. In their kindergarten sample small effects of naming were obtained after general ability was controlled for. Thus, specific effects of phonological awareness and verbal working memory in kindergarten on word decoding were not found.

The longitudinal study also revealed that vocabulary did not have a specific effect on reading achievement. This finding might be due to the reading comprehension test used in the study. This test measured the ability to understand referral words. Although the correct use of these words definitely adds to the comprehension of a text, vocabulary might not be very important as long as the words in the text are known.

Wagner et al. (1994) reported large effects of phonological awareness in kindergarten on word decoding in Grade 1. Naming, which was the only phonological ability important in our longitudinal study, did not exert an effect after phonological analysis was taken into account. Several differences between the study of Wagner et al. and our study may account for the different outcomes. Whereas Wagner et al. could distinguish a separate factor for phonological analysis, in our study this factor could not be detected because the mean performance on two of the three sound categorization tasks was hardly above chance level. However, the results of Wagner et al. indicate that at least two of their tasks were also too difficult. For sound categorization the performance was hardly above chance level. Performance on phoneme elision was near zero and the distribution was probably highly skewed. Thus, as in our study, the tasks to measure phonological analysis were very difficult for kindergarten children, probably indicating that these phonological abilities are hardly developed yet.

In contrast to the study of Wagner et al. (1994), we included a measure of general ability. The high relationship between phonological analysis and word decoding in the study of Wagner et al. might be due to general ability. In this respect the supplementary analysis of the data of the Wagner et al. (1993) study is of interest. Wagner et al. (1993) and Wagner et al. (1994) used very similar tasks to measure phonological abilities. The supplementary analysis showed that in kindergarten, except for naming, the relationship between phonological skills and word decoding was due to their common relationship to a general ability factor. These analyses suggest that the importance of phonological analysis in kindergarten for the prediction of Grade 1 performance might be overestimated in the Wagner et al. (1994) study, while the influence of naming is underestimated.

There is much evidence for a reciprocal causal relationship between the development of phonological abilities and the acquisition of word decoding. Indeed, in our supplementary analysis of Wagner et al. (1993) we found in Grade 2 clear effects of phonological abilities on word decoding even after general abilities were controlled for. Our results do, however, question the onset of this bi-directional relationship. Particularly, the results cast doubts about the importance of phonological abilities in kindergarten for the prediction of the acquisition of word decoding. One reason for this might be that kindergarten phonological abilities are not yet sufficiently developed to have much specific predictive value. Another reason might be that individual differences in early reading achievement primarily reflect more general abilities. Evidence on skill acquisition suggests that general cognitive abilities determine initial differences in acquisition, while eventually skill-specific abilities prevail (e.g., Ackerman, 1987, 1988). Thus, phonological abilities acquire their causal influence on the acquisition of word decoding after the early phases of reading acquisition when the specific mechanisms that underlie reading become more important. Children that appear to be unable to develop phonological abilities by that time might be called really 'at risk' for reading problems.

## REFERENCES

Ackerman, P. L. (1987). Individual differences in skill learning: An integration of psychometric and information processing perspectives. *Psychological Bulletin, 102*, 3-27.

Ackerman, P. L. (1988). Determinants of individual differences during skill acquisition. *Journal of Experimental Psychology: General, 117*, 288-318.

Anderson, R. C., & Freebody, P. (1981). Vocabulary knowledge. In J. T. Guthrie (Ed.), *Comprehension and teaching: Research reviews* (pp.77-117). Newark, DE.: International Reading Association.

Baddeley, A. D., & Gathercole, S. E. (1992). Learning to read: The role of the phonological loop. In J. Alegria, D. Holender, J. Junca de Morais, & M. Radeau (Eds.), *Analytic approaches to human cognition* (pp. 153-167). Amsterdam: Elsevier Science Publishers.

Bast, J. W. (1995). *The development of individual differences in reading ability.* Duivendrecht, The Netherlands: Vrije Universiteit, Paedologisch Instituut.

Bentler, P. M. (1989). *EQS structural equations program manual.* Los Angeles: BMDP Statistical Software.

Bentler, P. M. (1990). Comparative fit indexes in structural models. *Psychological Bulletin, 107*, 238-246.

Bleichrodt, N. D., Drenth, P. J. D., Zaal, J. N., & Resing, W. C. M. (1987). *Revisie Amsterdamse Kinder Intelligentie Test* [Revision of the Amsterdam Intelligence Test for Children]. Lisse, The Netherlands: Swets & Zeitlinger.

Brus, B. T., & Voeten, M. J. M. (1979). *Een-minuut-test* [One-minute-test]. Nijmegen, The Netherlands: Berkhout.

Carroll, J. B. (1993). *Human cognitive abilities: A survey of factor-analytic studies.* New York: Cambridge University Press.

De Jong, P. F., Klapwijk, M. J. G., & Van der Leij, A. (1995). Cognitieve en sociaal-emotionele vaardigheden van kleuters in relatie tot hun etnische afkomst [Cognitive and social-emotional abilities of kindergarten children as related to their ethnic origins]. *Pedagogische Studiën, 72*, 172-185.

De Jong, P. F., & Van der Leij, A. (1998). *School careers from 4 to 7: The relationship between cognitive development and the acquisition of reading and arithmetic.* Amsterdam: Vrije Universiteit, Department of Education.

Gathercole, S. E., Willis, C. S., Baddeley, A. D., & Emslie, H. (1994). The children's test of nonword repetition: A test of phonological working memory. *Memory, 2*, 103-127.

Gustafsson, J. E. (1984). A unifying model for the structure of intellectual abilities. *Intelligence, 8*, 179-203.

Gustafsson, J. E., & Balke, G. (1993). General and specific abilities as predictors of school achievement. *Multivariate Behavioral Research, 28*, 407-434.

Leseman, P. (1993). How parents provide young children with access to literacy. In L. Eldering & P. Leseman (Eds.), *Early intervention and culture* (pp. 149–171). Den Haag, The Netherlands: Unesco Publishing.

Mann, V. A., & Ditunno, P. (1990). Phonological deficiencies: Effective predictors of future reading problems. In G. Pavlidis (Ed.), *Perspectives on dyslexia* (Vol. 2, pp. 105–131). New York: Wiley.

Muthén, B. O. (1989). Latent variable modeling in heterogeneous populations. *Psychometrika, 54*, 557–585.

Perfetti, C. A., Beck, I., Bell, L., & Hughes, C. (1987). Phonemic knowledge and learning to read are reciprocal: A longitudinal analysis of first grade children. *Merrill-Palmer Quarterly, 33*, 283–319.

Schneider, W., & Näslund, J. C. (in press). The impact of early phonological processing skills on reading and spelling in school: Evidence from the Munich Longitudinal Study. In F. E. Weinert & W. Schneider (Eds.), *Individual development from 3 to 12: Findings from the Munich Longitudinal Study*. Cambridge: Cambridge University Press.

Schoonen, R., & Damhuis, R. (1992). *Taalplan Toetsen: Constructie en verantwoording van programmagebonden woordenschattoetsen ten behoeve van Taalplan Kleuters groep 1 en 2* [Vocabulary tests related to the method for language teaching Taalplan]. Amsterdam: University of Amsterdam, SCO–Department of Education.

Schroots, J. J. F., & Van Alphen de Veer, R. J. (1976). *Leidse Diagnostische Test: handleiding* [Leiden Diagnostic Test Battery: Manual]. Lisse: Swets & Zeitlinger.

Share, D. L., Jorm, A. F., Maclean, R., & Matthews, R. (1984). Sources of individual differences in reading acquisition. *Journal of Educational Psychology, 76*, 1309–1324.

Snow, C. E. (1991). The theoretical basis for relationships between language and literacy in development. *Journal of Research in Childhood Education, 6*, 5-10.

Snow, C. E. (1993). Linguistic development as related to literacy. In L. Eldering (Ed.), *Early intervention and culture* (pp. 132–147). Den Haag, The Netherlands: Unesco Publishing.

Staphorsius, G., Krom, R. S. H., & de Geus, K. (1988). *Frequenties van woordvormen en letterposities in jeugdlectuur* [Frequencies of word types and positions of letters in literature for the youth]. Arnhem, The Netherlands: Cito.

Vellutino, F., & Scanlon, D. M. (1987). Phonological coding, phonological awareness, and reading ability: Evidence from longitudinal and experimental study. *Merrill-Palmer Quarterly, 33*, 321–364.

Verhoeven, L. (1993). *Lezen met begrip 1* [Reading with comprehension 1]. Arnhem, The Netherlands: Cito.

Verhoeven, L., & Vermeer, A. (1986). *Taaltoets voor allochtone kinderen. Handleiding* [Language Test for children of ethnic minorities]. Tilburg, The Netherlands: Zwijsen.

Wagner, R. K., & Torgesen, J. K. (1987). The nature of phonological processing and its causal role in the acquisition of reading skills. *Psychological Bulletin, 101*, 192–212.

Wagner, R. K., Torgesen, J. K., Laughon, P., Simmons, K., & Rashotte, C. A. (1993). Development of young readers' phonological processing abilities. *Journal of Educational Psychology, 85*, 83–103.

Wagner, R. K., Torgesen, J. K., & Rashotte, C. A. (1994). Development of reading-related phonological processing abilities: New evidence of bi-directional causality from a latent variable longitudinal study. *Developmental Psychology, 30*, 73–87.

BENTE E. HAGTVET

# PRESCHOOL ORAL LANGUAGE COMPETENCE AND LITERACY DEVELOPMENT

Phonological problems have proved to be good predictors of reading difficulties (Bryant, Bradley, MacLean, & Crossland, 1989; Lundberg, Olofsson, & Wall, 1980), and training in phonological awareness appears to have a positive impact on early reading development (Ball & Blachman, 1991; Lundberg, Frost, & Petersen, 1988). Therefore, some have argued in favour of a causal link between phonological problems and reading difficulties (e.g., Høien & Lundberg, 1991). However, the hypothesis that reading difficulties are narrowly localized in a specific phonological dysfunction is challenged by *the verbal deficit hypothesis* most explicitly expressed by Vellutino (1979) who related reading difficulty to broader cognitive linguistic dysfunctions.

A basic assumption in the definition of specific reading disorders (dyslexia) is that the reading problem is unexpected, suggesting that the core language problem of dyslexia specifically affects written, but not oral language functioning (Lyon, 1995). Typically, normal use and comprehension of oral language in addition to normal intellectual functioning is assumed (Hoover & Gough, 1990; Stanovich, 1988).

While the oral language abilities of the dyslexic may appear quite normal at a superficial level, problems have been revealed in test situations. Poor readers of normal intelligence have been observed to perform poorer than normal readers when producing oral texts or monologues (Feagans & Short, 1984; Olson & Geva, 1983) and when producing syntactically complex sentences (e.g., Butler, Marsh, Sheppard, & Sheppard, 1985). They also score lower than normal readers on tests of receptive vocabulary (Share, Jorm, Maclean, & Matthews, 1984), tests of comprehension of complex syntax (Mann, Shankweiler, & Smith, 1984; Shankweiler & Crain, 1986), and on tests of comprehension of figurative language (Seidenberg & Berstein, 1986). Hence, there appears to be a discrepancy between the conceptualization of *specific* reading problem at a definitional level and the empirical basis on which the definition is built (Siegel, 1989).

Knowledge on oral language correlates of reading disability is usually - and for obvious reasons - empirically founded in school age children. Not until the child has documented problems in learning to read in school can one know for sure that the child has a reading problem. However, over the last decade longitudinal data have included the preschool period. This has contributed to a deeper understanding of the oral language precursors of reading problems.

Precursors of written language problems have been identified in a variety of language domains. Children at risk for reading problems have documented poor rhyming ability at age 3 to 4 (Bryant et al., 1989). They score low on phonemic awareness tasks at ages 5 and 6 (Bradley & Bryant, 1983; Elbro, this volume; Hagtvet, 1989; Lundberg, Olofsson, & Wall, 1980; Lyster, 1996). At age 2.5 delayed articulation and syntax were at risk signs in American children of dyslexic parents who later developed a reading problem (Scarborough, 1989, 1990). The same study showed that at age 3.5 delayed passive as well as active vocabulary were at risk factors, a finding which has been replicated in a British sample at age four (Gallagher, Frith, & Snowling, 1996). Also, Magnusson and Nauclér (1990) identified phonological and syntactic weaknesses in Swedish 6-year-olds who later became poor readers. Empirical research on oral language precursors of reading disabilities thus suggests potentially rather broad and complex problems.

Most of these studies of oral language precursors of reading problems have focused on self-selected groups of at-risk children (e.g., children of dyslexic parents, Gallagher et al., 1996; Scarborough, 1989, 1990), or children referred to speech therapists due to delayed and/or deviant language development in preschool (Catts, 1991; Bishop & Adams, 1990; Magnusson & Nauclér, 1990).

The present study focuses on the relation between preschool oral language abilities and later written language development in a random sample of normally functioning preschool children, i.e., children who showed no signs of deviancy or delay linguistically, cognitively or emotionally. Any problems in learning to read is therefore unexpected and by definition a specific reading problem.

The first issue of this study is the relation between early oral language abilities (ages 4, 6, and 9) and early written language development (ages 8 and 9). Secondly, the specificity issue is addressed, i.e., the relative contribution of syntactic, semantic and phonological oral language variables at age 6 to reading difficulties as measured at ages 8 and 9. Three groups of children were defined on the basis of their reading performance at ages 6 and 9: poor readers, average readers and early readers (i.e., children who learned to read before they started formal instruction in school). A comparison of the linguistic strengths of the early readers with the weaknesses of the poor readers was expected to shed light on the variables that are most critically involved in reading development.

A distinction is made between 1) everyday language abilities, as manifested in daily life contextualized communication, 2) linguistic awareness, i.e., the ability to view language as an object in its own right and with sensitivity to linguistic structure, and 3) comprehension and use of decontextualized, often complex, language. These distinctions may be relevant to reading development, but have often been neglected in the past. The assumption of the present study is that the written language problems many children unexpectedly experience may not be as unexpected once we go below the surface of everyday language and challenge the developing language system. Both linguistic awareness and decontextualized language are constructs which are having a developmental peak during the age period covered by this study and are therefore linguistically demanding to the age groups involved (Clark, 1973; Karmiloff-Smith, 1979).

A positive relation between linguistic awareness and reading ability has been documented in numerous empirical studies over the last 25 years (Bradley & Bryant, 1983; Fox & Routh, 1975; Lundberg & Tornéus, 1978; Mattingly, 1972; Tunmer, Herriman, & Nesdale, 1988). Good readers have been found to produce more coherent oral texts when retelling or creating stories (Feagans & Short, 1984; Olson & Geva, 1983). The relative importance of different aspects of linguistic awareness is, however, far from settled and the relation between mastery of decontextualized language and reading appears more soundly founded in logic than in empirical results (Snow, 1983). The verbal deficit hypothesis would predict poor readers to score lower than better readers on tasks of linguistic awareness and decontextualized language, while mastery of contextualized everyday language would presumably not differentiate between groups. On the basis of the phonological deficit hypothesis, one would, however, expect the oral language deficit of poor readers to be more specifically associated with awareness of phonological segments.

## METHOD

### Participants

Included in the study were 75 children (38 boys and 37 girls) who were randomly selected in the Oslo and Akershus county by the help of The Norwegian Bureau of Statistics. Children whose first language is not Norwegian, or with a sensory handicap, or a serious language problem were excluded from the sample at the outset.

Five subjects went to a branch of private schools (Rudolf Steiner Schools) which de-emphasizes reading in the first years of schooling, and were excluded from the data analysis when reading was involved. One of these subjects left the study after age 6. All other subjects stayed in the study until age 9. Therefore, most of the analyses included 70 participants.

All children were assessed four times, i.e., at ages 4, 6, 8, and 9. While assessments at ages 4 and 6 took place as close to the participants' respective birthdays as possible, the two last assessments were performed at the end of Grades 1 and 2, respectively.

The socio-economic background of the participants assumedly reflects the population distribution in the Oslo and Akershus county, but with a small overrepresentation of the upper socio-economic group (25% working class, 23% lower middle class, 20% middle class and 32% upper middle class; Hagtvet, 1996).

The children went to 64 different schools and were taught reading by means of 64 different methods. However, most of the teachers reported that they used a phonetic reading method, or some combination of phonics and whole language with an emphasis on phonics. Teaching the children to read and write in first grade is given top priority in all schools.

Up until August 1997 Norwegian children started school at age 7. By tradition there is a strong tendency among Norwegian kindergarten teachers as well as parents not to stimulate written language formally or informally before this age. Reading and writing should be taught by qualified specialists, i.e., primary school teachers, whereas kindergarten teachers should stimulate social, motor, creative or oral language and creative abilities (Nurss, 1988a, 1988b).

*Definition of reading groups*

Three reading groups were identified: poor, average, and early readers. Poor readers had a score less than the 25th percentile at the end of Grade 2 on two out of three reading tests: 1) Nonword reading, involved reading a list of nine short words with no meaning (Olofsson & Lundberg, 1985). The child's final score was a measure of accuracy corrected for speed. 2) Word reading (Olofsson & Lundberg, 1985), in which the children read 13 meaningful words of different length (regularly and irregularly spelled, e.g., ned, førstemann, regne). The score was a measure of accuracy corrected for speed. 3) In Sentence reading (Dugstad, 1978) the children read 24 short sentences with a simple content as cloze tasks. In the empty space at the end of each sentence the child had to fill in one out of five words which were presented as a list underneath each sentence, e.g., "You have to come .... (school, some, soon, us, bed)".

On the basis of the reading tests, 13 subjects were defined as poor readers. Defining poor readers by means of a simple cut-off-score principle does not of course guarantee that only children with specific reading disability were included in the sample. The identified poor readers were, however, all of average intelligence (average IQ=100; range: 90–115) and had no peripheral sensory deficits, diagnosed brain damage, or other debilitating physical problems. Neither had they suffered serious emotional or social disorders as a result of cultural disadvantage, and they had had adequate opportunity to learn.

Characteristics of the group of poor readers were contrasted with average and early readers, respectively. The early readers were 19 children, who taught themselves to read before they started school at age 7. This group was considered to be particularly interesting since the Norwegian culture by tradition de-emphasizes reading before school age. One might therefore assume that reading came especially easily to these children and that possible linguistic strengths of these children might shed light on the variables that are most critically involved in reading development. The average readers constituted the 38 children who were classified as neither poor nor early readers.

*Instruments*

The main purpose of the first assessment at age 4 was to standardize the Norwegian version of the Reynell Developmental Language Scales (Hagtvet & Lillestølen, 1985; Reynell, 1977). Additionally, clinical information on oral language abilities was collected, as were anamnestic data given by the parents. At the later assessments various aspects of written language abilities were at the center of attention, in addition to a variety of potential correlates, in particular oral language correlates. This chapter relates to a subsection of the variables included in the larger study (Hagtvet, 1996); the following variables are covered:

---

Phonemic awareness
 – Analysis & Synthesis (Olofsson & Lundberg, 1983; age 6)
Semantics
 – Picture description (content; Reynell, 1977; ages 4 and 6)
 – Vocabulary (WISC; Wechsler, 1974; ages 6, 9)
 – Homonym (Hagtvet, 1996; ages 6, 9)
Syntactic comprehension
 – Comprehension of negations, prepositions, etc. (Reynell, 1977; ages 4, 6)
 – Comprehension complex syntax (Rommetveit & Rommetveit, 1980; ages 6, 9)
 – Anaphoric reference (oral and in written cloze tasks; Hagtvet, 1996; age 9)
Syntactic/morphemic awareness
 – Grammatical closure (ITPA, Kirk, McCarthy & Kirk, 1968; ages 6, 9)
Reading
 – Nonword reading (Olofsson & Lundberg, 1985; age 9)
 – Word reading (Olofsson & Lundberg, 1985; age 9)
 – Word reading (Dugstad, 1978; age 8)
 – Sentence reading (corrected / uncorrected for speed; Dugstad, 1978; ages 8, 9)
 – Anaphoric reference (cloze text; Hagtvet, 1996; age 9)
 – Text reading (Hagtvet, 1996; age 9)
Intelligence.
 – Two nonverbal intelligence tests were used (Block design; Wechsler, 1974, and a visual memory task, Sandven, 1967).

The assessment battery also included observational procedures, or combinations of interviews and observations. For example, when the tester and the child at ages 6 and 9 were telling jokes to each others, the tester finally told a joke where the punch line played on the double meaning of the homonym, "finn hansen". Each of the two meanings of this homonym is well understood by Norwegian children at ages 6 and 9 (meaning 1 = Finn Hansen (first name and family name), meaning 2 = find Hansen (verb ("to find") and family name). The child was afterward interviewed about the meaning of the joke, and was asked "What does /finn hansen/ mean?".

During assessment, the tester evaluated the language functioning of the child clinically to get an impression of everyday language abilities. A five point scale was used to evaluate the extent to which the child interacted actively with the tester, took initiative, used clear articulation, used correct syntax, etc.

In addition to the test- and observational data, parents and teachers were interviewed about the subjects' past and present functioning, in particular in verbal domains.

*Recategorizations of variables*

The linguistic variables were recategorized into three groups: everyday language, linguistic awareness, and decontextualized language. Everyday language was measured by Picture description and by means of information about a child's functioning in informal verbal interactions as reported by the parents and testers. Everyday language presumably reflects what the child has mastered, but not what (s)he has not mastered. Children with a rather good language ability as reflected in everyday language might therefore still have problems with specific verbal tasks.

Linguistic awareness was assessed by tests for phonemic and syntactic awareness. Word definition tasks were also conceived of as measures of awareness, i.e., semantic awareness (Hagtvet, 1993).

Decontextualized language refers to the comprehension and use of language which is not contextualized in an explicitly defined or tacitly assumed here-and-now situation. A test of complex syntax (Rommetveit & Rommetveit, 1980) demanded from the child the ability to understand language devoid of contextual support.

*Procedures*

*Data collection.* At ages 4, 6, and 9 the children were assessed individually – on most occasions in their own homes by a psychologist, speech therapist or equally qualified tester. At age 8 the children were tested by their teachers in school, and all tests were group administered. Conversations with the children during assessments were taped and transcribed verbatim, and so was the reading of the children when they read aloud.

*Data analysis.* In order to find an answer to the first research question about reading abilities and oral language correlates, a number of group comparisons were performed. Data are presented descriptively and include a broad set of variables.

The second research question, concerning the relative contribution of syntactic, semantic and phonological oral language precursors to reading difficulties, was addressed by means of a series of fixed order multiple regressions with the different reading tasks at ages 8 and 9 (nonword reading, word reading, sentence reading with and without adjustment for speed, as well as text reading) as dependent variables. Four independent variables were entered stepwise into the multiple regression and always in the same order: (1) Intelligence, (2) Grammatical closure, (3) Vocabulary, and (4) Phonemic awareness. Thus, differences in nonverbal IQ were controlled for, before the relative importance of the different linguistic variables to reading was assessed. The order in which the linguistic variables were entered into the regressions was determined by their assumed relevance to reading with the presumably most influential variable on the basis of theory as well as bivariate correlations being entered last.

RESULTS AND DISCUSSION

*Linguistic and cognitive correlates of reading abilities*
The process of identifying correlates of reading abilities was carried out by means of observational data as well as by quantitative and qualitative information in test results.

According to information given by the parents at age 4 the early language development of the 13 at risk children, had in all cases been normal - or even early, as had the oral language development of the other reading groups. For example, more than 70% of the parents of the poor readers at age four reported that their child had produced her first word before the age of 15 months.

When the children were first seen at age 4, the testers' observations confirmed the parents' reports. No significant differences between reading groups were observed in articulation, spontaneous talk or pragmatic aspects of language (e.g., tendency to initiate verbal interactions during the assessment). At age 9 the poor readers still gave an overall impression of having normal oral language abilities as evaluated by the tester and the teachers of the children. Yet, in situations which were linguistically or socially demanding, the oral language abilities of the poor readers were reported at age 9 to be significantly poorer than the comparison groups. They were now, for example, less able to express themselves cohesively in class, and they took fewer verbal initiatives. The observational data on the subjects' everyday language presented above may be described as soft, in that they are subject to tester bias, e.g., by halo effects. Yet, they confirm and substantiate research which emphasizes the apparent normality of dyslexic children in other areas than reading and writing. They are also supported by test results.

Figure 1 presents an overall picture of the average developmental patterns for poor, average and early readers, respectively. To allow for a direct comparison of group trends, the average z-score for each variable for each of the groups is represented. At the left end of the horizontal axis are socio-economic background and oral language scores measured at age 4, then oral language variables at age 6 follow, and towards the right end are the variables measured at ages 8 and 9.

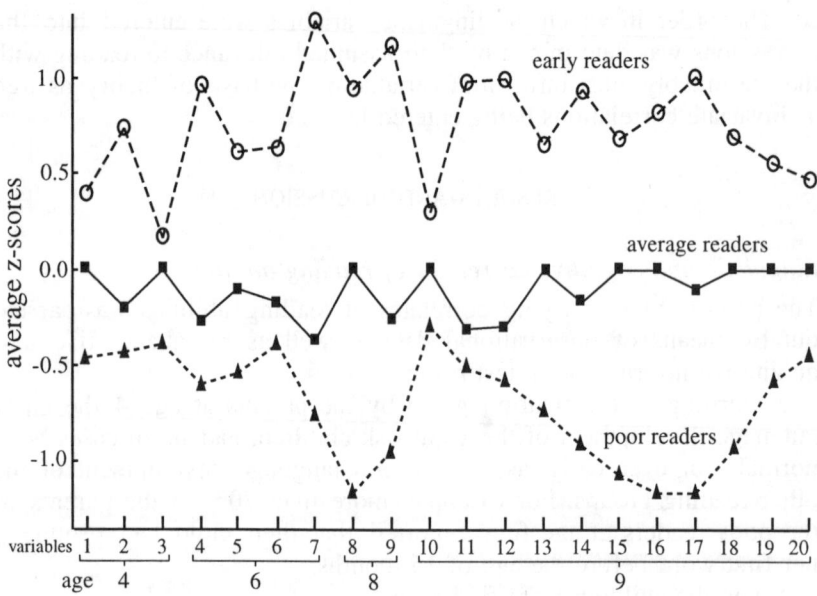

Fig. 1. Developmental trends for poor, average and early readers (mean z-scores for the variables: (1) Socio-econ. background, (2) Reynell total, (3) Picture description, (4) Vocabulary, (5) Grammatical closure, (6) Comprehension complex syntax, (7) Phonemic awareness, (8) Word reading, (9) Sentence reading, (10) Picture description, (11) Vocabulary, (12) Grammatical closure, (13) Comprehension complex syntax, (14) Oral cloze, (15) Nonword reading, (16) Word reading, (17) Sentence reading, speed adj., (18) Written cloze, (19) Block design, (20) Visual memory.

Two main characteristics stand out as striking when observing Figure 1. First, the relative achievement levels of the three groups are stable across time. The poor readers score below the average readers, who are below the early readers on every variable at every age level. Thus, the trend for poor reading ability at age 9 is to be associated with poor oral language competence as early as age 4.

Secondly, the pattern is, with a few exceptions, unexpectedly stable across language variables. The groups consistently differ on almost every variable at ages 4, 6, and 9. While Phonemic awareness is expected to differentiate strongly between the groups, the differentiating ability of Vocabulary, Grammatical Closure and Oral cloze is also considerable. Even the Reynell, a composite language abilities score, differentiates between the reading groups as early as at age 4.

At age 9 differences were found for decontextualized comprehension of syntax, but not at age 6, probably because of a floor effect at that age. A number of children at this age scored low because they were unable to solve a cognitive complexity and not because they did not comprehend decontextualized language per se.

One-way analysis of variance for the variables in Figure 1 showed that the mean differences, except for Picture description at ages 4 and 9, were statistically significant according to the overall F-test. Also, the differences between early and average readers is generally larger than the differences between the average and poor readers. This is of no surprise because the poor readers constitute the lower end of a distribution of reading abilities in a random sample. One would not expect this group with 'unexpected' poor reading abilities to show serious problems on tests of linguistic awareness and decontextualized language, although there were individual cases who did.

The verbal deficit hypothesis would perfectly predict the consistent trend: poor<average<early for almost every oral language variable, because all variables would be expected to be related to reading abilities. The findings do not support the phonological deficit hypothesis, although the fact that Phonemic awareness at age 6 shows a larger deviancy from the average curve in Figure 1 than the other variables is consistent with this hypothesis. Phonemic awareness is, however, rather skewed with early readers scoring very high at age 6, and thereby strongly influencing the average raw score, the $z$-scores and the significance testing. A similar trend as in Figure 1 is found when non-parametric methods of analyzing data are used (Hagtvet, 1996).

The data from the joke telling session confirmed the previous results. Figure 2 shows the relations between reading levels and ability to tell a joke with a punch line at age 6. Of the poor readers 54% ($n=7$) could not or would not tell a joke, while only 11% of the early readers reacted similarly. Of the early readers 78% told a joke with a punch line, as opposed to 23% (n=3) of the poor readers ($\chi^2$(4, n=67)=11.10, p=.03). At age 9, all the children were willing to and able to tell a joke with a punch line, independent of reading ability.

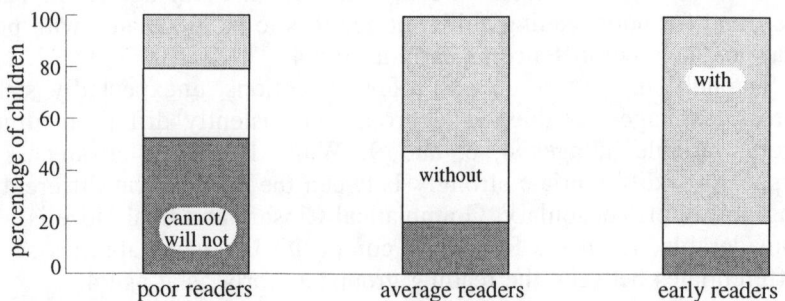

Fig. 2. Percentage of 6-year old children in each reading level group that is able to tell a joke, with and without a punch line.

Figure 3 shows the results when asked to explain the punch line in the experimenter's joke by defining the homonym, "finn hansen". Many poor readers (85%, n=11) were unable to give a definition, 15% defined one of the meanings, while none was able to define both. Among the early readers 25% (n=5) defined two meanings, 42% (n=8) gave one meaning and 32% (n=6) could or would not define the punch line ($\chi^2$ (4, n=69) = 15.98, p=.00). The average readers reacted more like the poor readers than like the early readers.

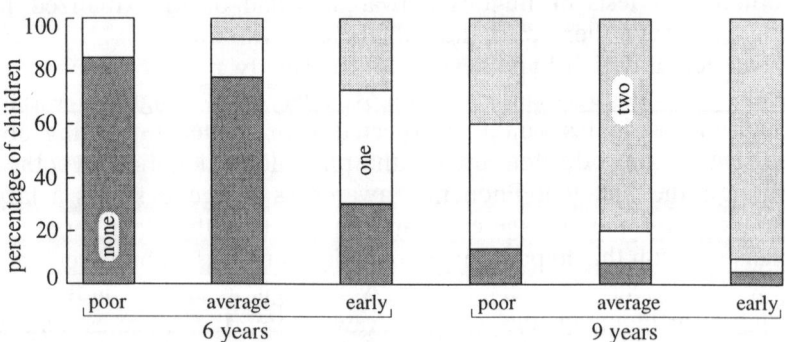

Fig. 3. Ability to define a homonym in the punch line of a joke at ages 6 and 9 as related to reading level.

At age 9, 90% of the early readers defined both meanings of the homonym. Only 38% of the poor readers did likewise, whereas 46% was able to define one meaning and two children were unable to give a definition at all. Thus, poor readers appeared to be at a loss when having to simultaneously handle the two meanings of the homonym "finn hansen". While this problem were most conspicuous at age 6, they were also prominent at age 9. Once again, the early readers appeared to excel in the very same task. Given the importance that participation in a group's humorous verbal exchanges has for group identification, and ultimately to self confidence, the social consequences of an inability to understand verbal jokes - and also to tell jokes - should not be underestimated.

*Relative contribution of precursors to reading difficulties*

The second research question of whether reading problems are primarily predicted by a narrow phonological dysfunction or by a broader linguistic problem, was addressed by multiple regression analyses with different aspects of reading as outcome measures and non-verbal IQ, Grammatical closure, Vocabulary and Phonemic awareness as predictor variables. Table 1 shows the $R^2$ change ($\Delta R^2$) and related $p$, for different runs, in addition to the simultaneous solutions.

With a few exceptions, for all outcome measures each independent variable which was entered into the analysis at each step contributed significantly to reading ($p$ for $\Delta R^2 \leq .05$). This indicates that syntactic, semantic and phonological variables are all typically uniquely related to reading, even after the influence of intelligence has been controlled for.

Phonemic awareness contributes unique variance to all reading scores, even after the influence from the other independent variables has been controlled for. This finding corroborates the large number of studies which identifies low phonemic awareness as a core problem in reading retardation.

Although it varies among reading tasks, the relative contribution of the other independent variables is, however, also substantial. For Text reading and Sentence reading, both Grammatical closure and Vocabulary contribute unique variance. For the two Word reading tasks, Grammatical closure does not contribute, whereas Vocabulary adds significantly to Word reading, but not to Nonword reading. For Nonword reading only phonemic awareness contributes unique variance. Thus, the relative importance of different language aspects to reading ability varies with the reading measure used.

The simultaneous solutions of the regression procedures showed that Grammatical closure and Vocabulary are about equal to Phonemic awareness in importance to Text reading (with beta coefficients reaching statistical significance). Only Phonemic awareness contributes significantly to Sentence reading (uncorrected for speed) at ages 8 and 9, and to Nonword reading. When speed is taken into account (for Sentence reading and Word reading), at age 9 reading scores are influenced by Vocabulary, but not by Grammatical closure.

TABLE 1
Four-step fixed order multiple regressions of Intelligence, Grammatic closure, Vocabulary and Phonemic awareness at age 6 on reading at ages 8 and 9

|  | Step | Variable | $R^2$ | $\Delta R^2$ | p | Simult.solution β | t | p | $R^2$ |
|---|---|---|---|---|---|---|---|---|---|
| Text reading | 1 | IQ | .10 | .10 | .00 | .04 | .31 | .75 | |
| age 9 | 2 | Grammatic closure | .21 | .11 | .00 | .23 | 2.04 | .05 | |
|  | 3 | Vocabulary | .31 | .10 | .00 | .27 | 2.16 | .03 | |
|  | 4 | Phonemic awareness | .34 | .03 | .06 | .23 | 1.87 | .07 | .34 |
| Sentence reading | 1 | IQ | .11 | .11 | .00 | .02 | .13 | .90 | |
| age 9 | 2 | Grammatic closure | .18 | .07 | .02 | .19 | 1.66 | .10 | |
|  | 3 | Vocabulary | .25 | .07 | .01 | .08 | .62 | .54 | |
|  | 4 | Phonemic awareness | .40 | .15 | .00 | .48 | 3.89 | .00 | .40 |
| Sentence reading * | 1 | IQ | .12 | .12 | .00 | .05 | .44 | .66 | |
| age 9 | 2 | Grammatic closure | .16 | .04 | .08 | .05 | .45 | .66 | |
|  | 3 | Vocabulary | .32 | .16 | .00 | .29 | 2.45 | .02 | |
|  | 4 | Phonemic awareness | .43 | .11 | .00 | .41 | 3.53 | .00 | .43 |
| Sentence reading | 1 | IQ | .10 | .10 | .01 | -.08 | -.79 | .43 | |
| age 8 | 2 | Grammatic closure | .16 | .01 | .04 | .11 | 1.08 | .28 | |
|  | 3 | Vocabulary | .31 | .15 | .00 | .14 | 1.32 | .19 | |
|  | 4 | Phonemic awareness | .59 | .28 | .00 | .67 | 6.34 | .00 | .59 |
| Word reading | 1 | IQ | .17 | .17 | .00 | .12 | .99 | .33 | |
| age 8 | 2 | Grammatic closure | .20 | .04 | .10 | .09 | .81 | .42 | |
|  | 3 | Vocabulary | .29 | .08 | .01 | .12 | .95 | .35 | |
|  | 4 | Phonemic awareness | .42 | .13 | .00 | .47 | 3.72 | .00 | .42 |
| Word reading * | 1 | IQ | .05 | .05 | .07 | -.02 | -.12 | .90 | |
| age 9 | 2 | Grammatic closure | .08 | .03 | .13 | .04 | .34 | .73 | |
|  | 3 | Vocabulary | .22 | .14 | .00 | .31 | 2.22 | .03 | |
|  | 4 | Phonemic awareness | .26 | .04 | .07 | .25 | -.08 | .07 | .26 |
| Nonword reading * | 1 | IQ | .04 | .04 | .10 | .01 | .05 | .96 | |
| age 9 | 2 | Grammatic closure | .07 | .03 | .17 | .13 | .94 | .35 | |
|  | 3 | Vocabulary | .09 | .02 | .24 | .03 | .17 | .81 | |
|  | 4 | Phonemic awareness | .14 | .05 | .05 | .29 | 2.00 | .05 | .14 |

* adjusted for speed

Thus, Phonemic awareness seems to be the most influential variable, most conspicuously for word decoding at age 8, for nonword decoding and sentence reading at ages 8 and 9 (unadjusted for speed). Grammatical closure is most influential when demands are made on comprehension as in Text reading, and Vocabulary is significantly related to outcome scores in tasks that make demands on the fast processing of sentences and words, in addition to text comprehension. The relative importance of these variables could, of course, be more precisely decided by reversing the order of entrance in the regression equations, but for the present purposes such detailed analyses were not deemed necessary.

The total amount of variance in reading scores explained by the four independent variables vary from small to large with $R^2$ ranging from .14 to .59. This indicates that a number of variables not included in the analyses are also rather heavily influencing the outcome measures, especially for Nonword reading.

Table 1 shows that the assessment of the relative importance of oral language variables to reading cannot be decided in general terms, but has to be contextualized in a specific aspect of reading. Although the actual operationalizations and selection of independent variables can always be questioned, the present data appear important as they suggest that a search for *the* core problem of reading disabilities in one variable and across tasks and situations may be too simplistic an approach for the complexities of the issues involved.

## CONCLUSIONS

The first part of the study identified oral language precursors of reading difficulties in a broad range of areas at ages 4 and 6. The data suggest that the difficulties are typically not observed in everyday communication, whereas they can still be traced in domains that demand manipulation of linguistic segments (linguistic awareness) and to some extent also command of decontextualized language. This indicates that the oral language precursors of poor reading may be subtle and not easy to detect. However, even when differences were identified, the group of at-risk children scored only marginally worse than the group of average readers, confirming the general impression of a marginal oral language problem - or weakness.

The results also support the view that the oral language precursors (and correlates) of reading problems are rather broadly linguistically localized, and data from the subjects' retelling and comprehension of verbal jokes substantiate this argument. Social verbal activities as joke telling makes linguistic shortcomings public knowledge, and such activities may therefore act as mediators of the low self concept which is often found in poor readers (Bryan & Bryan, 1991).

The second research question explicitly addressed the specificity issue. Multiple regression analyses indicated that for a number of reading measures, intelligence, grammatical knowledge, vocabulary and phonemic awareness all contributed uniquely to the total variance in reading scores. The analyses hence confirmed and substantiated the hypothesis, that reading scores to a large extent are composites of broadly based cognitive/linguistic subskills.

Phonemic awareness explained the most variance in almost every outcome measure, and also contributed uniquely after the influence from the other variables was controlled for. However, although phonology is important to reading ability during the two first years in school, syntactic and semantic aspects are also at work - for some reading measures even to the same degree as phonemic awareness. Such findings corroborate recent findings on oral language precursors of reading problems (Scarborough, 1989, 1990; Gallagher et al., 1996) and invite renewed interest in the role played by syntax and semantics in early reading.

Bowey and Patel (1988) argue that a general language delay would more often have been revealed in relation with reading difficulties if measurement instruments of general language had been more refined and also more developmentally relevant. They suggest that when general language abilities are carefully assessed, metaphonological abilities will not appear to contribute more unique variance to reading scores than general language abilities. The present results are consistent with this hypothesis in that a general language measure as the composite score of the Reynell differentiates moderately between the reading groups at age 4 (cf. Share et al., 1984; Butler et al., 1985).

These findings are also consistent with other studies where longitudinal research designs covering the preschool years have been applied (Bishop, 1991; Gallagher et al., 1996; Scarborough, 1989, 1990; Tallal, Curtis, & Kaplan, 1988). While these studies have studied language impaired children or self-selected at-risk groups, the present data indicate that a broad, but subtle, language deficit appears to be associated with reading problems even at the lower end of normal variation and in cases where no oral language problems could be identified on the basis of everyday oral language.

One might of course discard the relevance of the present findings to dyslexia by reference to the degree and quality of the reading problems of the subjects under study, and argue that the children were not "true dyslexics", but a combination of dyslexics and "late bloomers". However, all the poor readers were within the normal range intellectually (range: 90–115), and in the regression analyses IQ was controlled for. The low scores on tasks of linguistic awareness and decontextualized language of the at risk children cannot therefore be explained by reference to low cognitive functioning.

It is possible that different subgroups of poor readers show different profiles in oral language abilities and this was also indicated in the present study. However, rather than suggesting qualitatively different subgroups, the trend in the present data indicates quantitative rather than qualitative differences between the children. The poor readers all showed weaknesses in a whole range of linguistic awareness and decontextualized language skills. Thus marginal oral language problems are associated with quite serious reading problems. This may indicate that even a small problem may become a big one when many different problems coincide and mutually reinforce each other. This is an issue which should be pursued in future research.

The amount of variance in reading scores explained by the four independent variables in some cases was rather small. While this in some sense may be expected, because reading by definition is a complex cognitive task, it also challenges the specificity hypothesis which so strongly emphasizes phonology as *the* core issue. Yet, the results are not necessarily incompatible with the phonological core deficit hypothesis. A presumed primary phonological dysfunction may be hypothesized to develop in interaction with the rest of the language system right from the beginning, resulting in more or less subtle trade off with other language aspects. The phonological deficit hypothesis does, however, need to be elaborated into a more comprehensive developmental theory which also takes other developmental domains into account, including semantics and syntax or other relevant cognitive and emotional variables. Within such a developmental framework a problem in learning to read is seen as the end product of a complex developmental process where the reading outcome is the result of a large amount of mutually influencing variables, e.g., the degree of a primary problem, the environmental language input (including the method used for reading instruction) and the compensatory abilities within the child (e.g., linguistic, intellectual and emotional abilities).

## REFERENCES

Ball, E. W., & Blachman, B. A. (1991). Does phoneme awareness training in kindergarten make a difference in early word recognition and developmental spelling? *Reading Research Quarterly, 26*, 49–66.

Bishop, D. V. M. (1991). Developmental reading disabilities: The role of phonological processes has been overemphasized. *Mind and Language, 6*, 97–101.

Bishop, D. V. M., & Adams, C. (1990). A prospective study of the relationship between specific language impairment, phonological disorders and reading retardation. *Journal of Child Psychology and Psychiatry, 31*, 1027–1050.

Bowey, J. A., & Patel, R. K. (1988). Metalinguistic ability and early reading achievement. *Applied Psycholinguistics, 9*, 367–383.

Bradley, L. L., & Bryant, P. E. (1983). Categorizing sounds and learning to read - a causal connection. *Nature, 301*, 419–421.

Bryan, J. H., & Bryan, T. (1990). Social factors in learning disabilities: Attitudes and interactions. In G. T. Pavlidis (Ed.), *Perspectives on dyslexia, Vol. 2.* (pp. 247–281). London: Wiley.

Bryant, P. E., Bradley, L. L., MacLean, M., & Crossland, J. (1989). Nursery rhymes, phonological skills and reading. *Journal of Child Language, 16*, 407–428.

Butler, S. R., Marsh, H. W., Sheppard, M. J., & Sheppard, J. L. (1985). Seven-year longitudinal study of the early prediction of reading achievement. *Journal of Educational Psychology, 77*, 349–361.

Catts, H. W. (1991). Early identification of dyslexia: Evidence of a follow-up study of speech-language impaired children. *Annals of Dyslexia, 41*, 163–177.

Clark, E. V. (1973). Awareness of language. Some evidence from what children say and do. In A. Sinclair, R. J. Jarvella & W. J. M. Levelt (Eds.), *The child's* conception of language (pp. 17–43). Berlin: Springer-Verlag.

Dugstad, B. S. (1978). *Diagnostiske prøver for 2. og 3. skoleår* [Diagnostic tests for Grades 2 and 3]. Trondheim: Kontoret for pedagogisk utviklingsarbeid, Skolesjefen.

Feagans, L., & Short, E. J. (1984). Developmental differences in the comprehension and production of narratives by reading disabled and normally achieving children. *Child Development, 55*, 1727–1736.

Fox, B., & Routh, D. K. (1975). Analyzing spoken language into words, syllables and phonemes: A developmental study. *Journal of Psycholinguistic Research, 4*, 331–342.

Gallagher, A. M., Frith, U., & Snowling, M. J. (1996). *Language processing skills in pre-schoolers at risk of developmental dyslexia.* Un. of York, UK: Manuscript.

Hagtvet, B. E. (1989). Emergent literacy in Norwegian six-year-olds. From pretend writing to phonemic awareness and invented writing. In F. Biglmaier (Ed.), *Reading at the crossroads.* Proceedings of the 6th European Conference on Reading, Berlin.

Hagtvet, B. E. (1993). "'Dress' is birthday" and "'sleep' is night". Young children's word definition strategies. In A. Heen Wold (Ed.). *The dialogical alternative.* Oslo: Scandinavian Press.

Hagtvet, B. E. (1996). *Fra tale til skrift. Om prediksjon og utvikling av leseferdighet i fire- til åtteårsalderen* [From oral to written language. On the prediction and development of reading abilities during the age period four through eight]. Oslo: Cappelen.

Hagtvet, B. E., & Lillestølen, R. (1985). *Reynells språktest* [Reynell Developmental Language Scales - Norwegian version]. Oslo: Universitetsforlaget.

Hoover, W. A., & Gough, P. B. (1990). The simple view of reading. *Reading and Writing: An Interdisciplinary Journal, 2*, 127–160.

Høien, T., & Lundberg, I. (1991). *Dysleksi.* Oslo: Gyldendal.

Karmiloff-Smith, A. (1979). Language development after five. In R. Fletcher & M. Garman (Eds.). *Language acquisition. Studies in first grade development.* Cambridge, Mass: Cambridge University Press.

Katz, R. B. (1986). Phonological deficiencies in children with reading disability: Evidence from an object-naming task. *Cognition, 22*, 225–227.

Kirk, S. J., McCarthy, J., & Kirk. (1968). *Illinois Test of Psycholinguistic Ability.* Urbana: University of Illinois Press.

Lundberg, I., & Tornéus, M. (1978). Nonreaders' awareness of the basic relationship between spoken and written words. *Journal of Experimental Child Psychology, 25*, 404–414.

Lundberg, I., Olofsson, Å., & Wall, S. (1980). Reading and spelling skills in the first school years predicted from phonemic awareness skills in kindergarten. *Scandinavian Journal of Psychology, 21*, 159–173.

Lundberg, I., Frost, J. & Petersen, O. P. (1988). Long term effects of a preschool training program in phonological awareness. *Reading Research Quarterly, 28*, 263–284.

Lyon, G. R. (1995). Toward a Definition of Dyslexia. *Annals of Dyslexia, 45*, 3–27.

Lyster, S. A. (1996). *Preventing reading and spelling failure.* Doctoral dissertation, University of Oslo, Department of Special Education.

Magnusson, E., & Nauclér, K. (1990). Can preschool data predict language-disordered children's reading and spelling at school? *Pholia Phoniatria, 43*, 277–283.

Mann, V. A., Shankweiler, D. P., & Smith, S. T. (1984). The association between comprehension of spoken sentences and early reading ability: The role of phonetic representation. *Journal of Child Language, 11*, 627–643.

Mattingly, I. G. (1972). Reading, the linguistic process, and linguistic awareness. In J. F. Kavanagh & I. G. Mattingly (Eds.), *Language by ear and by eye*. Cambridge, Mass: MIT Press.
Nurss, J. (1988a). Development of written communication in Norwegian kindergarten children. *Scandinavian Journal of Educational Research, 32*, 33-48.
Nurss, J. (1988b). Written language environments for young children: Comparison of Scandinavian, British, and American kindergartens. *International Journal of Early Childhood, 20*, 45-53.
Olofsson, Å., & Lundberg, I. (1983). Can phonemic awareness be trained in kindergarten? *Scandinavian Journal of Psychology, 24*, 35-44.
Olofsson, Å., & Lundberg, I. (1985). Evaluation of long term effects of phonemic awareness training in kindergarten. Illustrations of some methodological problems in evaluation research. *Scandinavian Journal of Psychology, 26*, 21-34.
Olson, R. K. (1994). Language deficits in "specific" reading disability. In M. Gernsbacher (Ed.). *Handbook of psycholinguistics*. New York: Academic Press.
Olson, D. R., & Geva, E. (1983). Children's story-retelling. *First Language, 4*, 85-110.
Perfetti, C.A. (1985). *Reading ability*. New York: Oxford University Press.
Reynell, J. (1977). *Reynell developmental language scales (revised)*. Windsor: NFER.
Rommetveit, S., & Rommetveit, R. (1980). *Pek på* [The point-at-game]. Oslo: Tiden.
Sandven, J. (1967). Det teoretiske grunnlag for modenhetsprøving [Theoretical and methodological basis of testing cognitive functions]. Oslo: Universitetsforlaget.
Scarborough, H. S. (1989). Prediction of reading disability from familial and individual differences. *Journal of Educational Psychology, 81*, 101-108.
Scarborough, H. S. (1990). Very early language deficits in dyslexic children. *Child Development, 61*, 1728-1741.
Shankweiler, D. P., & Crain, S. (1986). Language mechanisms and reading disorder: A modular approach. *Cognition, 24*, 139-168.
Share, D. L., Jorm, A. Maclean, R., & Matthews, R. (1984). Sources of individual differences in reading acquisition. *Journal of Educational Psychology, 76*, 1309-1324.
Siegel, L. S. (1989). IQ is irrelevant to the definition and analysis of reading disability. *Canadian Journal of Psychology, 42*, 201-215.
Seidenberg, P., & Berstein, D. (1986). The comprehension of similes and metaphors by learning disabled and nonlearning disabled children. *Language, Speech and Hearing Services in Schools, 17*, 219-229.
Snow, C. E. (1983). Literacy and language: Relationships during the preschool years. *Harvard Educational Review, 53*, 165-189.
Stanovich, K. E. (1988). Explaining the differences between the dyslexic and the garden-variety poor reader: The phonological-core variable-difference model. *Journal of Learning Disabilities, 21*, 590-604.
Tallal, P, Curtis, S., & Kaplan, R. (1988). The San Diego longitudinal study: Evaluating the outcomes of preschool impairment in language development. In S. Berger & G. Mencher (Eds.), *International perspectives in communication disorders* (pp. 86-126). Washington DC: Gallandet University Press.
Tunmer, W. E., Herriman, M. L., & Nesdale, A. R. (1988). Metalinguistic abilities and reading. *Reading Research Quarterly, 23*, 134-157.
Vellutino, F. R. (1979). *Dyslexia: Theory and research*. Cambridge, MA: MIT Press.
Wechsler, D. (1974). *Wechsler Intelligence Scale for Children - Revised*. New York: The Psychological Corporation, 1949.

RALPH WESSELING AND PIETER REITSMA

# PHONEMICALLY AWARE IN A HOP, SKIP, AND A JUMP

The importance of phonological awareness in reading acquisition is beyond question. The last three decades has seen a substantial amount of research to demonstrate the intimate relationship between phonological awareness and the acquisition of literacy skills (cf. Stanovich, 1986, Adams, 1990, for reviews). However, many questions remain unanswered. Of interest in the present study is how phonological awareness develops from Kindergarten through to Grade 1. In order to examine this, a group of children are followed from Kindergarten into Grade 1 where they learn to read. Phonological skills are assessed three times throughout this period. The main issue is the relative growth in phonological awareness prior to reading instruction compared with the first few months of reading instruction.

A number of theoretical positions are possible regarding the causal nature between phonological awareness and reading acquisition. The first is that phonological awareness is a *prerequisite* for reading acquisition. For example, Liberman (1973) argued that phonological awareness preceded and predicted later reading success. Phonological awareness needs to be present before grapheme to phoneme correspondences can be mastered. Without an awareness of how spoken language can be divided into simple sound units the acquisition of phoneme-grapheme correspondences is doubtful. Studies by Bradley and Bryant (1983), Tornéus (1984), and Tunmer and Nesdale (1985) show that phonological awareness is a potent predictor of later reading success, more so than intelligence ratings and general language ability. This suggests prereading acquisition of phoneme awareness is necessary, or at least helpful for reading development (Juel, 1988).

However, there have also been studies that suggest development of phonological awareness is a *consequence* of learning about print. It is the consequence of finding out that letters represent sound that introduces the child to the concept of phonemes. Ehri (1979, 1989) argues that certain phonological manipulations such as phoneme deletion cannot be achieved without letter knowledge. Morais, Cary, Algeria, and Bertelson (1979) found that illiterate Portuguese adults lacked phonological awareness whereas their literate colleagues did display awareness of phonemes. This type of evidence builds a powerful case for the influence of reading experience on phoneme awareness. In concordance with this perspective are the findings of Johnston, Anderson, and Holligan (1996), who reported in a recent study that in the absence of explicit letter to sound knowledge a child is not likely to become phonemically aware.

*P.Reitsma, & L.Verhoeven (Eds.), Problems and Interventions in Literacy Development, 81—94.*
© *1998 Kluwer Academic Publishers. Printed in the Netherlands.*

These two positions and related research findings seem quite contradictory and opposing and hence a third position evolved that states that development of phonological awareness is *reciprocal* with reading development. Stanovich (1992) suggests that a minimal level of phonological awareness is required to learn to read, but that phonological awareness develops further as reading ability advances. Perfetti, Beck, Bell, and Hughes (1987) found evidence of reciprocal causation in a longitudinal study. They followed 82 children for one year and measured various phonological tasks four times. The results show that skills such as blending phonemes together are possible by the majority of children prior to learning read. However, phoneme deletion was a more difficult task requiring grapheme knowledge. A study by Hatcher, Hulme, and Ellis (1994) in the United Kingdom found that training phoneme awareness by itself was not very successful in developing reading ability, and that much better training effects were found when phonological awareness training was carried out simultaneously with the teaching of reading skills. A study by Liberman, Shankweiler, Fisher, and Carter (1974), tested the phoneme segmentation ability of three age groups. The results showed that pre-kindergarten children scored 0% correct, kindergarten children 17% correct and Grade 1 children 70%. These types of studies suggest that there is some type of reciprocal relationship between reading skill development and development of phonological awareness.

Thus it seems possible to hypothesize a gradual increase in phonological awareness during the pre-school period, with some children advancing further to a more sophisticated level of awareness than others. Preschool phonological awareness is largely the result of individual discovery and the variability is possibly quite large, with many children understanding little or nothing about phonemes and other children having already made significant insights. However, the influence of reading instruction is dramatic and applies to most if not all children.

The reciprocal view of phonological development is relatively quiet about the exact causes of phonological awareness development during the preschool period. Is it due to cognitive maturation or through environmental exposure to print? Studies by Morrison, Smith, and Dow-Ehrensberger (1995) and Bentin, Hammer, and Cahan (1991) studied the question of ageing and schooling on the development of phoneme awareness. They examined children who were of the same age but in different grades (i.e., kindergarten and Grade 1). Both ageing and schooling significantly increase phoneme awareness. However, children receiving reading instruction had much greater increases in phoneme awareness than the same age kindergarten children. A major flaw in these two studies is that neither took into account the development of print experience in the kindergarten children. Although the kindergarten children did not progress in reading ability, as measured by a reading test, they may very well have developed in letter to sound knowledge. The study by Johnston, Anderson, and Holligan (1996) found that kindergarten children who knew the letter sound correspondences of only 8 letters of the alphabet, could do some (more than one item correct) phoneme segmentation and deletion, even though they could not read text. This type of evidence throws doubt on the conclusion that phoneme awareness may develop based purely on maturational factors.

Phonological awareness is often referred to as an all or nothing concept. In practice this does not appear to be the case. Tests that measure phonological sensitivity differ in difficulty and seem to tap different levels of awareness and understanding of the concept involved. A thorough examination of reliability, validity and difficulty of phonological awareness tests was done by Yopp (1988). She found tests of rhyming and phoneme blending were relatively simple tasks, achievable to some degree by most preschoolers. More difficult tasks such as phoneme deletion are less likely to be accomplished by preschoolers. In the present study we monitored changes in phonological sensitivity measured by three tasks of varying complexity.

Many studies that examine the importance of phonological awareness in early reading acquisition have been done in English speaking countries. Written English has a relatively deep orthography, that is to say that the letters that are used in words do not have a one to one correspondence with a given phoneme. The implicit rules that govern these correspondences are complex and for this reason a good awareness of phonemes would seem crucial. However, there are some questions regarding the importance of phonological awareness in languages whose orthographies are more shallow than English. In a language such as Dutch, most words may be decoded using simple grapheme to phoneme correspondences. If this is the case then prereading levels of phoneme awareness may be much less crucial than for English speaking children. Also the effect of the type of teaching may have a profound effect on development. In the Netherlands, reading instruction curricula strive to make explicit the correspondences between phonemes and graphemes. The whole word method reading adopted in a number of English speaking countries tends to avoid this, as it is argued that in English these correspondences are numerous, varied and difficult to master. Therefore, we predict that the phonological awareness will be much more rapidly acquired by Dutch children than was reported in studies from English speaking countries (e.g., Liberman et al., 1974).

The specific predictions in this study were as follows:

1 Phoneme blending and phoneme segmentation tasks are possibly to complete earlier than phoneme deletion.
2 The rate of growth in phonological skills is less in kindergarten than in Grade 1. The study by Bentin et al. (1991) in Israel reported that prior to reading instruction children increased by 9% on phonological skills, but increased by 32% after introduction of a reading program. Which is similar to the Liberman (1973) study which reported a 17% and a 53% increase over this same period. We may expect a greater increase after the introduction of reading instruction because of the facilitating attributes of the Dutch orthography for phoneme awareness and related teacher activities.
3 The scores on the first and second kindergarten tests will be highly correlated, but kindergarten results will not correlate as highly with Grade 1 results. The individual differences in kindergarten are largely determined by effects of personal discovery from parental/ sibling and other factors, whereas development in Grade 1 is highly influenced by the quality and extent of teaching practices. It is likely that growth in skill is relatively independent of starting skills as measured by the kindergarten tests.
4 The present study attempts to replicate the findings by Johnston et al. (1996) who report that limited knowledge of letter sounds is sufficient to develop phonological awareness. They suggested that 8 letters is sufficient to be able to do at least one complicated phonological manipulation, such a phoneme deletion.

## METHOD

*Participants.* In total 120 children, 63 boys and 57 girls, from four primary schools took part in this study, at the time that testing began they were all in the second kindergarten year with an average age of 5 years and 10 months. The group of children was composed of Dutch (68%), Surinam (18%) and other ethnicity's, mainly Turkish and Moroccan (14%). According to their teachers, children taking part were all expected to continue on to Grade 1 in the following academic year. All schools were situated in the same geographical area and drew their school roll from families with similar socio-economic backgrounds. The same children were tested three times (T1, T2, & T3).

*Materials*

T1 January, halfway through the final preschool year the following tests were administered.

– A 98 item passive vocabulary test (Verhoeven, Vermeer, & Van de Guchte, 1986). The child is asked which out of four pictures best represents a word presented by the experimenter.

- A 27 item lower case letter test was administered. This test was presented on a A4 piece of paper and included all the letters of the alphabet (including "*ij*") used in Dutch. The child was given an unlimited period of time to indicate, by naming or pronouncing, as many letters as they knew.
- A short test of word recognition. Ten words commonly found in early readers were presented on a sheet and the child was asked if they could read any of them. No time limit was applied.
- Phoneme blending test - In total 26 segmented words are presented aurally via a computer and the child is asked to respond with the whole word. The stimuli contained 6 CV or VC words and 5 items in each of the following word structures, CVC, CCVCC, CVCC, CCVCC (see Table 1 for examples). Although containing no articulatory cues, normally present when viewing a human speaker, material was chosen for its clarity and ease of recognition in order to limit such perception difficulties. Words containing difficult to distinguish sounds like 'm' and 'n' (e.g., *maan*) were not used.
- Phoneme segmentation test - Whole words are aurally presented. In total there were 20 items (CV and VC, CVC, CCVCC, CVCC, and CCVCC, see Table 1) and the children are instructed to segment the words into their constituent phonemes.

TABLE 1
Examples of items in the PA tests.

| Type of item | Presented | Expected response | (English translation) |
|---|---|---|---|
| *Phoneme Blending test.* | | | |
| 6 CV items | /k/ /oe/ | /koe/ | (cow) |
| 5 CVC items | /b/ /oo/ /t/ | /boot/ | (boat) |
| 5 CVCC items | /k/ /i/ /s/ /t/ | /kist/ | (chest) |
| 5 CCVC items | /t/ /r/ /ei/ /n/ | /trein/ | (train) |
| 5 CCVCC items | /k/ /r/ /a/ /n/ /t/ | /krant/ | (paper) |
| *Segmentation test* | | | |
| 4 VC items | /uit/ | /ui/ /t/ | (out) |
| 4 CVC items | /kip/ | /k/ /i/ /p/ | (chicken) |
| 4 CVCC items | /melk/ | /m/ /e/ /l/ /k/ | (milk) |
| 4 CCVC items | /brok/ | /b/ /r/ /o/ /k/ | (chunk) |
| 4 CCVCC items | /klomp/ | /k/ /l/ /o/ /m/ /p/ | (clog) |
| *Initial Phoneme Deletion test* | | | |
| 8 CVC items | /map/, take /m/ away what do you have left? | | |
| | /ap/ | | |

- Initial phoneme deletion test - The child is asked to delete the initial phoneme of each of 8 CVC words and then provide the remaining cluster (VC, see Table 1 for an example). Note that unlike the other two phonological awareness tests, deletion contains only one level of complexity.

T2  In June, the end of kindergarten

New versions of the three phonological tests were administered. The format of these tests was the same as in the pretests, except that the words were different.

T3  January, 4 months after start of formal reading instruction

The same three phonological tests used in June were re-administered, although the order of item presentation was changed, with the constraint that the level of difficulty remained similar.

*Procedure*

The children were tested one at a time in a quiet area of the school. Total testing time was approximately 20 min at T1 and 10 min for testing at T2 and T3. The vocabulary test was done first, the child was told to pick the most suitable picture that represents a spoken word. The vocabulary test was stopped when the child failed to get more than two out of eight items correct. The letter recognition test was then placed on the desk and the child asked to indicate, by either naming or pronouncing, which letters they knew. When the letter test was completed the word recognition test was presented. The child was asked if they could read any of the words on the page.

For the phoneme awareness tests the child was asked to put on a headphone connected to a computer. The instructions for the tests were given by the computer which contained examples to which the child was expected to respond. The actual testing did not commence until the experimenter was satisfied that the task was clear to the child. Items were not repeated and corrective feedback was not provided during testing. When three items in a row were incorrectly answered the test was broken off and the next test started. The order of testing was phoneme blending, segmentation and lastly initial phoneme deletion. The same procedure was used for all three sessions.

To test our predictions a number of analysis will be done. Descriptive statistics and correlational analysis will be used to examine the questions on relative difficulty of various phonological tasks, and to track the children throughout the study. Also a structural diagram will be made in LISREL in order to examine the issue of predictability of Grade 1 ability based upon Kindergarten ability.

RESULTS

The mean test scores for the three measurement moments (T1, T2, & T3) are shown in Table 2. The vocabulary scores at T1 were within the range expected for the age group tested (Verhoeven et al., 1986). There were a few outliers, however, with children scoring as low as 12 and as high as 89 (maximum possible was 98). The letter test revealed that many children could name or pronounce a few letters at least. The word recognition test showed that only a few children were are able to read words. These three tests thus revealed much variability in letter, word knowledge and vocabulary knowledge halfway through kindergarten.

The tests used for phoneme blending and segmenting are designed to increase in difficulty and complexity Therefore, the absolute increase relative to the other tests cannot be measured by merely looking at the mean scores. The distribution for all three tests was strongly skewed towards zero at T1. Most children could do some blending items, only 9% of the subjects had scored zero items correct. Segmentation was more difficult with 55% of the children scoring zero items correct. The phoneme deletion test was the most demanding, most children (82% of sample) finding it impossible to do even one correctly. By examining the frequency plots in Figure 1 we can see that at T1 phoneme blending has a slightly greater spread than either segmentation or deletion, suggesting that blending is easier.

TABLE 2

Average test scores (and standard deviations) on three measurement moments and factor of increase between subsequent measurements.

|  |  | T1 | increase | T2 | increase | T3 |
|---|---|---|---|---|---|---|
| Phoneme Blending | max= 26 | 3.47 | 2.0 | 7.03 | 2.7 | 18.83 |
|  |  | (4.18) |  | (7.00) |  | (6.63) |
| Phoneme Segmentation | max= 20 | 2.94 | 2.1 | 6.07 | 2.7 | 15.73 |
|  |  | (5.00) |  | (5.39) |  | (4.67) |
| Phoneme Deletion | max= 8 | 0.66 | 2.6 | 1.69 | 3.9 | 6.64 |
|  |  | (1.74) |  | (2.22) |  | (2.38) |
| Vocabulary | max= 98 | 55.15 |  |  |  |  |
|  |  | (18.83) |  |  |  |  |
| Letter Identification | max= 27 | 6.43 |  |  |  |  |
|  |  | (6.82) |  |  |  |  |
| Word Recognition | max= 10 | 0.72 |  |  |  |  |
|  |  | (1.79) |  |  |  |  |

Between T1 and T2 there was a more than twofold (200%-260%) increase in phoneme awareness scores. The distribution of scores at T2 remains negatively skewed, but an increasing number of children were scoring across the entire range possible. The phoneme deletion tests remain very difficult for most children in the sample, 47% not being able to complete a single item correctly. From T2 to T3 (Kindergarten to Grade 1) there is a large increase in scores. By the fourth month of Grade 1 the scores on all three tests are strongly positively skewed. Overall, a 270% increase on test scores occurs from

T2 to T3, for blending as well as segmentation. The average on all three tests are within one standard deviation from the maximum possible scores. The most dramatic increase was found for initial phoneme deletion. At T2 the vast majority of children was unable to complete a single item correctly, but by T3 a 390% increase in average scores on deletion was measured.

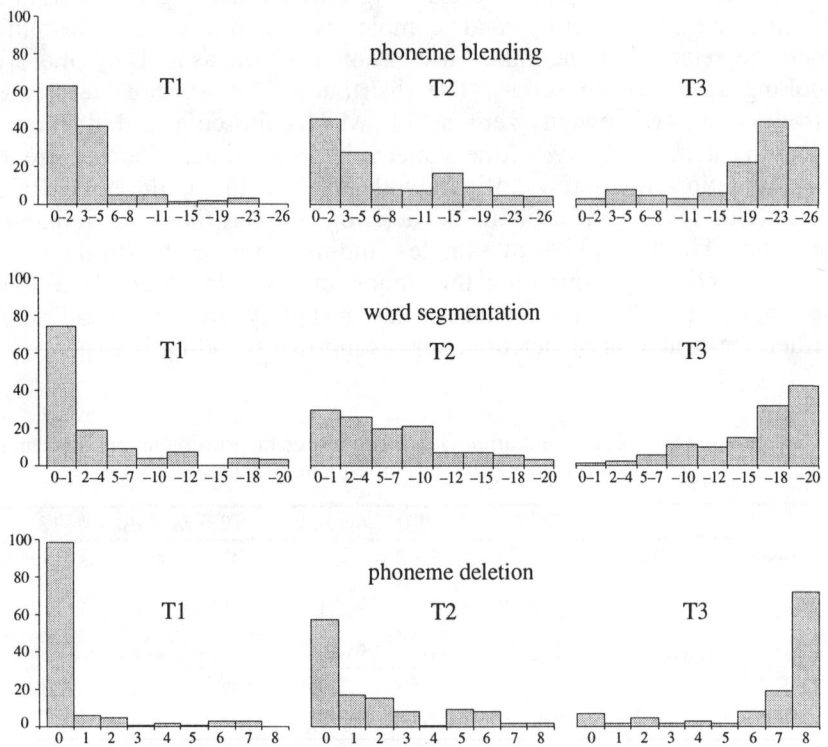

Fig. 1. Frequency plots for the three tests of phonological awareness at three moments of testing (T1, T2, and T3).

*Correlational analysis*

Correlation coefficients were calculated for the three measures of phoneme awareness and for all three test moments. The values are displayed in Table 3. The three tests have high positive inter-correlations at T1, thus a child that is good at one task is likely to be good on another. For the blending and segmentation tasks the correlation between the first test moment (T1) and the second (T2) is high, .67 and .65 respectively, but the correlations between kindergarten scores and Grade 1 scores are much lower (between .19 and .34). This would suggest that performance at T3 is not dependent on ability in pre-

TABLE 3
Correlations between the three phonological tasks at the three measurements.

|  | time | blnd.1 | blnd.2 | blnd.3 | seg.1 | seg.2 | seg.3 | del.1 | del.2 |
|---|---|---|---|---|---|---|---|---|---|
| blending | (2) | .67** | | | | | | | |
| blending | (3) | .19* | .29* | | | | | | |
| segmentation | (1) | .65** | .70** | .21* | | | | | |
| segmentation | (2) | .63** | .74** | .22* | .65** | | | | |
| segmentation | (3) | .28* | .38* | .42** | .27* | .34** | | | |
| deletion | (1) | .41** | .45** | .15 | .54** | .30** | .26* | | |
| deletion | (2) | .53** | .61** | .14 | .55** | .65** | .27* | .47** | |
| deletion | (3) | .23* | .22** | .49** | .24* | .27* | .55** | .17 | .16 |

*p<.05, **p<.001

school. For deletion similarly the preschool scores are also correlated, but there is no correlation between preschool ability and Grade 1 performance.

*Structural analysis*

In order to get an idea of the relative contributions of each variable measured at T1 to the development of phonological awareness, a structural model was constructed. The diagram in Figure 2 gives an overview of the development in phonological awareness over the three measurement moments. Phonological awareness is a latent variable comprised from the three phonological awareness tests.

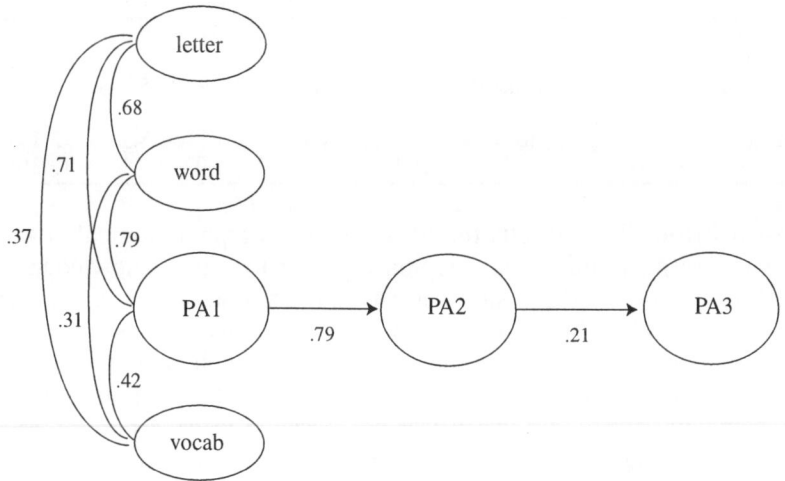

Fig. 2. Path diagram of the standardized solution of the best fitting structural model for the development in phonological awareness (PA) over the three measurement moments, $\chi^2=93.85$ (d.f.=49)

Vocabulary knowledge has a moderate correlation with phonological awareness, letter and word knowledge. Both word knowledge and letter knowledge strongly correlate with phonological awareness at T1. Approximately 80% of the variance in phonological awareness phonological awareness at T2 is explained by results of phonological awareness at T1. Phonological awareness in Grade 1 (T3) is predicted to a much lesser degree by kindergarten variables measured, 21% of the variance is explained by performance at T2.

*Absence of letter knowledge*

Knowledge of letters and words correlated highly (0.71 and 0.79, respectively) with the three measures of phonological awareness. The significance of letter knowledge is demonstrated in Table 4, which contains an analysis of children who at T1 had no letter or word knowledge (N=23). Their means, standard deviations and progression are presented. The initial levels of phoneme awareness were very low and the retest at T2 remained at a very low level. The transition to Grade 1, as measured at T3, shows enormous increases for all three tests. Both segmentation and blending increased by 600%, and achievement on the deletion test increased to 850%.

TABLE 4
Means, standard deviations, and progression on phoneme awareness tests of children who had no letter knowledge at T1 (N=23).

|  |  | T1 | increase | T2 | increase | T3 |
|---|---|---|---|---|---|---|
| Blending | max=26 | 1.78 | 1.4 | 2.57 | 6.0 | 15.48 |
|  |  | (1.20) |  | (3.75) |  | (7.61) |
| Segmentation | max=20 | 0.96 | 2.2 | 2.09 | 5.7 | 11.91 |
|  |  | (2.12) |  | (2.45) |  | (5.22) |
| Deletion | max= 8 | 0.35 | 1.7 | 0.61 | 8.5 | 5.17 |
|  |  | (1.47) |  | (1.23) |  | (3.39) |

It seems from these results that development of phonological awareness is dependent on the acquisition of letter to sound knowledge. In the Johnston et al. (1996) study, it was found that at least 8 letters were required before a child could do any explicit phoneme manipulations, like segmentation and deletion. In that study their analysis showed that it was possible to have letter knowledge without being phonemically aware, but that it was not possible to have phonological awareness in the absence of letter knowledge. They found only one child who fell into this latter category out of a sample of 49 children. We decided to do the same analysis with our sample. The 120 children were divided into four groups based on tests results at T1. As in the Johnston et al. (1996) study, we classed explicit phoneme awareness as the ability to do at least one segmentation or deletion item correctly. The same category was used for letter knowledge, the child needed to name or pronounce at least one letter correct. This created four groups: (a) those children who had letter knowledge and phoneme awareness; (b) letter knowledge and no phoneme awareness; (c) no letter knowledge, but phonemically aware; (d) absence of both letter knowledge and phoneme awareness.

TABLE 5

The number of children phonemically aware as a function letter knowledge

|  |  | Awareness + | No Awareness - |
|---|---|---|---|
| Letter Knowledge | + | 49 | 48 |
| No Letter Knowledge | - | 6 | 17 |

In Table 5 are the results of this analysis. It shows that it is possible to have knowledge of letter sounds and be phonemically aware or unaware. The children who had both letter knowledge and were phonemically aware knew 10 letters on average, whereas the children who knew some letters, but were not phonemically aware, knew about 5 letters. In the absence of letter knowledge a child is most likely to be phonemically unaware. These results reflect the pattern reported in the Johnston et al. (1996) study, except in one respect. Whereas they found only one child who had phoneme awareness in the absence of letter knowledge, we found 6 children in a group of 120.

## CONCLUSIONS AND DISCUSSION

The results of the study strongly suggest that schooling is a major influence on the development of phonological awareness. For all three measures of phoneme awareness there were large increases in scores from the end of kindergarten to the final measurement in Grade 1. Children who at the start of the study had no letter knowledge, barely progressed in phonological awareness during kindergarten, but increased significantly when exposed to literacy instruction in Grade 1. It would appear that the introduction of formal reading instruction was the major cause of this increase.

Furthermore, one consistent trend was that the correlations between the kindergarten scores and Grade 1 scores is fairly low, which suggests that Grade 1 achievement is relatively independent of kindergarten achievement. Concurrent teaching of phoneme awareness and reading skills seems to be sufficient to allow children to catch up, regardless of their initial skill relative to class mates.

The structural diagram supports this view and shows a similar pattern. The individual differences in phonological awareness skills at T2 are easily explained by ability differences at T1. However, Grade 1 levels of awareness are not predicted well by ability in kindergarten. The reading program used by schools may be providing sufficient support that even children who were unaware of phonemes during kindergarten are "pulled up" soon after starting Grade 1.

There seems to be variation in the difficulty of the three different types of phonological awareness tasks used for this study. Both phoneme blending and segmentation are tasks that can be done by a significant number of kindergarten children, who had mastered at least some of the simpler items in the tests (CV, VC, and CVC items). However, initial phoneme deletion (T1) seems too difficult for the vast majority of children. The same was found for scores at T2. But by T3 the majority of children are able to complete most items correctly. A possible explanation for this turn around is that children are learning letters and other reading skills which provide skills and resources to do the more complex phoneme manipulations. This evidence supports the reciprocal causation view of phonological awareness development in a loose form. The hallmarks of the reciprocal causation view are discernible in the present data: in the absence of letter knowledge, phonological awareness does not progress, and increases in letter knowledge at T1 correlate with higher phonological awareness at T1.

However, in a strict sense we have little proof that a reciprocal relationship is definitively present, because it is practically impossible to tease apart what actually occurred early on in Grade 1. Is it phonological awareness that fuels development in reading, or is the introduction of reading concepts that fuels the development of phonological awareness which in turn allows reading to develop? These questions cannot be answered with this study. The teaching program in the Netherlands is designed to stimulate reading skills and phonological skills simultaneously, making it quite difficult to get a detailed picture of what occurs at a microlevel in Grade 1.

If we examine these results in the broader sense, we conclude that even relatively simple tasks, such as blending, require knowledge of letter-sound correspondences to progress beyond very minimal levels of ability. Simpler phoneme awareness tasks such as rhyming and syllable blending may be possible without letter knowledge, as a number of studies have found that even four year old children can complete this type of task (e.g., Bradley & Bryant, 1983).

The lack of predictability of Grade 1 phoneme awareness achievement based on kindergarten scores may have important consequences for future research. Children's letter knowledge came out consistently as a predictor of phoneme awareness, especially for the phoneme deletion where it was the only predictor. It may be argued that some letter experience is crucial to these aspects of phoneme awareness development. In the Johnston et al. (1996) study the knowledge of eight letters was sufficient for children to be able to do phoneme manipulations. In the present study the children who at the start had no letter knowledge did not develop very much while in kindergarten. However, our results did show that 6 children could do some explicit phoneme manipulations even though they had scored zero on a test of letter knowledge. Children with letter knowledge and phonemic awareness could name 10 letters, and the children with letter knowledge but without phonemic awareness, could only name half as many. The introduction of letter-to-sound correspondences and other reading skills vastly increased the average scores on the phoneme awareness tests, by a factor of six to eight. Without the requirement to read, there is no reason to be phonologically aware, as demonstrated in the study by Morais et al. (1979).

These findings may be limited to languages that have a regular grapheme-to-sound system, like Dutch. Generalization may also be limited to countries that have an education system where these correspondences are made as accessible as possible. Children who at the start of Grade 1 have little or no phoneme awareness, may quickly become aware due to the relative ease by which phonemes are mapped onto graphemes. The importance placed on early phoneme awareness may not be as crucial for children learning to read in the Netherlands. In the Netherlands the aim of early reading acquisition is to make children aware of the mechanisms of reading as soon as possible. This is done by combining reading instruction with exercises designed to highlight the segmental nature of language and the correspondences between the sound segments and letters. A much closer examination of the development of print and letter knowledge in relation to phoneme awareness and reading development is required with special emphasis on the preschool period. The present study findings strongly suggest that the development of phoneme awareness goes hand in hand with the development of letter knowledge, and that early letter knowledge may actually start the process by which children become fully phonemically aware.

## REFERENCES

Adams, M. J. (1990). *Beginning to read: Thinking and learning about print.* Cambridge, MA: MIT Press.

Bentin, S., Hammer, R., & Cahan, S. (1991). The effects of aging and first grade schooling on the development of phonological awareness. *Psychological Science, 2*, 271–274.

Bradley, L. L., & Bryant, P. E. (1983). Categorizing sounds and learning to read - a causal connection. *Nature, 301*, 419–421.

Ehri, L. C. (1979). Linguistic insight: Threshold of reading acquisition. In T. Waller & G. MacKinnon (Eds.). *Reading research: Advances in theory and practice* (pp. 63–114). New York: Academic Press.

Ehri, L. C. (1989). The development of spelling knowledge and its role in reading acquisition and reading disability. *Journal of Learning Disabilities, 22*, 356–365.

Hatcher, P. J., Hulme, C., & Ellis, A. W. (1994). Ameliorating early reading failure by integrating the teaching of reading and phonological skills: The phonological linkage hypothesis. *Child Development, 65*, 41–57.

Johnston, R. S., Anderson, M., & Holligan, C. (1996). Knowledge of the alphabet and explicit awareness of phonemes in prereaders: the nature of the relationship. *Reading and Writing, 8*, 217–234.

Juel, C. (1988). Learning to read and write: A longitudinal study of 54 children from first through fourth grades. *Journal of Educational Psychology, 80*, 437–447.

Liberman, I. Y. (1973). Segmentation of the spoken word and reading acquisition. *Bulletin of the Orton Society, 23*, 65–77.

Liberman, I. Y., Shankweiler, D. P., Fischer, F. W., & Carter, B. J. (1974). Explicit syllable and phoneme segmentation in the young child. *Journal of Experimental Child Psychology, 39A*, 451–465.

Morais, J., Cary, L., Algeria, J., & Bertelson, P. (1979). Does awareness of speech as a sequence of phones arise spontaneously? *Cognition, 7*, 323–331.

Morrison, F. J., Smith, L., & Dow-Ehrensberger, M. (1995). Education and cognitive development: a natural experiment. *Developmental Psychology, 31*, 789–799.

Perfetti, C. A., Beck, J., Bell, L., & Hughes, C. (1987). Phonemic knowledge and learning to read are reciprocal: A longitudinal study of first grade children. *Merrill-Palmer Quarterly, 33*, 283–319.

Stanovich, K. E. (1986). Matthew effects in reading: some consequences of individual differences in the acquisition of literacy. *Reading Research Quarterly, 21*, 360–407.

Stanovich, K. E. (1992). Speculations on the causes and consequences of individual differences in early reading acquisition. In P. B. Gough, L. C. Ehri, & R. Treiman (Eds.), *Reading Acquisition* (pp. 307–342). Hillsdale, NJ: Erlbaum.

Tornéus, M. (1984). Phonological awareness and reading: A chicken and egg problem? *Journal of Educational Psychology, 76*, 1346–1358.

Tunmer, W. E., & Nesdale, A. R. (1985). Phonological segmentation skill and beginning reading. *Journal of Educational Psychology, 77*, 417–427.

Verhoeven, L., Vermeer, A., & Van de Guchte, C. (1986). *Taaltoets Allochtone Kinderen.* [Test of Dutch Language ability in Foreign Children]. Tilburg: Zwijsen.

Yopp, H. (1988). The validity and reliability of phonemic awareness tests. *Reading Research Quarterly, 23*, 159–177.

JANWILLEM BAST AND PIETER REITSMA

# THE SIMPLE VIEW OF READING:
# A DEVELOPMENTAL PERSPECTIVE

Nearly all reading problems are due to recognizing words or comprehending language (Daneman, 1991). The idea that reading consists of *only* two components, word recognition and language comprehension, has been called the 'simple view of reading' (Gough & Tunmer, 1986; Hoover & Gough, 1990). The simple view of reading does not hold that word recognition or language comprehension are simple themselves. Nor is the simple view model concerned with the determinants of individual differences in these abilities. The claim of this model is that only word recognition and language comprehension are necessary for reading success, neither being sufficient by itself.

Research evidence shows that a considerable amount of performance differences in reading comprehension can be explained by the combination of decoding and listening comprehension. Hoover and Gough (1990) report that, respectively, 72, 73, 78, and 85% of the reading comprehension variance in the first four grades could be explained. Other percentages found in the literature are: 44% for Grade 1 data (Dreyer & Katz, 1992), 79% for data gathered in Grade 3 through 5 (Carver, 1993), and 54% and 59% for students from respectively Grade 1 and 2 (Juel, 1994). Although these studies support the idea that both decoding ability and listening comprehension are important determinants of reading comprehension, the data seem not to indicate that both components are the *only* factors involved. However, several methodological and conceptual issues are not adequately resolved in these previous studies.

The first issue concerns different views on how decoding ability and listening comprehension are linked to reading comprehension. Hoover and Gough (1990) argue that reading comprehension is the product of listening comprehension and decoding ability. In an alternative view (Carver, 1993), reading level is simply the average of the word identification level and the listening comprehension level. The reason Hoover and Gough (1990) propose a multiplicative model instead of an additive one, is that the former model captures the relationship of necessity coupled with non-sufficiency (p. 132). No progress in reading skill can be found whenever decoding or listening comprehension is zero. The model in which reading comprehension is the product of decoding and listening comprehension tries to incorporate two different states into one single model. When either decoding ability or listening comprehension is zero, a product model

*P.Reitsma, & L.Verhoeven (Eds.), Problems and Interventions in Literacy Development, 95—109.*
© *1998 Kluwer Academic Publishers. Printed in the Netherlands.*

provides a better description of the data than an additive model. An additive model would nonsensically predict that even when decoding ability is zero an increase of comprehension in reading still can be found as a result of increasing listening comprehension. Questions can be raised about the validity of this situation. When children are beginning to learn to read a considerable amount of listening comprehension will already be present. A situation in which decoding ability is zero seems to be more realistic, but no one would than be interested in reading comprehension. Thus, the product model seems to be a superior model for nonexistent situations. However, when both decoding and listening comprehension are unequal to zero, the product model and the additive model are hard to distinguish empirically. Because of this similarity, and because cases with zero listening comprehension hardly exist, empirical evidence for the product model is scanty at best (Carver, 1993).

Secondly, according to Hoover and Gough (1990), the simple view of reading can only adequately be tested if the constructs are operationalized properly and if certain requirements of the data set are met. It is important to know how constructs are defined. Hoover and Gough (1990) define decoding as efficient word recognition, listening comprehension as the ability to use lexical information and derive sentences and discourse interpretations, and reading comprehension as the same ability with the difference that the comprehension process begins with print. In other words, a test for efficient word recognition and parallel materials to assess listening comprehension and reading comprehension must be used. Furthermore, decoding, listening - and reading comprehension must not be so highly developed that both the independence of component skills and their variability are restricted. Surprisingly also, Hoover and Gough (1990) defined decoding as the accuracy of pronunciation of pseudowords without regard for rate or efficiency (Carver, 1993). The other studies mentioned above do also not take the speed element of decoding ability into account. However, the speed element of decoding ability seems important. Apart from accuracy, rapid word recognition is necessary to create cognitive capacity to comprehend sentences. Moreover, with the exception of the study of Hoover and Gough (1990), no parallel measures were used to asses listening- and reading comprehension. Because the simple view is a model for the relation between latent abilities, measurement error of the independent and dependent observed variables must be taken into account. However, in none of the studies the relations between variables are corrected for attenuation due to unreliability of the empirical measures.

Finally, theoretical accounts of processes in beginning reading suggest that decoding is the most important skill in Grade 1 and 2.

Prior to Grade 3, growth in reading mainly consists of learning the printed form of words already in a child's spoken vocabulary. In the next grades general language comprehension becomes more important and the reading process is increasingly constrained by the demands of different reading materials and reading purposes. Therefore, it would be interesting to take into account the developmental aspects of the relation between listening comprehension, decoding, and reading comprehension. Also, from a longitudinal perspective the best predictor of future behavior often is past behavior. Cross-sectional analyses do not take these autoregressive effects of variables into account. It is possible that the contributions of listening comprehension and decoding to reading comprehension will be affected when the autoregressive effect of reading comprehension is added to a developmental model. Although in some previous studies longitudinal data were available (Hoover & Gough, 1990; Juel, 1994), only cross-sectional simple view analyses were performed. To our knowledge, with regard to the simple view of reading developmental aspects have not been studied yet.

In the present study data from a large scale longitudinal study (Bast & Reitsma, 1998) are used to test the suitability of the Simple View model and four research questions were posed: First, does the product of decoding and listening comprehension provide a better prediction of comprehension in reading than an additive model? Second, to what extent is empirical support for the product model dependent on the fact that respondents with zero decoding- or listening comprehension scores are present in the data? Third, what is the effect when measurement error of the observed measures is taken into account? Fourth, what is the effect when developmental aspects of the relation between decoding, listening comprehension and reading comprehension are included in the model?

In order to answer these research questions simple view analyses by means of standard multiple regressions are performed. Second, simulated data including subjects with zero listening comprehension or zero decoding are added to the data set, after which the standard simple view analyses are repeated. Third, cross-sectional latent variable models are specified to quantify the effect of measurement error. Finally, a longitudinal structural equation model is specified to study developmental aspects of the Simple View model.

## METHOD

### Samples

The present natural variation study tracked 235 Dutch children from 40 different schools through the early elementary grades. The reading curriculum was uniform across schools. In prospect of the distribution of a standard decoding test, children with really well developed beginning reading skills, the upper 25% of the distribution, or with very poor readiness skills, approximately the lowest 10% of the distribution, were excluded from the study in order to arrive at a sample of students that could be tracked the first three grades. Children at risk for non-promotion or referral to special education were excluded to minimize sample attrition. Children expected to be among the best readers of the group were excluded in an attempt to prevent problems with the ability range of the measurement instruments. At the end of Kindergarten the mean age of this sample (121 boys and 114 girls) was 74 months (*SD* 4 months, *min*= 64 *max*=88).

We will report about five different measurement occasions within a three year period. The first waves of data were gathered in Grade 1 in respectively March and June, that is after about, 6 and 9 months of reading instruction. The data gathering continued with two measurements in Grade 2 (March and June) and was completed with a measurement at the end of Grade 3.

*Procedure*

A total of 25 tests was used to represent the simple view variables. The majority of these tasks (22) were individually administered by postgraduate students, who received training to ensure standardized assessment procedures. The other three tasks were group administered. Because we tried to keep each testing session to 30 minutes or less, tests were administered in two or three sessions on separate days for each measurement occasion. The tasks were administered to all the children in a fixed order designed to maintain the child's interest, give priority to the most critical measures, and alternate more and less challenging tasks. Before starting each new task children were provided with practice items. The assignments were not given until the child understood the task requirements. Feedback and modeling were provided for the demonstration and practice trials only. For some of the tests there were exit rules. When the child failed a certain amount of items the task was terminated. Once the criterion for exit was met performance on subsequent items was not assessed assuming failure.

*Measures*

The same decoding measure was used for all five measurement occasions. In June Grade 1, 2, and 3 parallel measures for listening comprehension (as a proxy for linguistic comprehension) and reading comprehension skills were administered to the children. In order to be able to perform latent variable analyses, various measures were added to the data set. For listening comprehension, two measures were added in March and one test in June Grade 1 and June Grade 2. For reading comprehension, a second measure was added in June Grade 1, March Grade 2 and June Grade 3. At this last measurement occasion a third comprehension measure was added.

*Decoding ability.* The child was instructed to read aloud real words as fast and accurately as possible and the number of correct responses within a time limit of one minute was scored. The first measure (Brus & Voeten, 1973) consisted of 116 unrelated regular words that become progressively more difficult, ranging from simple monosyllabic CVC words to polysyllabic items containing blends, digraphs, and vowel variations. The second test (Verhoeven, 1992) consisted of 116 CVC words.

*Listening comprehension.* In March Grade 1 children had to listen to stories and then answer questions about them. The first test (LDT-Verhaaltje Vragen; Schroots & Van Alphen de Veer, 1976) consists of one story and 11 questions, the second one (TAK-Tekstbegrip; Verhoeven, Vermeer & Van de Guchte, 1986) of six short stories with 24 questions. The maximum score of both tests was 24.

In June Grade 1 two other instruments were used. The BELL (Form A; Van den Bos, 1992) consists of 39 unrelated and progressively more difficult sentences. The children listened to these sentences after which they had to choose the one picture of four that best described the meaning of the sentence. There was an exit rule of six wrong answers out of the last eight items. The second test (TVK-Zinsbouw Keuze; Van Bon, 1982) consists of 37 unrelated sentences with two pictures alternatives. The BELL (Form A or B) was also administered in June Grade 2 and 3.

In June Grade 2 the test was complemented with the TVK-Verzwegen Betekenissen (Van Bon, 1982), consisting of 37 unrelated sentences. Children had to choose the best visualization from two pictures.

*Reading comprehension.* At the end of Grade 1 two reading comprehension tests were administered. The first test (BELL, A or B; Van den Bos, 1992) is equivalent to the listening comprehension version, but here the children had to read the sentences themselves. There was an exit rule of three wrong answers out of the last four items. The BELL was administered as reading comprehension test with the same exit rule at every subsequent measurement occasion. The second test (Lees en Begrijp 1A; Van der Schoot, 1980) was group administered. For seven short sentences the child first had to choose from four alternatives the pictorial equivalent and for the next seven items the written equivalent. The last six items consisted of the completion of a short story by choosing the right sentence from four possibilities.

In March Grade 2 another measure (Aarnoutse, 1988) was added; a 36-item test for which students have 45 minutes to complete. Children had to read passages and then answer multiple-choice questions. In June Grade 3 two new reading comprehension tests were group administered to the students. The first measure (Aarnoutse, 1989) is a 30-item test, requiring to read passages and then answer multiple-choice questions. The second test (Schriftelijke Opdrachten 2; Brus & Van Bergen, 1973) comprised 32 simple assignments, such as adding elements to drawings or the underlining or circling of certain element of drawings. Because these assignments were given in a written form, this measure gives an indication of the reading comprehension level and the extent to which the child can use his reading skills to complete the tasks.

*Analyses*

First, descriptive statistics are computed for the decoding, listening comprehension, and reading comprehension measures to determine whether the selected data meet the criteria expressed by Hoover and Gough (1990), and whether respondents with zero decoding- or listening comprehension scores are present in the data set.

In order to find an answer to the first research question hierarchical multiple regressions with various combinations of independent and dependent manifest variables are performed. First, the linear combination of the decoding and listening comprehension variables is entered into the regression equation after which the product term is added at step two. Next, the order is reversed, that is, the product term is entered before the linear combination of the variables.

To answer the second research question, cases with zero scores for the listening comprehension or decoding variable are added to the data set. Twenty-seven cases are given the value zero for the Grade 1 decoding variable, zero for the Grade 1 reading comprehension variable, and different values for the listening comprehension variable, based on the empirical data from a random sample of the selected students. For 27 other cases the procedure for the decoding and listening comprehension variables are reversed. After adding the simulated data to the empirical data set, regression analyses are repeated for one specific combination of Grade 1 measures.

With regard to the third research question cross-sectional latent variable models are specified and estimated. A structural equation model consists of two parts: the measurement model and the structural equation model. The measurement model specifies how the latent variables are indicated by a set of observed measures. The structural equation model specifies the relationships among the latent variables, that is variables free of measurement error. The fit statistic to determine model fit is distributed as $\chi^2$ with the same number of degrees of freedom as the number of nonrecursive elements of the input covariance matrix minus the number of free parameters. A nonsignificant value for $\chi^2$ indicates a nonsignificant discrepancy between the model and the data. The $\chi^2$ statistic is a test of the null hypothesis of exact fit. Also, the hypothesis that the root mean square error of approximation (RMSEA, Browne & Cudeck, 1993) is less or equal to 0.05 is tested. Another measure for the overall fit of the model to the data is the Normed Fit Index (NFI). This measure has a value between 0 and 1, with values above .90 indicating acceptable fit (Bentler & Bonett, 1980).

Finally, a structural equation model is specified for the total set of 25 measures. A longitudinal model is specified in which the interrelations between the latent decoding, listening comprehension and reading comprehension variables are estimated, as well as the autoregressive effects of these latent variables. The cross-sectional- and longitudinal structural equation models are estimated by means of the LISREL 8.0 program (Jöreskog & Sörbom, 1993).

## RESULTS

*Descriptive statistics*

Table 1 displays the descriptive statistics and the intercorrelations between measures for each grade. The summary statistics show that skills in decoding, listening-, and reading comprehension are not so highly developed that the independence of component skills nor their variability are restricted.

The correlation between decoding and reading comprehension decreases with grade. The correlation between listening comprehension and reading comprehension did not increase systematically. As shown in Table 1, no students with zero listening comprehension or zero decoding scores are present in this data set. Therefore, 27 simulated cases with zero values for decoding and reading comprehension, and different values for listening comprehension based on a random sample were added to the data. As a result of this procedure the correlation between decoding and reading comprehension increases, while the correlation between listening comprehension and the other variables decreases. Next, 27 cases with zero listening comprehension were added, resulting in a higher correlation between listening comprehension and reading.

*Standard regression analyses*

The most important prediction of the simple view model is that the linear combination of listening comprehension and decoding explains a large part of the reading comprehension variance, but that the product of the two components significantly adds to this prediction.

To test this hypothesis, hierarchical multiple regressions were performed with reading comprehension as the dependent variable.

TABLE 1
Descriptive statistics and intercorrelations of variables

| Variables | 1 Decoding | 2 Listening | 3 Reading | 4 Product |
|---|---|---|---|---|
| *Grade 1 (N=235)* | | | | |
| 1. Decoding | | .13* | .47** | .90** |
| 2. Listening | | | .33** | .52** |
| 3. Reading | | | | .53** |
| Mean | 21.00 | 16.59 | 11.89 | 352.74 |
| Standard deviation | 9.05 | 3.64 | 5.37 | 186.09 |
| Range | 6-59 | 3-24 | 0-27 | 60-1121 |
| *Grade 2 (N=235)* | | | | |
| 1. Decoding | | .20** | .32** | .87** |
| 2. Listening | | | .43** | .64** |
| 3. Reading | | | | .46** |
| Mean | 42.77 | 24.41 | 17.76 | 1056.30 |
| Standard deviation | 12.90 | 4.75 | 5.45 | 415.99 |
| Range | 12-76 | 8-35 | 4-33 | 168-2584 |
| *Grade 3 (N=235)* | | | | |
| 1. Decoding | | .15** | .15** | .83** |
| 2. Listening | | | .32** | ..66** |
| 3. Reading | | | | .30** |
| Mean | 58.29 | 25.91 | 23.38 | 1519.24 |
| Standard deviation | 13.21 | 4.52 | 5.39 | 474.77 |
| Range | 23-95 | 13-37 | 8-35 | 585-2816 |
| *Grade 1 empirical and simulated data (N=262)* | | | | |
| 1. Decoding | | .11 | .66** | .93** |
| 2. Listening | | | .27** | .43** |
| 3. Reading | | | | .67** |
| Mean | 18.84 | 16.58 | 10.66 | 316.39 |
| Standard deviation | 10.69 | 3.60 | 6.24 | 206.38 |
| Range | 0-59 | 3-24 | 0-27 | 0-1121 |
| *Grade 1 empirical and simulated data (N=289)* | | | | |
| 1. Decoding | | -.01 | .52** | .76** |
| 2. Listening | | | .51** | .57** |
| 3. Reading | | | | .74** |
| Mean | 19.12 | 15.03 | 9.67 | 286.83 |
| Standard deviation | 10.67 | 5.93 | 6.70 | 217.04 |
| Range | 0-59 | 0-24 | 0-27 | 0-1121 |

* $p < .05$, ** $p < .01$

In Grade 1 the linear combination of decoding and listening comprehension variables accounted for 30% of the reading comprehension variance (see Table 2). For Grade 2 and 3, $R^2$ was respectively 24% and 12%. The product of these components did not account significantly for additional variance. Moreover, when reading comprehension was regressed on the product term first, the linear combination of decoding and listening comprehension did, except for Grade 1, significantly explain an additional portion of this variance.

TABLE 2
Summary of regression analyses

| Variable | $R^2$ | $R^2$ change | F change | p |
|---|---|---|---|---|
| | | Grade 1 | | |
| 1 Additive | .297 | .297 | 49.118 | .000 |
| 2 Product | .297 | .000 | .132 | .717 |
| 1 Product | .282 | .282 | 91.468 | .000 |
| 2 Additive | .298 | .016 | 2.627 | .074 |
| | | Grade 2 | | |
| 1 Additive | .237 | .237 | 35.967 | .000 |
| 2 Product | .243 | .006 | 1.968 | .162 |
| 1 Product | .213 | .213 | 62.962 | .000 |
| 2 Additive | .243 | .030 | 4.637 | .010 |
| | | Grade 3 | | |
| 1 Additive | .116 | .116 | 15.194 | .000 |
| 2 Product | .126 | .010 | 2.546 | .112 |
| 1 Product | .092 | .092 | 23.560 | .000 |
| 2 Additive | .126 | .034 | 4.440 | .013 |

TABLE 3
Summary of regression analyses with empirical and simulated data

| Variable | $R^2$ | $R^2$ change | F change | p |
|---|---|---|---|---|
| | Empirical data End Grade 1 (N=235) | | | |
| 1 Additive | .297 | .297 | 49.118 | .000 |
| 2 Product | .297 | .000 | .132 | .717 |
| 1 Product | .282 | .282 | 91.468 | .000 |
| 2 Additive | .298 | .016 | 2.627 | .074 |
| | After adding simulated decoding data (N=262) | | | |
| 1 Additive | .468 | .468 | 113.957 | .000 |
| 2 Product | .468 | .000 | .004 | .945 |
| 1 Product | .451 | .451 | 213.307 | .000 |
| 2 Additive | .468 | .017 | 4.223 | .016 |
| | After adding simulated listening comprehension data (N=289) | | | |
| 1 Additive | .534 | .534 | 164.136 | .000 |
| 2 Product | .551 | .021 | 13.720 | .000 |
| 1 Product | .541 | .541 | 338.150 | .000 |
| 2 Additive | .556 | .015 | 4.774 | .009 |

*Simulated data*

The results from the standard regression analyses provide no empirical support for the superiority of the product model. A reason could be that no cases with zero decoding or zero listening comprehension were present. Therefore, analyses were repeated after adding simulated data. The results of these analyses are summarized in Table 3.

After adding 27 cases with zero values for the decoding and reading comprehension variables the product term did not significantly add to the prediction of the reading comprehension scores. After adding another 27 cases with zero values for the listening- and reading comprehension variables, the product term explains an additional 2%. However, when the order of entering is reversed the linear combination of components also adds significantly to this prediction.

*Cross-sectional latent variable modeling*

Multiple measures of decoding, listening, and reading comprehension have been administered at the end of every grade. The results of one combination of measures is shown in Tables 1 and 2. On average, respectively, 27, 21, and 19% of the reading comprehension variance could be explained by various combinations of *all* the measures available. However, none of the relations between variables are corrected for attenuation due to the unreliability of these measures. In order to quantify the effect of measurement error the interrelations between multiple indicator latent variables are specified.

Figure 1 summarizes the results of three cross-sectional structural equation models in a path diagram. Only the structural part of the model is depicted. To assist interpretation, the common metric standardized solution is presented. Each latent variable has been standardized to a mean of zero and unit variance. Following typical convention, the ovals represent latent variables, and the paths between the latent variables represent path coefficients.

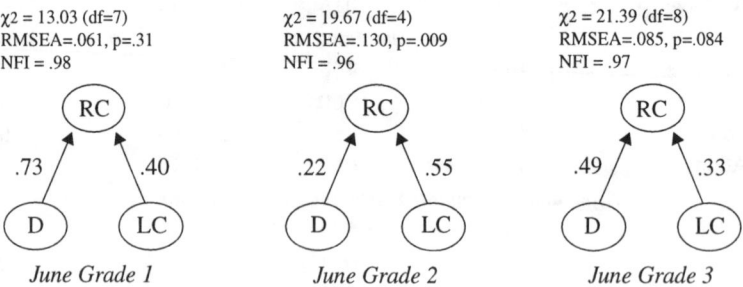

Fig. 1. Path diagrams of cross-sectional structural models in a standardized solution metric with listening comprehension (LC), reading comprehension (RC), and decoding ability (D).

All measures indicate acceptable model fit. At the end of Grade 1 69% of the latent variance in reading comprehension could be explained by decoding and listening comprehension. At that time decoding is a stronger predictor than listening comprehension. In Grade 2, 35% of the variance of reading comprehension could be explained by the combination of decoding and listening comprehension, with the latter being the strongest predictor at this point in time. In Grade 3 comprehension in reading seems to depend more on decoding ability than on listening comprehension again. Together, these variables explain 35% of the latent variance.

When one compares these results with those obtained by means of the multiple regression analyses, the large effect of measurement error is apparent. Especially in Grade 1, the difference between the attenuated and the unattenuated results is substantial.

*Longitudinal structural equation modeling*

The third type of analysis started with the specification of autoregressive models for decoding, listening-, and reading comprehension. When the same measurement instrument is repeatedly administered, nonrandom measurement error can be introduced by the particular assessment method. Therefore, correlations between measurement errors of identical decoding, listening comprehension, and reading comprehension measures at adjacent occasions were allowed. The overall fit of the model is moderate ($\chi^2$ = 731.54, df=257; RMSEA = .089, p<.001; NFI = .85). The percentage of latent reading comprehension variance at the end of every grade that could be explained by the autoregressive effect is, respectively, 0, 50, and 32%.

Model fit improved significantly ($\Delta\chi^2$ = 291.10, $\Delta$df = 4, p<.001) after adding the lead-lag relationships, that is the effects of decoding ability and listening comprehension on a previous time on reading comprehension at a latter time. In the present study, lead-lag relationships are considered suggestive of causal determination. When the longitudinal nature of the data is taken into account, respectively 89, 53, and 63% of the latent reading comprehension variance could be explained by the autoregressions and the joint effect of decoding and listening comprehension.

In Figure 2 the structural part of the final model is depicted in a standardized solution metric. Substantive interpretations of the path diagram suggest several findings of interest. First, the diagram indicates that individual differences in listening comprehension and decoding ability are very stable. However, after adding the lead-lag effects of decoding and listening comprehension a different picture emerges for reading comprehension. Although individual differences seem to be rather stable in Grade 2, there is no direct relation with individual differences in Grade 1 and Grade 3. Second, as expected the influence of decoding ability on comprehension in reading decreases from

Grade 1 to Grade 2, whereas the influence of listening comprehension increases. Unexpectedly, this pattern seems to change in Grade 3. Listening comprehension is still the stronger predictor, but the effect of decoding is slightly stronger than in Grade 2.

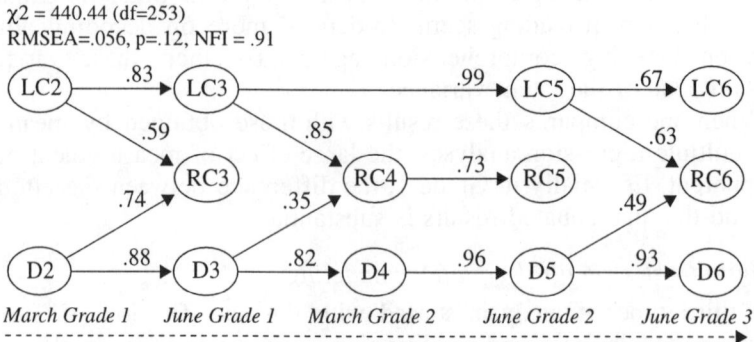

Fig. 2. Path diagram of a longitudinal structural model in a standardized solution metric with listening comprehension (LC), reading comprehension (RC), and decoding ability (D).

TABLE 4
Summary of results

| Analysis | % variance explained | Grade 1 | Grade 2 | Grade 3 |
|---|---|---|---|---|
| Multiple regressions (average) | | 27% | 21% | 19% |
| Multiple regressions (parallel) | | 31% | 24% | 12% |
| Multiple regressions (non-parallel) | | 25% | 19% | 23% |
| Cross-sectional latent variable | | 69% | 35% | 35% |
| Longitudinal latent variable | | 89% | 53% | 63% |

The results of the different analysis procedures used in this study are summarized in Table 4. In order to be able to perform latent variable modeling, multiple measures of every construct were administered. The average of the multiple regression analyses refers to the average of the variance that could be explained by different combinations of these observed measures. There was no difference between the two decoding measures in the prediction of the reading comprehension scores. However, differences were found for parallel listening and reading comprehension measures and non-parallel measures. In Grade 1 and 2 the use of parallel measures leads to a better prediction of reading comprehension, but the reverse is true for Grade 3. In general, the percentage of the variance in reading comprehension that could be explained by different combinations of observed measures is moderate.

As can be derived from Table 4, cross-sectional and longitudinal latent variable models, using the same set of observed measures and taking into account the measurement error and developmental aspects, lead to an significant improvement. The best prediction of comprehension in reading is obtained by a longitudinal latent variable model.

CONCLUSION AND DISCUSSION

The aim of the present study was to find empirical support for the Simple View of Reading. In the simple view model by Hoover and Gough (1990) it is hypothesized that reading comprehension consists of only two components, word decoding and listening comprehension, and that these abilities are related to reading comprehension in a multiplicative fashion.

The results of the regression analyses do not provide empirical support for the product model, and replicate the results of other studies (Dreyer & Katz, 1992; Carver, 1993). In the present study the findings of Hoover and Gough (1990) could only be confirmed after adding simulated data. However, even then, evidence for the superiority of the product model is not convincing and quite artificial conditions are required to demonstrate it. The present study indicates that decoding and listening comprehension are important predictors of reading comprehension. The strongest support for this notion was obtained by a longitudinal latent variable model. However, the simple view of reading also claims that listening comprehension and word recognition skills are the *only* components of reading. No empirical support could be found for this claim. Even when measurement error of the observed measures and developmental aspects are taken into account a considerable part of the variance of reading comprehension remains unexplained. Therefore, the question to be answered is: what are the sources of this residual variance?

According to Hoover and Gough (1990), the simple view can only adequately be tested if parallel materials to assess listening comprehension and reading comprehension are used. When parallel materials are used the only difference between reading comprehension and listening comprehension is that the reading process begins with print. However, the results of an experimental study of Sinatra (1990) suggest that the comprehension processes of listening and reading converge *only* at the word level. Qualitative differences between listening and reading comprehension with regard to the processing of sentences and texts exist. It could therefore be argued that the Simple View model is only valid for the comprehension of single words (Carver, 1997).

When qualitative differences between reading and listening processes exist, it is possible that individual differences in these processes depend upon different factors. For instance, working memory can be related in a different way to listening comprehension processes than to reading comprehension processes. In this case, the effect of working memory on reading comprehension is not partialled out by the factor listening comprehension. As a consequence, working memory could add to the prediction of comprehension in reading.

Moreover, when non-parallel tests are used comprising different materials sources of variance related to the differences between the measures may also emerge. Although parallel measures have been used for the standard regression analyses, in order to be able to perform latent variable analyses other measures were added. In Grade 2 these measures were not strictly parallel. Both tasks involved comprehension processes at the sentence level, but different materials were used. However, in Grade 3 the reading measures involved the comprehension of text passages, whereas the listening comprehension measure used sentence comprehension only. It could be argued that the finding that the effect of decoding slightly increased from Grade 2 to Grade 3 is caused by this difference in material. The simple correlations seem to support this line of reasoning. The correlation between decoding and reading comprehension at the sentence level decreases with every grade, while at the end of Grade 3 the correlation between decoding and comprehension at the text level is comparable to the values found in Grade 1. This would mean that empirical support for the simple view of reading is also to a certain degree dependent on the nature of the measures used.

The above mentioned issues could not be addressed fully in the present study and therefore demand further study. However, on basis of the present study it can be concluded that, although decoding ability and listening comprehension are important factors to predict progress in reading, they do not appear to be the only factors involved. In that respect, the Simple View of Reading seems to be too simple.

## REFERENCES

Aarnoutse, C. A. J. (1988). *Begrijpend leestest en leesattitudeschaal bestemd voor groep 4 van het basisonderwijs* [Second Grade Reading Comprehension test and Attitudes towards Reading scale]. Nijmegen: Berkhout.

Aarnoutse, C. A. J. (1989). *Begrijpend leestest en leesattitudeschaal bestemd voor groep 5 van het basisonderwijs* [Third Grade Reading Comprehension test and Attitudes towards Reading scale]. Nijmegen: Berkhout.

Bast, J. W., & Reitsma, P. (1998). Analyzing the development of individual differences in terms of Matthew effects in reading: results from a Dutch longitudinal study. *Developmental Psychology, 34*, 6.

Bentler, P. M., & Bonett, D. G. (1980). Significance tests and goodness of fit in the analysis of covariance structures. *Psychological Bulletin, 88*, 588–606.

Browne, M. W., & Cudeck, R. (1993). Alternative ways of assessing model fit. In K.

A. Bollen, & J. Scott Long (Eds.), *Testing structural equation models* (pp. 136–162). London: Sage.

Brus, B. T., & Van Bergen, J. B. A. (1973). *Schriftelijke opdrachten: verantwoording en handleiding* [Written assignments: Manual]. Nijmegen: Berkhout.

Brus, B. T., & Voeten, M. J. M. (1973). *Een Minuut Test: verantwoording en handleiding* [One minute test: Manual]. Nijmegen: Berkhout.

Carver, R. P. (1993). Merging the Simple View of Reading with rauding theory. *Journal of Reading Behavior, 25*, 439–455.

Carver, R. P. (1997). Reading for one second, one minute, or one year from the perspective of rauding theory. *Scientific Studies of Reading, 1*, 3–43.

Daneman, M. (1991). Individual differences in reading skills. In R. Barr, M. Kamil, P. Mosenthal, & P. D. Pearson (Eds.), *Handbook of reading research. Volume II* (pp. 512–538). New York: Longman.

Dreyer, L., & Katz, L. (1992). An examination of "the Simple View of Reading". In C. K. Kinzer, & D. J. Leu (Eds.), *Literacy research, theory, and practice: views from many perspectives* (pp. 169–175). Chicago: National Reading Conference.

Gough, P. B., & Tunmer, W. E. (1986). Decoding, reading, and reading disability. *Remedial and Special Education, 7*, 6–10.

Hoover, W. A., & Gough, P. B. (1990). The Simple View of Reading. *Reading and Writing, 2*, 127–160.

Jöreskog, K. G., & Sörbom, D. (1993). *LISREL 8- User's reference guide*. Chicago: Scientific Software International, Inc.

Juel, C. (1994). *Learning to Read and Write in one elementary school*. New York: Springer-Verlag.

Schroots, J. J. F., & Van Alphen de Veer, R. J. (1976). *Leidse diagnostische tests: handleiding* [Leyden diagnostic tests: Manual]. Lisse: Swets & Zeitlinger.

Sinatra, G. M. (1990). Convergence of listening and reading processes. *Reading Research Quarterly, 2*, 115–130.

Sticht, T. G., & James, J. H. (1984). Listening and reading. In P. D. Pearson (Ed.), *Handbook of reading research. Volume I* (pp. 293–317). New York: Longman.

Van Bon, W. H. J. (1982). *Taaltests voor kinderen: handleiding* [Language tests for children: Manual]. Lisse: Swets & Zeitlinger.

Van den Bos, K. P. (1992). *De BELL-Test: Begrijpend lezen en -luisteren* [The BELL test: reading- and listening comprehension]. Groningen: Rijksuniversiteit.

Van der Schoot, F. C. J. (1980). *Lees en begrijp 1a* (Read and comprehend 1a). Arnhem: Cito.

Verhoeven, L. (1992). *Drie-Minuten-Toets* [Three minutes test]. Arnhem: Cito.

Verhoeven, L., Vermeer, A., & Van de Guchte, C. (1986). *Taaltoets Allochtone Kinderen* [Language test for children from a non-Dutch background]. Tilburg: Zwijsen.

# PART 2

# PROBLEMS IN LITERACY DEVELOPMENT

INÊS GOMES AND SÃO LUÍS CASTRO

# LANGUAGE PROCESSING AND SCHOOLING IN EUROPEAN PORTUGUESE

Does literacy and schooling affect the way language is processed? The status of this question is not unequivocal, probably because of the inherent difficulty of assessing deep characteristics of language processing independently of the more superficial layers at which schooling and literacy clearly affect awareness of the structure and elements of language. One line of research has sought to discover differences in segmentation skills that access deep structures of the language processing system. A seminal study by Morais, Cary, Alegria and Bertelson (1979) showed that illiterates have a limited awareness of speech as a sequence of phones (cf. Morais, Bertelson, Cary, & Alegria, 1986). Morais et al. (1979) tested Portuguese illiterates and ex-illiterates, who had learned to read only as adults. The tasks involved deleting or adding a phoneme at the beginning of utterances, which were presented orally. Differences between illiterate and ex-illiterate adults provided evidence that reading instruction stimulates the development of awareness of phonemes. Other studies also suggested that reading instruction stimulates the development of phonemic awareness (Liberman, Shankweiler, Fischer, & Carter, 1974; Alegria, Pignot, & Morais, 1982; Bentin, Hammer, & Cahan, 1991).

A related line of work provided evidence for changes in language processing as a result of literacy and schooling by demonstrating that illiterates and low-schooled adults do not have access to a segmental representation of speech in tasks where the explicit manipulation of phonemes is not required. For the recognition of words presented dichotically, illiterate and low-schooled adults gave proportionally fewer single-segment errors and more global errors, in contrast to adults with higher schooling who showed the reverse pattern of errors (Morais, Castro, Scliar-Cabral, Kolinsky, & Content, 1987). A similar result was observed in children by Castro (1993). Illiterate adults also make proportionally more global errors, and less single-segment errors in the identification of words embedded in noise, than low-schooled adults (Castro & Morais, 1997).

Another influence of schooling on deep structures of language processing has been reported with regard to the lateralization of language. Clinical studies revealed that unilateral right lesions are more often associated with language deficits in illiterates and low-schooled adults than in adults with a higher degree of schooling (e.g., Joanette, Lecours, Lepage, & Lamoureux, 1983). Behavioural studies have shown that the right ear advantage for language is a less reliable result in illiterates and low-schooled adults than it is in adults with a higher degree of schooling (Damásio, Damásio, Castro-Caldas, & Hamsher, 1979; Castro & Morais, 1987). It may be that schooling stimulates the development of processing strategies or devices that are strongly lateralized.

In order to assess the structure of the language processing system an interesting instrument has recently been developed. The test battery PALPA (Psycholinguistic Assessments of Language Processing in Aphasia), developed in English by Kay, Lesser and Coltheart (1992), is based on a cognitive model of language processing and was designed to enable assessment of language related performance disorders. The battery consists of 60 component tests, that address auditory processing, reading and spelling, picture and word semantics, and sentence comprehension skills. Each task of PALPA was designed to provide specific information about the integrity and the functioning of partly autonomous brain modules. The model of the language system that formalizes these underpinnings of the PALPA test battery was developed by Coltheart and collaborators (Kay et al., 1992; Coltheart, Curtis, Atkins, & Haller, 1993).

The aim of our study is to use some of the subtests of the PALPA instrument to assess the changes occurring in the language processing system during schooling and literacy. Overall, this set of tasks provides information about cognitive processes involved in recognition, comprehension and production of spoken and written words and sentences. Qualitative analysis can be used in addition to evaluation of test scores to elucidate specific changes in the language processing system with development and schooling.

To appreciate the effects of schooling dissociated from age, we observed 4 groups of children (from Grade 1 to Grade 4) and 2 groups of adults (low schooling vs. high schooling). Low schooling consists of 4 years of elementary school (the same level of schooling as that the oldest children), and high schooling of between 9 and 12 years of schooling. We also monitored gender differences in our analysis and had approximately balanced gender ratios in all groups.

## METHOD

*Participants*

Eighty kindergarten children, 160 school children, and 80 adults participated in the study (cf. Table 1). All school children attended the respective grade for the first time, with the exception of 10 children that were excluded from data analysis.

TABLE 1
Mean Age and Gender for Each Subgroup of Children and Adults

| Group | Age | | Gender | |
|---|---|---|---|---|
| | M | SD | Female | Male |
| Year 4 | 4.4 | .3 | 21 | 19 |
| Year 5 | 5.5 | .4 | 16 | 24 |
| Grade 1 | 6.7 | .4 | 19 | 20 |
| Grade 2 | 7.5 | .4 | 15 | 22 |
| Grade 3 | 8.7 | .4 | 18 | 21 |
| Grade 4 | 9.6 | .4 | 14 | 20 |
| Schooling 4 | 48.3 | 6.8 | 18 | 22 |
| Schooling 9/12 | 41.1 | 5.9 | 20 | 20 |

*Materials*

A set of six reading, one auditory processing, and one sentence comprehension tasks from the PALPA test battery was translated and adapted to Portuguese language. The reading tasks were as follows:

*Letter discrimination: Mirror reversal* requires discrimination between the correct form of a letter and its mirror-reversed form. Letters whose mirror-reversed form is another letter (d/b) and symmetrical letters (A/i) were not used. The complete set of stimuli comprises of 18 letters, each in the correct and in the mirrored orientation. The task is to mark the correctly oriented letters on an answering sheet.

*Letter discrimination: Between case matching* assesses the ability to identify the same letter in upper case and in lower case. The participant is required to match a given letter in upper case to its lower case form. The cases are reversed in a second task (e.g., select from *F* and *T* the letter matching *t*). All 26 alphabet letters are used on both tasks[1].

*Letter discrimination: Letters in words and nonwords.*

Thirty pairs of five-letter words, one in upper, and one in lower case, are presented and the task is to mark which pairs are identical words. Thirty pairs of nonwords were added. Same pairs consist of same letter items (e.g., CARRO-carro) and different pairs differed in just one letter, either at the first position (**t**inta-PINTA), in the middle position (BANCO-ba**r**co), or at the end of the string (RRBAA-rrbao).

*Letter naming and sounding.*

This test is composed of two different tasks: saying the name of the letter, and saying how the letter sounds. Due to the specific characte-

---

[1] Since 1990, the Orthographic Agreement for Portuguese between Portugal and Brazil defines the alphabet as composed by 26 letters (cf., Bergström, M., & Reis, N. [1996]. Prontuário ortográfico e guia da língua portuguesa [Orthographic prontuario and guide of Portuguese language]. Lisbon: Editorial Notícias.). This added the letters 'k', 'w' and 'y', which are not traditionally part of the European Portuguese alphabet. These three letters continue to be used primarily to transcribe foreign names and words, and are not very common in daily life.

ristics of Portuguese spelling, the stimuli for sounding include ç, diacritics (ó and ã), a nasal diphthong and digraphs (en; rr, ss, ch, nh, lh, qu, and gu); the consonant h was excluded, since it is not pronounced. The Portuguese version of the test has 52 stimuli (26 x 2 cases) for naming, and 72 (36 x 2) for sounding.

*Oral reading – Sentences.*
Thirty-six active, passive or comparative sentences (12 of each type) were presented to be read aloud and were used to test whether reading preserves meaning and syntactical properties of the sentence. A distinction was made between reversible and non-reversible sentences, sentences with a verb that is directional or not directional (active and passive sentences only), and sentences using a single adjective or an additional verbal complement (comparative sentences only). The various combinations of these factors lead to a total of nine different types of sentences. The sentences are built from a restricted set of six animate referents (man, girl, horse, cat, dog, chicken) and eleven verbs. The set of referents is almost the same as in the English version; three verbs and one adjective were changed because a direct translation was not suitable. The sentences used in this task are a subset of those used to assess sentence comprehension.

*Auditory Processing – Repeating sentences.*
This task is analogous to the previous one, except that the participant is required to repeat the sentences instead of reading them aloud.

*Sentence Comprehension – Pointing span for Noun-Verb sequences.*
In the pointing span test, a string of three words is presented auditorily with a sentence-like intonation. Participants have in front of them pictures representing eight words and have to point to the pictures in the same order as they were presented. Twelve noun-verb and noun-verb-noun strings were used with a structure of S–V and S–V–O (subject, verb, object), respectively. The sentences are grammatically anomalous in that verbs were not conjugated and no articles were used. The sentences are also semantically anomalous (for example: "pin boil" or "hat cut shed"). A restricted set of four nouns and four verbs serves to construct a set of phrases. These are combined into 6 different types of strings: SV, SVO, SV/SV, SVO/SV, SV/SV/SV, and SVO/SVO. Strings containing more than one phrase never contain the same phrase twice. Overall, two variants of each type of string are prepared.

The six types of strings are used sequentially in increasing order of complexity as listed above. A staircase procedure is used in which successful performance on a particular type of string is followed by the next more complex type of string. If subjects fail at a particular type of string, the next shorter type of string is used on the next trial. The type of string beyond which subjects never advance is the primary measure in this test.

*Procedure*

Participants were tested individually in a quiet room. School children from third grade onwards and adults were presented with all tasks. Kindergarten children and the first two grades were presented only with those tasks they are considered capable of.

*Analysis*

We have computed ANOVAs by subject and by item on the number of correct responses (or errors); corresponding results are reported as $F_1$ and $F_2$, respectively. Schooling and Gender were systematically included as between-subjects factors in the analysis by subject. Because the size of groups varied due to the exclusion of students repeating a grade, the analyses by item were computed on the proportion of errors (relative to $n$), after an arc sine transformation ($Y'=2\arcsin[Y]^{1/2}$). When reporting inferential statistics, we included the mean squared error as estimator of the subjects' error variance.

## RESULTS

*Letter Discrimination: Mirror Reversal*

We will consider two types of errors separately: normal errors - failing to mark a correctly oriented letter, or mirror errors - marking a mirror-reversed letter. Results were analyzed separately for children and adults.

*Children.* As shown in Table 2, more errors were made on mirror-reversed letters than there were failures to mark normal letters. Almost all older children marked all correctly oriented letters, but only about half avoided marking any mirror-reversed letters. ANOVAs, which included Orientation (Normal vs. Reversed) as an additional factor, revealed that this effect was significant by item ($F_2(1,136)=10.48$, MSE=0.10, p=.001), and almost reached significance by subject ($F_1(1,69)=3.64$, MSE=5.73, p=.06). The interaction effect of Orientation x Schooling was also significant ($F_1(3,69)=3.37$, MSE=5.73, p=.02; $F_2(3,136)=7.40$, MSE=.10, p<.001). This is probably due to the fact that the second graders did not perform worse with mirror-reversed letters. The number of errors decreased from the lower two grades to the upper two grades. The effect of Schooling was indeed significant ($F_1(3,69)=7.70$, MSE=9.06, p<.001; $F_2(3,136)=31.94$, MSE=.10, p<.001). Tukey tests confirmed that the differences between Grades 1 and 2, and Grades 3 and 4, were not significant, but the difference between Grades 2 vs. 3 was, as were the comparisons of Grade 1 vs. 4, and 2 vs. 4.

TABLE 2
Letter Discrimination: Mirror Reversal Task - mean errors (and SD), percentage of participants (%n) with the maximum score, and the discriminability index d'

|  | group | errors normal | errors mirror | %n normal | %n mirror | d' |
|---|---|---|---|---|---|---|
| Children | Grade 1 | 1.3 (1.5) | 3.5 (3.6) | 50 | 30 | 3.3(1.8) |
|  | Grade 2 | 4.4 (5.2) | 3.1 (2.5) | 17 | 6 | 2.2(1.4) |
|  | Grade 3 | 0.9 (1.8) | 2.3 (2.9) | 63 | 21 | 3.7(1.4) |
|  | Grade 4 | 0.1 (0.3) | 1.0 (1.3) | 90 | 40 | 4.7(0.9) |
| Adults | Schooling 4 | 0.1 (0.3) | 1.3 (1.3) | 90 | 35 | 4.5(0.9) |
|  | Schooling 9–12 | 0.0 -- | 0.3 (0.4) | 100 | 75 | 5.4(0.6) |

Note. Values enclosed in parentheses show standard deviations.

These results were also analyzed by calculating the discriminability index d', which is independent of response bias (e.g., MacMillan & Greelman, 1991). Correct answers to normally oriented letters were considered hits, so that failures to mark normally oriented letters correspond to omissions; incorrect responses to mirror-reversed letters were considered false alarms. The remaining cases then were correct rejections. These percentages were used to calculate the discriminability index for each participant. As shown in Table 2, average discriminability was highest in Grade 4. An ANOVA confirmed the effect of Schooling on d' values ($F_1(3,72)=9.42$, MSE=2.02, p<.001); Tukey tests showed that significant differences occur between Grades 1 vs. 4, 2 vs. 3, and 2 vs. 4.

Errors occurred in all stimuli, but they were particularly frequent in the reversed g and n. These letters accounted for 18% of all errors. The fact that in all groups errors were made about half of the time when the mirror-reversed g was presented, was probably due to the font used, in which the printed mirror-reversed g was very similar to a hand-written normal $g^2$.

*Adults.* Participants with a high level of schooling (Schooling 9-12) made no errors when responding to correctly oriented letters, and 15 (of 20) performed flawlessly also when responding to the mirror-reversed forms. The performance of participants with a low level of schooling (Schooling 4) was slightly lower with two subjects not perfect on normally oriented letters, and only seven errorless on mirror-reversed letters. The difference between Schooling 4 and

---

[2] However, the results reported here are not an artefact due to the presence of this mirror-reversed 'g', since if this item is excluded from data analysis the main (statistical) results remain.

Schooling 9-12 was significant ($F_1(1,36)=1.27$, MSE=.52, p=.001; $F_2(1,68)=5.06$, MSE=.08, p=.03), as was the difference between normally oriented and mirror-reversed letters ($F_1(1,36)=18.77$, MSE=.52, p<.001; $F_2(1,68)=7.03$, MSE=.08, p=.01). The interaction Schooling x Orientation was significant only by subject ($F_1(1,36)=-7.86$, MSE=.52, p=.008), possibly because adults perform at the ceiling level. The SDT analysis showed that d's were, on average, significantly higher in the Schooling 9-12 group ($F_1(1,38)=12.07$, MSE=.60, p=.001). Almost half of the errors (13 in 32) came from adults in the Schooling 4 group accepting the reversed g as normal; the next frequent error was observed for the reversed n (6:32 in the same group).

*Letter Discrimination: Upper – Lower Case Matching*
**Children.** Performance was very close to the maximum possible. Errors diminished markedly from Grade 1 to Grade 3. In Grades 3 and 4 most children reached the maximum score (see Table 3). Variability is large among first graders. The effect of Schooling was significant only by item ($F_2(3,100)=3.73$, MSE=.07, p=.01); Scheffé tests indicate that only the difference between Grades 1 and 3 is significant.

TABLE 3
Mean Errors (and SD) and percentage of participants (%n) with maximum scores in the letter matching tasks

| Group | | Upper-Lower matching errors | | %n | Lower-Upper matching errors | | %n |
|---|---|---|---|---|---|---|---|
| Children | Grade 1 | 1.2 | (2.1) | 60 | 3.3 | (5.0) | 55 |
| | Grade 2 | 0.6 | (0.8) | 63 | 1.1 | (3.3) | 72 |
| | Grade 3 | 0.2 | (0.4) | 84 | 0.7 | (1.4) | 65 |
| | Grade 4 | 0.4 | (0.8) | 78 | 1.3 | (3.6) | 73 |
| Adults | Schooling 4 | 0.1 | (0.4) | 85 | 0.2 | (0.4) | 85 |
| | Schooling 9-12 | 0.0 | -- | 100 | 0.0 | -- | 100 |

Errors were observed in 18 letters. Most errors (40%) consist of matching lower case d with upper case B, and, conversely, b with D. This right-left confusion occurred in all groups, but more strongly so in the first and second graders. Discrimination between target letter and distractor was also more difficult when structural features were shared, such as in t and f for T, or i and j for J; this accounted for 20% of all errors. Of eight letters for which no errors were observed, five have structurally similar upper and lower case forms that facilitated the process of matching (O, P, S, V, and X).

**Adults.** Only three of all 40 adults made some errors in this task. The three adults belonged to the group with low schooling. No significant effects were obtained.

*Letter Discrimination: Lower – Upper Case Matching*
*Children*. Slightly more errors were observed here than in the previous task. Again, first graders showed variable results, and older children performed somewhat better than the younger ones (see Table 3, right half). The effect of Schooling was significant by item only ($F_2(3, 100)=15.83$, MSE=.08, $p<.001$); Scheffé tests showed that first graders performed significantly worse than all the other groups.

Errors were observed in all letters. The largest percentage errors (15%) occurred with o and q, probably because in both cases target and distractor were structurally similar (O vs. Q). Errors were also more frequent when lower and upper case form have identical form and differ in size only (e.g., v and s).

*Adults*. The pattern of results matches very closely that of the analogous task (upper - lower case matching): adults with Schooling 9-12 performed 100% correct, and 3 adults with Schooling 4 made each one an error (two errors for i, and one error for o).

TABLE 4
Letter Discrimination in words and nonwords task - mean errors (and SD) and percentage of participants (%n) with the maximum score

| | | errors | | % n | |
|---|---|---|---|---|---|
| | Group | words | nonwords | words | nonwords |
| Children | Grade 1 | 3.5 (0.3) | 3.4 (2.8) | 20 | 5 |
| | Grade 2 | 0.3 (0.7) | 0.1 (0.3) | 79 | 89 |
| | Grade 3 | 1.5 (1.5) | 1.8 (2.1) | 35 | 40 |
| | Grade 4 | 0.0 -- | 0.6 (0.8) | 100 | 53 |
| Adults | Schooling 4 | 0.2 (0.5) | 1.0 (1.7) | 85 | 60 |
| | Schooling 9-12 | 0.2 (0.4) | 0.4 (0.8) | 85 | 75 |

*Letter Discrimination: Letters in Words and Nonwords*
*Children*. Performance improved from Grade 1 to Grade 4, where it reached the ceiling in the word condition. Interestingly, only about half of the fourth graders reached this level when the stimuli were nonwords (see Table 4). ANOVAs, including Lexicality as an additional factor (within-subject in the analysis by subject), showed that the effect of Schooling was significant ($F_1(3, 66)=12.94$, MSE=6.40, $p<.001$; $F_2(3, 232)=83.55$, MSE=.06, $p<.001$); Schooling interacted significantly with Lexicality in the analysis by item only ($F_2(3, 232)=2.66$, MSE=.06, $p=.04$). Even though there are very few errors in Grades 3 and 4, they occur more often for nonwords than for words; this advantage of words is not observed in Grade 1 and 2. Lexicality by itself was not significant. An inspection of results on different pairs broken down by position suggested that there were more errors in the final position for words and in the initial and final

positions for nonwords. However, an ANOVA including Position did not reveal a significant effect.

*Adults.* Performance of both adult groups was almost perfect. However, there was a small significant disadvantage for nonwords ($F_1(1,36)=7.53$, MSE=.66, p=.009; $F_2(1,116)=12.57$, MSE=.04, p<.001). Adults with Schooling 4 performed at a slightly lower level than adults with Schooling 9-12, in the nonword condition only. The difference between these two groups was significant by item only ($F_2(1, 116)=4.49$, MSE=.04, p=.03).

*Letter Naming and Sounding*
*Children.* Results show a clear improvement on letter naming, from Grade 1 to Grade 4 (cf. Table 5). The effect of Schooling was significant ($F_1(3, 68)=9.36$, MSE=28.01, p<.001; $F_2(3, 204)=21.48$, MSE=.24, p<.001). Scheffé tests reveal that the only significant differences are those between Grade 4 and all the other grades. Errors in naming were seen in all letters, except A and U. Errors were more frequent in K, W, and Y, which alone accounted for 47% of all errors. In the Sounding task, performance improved from Grades 1 to 4 ($F_2(3,68)=106.56$, MSE=90.95, p<.001; $F_2(3,284)=111.2$, MSE=.49, p<.001). Differences between all groups were significant. Errors occurred in all stimuli; they were more frequent in K, W, Y, S, and G (together 30%), and in the digraphs NH and LH (together 22%).

TABLE 5
Letter Naming and Sounding task - mean errors (in percent, and SD in parentheses), and percentage of participants (%n) with the maximum score

|  | Group | % errors naming | % errors sounding | %n naming | %n sounding |
|---|---|---|---|---|---|
| Children | Grade 1 | 18.0 (16) | 80.0 (10) | 15 | 0 |
|  | Grade 2 | 13.0 (5) | 48.0 (11) | 0 | 0 |
|  | Grade 3 | 10.0 (11) | 29.0 (21) | 26 | 0 |
|  | Grade 4 | 1.0 (2) | 7.0 (3) | 79 | 5 |
| Adults | Schooling 4 | 0.8 (3) | 0.6 (2) | 90 | 90 |
|  | Schooling 9-12 | 0.0 | 0.0 | 100 | 100 |

*Adults.* Participants with a high level of schooling named all letters correctly; two participants from the group with a low level of schooling misnamed 8 letters (cf. Table 5). Though very small, this difference was significant in the analysis by item ($F_2(1,102)=6.43$, MSE=.01, p=.01). Similar results were obtained in the Letter Sounding task. Only two adults from the low schooling group made 2 and 6 errors, respectively. Again, this difference was significance by item only ($F_2(1,142)=6.24$, MSE=.01, p=.01). In both tasks, errors appeared in the letters k, w and y. These letter names are foreign sounding and not very common. For example, w is named as in English (double u).

*Oral Reading: Sentences*
*Children.* This task was presented only to third and fourth graders, who performed very well (cf. Table 6). Only three children of Grade 3 made a total of 12 errors. The difference between Grades 3 and 4 is significant by item only ($F_2(1,70)=10.90$, MSE =.03, p=.001).

Ten of the 12 errors consisted of replacing targets by words with a similar orthographic and phonological form (e.g., 'lembrar' instead of 'lamber'; or 'lavado' instead of 'levado'). The remaining two errors consisted of failing to read the passive verb, while maintaining the referents in the presented order (e.g., reading 'the horse's *pulling* the man' instead of '*was pulled by* the man'). On the whole, more errors were observed in passive than in active sentences (6 against 3). The other 3 errors occur in sentences with a comparative adjective.

*Adults.* All adults read correctly the 36 sentences.

TABLE 6
Sentence Reading and Sentence Repetition tasks – mean errors (and SD) and percentage of participants (%n) with the maximum score

|  | Group | reading task errors | %n | repetition task errors | % n |
|---|---|---|---|---|---|
| Children | Year 4 | – | – | 5.2 (3.8) | 5 |
|  | Year 5 | – | – | 0.9 (1.3) | 55 |
|  | Grade 1 | – | – | 1.4 (1.1) | 25 |
|  | Grade 2 | – | – | 0 – | 100 |
|  | Grade 3 | 0.6 (1.9) | 85 | 1.4 (1.6) | 32 |
|  | Grade 4 | 0 – | 100 | 0.2 (0.5) | 89 |
| Adults | Schooling 4 | 0 – | 100 | 0 – | 100 |
|  | Schooling 9-12 | 0 – | 100 | 0 – | 100 |

*Repetition: Sentences*
*Children.* The results show clearly that there is a sharp increase in the ability to repeat sentences from 4 years to 5 years of age (cf. Table 6, right half). An ANOVA, including Group instead of Schooling, revealed that this effect was significant ($F_1(5,105)=20.03$, MSE=3.49, p<.001; $F_2(5,210)=28.13$, MSE=.08, p<.001). Four-year-olds make significantly more errors than all the other groups (Scheffé tests, both by subject and by item). Differences between Grades 1 vs. 2, 2 vs. 3, and 3 vs. 4 were significant only in the analysis by item.

Almost all of the repetition errors consisted of replacing target words by related words. These accounted for 67% of all errors. Different types of substitutions were observed. One that was very frequent in all groups, except in the 4th graders, consisted of replacing a target word by a word that was correctly repeated in the previous sentence (e.g., instead of "The *dog's* conducting the girl", the child repeated "The *horse's* conducting the girl", where 'horse' had been correctly repeated in the previous sentence - "The man's thinner than the *horse*"). Two other substitutions occurred rather frequently until the fourth grade: replacing the Portuguese contraction of 'by + the' ("por + o = pelo") by the preposition alone, 'by' ("por"), and exchanging 'less' with 'more'. Partial repetition or complete absence of response was particularly frequent in 4-year-olds and in the third graders. Interestingly, they are almost nonexistent in the remaining groups. On the whole, there were more errors in passive sentences, followed by errors in sentences with a comparative word, with the smallest number of errors in active sentences (error ratios 82:65:31).

*Adults.* All participants repeated correctly the 36 sentences.

TABLE 7
Pointing Span task - mean correct responses broken down by gender, and percentage of participants (%n) with the maximum score

|  | Group | correct responses | | | | %n |
|---|---|---|---|---|---|---|
|  |  | female | | male | |  |
| Children | Year 4 | 4.8 | (2.9) | 3.6 | (1.9) | 5 |
|  | Year 5 | 3.4 | (2.2) | 3.5 | (1.0) | 0 |
|  | Grade 1 | 6.0 | (2.1) | 7.6 | (2.5) | 5 |
|  | Grade 2 | 5.0 | (1.0) | 6.9 | (2.2) | 0 |
|  | Grade 3 | 7.0 | (1.3) | 5.7 | (1.4) | 0 |
|  | Grade 4 | 9.8 | (1.5) | 8.4 | (2.8) | 0 |
| Adults | Schooling 4 | 7.0 | (1.8) | 8.3 | (1.6) | 0 |
|  | Schooling 9-12 | 9.4 | (1.9) | 10.7 | (1.9) | 30 |

*Pointing Span for Noun-Verb Sequences*

*Children.* Performance was clearly worse in both groups of kindergartners, and better in 4th graders (see Table 7). An ANOVA showed a significant effect for Group ($F_1(5,101)=14.59$, MSE=4.14, $p<.001$; $F_2(5,66)=2.30$, MSE=.99, $p=.05$). Scheffé tests indicated that 4- and 5-year-olds did not differ significantly, and 5-year-olds were performing significantly less than any of the older groups. The interaction Group x Gender was also significant ($F_1(5,101)=2.35$, MSE= 4.14, $p=.04$), indicating that possibly one gender outperformed the other in some age groups, while the reverse happened in other groups.

Most of the kindergartners reached only the SVO string. From Grade 1 to 3, most children reached SV/SV or SVO/SV string; but it was only in Grade 4 that a reasonable number of children reached more complex and lengthy strings, like SV/SV/SV and SVO/SVO.

*Adults.* Seventeen out of 20 participants with a high level of schooling reached the lengthier, more complex sequences (6 items), whereas only 8 out of 20 with a low level of schooling had equivalent performance. This between-group difference was significant by subject only ($F_1(1,36)=17.78$, $MSE=3.24$, $p<.001$). This was the only task where an effect of Gender was found ($F_1(1,36)=5.22$, $MSE=3.24$, $p=.02$). Male participants performed better than female participants.

## CONCLUSIONS AND DISCUSSION

From this preliminary study we can draw a set of conclusions. First of all, the test battery developed by Kay et al. (1992) turns out to be a sensitive instrument to monitor specific changes of the language processing system during development and schooling. Furthermore, it was found that schooling affects low level components of the language processing system such as letter discrimination, letter naming, and letter sounding. Moreover, changes that were detectable in the sentence repetition and pointing span tasks occurred early and were probably not directly related to schooling. Specifically, we found significant differences between first graders and more advanced students in two (analogous) tasks of single letter discrimination, case matching starting from upper-to-lower case, and case matching starting from lower-to-upper case. For adults, no effect for schooling was found on these tasks. Taken together, this outcome suggests that discrimination between single upper and lower case letters is mastered in the acquisition phase of literacy, becoming an automatic pattern recognition skill early during the learning process.

By contrast, case discrimination done in a more complex context of letter strings that may be words or non-words, develops later during reading acquisition (after the first two years of schooling) and is affected by levels of schooling. Although in children the effect of lexicality per se did not reach significance, it did interact with grade; thus, as children become skilled readers, their performance on case discrimination becomes affected by the lexical status of the letter string. Indeed, lexicality was significant in the adults groups: they discriminated better in the context of words.

Even though knowledge of letter names can be acquired before going to school, our results show that in Portugal this knowledge is still enhanced in the course of the first three years of school attendance. Fourth graders performed at a significantly higher level than third graders, who did not differ significantly from first graders. Interestingly, an effect of schooling was also observed in the adult groups, where adults with a high level of schooling performed better than adults with only a low level of schooling. However, this is primarily an artifact of the letters 'k', 'w', and 'y', that at the time of their schooling were not a part of the Portuguese alphabet.

Knowing the name of a letter is not necessarily relevant to reading. By contrast, given the consistent orthography of Portuguese, knowing the sound of a letter is relevant. Our data provide evidence for a very gradual development of the mastery of letter-to-sound correspondences. As with naming, there is also a difference between the two groups of adults. Both children and adults frequently made errors for the letters 'k', 'w' and 'y', in naming and sounding. This is, however, an artifact because they are foreign sounding imports from Brazilian Portuguese (cf. footnote 1). Frequent errors occurred also with 's' and 'g' and this might be related to intricacies of Portuguese spelling. The sounding of 's' and 'g' is governed by strict contextual rules that admit no exceptions (initial 's' is read /s/, intervocalic 's' is read /z/; followed by 'e' or 'i', 'g' is read as a voiced palatal fricative, but if followed by 'a', 'u' or 'o', it is read as the voiced velar stop). However, the mapping from sound-to-print is ambiguous. For example, words whose first consonant is the voiced palatal fricative may be spelled either with 'g' or with 'j'; intervocalic /z/ may be spelled with 's' or with 'z'. Thus, the errors observed in the sounding of 's' and 'g' might be related to the ambiguity in the sound to spelling mapping.

Discrimination between the correct form and the mirror-reversed form of written letters did not improve significantly from the third to the fourth grade. By contrast, an effect of schooling was observed for adults. The fact that the same result was observed with d' values rules out an explanation invoking response bias, that is, a strategy in which uncertainty about whether a letter form is correct or not leads to acceptance as a correct form of the item. Adults with only a low level of schooling show basically the same discriminability as eight and nine-year-old children. It appears, however, that practice or increased experience with printed matter increases the ability to discriminate: Adults with a more advanced level of schooling display significantly better average discriminability. This merits attention because it is of relevance to the interpretation of adult results in more general settings. For example, a neuropsychologist assessing aphasic damage would risk misinterpreting as a visual deficit what is no more than a characteristic of the premorbid state of the language system.

In sentence repetition, differences were observed between 4-year-olds and older children. A relatively high proportion of errors in these 4-year-olds consisted of an interesting kind of perseveration: repeating in the next sentence a word from the previous one. Furthermore, errors were more frequent in passive than in active sentences. The fact that these errors diminished in the course of the following years indicates that spoken language processing, particularly processing of complex structures as (passive) sentences, undergoes significant improvement before entering school.

Processing of spoken language is also involved in the pointing span task. Older children performed significantly better than children aged five, but among children at school no differences were found. In adults, however, a lower degree of schooling was associated with a smaller span, showing that subtle aspects of language processing in adults are affected by experiential variables like degree of schooling.

Finally, it is worth noting that the effect of gender was never significant, with the exception of the pointing span task. Only among adults did male participants perform better than females. This pattern of results matches a general trend pointed out by Fausto-Sterling (1992): when systematic gender differences in cognitive abilities are found, they tend to occur later in the life span, thus making it more difficult to disentangle biological factors from what is the product of social and experiential variables.

### ACKNOWLEDGEMENTS

This work has been partially subsidized by 'Centro de Psicologia da Universidade do Porto' (CPSI50, 'Linha 2'). I. Gomes was supported by a JNICT grant (PRAXIS XXI/BD/4529/94).

### REFERENCES

Alegria, J., Pignot, E., & Morais, J. (1982). Phonetic analysis of speech and memory codes in beginning readers. *Memory and Cognition, 10,* 451–456.

Bentin, S., Hammer, R., & Cahan, S. (1991). The effects of aging and first grade schooling on the development of phonological awareness. *Psychological Science, 2,* 271–274.

Castro, S. L. (1993). *Alfabetização e percepção da fala* [Literacy and speech perception]. Lisbon: Instituto Nacional de Investigação Científica.

Castro, S. L., & Morais, J. (1987). Ear differences in illiterates. *Neuropsychologia, 25,* 409–417.

Castro, S. L., & Morais, J. (1997). *Listening to phonemes as a way to recognize words.* Manuscript in preparation.

Coltheart, M., Curtis, B., Atkins, P., & Haller, M. (1993). Models of reading aloud: Dual-route and parallel-distributed-processing approaches. *Psychological Review, 100,* 589–608.

Damásio, H., Damásio, A. R., Castro-Caldas, A., & Hamsher, K. De S. (1979). Reversal of ear advantage for phonetically similar words in illiterates. *Journal of Clinical Neuropsychology, 1,* 331–338.

Fausto-Sterling, A. (1992). *Myths of gender. Biological theories about women and men* (2nd ed.). New York: Basic Books.

Joanette, Y., Lecours, A. R., Lepage, Y., & Lamoureux, M. (1983). Language in right-handers with right-hemisphere lesions: A preliminary study including anatomical, genetic and social factors. *Brain and Language, 20,* 217–248.

Kay, J., Lesser, R., & Coltheart, M. (1992). *Psycholinguistic assessments of language processing in aphasia: PALPA.* Hove: Lawrence Erlbaum Associates.

Liberman, I. Y., Shankweiler, D. P., Fischer, F. W., & Carter, B. (1974). Explicit syllable and phoneme segmentation in the young child. *Journal of Experimental Child Psychology, 18,* 201–212.

MacMillan, N. A., & Greelman, C. D. (1991). *Detection theory: A users guide.* Cambridge, Ma: Cambridge University Press.

Morais, J., Castro, S. L., Scliar-Cabral, L., Kolinsky, R., & Content, A. (1987). The effects of literacy on the recognition of dichotic words. *Quarterly Journal of Experimental Psychology, 39A,* 451–465.

Morais, J. (1987). Phonetic awareness and reading acquisition. *Psychological Research, 49,* 24–29.

Morais, J., Bertelson, P., Cary, L., & Alegria, J. (1986). Literacy training and speech segmentation. *Cognition, 24,* 45–64.

Morais, J., Cary, L., Alegria, J., & Bertelson, P. (1979). Does awareness of speech as a sequence of phones arise spontaneously? *Cognition, 7,* 323–331.

CARSTEN ELBRO

# READING–LISTENING DISCREPANCY DEFINITIONS OF DYSLEXIA

In the often cited words of the World Federation of Neurology (1968), specific developmental dyslexia is "a disorder manifested in difficulty in learning to read *despite* conventional instruction, adequate intelligence, and sociocultural opportunity. It is dependent upon fundamental cognitive disabilities which are frequently of constitutional origin" (Critchley, 1970, italics added). As pointed out by Stanovich (1991, 1992, 1994) among others, the 'unexplained' and therefore 'unexpected' aspects of dyslexia are central to this definition as well as to many of its variants. Dyslexia is 'unexpected' in the sense that the learner exhibits a *discrepancy* between potential (adequate intelligence) and achievement (difficulty in learning to read) (Harris & Hodges, 1981, 1995; Harris & Sipay, 1980; Skowronek & Marx, 1993). If the difficulties in learning to read had obvious causes, such as severe mental retardation, poor vision, deafness or lack of knowledge of the language of the text, there would be little need for a special term, because the difficulties could be diagnosed and treated without reference to reading. The challenge to both dyslexia research and education is this apparent paradox that there are children, young persons, and adults who experience severe difficulties in learning to read for no apparent reason.

The notion of a discrepancy between potential and achievement directly raises three questions: 1) Which abilities and opportunities constitute a person's potential for learning to read and write? 2) Which aspects of reading and writing acquisition are the best indicators of achievement? 3) How should the discrepancy be assessed; when is it sufficiently large to justify the use of the label dyslexic?

These three questions are discussed in this chapter. After a few general remarks about the assessment of definitions, the chapter opens with a brief presentation of the shortcomings of some of the traditional solutions which use IQ as a measure of potential. The body of the chapter is devoted to studies which have attempted to use *listening comprehension* as measures of potential. These studies differ from each other in several ways. For example, reading and listening abilities have been compared at different linguistic levels. Some have compared reading and listening abilities with whole texts, while others have used short passages or even single words. While the results with whole texts are mixed and difficult to interpret, the results at the word level seem more clear and promising.

## CRITERIA FOR ASSESSMENT OF DEFINITIONS

One obvious way to assess various definitions of dyslexia would be to evaluate them as tools: how good are they at what they are supposed to do? Definitions are used to serve many purposes, such as to delimit a group of poor readers for further study, to ease the exchange of information about this group or about single members of it, to allocate special resources to members of the group, to predict the reading development in groups and in individuals, and to guide the dyslexics themselves. Hence a good definition should make it easy to serve some or all of these purposes well. However, to my knowledge, no published studies have attempted to assess different dyslexia definitions in terms of their general usefulness.

In most research pertaining to the definition of dyslexia, one or more of the following criteria for assessment have been applied:

1. Definitions have been judged on logical grounds, i.e., they have been assessed according to their clarity, internal consistency, possible circularity, etc. (Skowronek & Marx, 1993; Stanovich, 1988, 1991; Tønnesen, 1995).

2. Definitions of dyslexia have been judged against practice (external validity). The questions are: Are those poor readers included by the definition the same as those who are seriously falling behind their peers in school, especially those who are referred to remedial teaching or special education? Are there good reasons why some poor readers may not be included by the definition, reasons which are also acknowledged by educational practice? In other words, the general methodology has been to match theoretically defined groups of dyslexics and normal readers as closely as possible to clinically defined groups (Bedford-Feuell, Geiger, Moyse, & Turner, 1995; Nielsen, & Petersen, 1992; Spring & French, 1990).

3. Definitions of dyslexia have been judged on the basis of their predictive validity: do poor readers included in the definition have a particular (poor) prognosis as concerns aspects of their reading development? One example would be the long lasting problems with phonological recoding (Bruck, 1990; Elbro, Nielsen, & Petersen, 1994; Scarborough, 1984). Another example is provided by prospective prediction studies which have found particular difficulties in word decoding (and phonological processing) to be highly predictive of general reading abilities at a later point in time (Juel, 1988; Shaywitz, Fletcher, Holahan, & Shaywitz, 1992). Assuming a genetic link in dyslexia (cf. 'of constitutional origin'), predictive validity might even be extended to include the offspring of dyslexics: to what extent do children of dyslexics (according to various definitions) develop the same problems as their parents (Elbro, Borstrøm, & Petersen, 1998;

Gilger, Pennington, & DeFries, 1991; Høien, Lundberg, Larsen, & Tønnesen, 1989; Scarborough, 1989)?

4. Subjective validity is yet another basis for evaluation of definitions: do poor readers identified by the definition describe their reading (problem) in a manner which is clearly different from other readers (Elbro, Møller, & Nielsen, 1995; Elbro et al., 1994; Scarborough, 1984)?

## IQ AS POTENTIAL

Potential for learning to read has usually been defined as 'intelligence', as this construct is measured by standard tests (Rutter & Yule, 1975; Stanovich, 1991, 1994; Stanovich & Siegel, 1994). A school child is dyslexic if he or she has a reading score which is, for example, two standard deviations below the level predicted by his or her 'intelligence'. Moreover, this discrepancy should not be easily explained by sensory deficits, gross neurological disorders or, for instance, lack of opportunity to learn to read (Critchley, 1970). This definition was strongly advocated by Rutter and Yule (1975), who reported several differences between discrepant poor readers and non-discrepant (low IQ) poor readers. The discrepant poor readers were more often boys than girls (3:1), they exhibited fewer signs of neurological disorders, motor development was more often normal, yet surprisingly, the prognosis was poorer for the discrepant poor readers than for the low IQ poor readers (Yule, 1973).

The discrepancy definition based on IQ-comparisons has later run into considerable trouble. Traditional IQ-tests seem to be poor measures of potential for the acquisition of basic decoding skills in reading. The correlation between non-verbal skills and reading acquisition is modest, and many children with low IQ (e.g., between 80 and 90) learn to read without problems (Siegel, 1989). Furthermore, poor readers with low IQ (non-discrepant backward readers) have *not* been found to differ from (discrepant) poor readers with high IQ in terms of type of decoding difficulties, phonological skills, or genetic characteristics (Fletcher, Shaywitz, Shankweiler, Katz, Liberman, Stuebing, Francis, Fowler, & Shaywitz, 1994; Siegel, 1988; Stanovich & Siegel, 1994; a summary is given by Lyon, 1995). Neither has the predictive validity reported by Rutter and Yule (1975) been found by other researchers: The prognosis is not better for reading disabled children with low IQ than for children with high IQ, rather worse if anything (Shaywitz et al., 1992). Furthermore, it remains to be seen whether the most suitable type of remediation is different for low-IQ and discrepant high-IQ children (Lyon, 1995). Finally, there is no indication that the prediction of reading difficulties in children gains precision from the inclusion of the IQ of the parents (Scarborough, 1990).

Furthermore, a major problem arises with teenagers and adults because reading experiences are likely to feed back into the presumed potentials for reading. Since 'reading makes you smarter' (Stanovich, 1993), the gap between the poor reader's reading and IQ score will tend to diminish with age. This problem of feed-back is not unique to IQ-based definitions, but also applies to definitions based on vocabulary and other language skills.

If one gives up intelligence as a standard measure of potential there are two possibilities: one is to abandon the idea of discrepancy – but not necessarily all exclusionary criteria (cf. Lyon, 1995). Another possibility is to look for more valid measures of potential.

## LISTENING COMPREHENSION AS POTENTIAL

An old idea is to compare reading comprehension with listening comprehension. In 1925 Samuel Orton relates that his first patient described his reading problem in the following way: "Mother says there is something funny about me, because you could read anything to me and I'd get it right away, but if I read it myself I couldn't get it" (cited in Critchley, 1970: p. 8). It seems intuitively reasonable to say that a person has a *specific* reading handicap if he or she is unable to read a text but perfectly capable of understanding the text when it is read aloud. This idea has indeed been around for a long time and it has recently received new interest. For instance, Stanovich (1992) concludes that "much more basic psychometric work needs to be done in order to develop a principled method of discrepancy measurement from listening comprehension or some other verbal aptitude indicator" (p. 136). This possibility has also been recommended by Aaron (1989, 1991), Durrell (1969), Gough and Tunmer (1986), Lyon (1995), Stanovich (1994), among others. As noted by Sticht and James (1984), there appears to be a common core of comprehension processes in both reading and listening comprehension. The development of reading comprehension cannot exceed the capabilities of this common core. Yet, reading ability can lag behind listening ability, as in young children – and in some poor readers who might be termed dyslexic. Given the intuitive appeal of this line of thinking, surprisingly little published research has been based on it.

Below, three types of attempts are presented to derive such a new discrepancy measure between reading and listening comprehension. The first is concerned with comprehension of whole texts; the second employs sentences and short passages; and the third employs single words.

## Comprehension of spoken text versus written text

Prototypical reading involves comprehension of whole texts. So, an obvious way of defining dyslexia would be as a discrepancy between listening and reading comprehension of whole texts, such as a newspaper article, a report, a short story, or coherent sets of instructions (Aaron, 1989; Bedford-Feuell et al., 1995; Royer, Sinatra, & Schumer, 1990; Sticht & James, 1984).

One of a few published studies which have attempted to go in this direction was reported by Bedford-Feuell et al. (1995). The listening and reading comprehension of five groups of 10 children was investigated using the sentence verification technique (cf. Royer et al., 1990). The groups were 9–10 and 13–14 years old children with either 'moderate learning difficulties' or 'specific learning difficulties' (dyslexia), and a normal control group of 9–10-year-old children.

The dyslexics performed well in the listening condition, but poorly in the reading condition, whereas the normal controls performed equally well in both conditions. The children with moderate learning difficulties performed relatively poorly in both conditions, but worst in the reading condition. The observed discrepancies between reading and listening performance were most marked with the most difficult text passages.

However, with only 10 participants in each of the groups, these results should be interpreted cautiously. Also, no data are presented about the reading-listening comparison in the older participants, so it is difficult to judge whether the discrepancy decreases with age.

It is possible that the poor readers showed poor language comprehension because they were unfamiliar with the written text genres, because they were unaccustomed with the relatively high information density of written texts, or because they were less able to process the syntactic structures of written text. Poor listening could be, to some extent, a by-product of poor reading. It is also possible that the differences are caused by difficulties with working memory – that the poor readers are less efficient at keeping new information in phonological working memory while they try to integrate it in a suitable framework of understanding (e.g., Bar-Shalom, Crain, & Shankweiler, 1993; Crain & Shankweiler, 1990; Mann, Shankweiler, & Smith, 1984; Oakhill & Yuill, 1996). In any case, the results did not support the idea of a *specific* reading disability although the courses for the adult dyslexics were based on such an idea.

It is important to consider the possibility that listening comprehension of text may be influenced by reading skill. This possibility is a threat to the validity of a discrepancy definition. For instance, Snyder and Downey (1991) reported that the gap between good and poor readers' retelling of stories appears to increase between the ages of 9;11 and 12;6. This study, as well as longitudinal studies of the development of listening comprehension in good and poor readers (e.g., Juel, 1988) suggest that poor reading may have detrimental consequences for the development of listening comprehension at the text level.

A study carried out in our group (Nielsen & Petersen, 1992) with *adult* poor readers and normal controls failed to find a discrepantly low reading performance among the poor readers. The participants were 86 adults from local remediation courses and 29 adults with equally low educational status selected from other courses for adults who prepare for an examination equivalent to a 9th or 10th grade school leaving examination. The 86 poor readers were probably best described as 'garden variety poor readers' because of possible accompanying difficulties in other areas than reading, but similarly the 29 normal controls might be described as 'garden variety normal readers' because of similar variations in other skills than reading. The texts were typical newspaper texts: newspaper advertisements, letters to the editor, and short news articles. Three texts were to be read, and three to be listened to by each participant. Great care was taken to make listening and reading conditions as similar as possible. The participants were asked to read or listen to each of the three texts in turn and to answer five multiple choice questions about each text.

The results indicated that the poor readers had difficulties in *both* reading and listening. They scored 8.6 (SD = 2.9) and 10.9 (SD = 3.0) correct out of 15 in the listening and the reading conditions, respectively, whereas the normal controls' scores were 10.7 (SD = 2.1) and 12.5 (SD = 1.6). A MANOVA with two groups (repeated measures) and two conditions revealed main effects of groups ($F(1,113) = 12.0$, $p = 0.001$, and of condition ($F(1,113) = 63.8$, $p < 0.001$), but the interaction between groups and conditions was not significant ($F(1,113) < 1$). These results indicate that the poor readers scored equally below the level of the normal readers in both reading and listening. These results were similar to those reported by Royer, Sinatra and Schumer (1990) who used the sentence verification technique.

Obviously, a child who reads less than other children is less exposed to written discourse structures. Understanding and memory for stories require some analysis and representation of the structure of the text. Without some idea of the text structure, the reader or listener will hardly be able to remember the whole text, nor will he or she be able to distinguish between more and less important parts of the story (Cain, 1996). It is likely that exposure to written texts furthers the appreciation of and implicit knowledge of story structure. And this knowledge may also be useful when children are listening to written stories read aloud.

Furthermore, comprehension and recall of stories depend upon a well-functioning working memory. It is possible that poor reading comprehenders have less efficient working memory (as mentioned above), and if that is true, poor working memory may be a common obstacle in both reading and listening comprehension – and thus narrow down a possible gap between reading and listening comprehension.

*Comprehension of spoken versus written passages*

In order to reduce the influence of knowledge of story structure, and working memory in particular, on comprehension, attempts have been made to compare reading and listening at the level of short passages and single sentences (Aaron, 1991).

Spring and French (1990) asked students from grades 4 to 6 to read half of the items of the PIAT reading comprehension subtest and to listen to the other half. The groups consisted of only 15 poor readers and 15 normal readers, and a significant interaction was found between groups and type of presentation (reading or listening). While the two groups performed at the same level in the listening condition, the poor readers were significantly outperformed by the normal controls in the reading condition. It should be noticed, however, that much of the variation in difficulty of the test items appears to stem from their vocabulary. Examples provided by the authors include the following: "After an incredible performance, the outstanding athlete was exhausted". "The aggravated chauffeur had to remove the luggage prior to replacing the punctured tire". This is hardly everyday spoken English, but more likely to occur as written, school-related prose. Whilst this imbalance does not explain away the results reported by Spring and French, it makes the tasks under both conditions more dependent on familiarity with written language rather than spoken.

As a part of a study of brain correlates of dyslexia (Dalby, Elbro, & Stødkilde-Jørgensen, 1998), a technique was adopted similar to that used by Spring and French (1990). Every other item from two standard reading tests (SL60 and SL40, Nielsen, Kreiner, Poulsen & Søegård, 1986) was presented orally to the participants, while the rest were read by the participants themselves. The items (50 in each condition) were short passages, mostly single sentences, consisting of from 3 to 28 words. Following each passage, the participants saw five pictures and were asked to select the one illustrating the contents of the passage. The participants were recruited from a special school for children and adolescents with specific spoken language and/or written language impairments (The Speech and Hearing Institute in Århus).

In all cases we were told by the school that the reading disabilities were considered to be specific. There were ten age-matched boys in each group. As expected, a large effect of modality was found in the dyslexic group, with mean scores of 49.2 (SD = 0.3) and 24.6 (SD = 21.5) in the listening and the reading condition, respectively. However, the normal control group performed at ceiling in both listening and reading with mean scores of 49.9 (SD = 0.4) and 49.5 (SD = 0.5). Consequently, one cannot rule out the possibility that the normal controls would have outperformed the dyslexics not only in reading, but also in listening comprehension given a more difficult test. Yet, it is hard to see how the listening condition could be made more difficult without introducing unusual words and phrases, without syntactically complex structures which are more unlikely to occur in speech than in writing – and without added demands on working memory.

Aaron (1991) has advocated for the development of a standardized listening comprehension test which is relatively independent of differences in memory, attention, motivation, vocabulary, and the coherence and complexity of sentences. This seems an unrealistic task if this independence is to be a feature of the test itself. It is hard to see where the sources of variation in item difficulty should come from; and a test with, for instance, only relatively easy items would yield exactly the ceiling effects that we (and possibly others) have encountered.

Furthermore, even with short passages and sentences, there are theoretical arguments against the validity of definitions based on a discrepancy between reading and listening comprehension: first, the passages used to test listening comprehension are typically written language read aloud to the participants; and good readers are likely to have an advantage over poor readers with written sentences structures because they have been exposed to more written language. Secondly, the listening conditions also resemble reading conditions because they are decontextualized with contents unrelated to the particular setting (classroom or test room).

There is solid empirical evidence that poor readers tend to lag behind good readers in listening comprehension even with sentences and short passages. For example, Juel (1988) followed groups of good and poor readers from grade one to grade four, and found an increasing gap between the groups, not only in reading, but also in listening comprehension. While the two groups of children started out at comparable and age equivalent levels of listening comprehension, the poor readers were clearly falling behind the better readers in grade three. And in grade four the average difference was equivalent to no less than 2 grades. This means that the poor readers are likely to be poor both in reading and listening comprehension from about grade three, and that they are unlikely to exhibit any large discrepancy between reading and listening comprehension. For this and the above reasons, comparisons at the passage level between reading and listening comprehension may be a much less sound and easy way to proceed towards a definition of dyslexia than would be expected. The question now arises whether the word level offers a better ground for comparisons.

*Spoken word knowledge versus word decoding*
A large corpus of research have demonstrated that most poor readers with at least average IQ (dyslexics according to the traditional definition) are hampered by word decoding difficulties, rather than comprehension difficulties, and that slow and inaccurate phonological recoding appears to be a core symptom (Rack, Snowling, & Olson, 1992; Stanovich & Siegel, 1994). Recent studies of adults have provided quite strong evidence that early difficulties in learning to read are still observable many years later. Even in cases where the adults have reached a level of fluent reading, it is still possible to discern problems with phonological recoding (Bruck, 1990; Elbro et al., 1994; Pennington, Van Orden, Smith, Green & Haith, 1990). Problems with phonological processes in reading are the most persistent ones discovered so far and good candidates for a defining difficulty in dyslexia (Elbro, 1990; Lyon, 1995; Wimmer, 1996).

Therefore, a comparison of reading and listening abilities at the single word level seems to have two advantages over comparisons at higher linguistic levels: first, it dramatically reduces possible listening difficulties caused by poor phonological working memory and unfamiliarity with written language structures; secondly, it focuses on aspects of reading where poor readers are most likely to have particular difficulties.

Below results are presented from a new analysis of data from adults with and without a history of difficulties in learning to read (Elbro et al., 1994). The aims of this analysis were to assess how well a regression based definition of dyslexia matches the reading histories of the adults, and to compare this match with a simple cut-off definition solely based on reading data. Thus the overriding question was whether comparisons with spoken language skills in the form of receptive vocabulary did at all improve the match to the reading histories of the adults.

The adults were recruited by means of public advertisements for adults with a history of difficulties in learning to read which had lasted for more than a year and consisted in more than just low reading speed. It did not matter whether the adults considered the difficulties to have been remediated or not (cf. Scarborough, 1991). The controls without difficulties were the spouses of the affected adults. We asked the adults to solve four reading tasks: a reading comprehension task, single word reading, non-word reading, and pseudo-homophone detection. The two last-mentioned tasks provided by far the best match to the self-reported reading histories of the adults (see Elbro et al., 1994, and Table 1 below) and were selected for further analysis. They were the two measures of skills in phonological recoding in reading: a simple non-word reading test (40 isolated non-words to be read as accurately and quickly as possible), and a pseudo-homophone test (which letter string may sound like a real word when read aloud: tro – *sil* – tys – sof? Expected response: *sil* since this is a homophone with the real word *sill*). A combined reading score was calculated as the averaged z-scores from the two tests of phonological recoding in reading.

This combined reading score was evaluated against two measures of receptive vocabulary, one deliberately selected because of its presumed low demands on phonological processing, and another with strong demands on phonological representation (Grønborg et al., 1993, test E with 21 items, and test C with 19 items, respectively). In the first vocabulary test participants hear a word and are asked to point out the correct picture from a choice of three. The pictured objects belong to the same semantic field, but the their names are very different. In the second test, participants were asked to identify a synonym of a spoken target word given three similarly sounding choices (e.g., 'capital punishment' is that the same as excursion, excavation, or execution?). The first test with picture selection did not correlate significantly with the combined reading measure in the normally reading adults ($r=0.01$, $n=56$, n.s.); the correlation was positive and significant in the total population ($r=0.23$, $n=158$, $p<0.01$). Yet, that is most likely a simple effect of the differences in mean scores of the two groups.

As would be expected due to a common load on phonological processes, the second vocabulary measure correlated positively with the combined reading measure, $r=0.32$ ($n=56$, $p<0.05$) in the normal group, $r=0.53$ ($n=102$, $p<0.001$) in the group with a history of reading difficulties, and $r=0.60$ ($n=158$), $p<0.001$ across both groups. Consequently, this measure of receptive vocabulary made it possible to set up and assess a regression based definition. Figure 1 gives a graphical representation of the regression-based definition: dyslexia is defined as a reading score below one standard error from the regression line in adults with no history of reading problems.

The regression based definition gave a good fit to the reported histories of reading difficulties. However, 13 of the 102 adults reporting reading difficulties scored above the −1 SE criterion; they read better than expected. Similarly, among the 56 normal readers, 7 were misclassified by the regression definition as dyslexic. It seems evident from Figure 1 that the regression definition failed to include some non-discrepant poor readers (with scores between $Z = -1$ and $Z = -2$ and relatively poor vocabulary). The fact that these readers reported a history of difficulties in learning to read suggests that their difficulties were perceived in their own right – regardless of a receptive vocabulary which may have been slightly depressed even in the elementary grades.

In comparison, a simple cutoff definition with no reference to vocabulary provided an even better match to the reading histories. Using again the adults with no history of reading difficulties as basis for the definition, a cutoff point corresponding to a reading score of −1 SD was selected. With this criterion, only 10 adults with reported reading difficulties, and 6 normal readers were misclassified.

In conclusion, the data provided no indication that a decoding-vocabulary discrepancy definition gave a better fit to the self-reported histories of difficulties in learning to read than a simple cutoff definition without reference to vocabulary.

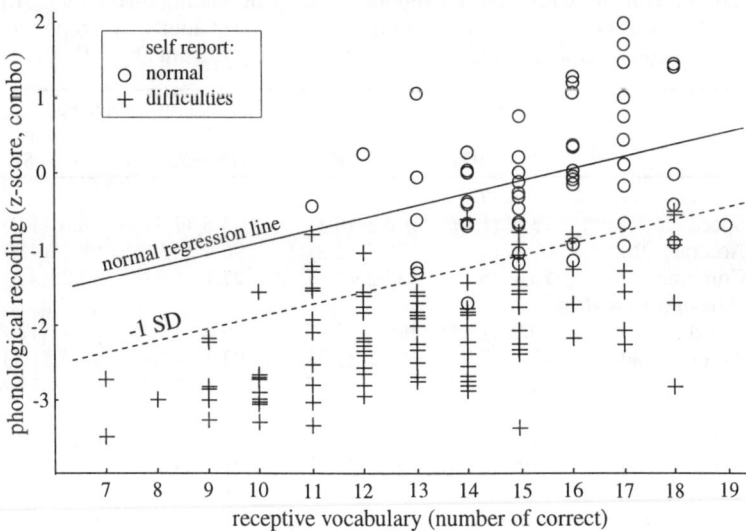

Fig. 1. Listening-reading discrepancy definition of dyslexia in adults. It includes adults with a phonological recoding score below one standard error from the expected level given their receptive vocabulary.

## STABILITY OF A SIMPLE READING-BASED DEFINITION

The participants in this study were recruited by means of public announcements for parents with a history of reading difficulties. This means that the subjects were self-referred. Therefore, the differences between good and poor readers may have been greater in this first sample than in a random sample. Adults with a particularly painful history may be more aware of their difficulties and thus more likely to enlist for the study than adults with only mild symptoms.

We have continued to collect data from adults with and without histories of reading difficulties, and we can now compare the results from the self-referred sample with data from a randomly selected sample of adults. This new sample consists of parents we have contacted via their children as we screened whole school classes for control children for a study of early precursors of dyslexia (Elbro, Borstrøm & Petersen, 1998). We routinely asked all parents whether they had experienced severe difficulties in learning to read, and in all positive cases, we interviewed and tested both parents. The mean scores in this new sample and in the self-selected sample are shown in Table 1.

TABLE 1
Reading skills in adults (means with standard deviations in parentheses) among adults with and without a self-reported history of reading difficulties. All differences on the four combined measures between adults with reported difficulties and reported normal reading are significant at $p < 0.001$.

|  | Self-referred | | Randomly selected | |
| --- | --- | --- | --- | --- |
|  | Difficulties (N = 102) | Normal (N = 56) | Difficulties (N = 35) | Normal (N = 18) |
| *Passage comprehension (n = 40)* | | | | |
| Speed[a] | 5.2 (1.0) | 6.5 (0.8) | 5.6 (1.2) | 6.6 (1.0) |
| Accuracy (%) | 97.7 (3.7) | 98.7 (2.3) | 96.9 (4.9) | 98.2 (4.4) |
| Combined[b] | 25.4 (5.1) | 32.2 (4.3) | 27.1 (5.3) | 32.2 (4.3) |
| *Word reading (n = 40)* | | | | |
| Speed | 66.9 (19.6) | 90.5 (23.6) | 69.6 (15.7) | 83.1 (12.8) |
| Accuracy (%) | 92.8 (7.9) | 99.5 (1.3) | 92.1 (8.2) | 99.4 (1.1) |
| Combined | 62.7 (20.5) | 90.0 (23.5) | 64.7 (17.3) | 82.6 (12.8) |
| *Non-word reading (n = 40)* | | | | |
| Speed | 34.9 (14.4) | 63.7 (16.3) | 38.2 (14.4) | 61.3 (12.1) |
| Accuracy (%) | 67.5 (21.9) | 95.9 (6.4) | 71.1 (18.2) | 94.4 (7.4) |
| Combined | 24.0 (12.7) | 61.1 (16.7) | 28.8 (15.2) | 58.5 (14.4) |
| *Pseudo-homophone detection* | | | | |
| Speed[a] | 4.5 (1.4) | 6.5 (1.1) | 4.7 (1.4) | 6.9 (2.6) |
| Accuracy (%) | 70.4 (22.1) | 92.3 (9.4) | 71.1 (20.7) | 87.2 (16.3) |
| Combined[b] | 11.8 (5.5) | 25.5 (6.9) | 13.2 (6.1) | 25.1 (9.6) |

[a] - passages / items per min., all others in words per min.
[b] - number of correctly read passages / items in 5 minutes; others are number of correctly read words per min

Of the 24 mean values in the groups of randomly selected adults, only one value differed significantly from the mean in the self-referred groups: passage comprehension speed was slightly higher among the randomly selected adults with a history of reading difficulties than in the similar group of self-referred adults. The general pattern was, however, quite closely repeated in the randomly selected adults.

Using exactly the same cutoff point as in the first study (combined Z-score below $-1$ based on the original normal controls), 14 of 19 adults with no history of reading difficulties were classified "correctly" while 30 of 34 adults with a history of reading difficulties were classified "correctly". This corresponds to a 83% match between the cutoff definition and the self-reported reading histories of the adults. As expected, this match is slightly, but not much lower than the match of 90% in the self-referred sample.

In sum, a simple cutoff definition based upon phonological recoding difficulties appears to yield a very good match to the adults' initial problems in learning to read. The definition seems to be both externally valid and reliable.

## DISCUSSION

Recent criticism of the role of IQ in definitions of dyslexia has led to renewed considerations of discrepancy definitions based on comparisons of reading and listening comprehension abilities (Stanovich, 1992, 1994). With respect to this idea, three related questions have been discussed in this chapter: 1) which aspects of listening comprehension should be used as measures of potential for reading? 2) which aspects of reading ability are the best indicators of achievement? and 3) how should a discrepancy between potential and achievement be assessed?

Obviously, some exclusionary criteria are necessary in a definition of dyslexia; some children obviously lack potential for learning to read – or any other academic skill for that matter. Sensory deficits, signs of gross neurological disorders, severe mental retardation, and unfamiliarity with the language to be read are among the most obvious candidates (Critchley, 1970). A first question is whether there are such obvious obstacles to the process of learning to read which are not usually noticed and if possible already treated before school entry. Except for some special requirements in the language domain (with particular emphasis on phonology), it remains to be demonstrated that learning to read requires physical functions and mental abilities which are not also required by many other everyday activities of young children. This first question might also be extended to include poor reading as a function of poor instruction. One might wish to narrow down the concept to only those children who fail to respond to some standard remedial treatment (Berninger & Abbott, 1994).

A second question about exclusionary criteria concerns children attending ordinary schools: should possible cases of dyslexia be judged against the potential of each child, i.e., should one use a discrepancy-based definition? The studies referred in this chapter have focused on the possibility of judging reading difficulties against spoken language comprehension. The successful studies appear to be few (if any), and there are both theoretical and empirical arguments against such a discrepancy measure.

The first theoretical difficulty is that as better measures of potential (than IQ) are discovered and applied, still fewer children will develop a discrepantly low reading ability – so that most babies will be thrown out with the bath water. Increased insight into predictors of reading and reading difficulties is obviously of practical importance for early intervention, but it does not make a specific and severe reading problem less deserving of a label. And the nature and causes of such problems still need to be explored.

The second difficulty is that successful reading experiences feed back into most of the known potentials for reading. This is certainly the case for some of the strongest predictors known, such as phonological awareness, morphological and syntactic awareness, and receptive and productive vocabulary (Stanovich, West, Cunningham, Cipielewski, & Siddiqui, 1996). So while normally developing readers advance rapidly on measures of potential for reading, poor readers are lagging still more behind. Consequently, poor readers are likely to exhibit a diminishing discrepancy between potential and achievement over time.

The results from the last mentioned study might, in fact, be interpreted as empirical support for this theoretical argument. In this study, a subgroup of adults with a history of early reading difficulties *and* low receptive vocabulary scores (between 10 and 12 correct, see Figure 1) were *lower* on vocabulary than expected by the regression-based definition. However as mentioned above, it is just as likely that their reading problems were noticed initially by themselves and by adults – without reference to their vocabulary.

Anyway, the empirical evidence did *not* support the notion of a discrepancy-based definition. A simple cutoff definition based solely on phonological recoding difficulties in reading fared even slightly better than the regression-based definition. This result is very much in line with the recent working definition proposed by The International Dyslexia Society. They define dyslexia as "a specific language-based disorder of constitutional origin characterized by difficulties in single word decoding, usually reflecting insufficient phonological processing" (Lyon, 1995, p. 9). In other words, skills in phonological recoding in reading appear among the most sensitive indicators of reading achievement. And, vice versa, problems in acquiring these skills are reliable indicators of fundamental problems in reading.

Of course, the identification of such core processes should not lead to a neglect of other possible types of reading difficulties, such as specific problems with automaticity in decoding, poor knowledge of less frequent letter-sound relationships (Wimmer, 1993), or specific reading comprehension problems (Oakhill & Yuill, 1996). However, the identification of phonological recoding difficulties can be seen as a first step of an analytical approach. The second step would be to delineate and study other difficulties in reading. A third step would then be to formulate and answer questions about the relations between different kinds of problems in reading.

Before completely abandoning definitions based on reading-listening discrepancies, one should consider the external criteria against which formal definitions are usually judged. Almost all the studies referred have employed a 'one-shot' method with clinical data, school classification or personal judgements as the bases for external validation. So in these studies, the best formal definition is one which 'just' matches already existing criteria, conventions, and idiosyncrasies. This is a potential problem. However, the studies still identify students almost all of whom experience very long-lasting, and handicapping, problems. Moreover, definitions such as the ones applied above offer a formal, well-defined, reproducible basis for communication of results and for studies of possible causes and consequences of dyslexia.

Yet, it is still possible that a discrepancy definition might be superior to cutoff definitions in other ways, such as in terms of prospective predictive validity, or in terms of educational usability. Other, preferably longitudinal methods are needed to throw light on these possibilities.

## ACKNOWLEDGEMENTS

This research was supported by a grant from the Danish Research Council (5-25-98-85). The author is grateful for this support. As for the contents, I would like to thank my collaborators Ina Beining Borstrøm and Dorthe Klint Petersen for help with the data collection and constructive discussions and suggestions. We are particularly grateful to all the participating adults.

## REFERENCES

Aaron, P. G. (1989). *Dyslexia and Hyperlexia*. Dordrecht, The Netherlands: Kluwer.

Aaron, P. G. (1991). Can reading disabilities be diagnosed without using intelligence tests? *Journal of Learning Disabilities, 24,* 178–186.

Bar-Shalom, E. G., Crain, S., & Shankweiler, D. P. (1993). A comparison of comprehension and production abilities of good and poor readers. *Applied Psycholinguistics, 14,* 197–227.

Bedford-Feuell, C., Geiger, S., Moyse, S., & Turner, M. (1995). Use of listening comprehension in the identification and assessment of specific learning difficulties. *Educational Psychology in Practice, 10,* 207–214.

Berninger, V. W., & Abbott, R. D. (1994) Redefining learning disabilities. Moving beyond aptitude–achievement discrepancies to failure to respond to validated treatment protocols. In G. R. Lyon (Ed.), *Frames of Reference for the Assessment of Learning Disabilities. New View on Measurement Issues* (pp. 163–183). Baltimore: Paul H. Brookes.

Bruck, M. (1990). Word recognition skills of adults with childhood diagnoses of dyslexia. *Developmental Psychology, 26,* 439–454.

Cain, K. (1996). Story knowledge and comprehension skill. In C. Cornoldi & J. V. Oakhill (Eds.), *Reading Comprehension Difficulties. Processes and Intervention* (pp. 167–192). Mahwah, N.J: Erlbaum.

Crain, S., & Shankweiler, D. P. (1990). Explaining failures in spoken language comprehension by children with reading disabilities. In D. A. Balota, G. B. Flores d'Arcais & K. Rayner (Eds.), *Comprehension processes in reading* (pp. 539–555). Hillsdale, N.J: Erlbaum.

Critchley, M. (1970). *The dyslexic child*. London: Heinemann.

Dalby, M. A., Elbro, C., & Stødkilde-Jørgensen, H. (1998). Temporal cortex asymmetry and dyslexia: An in-vivo study using MRI. *Brain and Language, 62,* 51–69.

Dunn, L. M., & Dunn, L. M. (1981). *Peabody Picture Vocabulary Test-Revised*. Circle Pines, MN: American Guidance Service.

Durrell, D. D. (1969). Listening comprehension versus reading comprehension. *Journal of Reading, 12,* 455–460.

Elbro, C. (1990). *Differences in Dyslexia. A Study of Reading Strategies and Deficits in a Linguistic Perspective*. Copenhagen: Munksgaard.

Elbro, C., Borstrøm, I., & Petersen, D. K. (1998). Predicting dyslexia from kindergarten. The importance of distinctness of phonological representations of lexical items. *Reading Research Quarterly, 33,* 36–60.

Elbro, C., Møller, S., & Nielsen, E. M. (1995). Functional reading difficulties in Denmark. A study of adult reading of common texts. *Reading and Writing: An Interdisciplinary Journal, 7,* 257–276.

Elbro, C., Nielsen, I., & Petersen, D. K. (1994). Dyslexia in adults: Evidence for deficits in non-word reading and in the phonological representation of lexical items. *Annals of Dyslexia, 44,* 205–226.

Fletcher, J. M., Shaywitz, S. E., Shankweiler, D. P., Katz, L., Liberman, I. Y., Stuebing, K. K., Francis, D. J., Fowler, A. F., & Shaywitz, B. A. (1994). Cognitive profiles of reading disability: Comparisons of discrepancy and low achievement definitions. *Journal of Educational Psychology, 86,* 6–23.

Gilger, J. W., Pennington, B. F., & DeFries, J.C. (1991). Risk for reading disability as a function of parental history in three family studies. *Reading and Writing: An Interdisciplinary Journal, 3,* 205–217.

Gough, P. B., & Tunmer, W. E. (1986). Decoding, reading, and reading disability. *Remedial and Special Education, 7,* 6–10.

Grønborg, A., Lund, J., Møller, O. S., & Pedersen, H. (1993). *Ordkendskabstesten*

[The word knowledge test]. Herning: Special-pædagogisk Forlag.
Harris, A. J., & Sipay, E. R. (1980). *How to increase reading ability*. 7th ed. New York: Longman.
Harris, T. L., & Hodges, R. E. (Eds.) (1981). *A Dictionary of Reading and Related Terms*. Newark, Delaware: The International Reading Association.
Harris, T. L. ,& Hodges, R. E. (Eds.) (1995). *The Literacy Dictionary. The Vocabulary of Reading and Writing*. Newark, Delaware: International Reading Association.
Høien, T., Lundberg, I., Larsen, J. P. & Tønnesen, F. E. (1989). Profiles of reading related skills in dyslexic families. *Reading and Writing: An Interdisciplinary Journal, 1,* 381–392.
Juel, C. (1988). Learning to read and write: A longitudinal study of 54 children from first through fourth grades. *Journal of Educational Psychology, 80,* 437–447.
Lyon, G. R. (1995). Towards a definition of dyslexia. *Annals of Dyslexia, 45,* 3–27.
Mann, V. A., Shankweiler, D. P., & Smith, S. T. (1984). The association between comprehension of spoken sentences and early reading ability: the role of phonetic representation. *Journal of Child Language, 11,* 627–643.
Nielsen, J. C., Kreiner, S., Poulsen, A., & Søegård, A. (1986). *Sætningslæseprøverne SL60 & SL40. SL–håndbog*. Copenhagen: Dansk Psykologisk Forlag.
Nielsen, I., & Petersen, D. K. (1992). *Diavok. Et materiale der afdækker eventuelle læse- og stavevanskeligheder*. Copenhagen: AOF.
Oakhill, J. V., & Yuill, N. (1996). Higher order factors in comprehension disability: Processes and remediation. In C. Cornoldi & J. V. Oakhill (Eds.), *Reading Comprehension Difficulties. Processes and Intervention* (pp. 69–92). Mahwah, NJ: Lawrence Erlbaum.
Pennington, B. F., Van Orden, G. C., Smith, S. D., Green, P. A., & Haith, M. M. (1990). Phonological processing skills and deficits in adult dyslexics. *Child Development, 61,* 1753–78.
Rack, J. P., Snowling, M. J., & Olson, R. K. (1992). The nonword reading deficit in developmental dyslexia: A review. *Reading Research Quarterly, 27,* 28–53.
Rodgers, B. (1983). The identification and prevalence of specific reading retardation. *British Journal of Educational Psychology, 53,* 369–373.
Royer, J. M., Sinatra, G. M., & Schumer, H. (1990). Patterns of individual differences in the development of listening and reading comprehension. *Contemporary Educational Psychology, 15,* 183–196.
Rutter, M., & Yule, W. (1975). The concept of specific reading retardation. *Journal of Child Psychology and Psychiatry, 16,* 181–197.
Scarborough, H. S. (1984). Continuity between childhood dyslexia and adult reading. *British Journal of Psychology, 75,* 329–348.
Scarborough, H. S. (1989). Prediction of reading disability from familial and individual differences. *Journal of Educational Psychology, 81,* 101–108.
Scarborough, H. S. (1990). *A comparison of methods for identifying reading disabilities in adults*. Unpublished manuscript. Brooklyn College, City University of New York, NY.
Scarborough, H. S. (1991). Antecedents to reading disability: Preschool language development and literacy experiences of children from dyslexic families. *Reading and Writing: An Interdisciplinary Journal, 3,* 219–233.
Shaywitz, B. A., Fletcher, J. M., Holahan, J. M., & Shaywitz, S. E. (1992). Discrepancy compared to low achievement definitions of reading disability. *Journal of Learning Disabilities, 25,* 639–648.
Siegel, L. S. (1988). Evidence that IQ scores are irrelevant to the definition and analysis of reading disability. *Canadian Journal of Psychology, 42,* 201–215.
Siegel, L. S. (1989). IQ is irrelevant to the definition of learning disabilities. *Journal*

*of Learning Disabilities, 22,* 469–486.
Skowronek, H., & Marx, H. (1993). Disorders of written language development: Definitions and overview. In G. Blanken (Ed.), *Linguistic Disorders and Pathologies. An International Handbook* (pp.711–723). Berlin: Walter de Gruyter.
Snyder, L. S., & Downey, D. M. (1991). The language–reading relationship in normal and reading-disabled children. *Journal of Speech and Hearing Research, 34,* 129–140.
Spring, C., & French, L. (1990). Identifying children with specific reading disabilities from listening and reading discrepancy scores. *Journal of Learning Disabilities, 23,* 53–58.
Stanovich, K. E. (1988). Explaining the differences between the dyslexic and the garden-variety poor reader: The phonological-core variable-difference model. *Journal of Learning Disabilities, 21,* 590–604.
Stanovich, K. E. (1991). Discrepancy definitions of reading disability: Has intelligence led us astray? *Reading Research Quarterly, 26,* 7–29.
Stanovich, K. E. (1992). The theoretical and practical consequences of discrepancy definitions of dyslexia. In M. Snowling & M. Thomson (Eds.), *Dyslexia. Integrating Theory and Practice* (pp. 125–143). London: Whurr.
Stanovich, K. E. (1993). Does reading make you smarter? Literacy and the development of verbal intelligence. In H. Reese (Ed.), *Advances in child development and behavior* (vol. 24, pp. 133–180). San Diego, CA: Academic Press.
Stanovich, K. E. (1994). Problems in the differential diagnosis of reading disabilities. In R. M. Joshi & C. K. Leong (Eds.), *Reading Disabilities: Diagnosis and Component Processes* (pp. 3–32). Dordrecht: Kluwer.
Stanovich, K. E., & Siegel, L. S. (1994). Phenotypic performance profile of children with reading disabilities: A regression-based test of the phonological-core variable-difference model. *Journal of Educational Psychology, 86,* 24–53.
Stanovich, K. E., West, R. F., Cunningham, A. E., Cipielewski, J., & Siddiqui, S. (1996). The role of inadequate print exposure as a determinant of reading comprehension problems. In C. Cornoldi & J. V. Oakhill (Eds.), *Reading Comprehension Difficulties. Processes and Intervention* (pp. 15–32). Mahwah, NJ: Lawrence Erlbaum.
Sticht, T. G., & James, J. H. (1984). Listening and reading. In P. D. Pearson (Ed.), *Handbook of Reading Research* (pp. 293–317). NY: Longman.
Tønnesen, F. E. (1995). On defining 'dyslexia'. *Scandinavian Journal of Educational Research, 39,* 139–156.
Wimmer, H. (1993). Characteristics of developmental dyslexia in a regular writing system. *Applied Psycholinguistics, 14,* 1–33.
Wimmer, H. (1996). The early manifestation of developmental dyslexia: Evidence from German children. *Reading and Writing: An Interdisciplinary Journal, 8,* 171–188.
Yule, W. (1973). Differential prognosis of reading backwardness and specific reading retardation. *British Journal of Educational Psychology, 43,* 244–248.

HEINZ MAYRINGER,
HEINZ WIMMER, AND KARIN LANDERL

# PHONOLOGICAL SKILLS AND LITERACY ACQUISITION IN GERMAN

The study reported here investigated the relationship between phonological skills and literacy development in German. It focuses on poor phonological skills and difficulties in reading and spelling. Previous findings showed that for English children there is a substantial predictive relationship between phonological awareness and later success in learning to read (see reviews by Goswami & Bryant, 1990; Wagner & Torgesen, 1987). Our findings with German-speaking children were disappointing. Wimmer, Landerl, Linortner, and Hummer (1991) used a vowel substitution task at the beginning of first grade and found only moderate correlations in the range of .30 to .40 with reading and spelling measures at the end of first grade. Wimmer, Landerl, and Schneider (1994) relied on Bradley and Bryant's (1985) alliteration and rhyme oddity detection task, but again the correlations with reading and spelling at the end of first grade were low (between .20 and .30). However, there was a gain in predictive importance of the rhyme detection task for reading and spelling differences in third and fourth grade.

Two main reasons may be responsible for our disappointing prediction results with German-speaking children. One is that phonological awareness tasks are rather difficult for our children at the beginning of first grade. Indeed, about a third of the children in Wimmer et al.'s (1991) study did not show a single correct response on the vowel substitution task. Bradley and Bryant's (1985) alliteration and rhyme oddity detection task–particularly the alliteration part–was also difficult. This is attributable to the fact that at school entry many children in German-speaking countries know very few letters and have no reading skills at all. This in turn is related to a kindergarten philosophy (shared by most parents) that discourages any reading preparation, such as letter teaching, before school. The high difficulty of the phonological awareness tasks may have masked important differences between children and, thus, could be responsible for the observed low correlations with later literacy achievement. For this possibility speaks the finding by Wimmer et al. (1991) that all of the few children with high phonological awareness scores exhibited good reading achievement, but that about half of the many children who showed poor phonological awareness were also normal readers at the end of first grade.

The hypothesis that in German a high difficulty of phonological awareness tasks is responsible for their low predictive associations with reading development, however, is disconfirmed by findings of the Munich longitudinal study (Näslund, 1990; Näslund & Schneider, 1993; Schneider & Näslund, 1993). In this study phonological tasks were applied that ranged from difficult to very easy. The very easy phonological awareness tasks as well as naming speed were only moderately related to later reading speed and the rather difficult onset oddity detection task correlated even somewhat higher with reading speed than the easy tasks. In predicting poor spelling the rather easy combined oddity detection task was of limited success.

Another main reason for poor predictive associations between phonological skills and learning to read could be that children in German-speaking countries, in contrast to English and American children, are exposed to a very systematic phonics instruction in first grade, which introduces all necessary grapheme-phoneme relations and directly attempts to induce children to phonological recoding as word recognition strategy. It seems conceivable that such a systematic phonics-oriented teaching reduces the importance of phonological skill differences between children. In particular, one could expect that such a teaching approach may have the effect that even children with poor phonological skills can successfully start into reading.

The aim of the present work was to develop easy phonological tasks that should allow reliable differentiation among our preliterate school beginners. Two tasks were applied to assess phonological awareness. One task required to identify segments at the beginnings of words, a second task examined rhyme detection ability. Instead of the complex oddity detection format a straightforward detection procedure with little memory demands was used. Based on the finding that dyslexic children have difficulties in producing morphological forms that require a phonological change of the base form (Fowler & Liberman, 1995; Shankweiler et al., 1995), a plural formation task was also included. Furthermore, a pseudoword repetition task was used because dyslexic children appear to have difficulties with the accurate repetition of pseudowords (Brady, Mann, & Schmidt, 1987; Snowling, Goulandris, Bowlby, & Howell, 1986) and because pseudoword repetition predicts later reading achievement (Gathercole & Baddeley, 1993). We considered the pseudoword repetition task and the plural formation task to be phonological processing tasks. Two tasks were included to assess naming speed and articulation rate. Naming speed was consistently found to be impaired in dyslexic children (Bowers & Wolf, 1993) and was also found to be predictive for reading development (Wolf, 1991; Catts, 1991). For articulation rate a correlation with reading was reported (Das & Mishra, 1991).

## METHOD

### Participants and administration

At the beginning of first grade 623 boys, aged between 70 and 97 months ($M = 81.0$, $SD = 5.0$), were tested. The sample was restricted to boys to increase the number of children with difficulties in reading or spelling. Except for two schools, all schools of the city of Salzburg participated in the longitudinal study with all of their first-grade classes. Additionally, a few schools out of Salzburg participated. Criterion for the selection of these schools was proximity to the institute or the residence of an experimenter. The children came from 77 classes out of 31 schools. Prerequisite for participation was German as the native language. Results presented here are based on a sample of 567 boys. Three classes (31 children) were excluded because most of the children showed very poor reading and spelling achievement, apparently due to a rather less demanding, creativity-oriented teaching. These three classes came from one school in an neighbourhood of Salzburg with a high proportion of upper-class families so that other than instructional reasons for the poor reading performance at the end of first grade are unlikely. Further 16 boys of the original sample were lost because they were downgraded to a preparatory class. Nine children dropped out for other reasons.

Children´s phonological skills and letter knowledge were tested at the beginning of first grade, the large majority (almost 95%) between end of September and end of October. Because formal reading instruction proceeds very slowly in the school district of Salzburg – not more than five to six letters were introduced until the end of the testing period – the assessment of phonological skills can be considered to be right at the beginning of reading instruction. Reading, spelling, and intelligence were assessed in May of first grade.

The phonological tasks were administered individually in a quiet room in the school. The tasks reported here constituted the bulk of a battery including also tests for fine motor speed, speed of visual discrimination, and handedness. Administering the whole battery took about 30 min per child. Reading achievement was also tested individually. Spelling and intelligence were assessed by a group test.

### Measures at school entry

*Alliteration detection.* The child's task was to identify the word among three choices that starts with a certain phonological segment. To make the task easy, the experimenter directly specified this segment. Memory load was intended to be minimized by using sheets that depicted by line drawings the referents of the three words of an item. The experimenter first named the pictures and then asked the child to pick the word starting with the specified sound (e.g., Nase–Lade–Rabe: Which one starts with la?). For the first half of the 16 items the first syllable had to be identified. These items also can be described as alliteration detection because the choices of an item had the same first vowel and the only difference was the initial phoneme. For the second eight items the first consonant was the crucial segment. To facilitate perception, this consonant was always a continuant. Each of the two blocks was preceded by two practice items. Item analyses were conducted on a subsample (N=108) of the large longitudinal sample. None of the items had to be excluded.

*Rhyme detection.* For each of the 16 items the experimenter presented a target word and two choices, one of which rhymed with the target word (e.g., What rhymes with Feld: Geld or Gold?). The non-rhyming alternative differed from the rhyming one in either the vowel (eight items) or the final consonant (eight items). Three practice items introduced the task. The items were presented in a randomized sequence, which was the same for all children. As a consequence of the item analysis, one final-consonant item, which was answered at chance level and had a low item-scale correlation, was excluded.

*Plural formation.* A single object, represented on the left side of a sheet, was named by the experimenter. On the right side the object was shown twice, and the child should name the objects in plural form (experimenter: There is one Frosch, child: There are two Frösche). Eight of the presented words change their stem if made plural, eight words do not change their stem. In the latter case only a grammatical morpheme is added at the end of the word. The task started with two practice items. Three items were excluded from the final scale. Two words were eliminated because it had to be recognized that in dialect these words are frequently not changed when used in plural. In addition, the most difficult item was excluded.

*Pseudoword repetition.* In this task the child should repeat immediately single three-syllable pseudowords (e.g., fiwofi, bowiba). The idea behind the phonological structure of the 16 items was to induce assimilation errors for the syllable that did not share the onset of the two other syllables (e.g., fifofi for fiwofi). Four practice items introduced the task. Because of a negative item-scale correlation, one item was excluded from the test.

*Articulation rate.* Word triples should be repeated as often as possible within 10 s. To reduce memory load, the words of a triple were semantically closely related to one another. The two used sequences were Hund–Katze–Maus (dog–cat–mouse) and Messer–Gabel–Löffel (knife–fork–spoon). The child was first presented with the three words and had to repeat them. To verify whether the instruction was understood, a short practice trial preceded the test trial.

*Naming speed.* This task was modelled after Denckla and Rudel's Rapid Automatized Naming test (1976). In each of two trials five objects, repeated four times, had to be named. The object drawings were presented on pages with four lines of five objects. For each line the order of the objects was different. The words of the first trial started with different consonant clusters (Kran, Frosch, Blatt, Schloß, Brot), whereas the words of the second trial started with the same single consonant (Buch, Bett, Bär, Baum, Ball). Two practice trials introduced the task. The first practice trial presented the five pictures, and the child was asked to name them. The second practice trial comprised two lines with five objects each and introduced the child to the rapid naming procedure.

*Letter knowledge.* The letters S, A, O, M, E, T, N, I, F, R, U, D, B, G, L, K, P, H, W were presented simultaneously as capitals. Letters that are less known by German-speaking children at school entry were not included. Upper case letters were chosen because it is very seldom that a child can name a lower case letter, but not the corresponding upper case letter, whereas the opposite is very frequent. First, the child was asked to point out and name the letters he knew, without being restricted to a predetermined order. To ensure that the child did not overlook a letter, the experimenter then pointed at those letters the child had not named by himself.

*Measures at end of First Grade*

A problem in constructing the reading and spelling tests for the end of first grade was that because of the very slow pace of reading instruction in the schools in Salzburg, children could not be expected to have learned all graphemes at that time. To construct common tests for all children, the teachers of all participating classes were asked at the beginning of the second term which letters would be introduced in their classrooms until the testing period started. The resulting list of common letters included the vowels A, E, I, O, U, and the consonants M, N, R, S, T.

*Reading.* The individual reading test consisted of a list of 10 words and a list of 10 pseudowords. For each of these lists a parallel form was created. By varying the lists from child to child, we wanted to reduce the odds that a child could profit by hearing from a classmate which items were to be read. The words of one form were Ente (duck), essen (eat), Messer (knife), Nase (nose), Ritter (knight), Rosine (raisin), rot (red), See (lake), Sonne (sun), Tasse (cup). Pseudowords were created by changing the vowels of the words: onta, assen, misser, nusi, rutter, rasoni, ret, saa, senno, tisso. Each list was preceded by a practice list with four words or pseudowords. These practice lists were read twice, the first time without any further instruction and the second time with the request to read as fast as possible but nevertheless carefully to avoid errors.

Three degrees of deviation from the correct reading were scored. One point was scored when in a reading of an item two visually similar graphemes were confused (a–o, t–l, t–f, T–F, R–B–P) or when two similar phonemes were confused (o–u, e–i, m–n). For word items one point was also scored when the stem morpheme was correctly read, but a wrong ending was produced (e.g., Enten, which is the plural form of Ente). Two error points were given when visual or phonological confusability could not explain the misreading of a grapheme. Two points were also scored when a phoneme was added or deleted or when the positions of two phonemes within an item were exchanged. When an item was distorted more seriously, including letter naming or refusals, the maximum score of three error points was given. The results presented are based on raw data.

For six children it was obvious from their performance on the practice sheet that they were unable to produce correct readings for any of the words or pseudowords. These children were assigned the highest possible error scores and the highest reading times observed in the sample.

*Spelling.* The spelling test, administered as a group test, consisted of 10 words: Mist (dust), Mitte (middle), Monat (month), munter (awake), Rast (rest), rennen (run), rosten (rust), summen (hum), Tasten (keys), turnen (to do gymnastics). The experimenter first presented a sentence. Then the target word of the sentence was repeated with a natural pronunciation, that is, not in an artificial, grapheme oriented manner. Because there were differences between the classes on how intensive words with double consonants were practised, children's spellings were judged according to phonological acceptability and not according to orthographical correctness. Spelling errors were scored in a similar way as reading errors, with two additional types of one-point errors: A consonant cluster was reduced to one consonant (e.g., Mit instead of Mist), or a single letter was written for two phonemes when the letter name sounds like the two phonemes (e.g., turnn for turnen).

*Intelligence.* To assess nonverbal intelligence, three scales of the Primary Test of Cognitive Skills (Huttenlocher & Cohen Levine, 1990) were applied as group test. The three scales were the nonverbal subtests, spatial sequences, spatial integration, and spatial concepts. Because no norm data for Austrian children are available, the raw points of each scale were standardized within the present sample. The sum of these standardized values was again standardized and finally transformed into an IQ.

## RESULTS

Descriptive statistics of all variables are presented in Table 1. In addition, split-half reliabilities are given for the predictors. From Table 1 it is evident that the phonological awareness tasks and the plural formation task were easy, whereas in the pseudoword repetition task more errors occurred. For the alliteration task there was no substantial difference in difficulty between syllable detection and phoneme detection (83% vs. 78%). Similarly, for the rhyme detection task there was no difference between the vowel items and the end-consonant items (90% vs. 89%), but it has to be noted that the most difficult end-consonant item was deleted. The reliability of the phonological awareness tasks and the phonological processing tasks was satisfactory. The reliability coefficients for naming speed and articulation rate were lower, probably because the two parts of each task were not strictly parallel.

TABLE 1
Descriptive Statistics and Reliabilities

| Measure | M | Median | SD | Reliability |
|---|---|---|---|---|
| *Phonological predictors* | | | | |
| Alliteration detection (% correct) | 81 | 88 | 18 | .74[a,b] |
| Rhyme detection (% correct) | 90 | 93 | 13 | .73[a,b] |
| Plural formation (% correct) | 83 | 85 | 16 | .86[a,b] |
| Pseudoword repetition (% correct) | 67 | 67 | 20 | .85[a,b] |
| Articulation rate (words/s) | 2.17 | 2.20 | 0.40 | .60[c] |
| Naming speed (s/object) | 1.35 | 1.30 | 0.29 | .66[c] |
| Letter knowledge (max = 19) | 7.49 | 5.00 | 6.21 | |
| *Reading* | | | | |
| Words Speed (s/word) | 3.0 | 2.4 | 2.7 | |
| Accuracy (% of max. error score) | 6 | 0 | 12 | |
| Pseudowords Speed (s/word) | 3.3 | 2.7 | 3.2 | |
| Accuracy (% of max. error score) | 7 | 3 | 14 | |
| *Spelling* | | | | |
| Phonetic (% of max. error score) | 10 | 3 | 15 | |
| Orthographic (% errors) | 50 | 50 | 19 | |

[a] N = 108, adjusted for test length, [b] Parallel halves, [c] Correlation between two parts of the task.

The mean letter knowledge was rather low. Although the main testing period lasted from end of September to end of October, no increase in letter knowledge was observed (7.3 at the beginning and 7.6 at the end of this period). Furthermore, there was no increase of performance on any of the phonological predictor tasks over the weeks of testing. None of the six correlations between task performance and weeks in school were higher than .09.

At the end of first grade the present children were slow, but rather accurate readers and they had little difficulty to produce phonologically accurate spellings. The mean reading time of 3 s for the short, simple words indicates that the children tended to slowly recode the words. This reliance on recoding is also evident from the finding that there was little difference between word reading and pseudoword reading. The correlations between word and pseudoword reading were .74 and .93 for error scores and time, respectively. The spelling scores indicate that children often did not know the correct spelling, but were able to produce a phonologically acceptable spelling. Of the orthographically incorrect spellings 75% were phonologically accurate.

Table 2 gives the correlations among the predictors, letter knowledge, and intelligence, as well as the correlations of these variables with the reading and spelling measures. To simplify further analyses, a combined score of reading and spelling was formed. This seems to be warranted by the substantial correlations between the individual literacy measures, ranging from .52 (reading time with spelling errors) to .74 (reading time with reading errors). For the combined score the standardized values of reading time, reading errors, and spelling errors were added, and the sum was standardized again.

TABLE 2
Correlations among the predictors, letter knowledge, and nonverbal intelligence and their correlations with reading and spelling

|  |  | (1) | (2) | (3) | (4) | (5) | (6) | (7) | (8) |
|---|---|---|---|---|---|---|---|---|---|
| (1) | ALLITER |  |  |  |  |  |  |  |  |
| (2) | RHYME | .32 |  |  |  |  |  |  |  |
| (3) | PLURAL | .37 | .36 |  |  |  |  |  |  |
| (4) | PSEUDO | .35 | .29 | .38 |  |  |  |  |  |
| (5) | ARTIC | .30 | .21 | .32 | .26 |  |  |  |  |
| (6) | NAMING | -.20 | -.20 | -.22 | -.15 | -.37 |  |  |  |
| (7) | LETTER | .44 | .26 | .25 | .30 | .21 | -.25 |  |  |
| (8) | IQ | .28 | .24 | .27 | .15 | .17 | -.12 | .26 |  |
| (9) | READ.T | -.16 | -.14 | -.10 | -.14 | -.13 | .29 | -.26 | -.09 |
| (10) | READ.E | -.21 | -.20 | -.15 | -.13 | -.12 | .24 | -.18 | -.08 |
| (11) | SPELL.E | -.33 | -.22 | -.24 | -.20 | -.23 | .23 | -.24 | -.15 |
| (12) | RSTOT | -.27 | -.22 | -.19 | -.18 | -.18 | .29 | -.26 | -.12 |

*Note.* Correlations ≥ .09 are significant at a level of $p < .05$. ALLITER = alliteration detection; RHYME = rhyme detection; PLURAL = plural formation; PSEUDO = pseudoword repetition; ARTIC = articulation rate; NAMING = naming speed; LETTER = letter knowledge; READ.T = reading time; READ.E = reading error points; SPELL.E = spelling error points; RSTOT = combined reading and spelling score.

From Table 2 it is evident that the correlations among and between the phonological awareness and the phonological processing measures were in the range between .30 and .40. The association between the naming speed measures on the one hand and the phonological awareness and the phonological processing measures on the other tended to be lower (between .20 and .30). Letter knowledge was substantially associated only with alliteration detection. The correlations between the predictors and the reading and spelling criterion measures tended to be rather small, the highest being around .30.

In a next step we analyzed the relative influence of the predictors. For each criterion measure a multiple regression analysis was performed to determine whether any unique contribution of the predictors to the variance of the criterion measure was given, when variance explained by letter knowledge and nonverbal intelligence was controlled for. The phonological tasks were entered by method stepwise. The results of these multiple regression analyses are shown in Table 3.

TABLE 3
Multiple regressions of reading and spelling measures by nonverbal intelligence, letter knowledge, and phonological tasks

| Criterion | Predictor | Step | $R^2$ | $R^2$ change | final Beta |
|---|---|---|---|---|---|
| Reading time | IQ | 1 | .01 | .01 | -0.02 |
|  | Letter knowledge | 2 | .07 | .06 | -0.19 |
|  | Naming speed | 3 | .12 | .05 | 0.24 |
| Reading errors | IQ | 1 | .01 | .01 | 0.02 |
|  | Letter knowledge | 2 | .03 | .03 | -0.06 |
|  | Naming speed | 3 | .07 | .04 | 0.18 |
|  | Rhyme detection | 4 | .09 | .02 | -0.12 |
|  | Alliteration detection | 5 | .10 | .01 | -0.12 |
| Spelling errors | IQ | 1 | .02 | .02 | -0.03 |
|  | Letter knowledge | 2 | .07 | .04 | -0.08 |
|  | Alliteration detection | 3 | .12 | .06 | -0.23 |
|  | Naming speed | 4 | .15 | .02 | 0.14 |
|  | Plural formation | 5 | .15 | .01 | -0.10 |
| Combined literacy score | IQ | 1 | .02 | .02 | -0.01 |
|  | Letter knowledge | 2 | .07 | .06 | -0.12 |
|  | Naming speed | 3 | .12 | .05 | 0.21 |
|  | Alliteration detection | 4 | .14 | .02 | -0.14 |
|  | Rhyme detection | 5 | .15 | .01 | -0.10 |

For each criterion measure there were unique contributions by phonological measures. For reading time only naming speed was of additional importance, whereas for the error scores and the combined literacy score beside naming speed the phonological awareness measures and plural formation (for spelling) significantly explained variance. As indicated by the beta weights of the predictors in the final model, for each of the criterion measures naming speed or other phonological predictors were at least as important as letter knowledge and nonverbal intelligence.

Table 4 shows the reading and spelling achievement of children with low phonological performance. The reasoning was that true effects of phonological impairments on reading and spelling performance may not be revealed by the correlations for the whole sample. For this step all children with IQ scores lower than 85 were excluded because the interest was on the role of phonological impairments in reading and spelling development. For each predictor we tried to select as closely as possible the 5% of children with the poorest performance and compared the literacy achievement of these children with the literacy achievement of the rest of the sample. In addition, a group of about 5% phonologically impaired children was formed on the basis of a combined phonological score. For this score, it was counted on how many tasks the child was in the group with poor phonological performance. Then those 5% of children were selected that had the highest value on this count. Table 4 gives the means and medians on the combined reading and spelling score for phonologically impaired children and for the rest of the (normal) sample.

TABLE 4
Literacy achievement of children with poor vs. normal phonological skills

| Measures and Groups | | M | Mdn | t (480) | p | % poor |
|---|---|---|---|---|---|---|
| Alliteration detection | Poor (5.4%) | 0.77 | 0.22 | 4.20 | < .001 | 38 |
| | Normal (94.6%) | -0.07 | -0.28 | | | |
| Rhyme detection | Poor (4.6%) | 0.70 | 0.11 | 3.51 | < .001 | 27 |
| | Normal (95.4%) | -0.06 | -0.28 | | | |
| Plural formation | Poor (5.2%) | 0.33 | 0.00 | 1.84 | .07 | 32 |
| | Normal (94.8%) | -0.04 | -0.27 | | | |
| Pseudoword repetition | Poor (4.1%) | 0.41 | -0.23 | 1.98 | .049 | 10 |
| | Normal (95.9%) | -0.04 | -0.27 | | | |
| Articulation rate | Poor (5.2%) | 0.47 | -0.03 | 2.53 | .01 | 28 |
| | Normal (94.8%) | -0.05 | -0.28 | | | |
| Naming speed | Poor (5.2%) | 0.58 | 0.14 | 3.11 | .002 | 40 |
| | Normal (94.8%) | -0.06 | -0.28 | | | |
| Phonological total score | Poor (5.0%) | 0.77 | 0.16 | 4.00 | < .001 | 38 |
| | Normal (95.0%) | -0.07 | -0.28 | | | |

Table 4 shows that children with low scores on the single predictors and on the combined phonological risk score have poorer literacy achievement than the rest of the sample, but the deficits were small. In no case was the score more than one standard deviation above the mean of the whole sample. For plural formation and pseudoword repetition the differences were of borderline significance. The differences between children with poor phonological skills and the rest of the sample are even lower when instead of the means the medians are considered. From the medians of the phonologically impaired children (close to the standardized mean of zero) it is obvious that the majority of these children showed reading and spelling achievement in the normal range. This is also evident from the last column of Table 4, which indicates how many per cent of the children in the groups with poor phonological skills showed poor literacy achievement at the end of first grade. A child was classified as poor in reading and spelling when the percentile corresponding to the child's combined reading and spelling score was less than 16. About 40% of the children with low scores on alliteration detection, naming speed, and the combined phonological score were poor readers or spellers at the end of the first year in school. A chance level of 15% has to be taken into account when interpreting these percentages.

## DISCUSSION

In the introduction two explanations were put forward why typical phonological awareness measures may show poorer predictive associations with reading achievement for German-speaking children than for English or American children. The hypothesis was that the difficulty of typical phonological awareness tasks for German-speaking children at the beginning of school may mask important differences between children in phonological skills, and may be responsible for the observed poor predictive associations. Tasks that require phoneme segmentation, or alliteration and rhyme oddity detection (Bradley & Bryant, 1985), were thought to be difficulty for German-speaking children because they do not receive any reading preparation in kindergarten. The present results speak against the stated hypothesis. Our attempts to devise easy phonological awareness tasks were successful, that is, our alliteration and rhyme detection tasks proved to be relatively easy. Furthermore, the phonological processing tasks (pseudoword repetition and plural formation) do not require metaphonological awareness and a lack of reading preparation should not be detrimental for these tasks. The same argument holds for naming speed and articulation rate. However, main results were that all the correlations between the individual phonological measures and the criterion measures were low, that the phonological predictors together explained only a minor proportion of reading and spelling variance (maximally 12%), and–most important–that quite a few of those children with very poor performance on the phonological predictors exhibited literacy achievement in the normal range.

The present findings with easy phonological predictors correspond well with the results of the Munich longitudinal study (Näslund, 1990; Näslund & Schneider, 1993). Several of the predictor measures of the Munich study were rather easy: Syllable counting, rhyme detection, and sound to word matching. As in the present study, a pseudoword repetition task and a naming speed task were included. In both studies phonological skills were assessed before or at the beginning of institutional reading instruction, and literacy skills were examined after the first year in school. In both studies reading speed for words and pseudowords showed very low associations with the easy phonological awareness measures (below .20) and a somewhat higher association with naming speed (around .30). The only difference is that pseudoword repetition was somewhat higher correlated with reading speed in the Munich sample (.28) than in our sample (.14). Interestingly, the rather difficult onset oddity detection task of the Munich study was higher related to reading speed (about .35) than the phonological awareness tasks with lower difficulty.

The low predictive associations between phonological skills and learning to read among German-speaking children may has to do with the phonics teaching approach these children are exposed to. Reading instruction proceeds very slowly, and although in other Austrian and German school districts all letters are introduced before Christmas, in our school district the introduction of letters is extended to the end of first grade. The motivation of this policy is to provide ample learning opportunities for the first crucial steps into reading and spelling. Further characteristics of the synthetic phonics approach are that children are directly introduced to word identification via phoneme blending. The first letters are for vowels and continuants, for which phoneme blending is easy to demonstrate and to practice. Children are encouraged to utter their blending attempts so that the teacher can check and correct. The high consistency of the German orthography in the grapheme-phoneme direction reinforces the use of phonological recoding because in most cases it leads to successful recognition. The majority of children succeeded in acquiring phonological recoding because at the end of first grade very few errors occurred in reading of both words and pseudowords. The reliance on phonological recoding has the additional effect that the phoneme sequences of successfully identified words become rather obvious. This may explain why the children also had little difficulty to spell words in phonologically acceptable ways. Even most of those children with the poorest scores on the phonological predictors committed few reading and spelling errors. Obviously, the described teaching approach leads even children with very poor phonological skills to basic phonological recoding in reading and phonemic segmentation in spelling.

Considering the low frequency of reading and spelling errors, one may speculate that for reading time as criterion measure a more substantial relationship with the phonological predictors could be found. In fact, there were large differences between children in reading time. From a theoretical standpoint it could be supposed that the mentioned teaching approach may be highly successful in establishing word recognition via phonological recoding, but has little direct effect on the efficiency of the process. However, there was little evidence for a more substantial relationship of phonological predictors to reading speed than to errors. The correlations between the phonological predictors and reading time were low and of similar size as for errors. Thus, whether speed or accuracy aspects of literacy achievement are considered, phonological skills played a minor role in the first steps of reading and spelling development.

The present negative findings about the role of phonological deficits in learning to read and to spell German should be interpreted cautiously, because literacy skills were assessed only at an early stage of reading and spelling development so far. A recent prediction study in Bielefeld (Marx, Jansen, Mannhaupt, & Skowronek, 1993) attained higher prediction results for a reading and spelling assessment at the end of second grade. Marx et al. used easy phonological awareness tasks, and also included tasks that were subsumed under the label attention and memory. The calculated risk score was based on the performances on all of these tasks at two times of measurement in kindergarten. Of those children classified as being at risk for difficulties in literacy development, 77% performed poor on a combined measure of reading and spelling at the end of second grade (chance level was 17%). The difference to our present results is remarkable. A possible explanation is that the assessment of reading and spelling at the end of first grade was too early, particularly with respect to the pace of local reading instruction. Because of the teaching approach even the phonologically poor children have not failed to acquire the basic recoding procedures in reading and spelling. Children with poor phonological skills may fail later when word recognition should become direct and automatized and when spellings are expected to be orthographically correct. This hypothesis fits with other findings among German-speaking children. Dyslexic children identified in later grades of primary school did show difficulties on rapid visual naming tasks (Wimmer, 1993) and on a spoonerism task–requiring complex phonological processing (Landerl, Wimmer, & Frith, 1997). Also, specific difficulties in reading nonwords were found (Wimmer, 1996b). The stated hypothesis furthermore fits with Wimmer et al.'s (1994) finding that differences in rhyme oddity detection at the beginning of school was of little predictive importance for the end of first grade, but gained in predictive value for later reading and spelling.

On the other hand, even in German it would be somewhat surprising, if phonologically poor children showed normal literacy development at the beginning but fell short of their peers later on. After all, Wimmer (1996a) found that dyslexic children diagnosed at the end of fourth grade had exhibited segmentation and blending difficulties in first grade, and Klicpera and Schabmann (1993) reported a high stability of reading difficulties among German-speaking children from the middle of second grade to the end of eighth grade.

ACKNOWEDGEMENTS

The present work was supported by the Austrian Science Foundation (Grant No. P09911-HIS). Thanks are due to Winfried Kain for his help in task development.

REFERENCES

Bowers, P. G., & Wolf, M. (1993). Theoretical links among naming speed, precise timing mechanisms and orthographic skill in dyslexia. *Reading and Writing, 5,* 69-85.

Bradley, L. L., & Bryant, P. E. (1985). *Rhyme and reason in reading and spelling.* Ann Arbor, MI: University of Michigan Press.

Brady, S. A., Mann, V. A., & Schmidt, R. (1987). Errors in short-term memory for good and poor readers. *Memory and Cognition, 15,* 444-453.

Catts, H. W. (1991). Early identification of dyslexia: Evidence from a follow-up study of speech-language impaired children. *Annals of Dyslexia, 41,* 163-177.

Das, J. P., & Mishra, R. K. (1991). Relation between memory span, naming time, speech rate, and reading competence. *Journal of Experimental Education, 59,* 129-139.

Denckla, M. B., & Rudel, R. G. (1976). Naming of object-drawings by dyslexic and other learning disabled children. *Brain and Language, 3,* 1-15.

Fowler, A. E., & Liberman, I. Y. (1995). Morphological awareness as related to early reading and spelling ability. In L. B. Feldman (Ed.), *Morphological aspects of language processing* (pp. 157-188). Hillsdale, NJ: Erlbaum.

Gathercole, S. E., & Baddeley, A. D. (1993). Phonological working memory: A critical building block for reading development and vocabulary acquisition? *European Journal of Psychology of Education, 8,* 259-272.

Goswami, U., & Bryant, P. E. (1990). *Phonological skills and learning to read.* Hove, U.K.: Erlbaum.

Huttenlocher, J., & Cohen Levine, S. (1990). *Primary Test of Cognitive Skills.* Monerey, California: Macmillan/McGraw-Hill.

Klicpera, Ch., & Schabmann, A. (1993). Do German-speaking children have a chance to overcome reading and spelling difficulties? A longitudinal survey from the second until the eighth grade. *European Journal of Psychology of Education, 8,* 307-323.

Landerl, K., Wimmer, H., & Frith, U. (1997). The impact of orthographic consistency on dyslexia: A German-English comparison. *Cognition, 63,* 315-334.

Marx, H., Jansen, H., Mannhaupt, G., & Skowronek, H. (1993). Prediction of difficulties in reading and spelling on the basis of the Bielefeld Screening. In H. Grimm & H. Skowronek (Eds.), *Language acquisition problems and reading disorders: Aspects of diagnosis and intervention* (pp. 219-241). Berlin, New York: Walter de Gruyter.

Näslund, J. C. (1990). The interrelationships among preschool predictors of reading acquisition for German children. *Reading and Writing, 2,* 327-360.

Näslund, J. C., & Schneider, W. (1993). Emerging literacy from kindergarten to second grade: Evidence from the Munich Longitudinal Study on the Genesis of Individual Competencies. In H. Grimm & H. Skowronek (Eds.), *Language acquisition problems and reading disorders: Aspects of diagnosis and intervention* (pp. 295-318). Berlin, New York: Walter de Gruyter.

Schneider, W., & Näslund, J. C. (1993). The impact of early metalinguistic competencies and memory capacity on reading and spelling in elementary school: Results of the Munich Longitudinal Study on the Genesis of Individual Competencies (LOGIC). *European Journal of Psychology of Education, 8,* 273-287.

Shankweiler, D. P., Crain, S., Katz, L., Fowler, A. E., Liberman, A. M., Brady, S. A., Thornton, R., Lundquist, E., Dreyer, L., Fletcher, J. M., Stuebing, K. K., Shaywitz, S. E., & Shaywitz, B. A. (1995). Cognitive profiles of reading-disabled children: Comparison of language skills in phonology, morphology, and syntax. *Psychological Science, 6,* 149-156.

Snowling, M., Goulandris, N., Bowlby, M., & Howell, P. (1986). Segmentation and speech perception in relation to reading skill: A developmental analysis. *Journal of Experimental Child Psychology, 41,* 489-507.

Wagner, R. K., & Torgesen, J. K. (1987). The nature of phonological processing and its causal role in the acquisition of reading skills. *Psychological Bulletin, 101,* 192-212.

Wimmer, H. (1993). Characteristics of developmental dyslexia in a regular writing system. *Applied Psycholinguistics, 14,* 1-33.

Wimmer, H. (1996a). The early manifestation of developmental dyslexia: Evidence from German children. *Reading and Writing, 8,* 171-188.

Wimmer, H. (1996b). The nonword reading deficit in developmental dyslexia: Evidence from children learning to read German. *Journal of Experimental Child Psychology, 61,* 80-90.

Wimmer, H., Landerl, K., Linortner, R., & Hummer, P. (1991). The relationship of phonemic awareness to reading acquisition: More consequence than precondition but still important. *Cognition, 40,* 219-249.

Wimmer, H., Landerl, K., & Schneider, W. (1994). The role of rhyme awareness in learning to read a regular orthography. *British Journal of Developmental Psychology, 12,* 469-484.

Wolf, M. (1991). Naming speed and reading: The contribution of the cognitive neurosciences. *Reading Research Quarterly, 26,* 123-141.

NATHALIE GENARD, PHILIPPE MOUSTY, ALAIN CONTENT, JESUS ALEGRIA, JACQUELINE LEYBAERT & JOSÉ MORAIS

# METHODS TO ESTABLISH SUBTYPES OF DEVELOPMENTAL DYSLEXIA

Do the developmental dyslexics form a homogeneous population, with a unique underlying impairment, or do they form distinct subgroups, thus opening up the possibility for different sources of impairment? In this chapter we compare different methods to subgroup dyslexic children and discuss the methodological implications.

Numerous studies carried out suggest the existence of two distinct profiles of developmental dyslexia (Boder, 1973; Mitterer, 1982). Phonological dyslexics have difficulty in reading PWs (PWs) in the absence of a regularity effect while surface dyslexics are indexed by the presence of many regularization errors in their reading of irregular words (IWs). However, more recent studies examining large samples of dyslexic children show that most of them are impaired on both PW and IW reading (Castles & Coltheart, 1993; Manis, Seidenberg, Doi, McBride-Chang, & Petersen, 1996; Murphy & Pollatsek, 1994). Given these findings, some authors talk about a continuous distribution of dyslexic children who differ primarily in the severity of their reading deficits (Ellis, 1985; Murphy & Pollatsek, 1994; Wilding, 1989). From the extreme ends of this continuum, however, the two distinct dyslexic patterns may be isolated, even if many dyslexics are found somewhere between (Ellis, 1993; Murphy & Pollatsek, 1994; Seymour, 1986; Wilding, 1989, 1990).

A first commonly used method to identify subtypes of dyslexic children is to compare them with normal chronological age matched children (CA group) on independent measures of their ability to read PWs and IWs as indexes of the phonological and the lexical procedures, respectively (Castles & Coltheart, 1993; Manis et al., 1996). A cutoff criterion computed on the CA group performances for each reading task (e.g., one SD below means or a specified confidence limit below the regression lines) is chosen in order to evaluate the dyslexic children's performances. Castles and Coltheart (1993), for example, examined 53 reading disabled children and regressed separately each reading task on age. Using 90% confidence intervals as a cutoff criterion, they found 10 cases of surface dyslexia for whom IW reading was low while PW reading was within the normal age range, and 8 cases of phonological dyslexia who showed the opposite pattern. The majority of cases exhibited a mixed pattern with low scores on both IWs and PWs. Relatively similar proportions were observed by Manis et al. (1996).

Although this method allows one to identify quite simply the rather "pure" cases of each distinct profile, it does not take into account the relationship between the two reading skills in order to isolate children who are more impaired in one task relative to the other. For this purpose, Castles and Coltheart (1993) proposed an alternative procedure, also based on the regression technique. They first regressed PW reading on IW reading for their CA comparison group and found a significant linear relationship between the two reading skills. When the 90% confidence intervals established for the CA group were used, 29 out of their 53 dyslexics fell below the confidence interval for PW reading, given their level of IW reading (thus fitting the phonological profile), whereas only 16 dyslexics fell below the confidence interval for IW reading, given their level of PW reading (thus fitting the surface profile). Castles and Coltheart concluded that the phonological and surface dyslexic profiles were quite common in the developmental dyslexic population (85% of their sample). Very similar results have been reported by Manis et al. (1996) who used the same method with a 95% confidence interval criterion.

This method does not avoid the arbitrary character of the placement of the cutoff limits along the children's distribution. Therefore, we compared the effects of three cutoff criterion's on the relative proportions of dyslexics fitting either the surface or the phonological profile. In addition to a CA comparison group, we included a reading-level matched group (RL group). One rationale for using such a group is that the comparison may be informative regarding the delay or deviance status of dyslexics' word recognition abilities. Manis et al. (1996) found that the surface dyslexics (but not the phonological ones) showed similar performance patterns to younger normally achieving readers, suggesting that surface dyslexics are delayed and not deviant. Moreover, the reading-match design may be adopted in another perspective. By definition, dyslexics must be less efficient readers than CA controls. Thus, it is impossible to know whether their word recognition deficits constitute a determinant or a consequence of reading efficiency. To resolve this problem, one strategy is to compare dyslexics with younger normal readers of the same reading level. If a difference persists, then one may conclude that it is not consequential to reading efficiency.

However, the RL-match design has its own weaknesses. Dyslexics may differ from younger normals in many respects, due to longer linguistic experience, educational courses, or general cognitive maturation. The fact that dyslexics are equated to younger normals on reading efficiency does not imply that the two groups use identical word identification processes and comparable procedures to reach a given proficiency level. For instance, poor readers tend to compensate their word recognition deficiencies by using to a greater extent sentence or discourse context (Stanovich, 1980). Furthermore, it is largely admitted that the development of decoding skills is faster than the development of lexical recognition processes (Frith, 1985). Therefore, one could argue that the reading-match analysis favours the assimilation of surface dyslexics and the discrimination of phonological dyslexics, with regards to the limits based on younger readers' performances. Consequently, it is difficult to draw conclusions about the causal relations between reading level and the IW deficit of the surface dyslexics.

The tests used to match the group are usually standardized tests of isolated word reading (Ellis, McDougall, & Monk, 1996; Manis et al., 1996; Murphy & Pollatsek, 1994). We consider that reading comprehension tests, involving a wider range of linguistic abilities, may be more appropriate as measures of reading efficiency. We also propose a new method that allows us to tackle the causal influence of reading efficiency in a different way. It consists in comparing dyslexics to CA while controlling statistically for the variability in reading efficiency.

Finally, our sample was formed by French-speaking children. Whereas English is characterized by the opacity of spelling to sound mappings, other languages like for instance German (Wimmer, 1996a, 1996b) have a more transparent writing system. Given that French can be considered as halfway between these languages regarding the consistency of the grapheme-phoneme relations, it seems of interest to examine whether linguistic characteristics of the writing system affect the incidence of subtypes.

## METHOD

### Participants

The dyslexics were 75 (25 girls and 50 boys) French-speaking children, coming from special education classes at public schools in the Brussels area. They were detected as presenting reading problems but not intellectual ones by an official institution. To be selected for the study, children had to fall within the age range 9–12, attain an IQ score of 80 or above on the Wechsler Intelligence Scale for Children - III. Most of them (69 out of 75) scored at the lowest quartile on the Lobrot L3 reading comprehension test described below.

The control data came from a previous longitudinal study (Leybaert, Alegria, Deltour, & Skinkel, 1994) of reading, spelling and metaphonological abilities. Children were examined at second and fourth grade. The data from the second grade readers (147 girls and 109 boys) served for the RL comparison, since the mean reading comprehension of the normal cohort closely matched the dyslexics' average score. The data from the same cohort (132 girls and 99 boys) at fourth grade was used for the AC comparison. All were French monolingual speakers and were recruited from twenty public schools. None had ever been identified as presenting reading problems.

*Materials and procedure*

The children were tested individually in a single session that lasted about 30 minutes. The session included a reading comprehension test, a PW reading task and a word reading task. No feedback on correctness of responses was given for any test.

Overall reading efficiency was assessed through a standardized reading comprehension test (Lobrot, 1973, subtest L3). This silent reading test consists of 36 sentences with a missing word. Five alternatives are proposed on each trial and children have to choose the correct one in order to make sense to the sentence. Children complete as many sentences as they can in 5 minutes. The subject's score is the percentage of correct responses obtained in this period of time. The test provides a global measure of reading comprehension that includes both specific (efficient written word identification procedures) and non-specific (general linguistic and cognitive knowledge) abilities.

For the PW reading task, 24 PWs were extracted from the MIM test of the BELEC battery (Mousty, Leybaert, Alegria, Content, & Morais, 1994). Items varied as a function of length (items of 5 letters and items from 9 up to 12 letters) and complexity. Stimuli were grouped on six-item cards. Children were asked to read aloud each card.

The word reading task consisted of the test REGUL from the BELEC battery (Mousty et al., 1994). Children were asked to read aloud 24 regular words (RWs) and 24 IWs matched on frequency and length (same number of letters and syllables). Items were administered by condition on six-item cards.

RESULTS

The mean percentages of correct responses for each reading task are provided in Table 1 for the dyslexic sample and the two comparison groups. As expected, the difference between dyslexics and the CA group is highly significant for the Lobrot L3 reading comprehension test, $t(304) = 12.17$ ($p<.001$). Differences between these groups are also highly significant both for PW reading, $t(304) = 12.39$ ($p<.001$), and IW reading, $t(304) = 19.02$ ($p<.001$). Dyslexics also performed more poorly on RWs, $t(304) = 11.01$ ($p<.001$). Significant differences between dyslexics and the RL group are also observed for the three tests ($t(329) = 6.73$, $p<.001$; $t(329) = 3.97$, $p<.001$; $t(329) = 4.87$, $p<.001$; respectively for PWs, IWs and RWs).

TABLE 1
Mean percentages of correct responses for each reading task
for dyslexics and comparison groups

|                | Dyslexics    | Normal readers |              |
|                |              | CA group       | RL group     |
|----------------|--------------|----------------|--------------|
| Age (years)    | 10.21        | 9.10           | 7.10         |
| Lobrot L3      | 34.5 (21.8)  | 63.2 (16.3)    | 33.1 (16.4)  |
| Pseudowords    | 55.1 (16.3)  | 78.0 (13.0)    | 70.3 (17.4)  |
| Irregular words| 41.9 (18.0)  | 81.0 (14.6)    | 51.9 (19.4)  |
| Regular words  | 75.6 (20.5)  | 96.6 ( 4.9)    | 85.9 (14.7)  |

The scores of the CA group do not reveal a significant difference between IW reading (81%) and PW reading (78 %), t(230) = 2.332, p=.09. A different pattern of results can be seen in English (Castles & Coltheart, 1993; Manis et al., 1996; Murphy & Pollatsek, 1994). Their subjects were less accurate on IW reading than on PW reading. With regard to the RL group, the same pattern of performance is found in all of the studies, regardless of the language. The younger children showed a higher performance on PW reading (70%) than on IW reading (52%), t(255) = 11.29, p<.001.

*CA comparison on independent measures*

The simplest procedure to identify dyslexic subtypes is to use independent cutoff values for the two dimensions: PW and IW reading. If it is assumed that the distribution of each score is normal, a lower limit can be computed by subtracting 1.96 SD from the CA group mean. This should be expected to isolate the lowest 2.5% performers. The resulting partition is given in Table 2. The most salient result is that a clear disproportion arises between the phonological and surface subtypes. To provide a direct comparison with previous studies, we also estimated the cutoff values as one SD below the CA group means. According to these criterion, 50 out of the 75 dyslexics (67%) were poor in both PW and IW reading, 2 subjects (3%) were low in PW reading only and 17 (23 %) were low in IW reading only.

TABLE 2
Incidence of the different dyslexic subtypes obtained in this study and in the previous English studies

|              | This study with 1.96 SD | This study with 1 SD | Manis et al. with 1 SD | Castles & Coltheart with 1SD |
|--------------|-------------------------|----------------------|------------------------|------------------------------|
| Severe       | 48%                     | 67%                  | 76.5%                  | 60.4%                        |
| Phonological | 4%                      | 3%                   | 9.8%                   | 15.1%                        |
| Surface      | 29%                     | 23%                  | 9.8%                   | 17.0%                        |
| Normal       | 19%                     | 8%                   | 3.9%                   | 7.5%                         |

The frequency of "pure" cases of phonological and surface dyslexia is close to the proportions obtained by Castles and Coltheart, and Manis et al. (26%, 32%, and 20%, respectively). One striking difference, however, appears in the relative proportion of the two subtypes. Whereas previous studies showed nearly equal proportions of surface and phonological cases, our data suggest a higher incidence of developmental surface dyslexia.

*CA comparison on interrelated measures*

As mentioned before, this technique does not take into account the relation between the two dimensions. An alternative approach is to classify as surface dyslexics those individuals who score lower than expected on IWs, given their performance on the other dimension. Conversely, phonological dyslexics would correspond to children presenting the opposite pattern. This approach seems particularly suitable when a correlation does exist between the two measures.

Therefore we first examined the relation between PW and IW reading in the CA group. There is a statistically reliable linear relationship between PW and IW reading, $F(1,229) = 101.5$, $p < .001$, with 31% of the variance in one task accounted for by variation in the other. For PW reading, the slope of the regression line is .49 and the intercept 38.0. For IW reading, the slope is .62 and the intercept 32.5. The residual variances provide estimates of the range of normal variation around the regression lines, and were taken to determine the cutoffs. Standard deviations of the residuals are 12.1 and 10.8 for IW reading and PW reading, respectively.

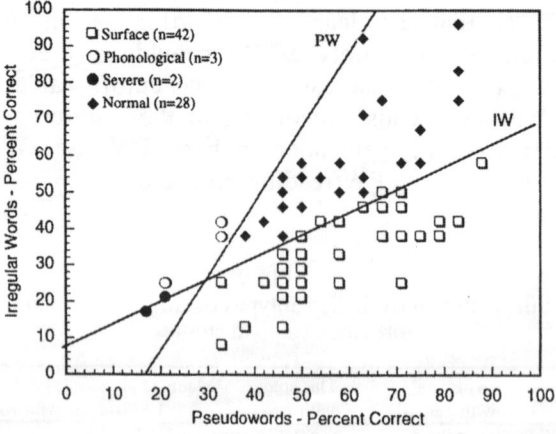

Fig. 1. Irregular word by pseudoword reading for dyslexic subjects, with a cutoff score of 1.96 SD below the CA group scores for both regressions.

As there is a clear relationship between the two variables, predicted values based on the CA group data were used to identify dyslexic subjects who were performing below expectations on either task relative to the other. For PW reading, the cutoff was determined as the predicted value based on IW reading minus 1.96 SD of the residual variance. Similarly, the cutoff for IW reading was estimated in exactly the same manner. Figure 1 displays the distribution of our dyslexic sample together with the low cutoff lines. The IW line corresponds to the regression of IW reading as a function of PW reading minus 1.96 SD of the residual IW reading scores. Thus, any point below the line corresponds to lower than expected IW reading. Conversely, the PW line corresponds to the regression of PW reading on IW reading (minus 1.96 SD), so that any point to the left of the PW line corresponds to lower than expected PW reading.

Three out of 75 dyslexic subjects fell below the limit for PW reading, while being in the normal range for IW reading. These subjects had markedly lower PW reading than would be expected among normally developing readers, based on their performance on IW. These 3 cases were called the phonological dyslexics. Conversely, 42 subjects were below the limit for IW reading only. These subjects were much poorer at reading IWs than would be expected based on their PW reading scores. These cases were called the surface dyslexics. Two cases were below both limits and could not be classified as either phonological or surface dyslexics because they had equally severe deficits on both tasks.

Mean values for the different tests are shown in Table 3 for the subgroups that emerged from this analysis as well as for the CA comparison group. The phonological and surface dyslexic subgroups were comparable in reading comprehension (Lobrot L3). The phonological dyslexics performed at a lower level in RW and PW reading compared to surface dyslexics. However, they obtained similar scores on IW reading, corresponding to the observation that all three children identified as phonological dyslexics had relatively poor performance on PWs. Both subgroups performed significantly lower than the CA group in PW and IW reading as well as in other measures.

TABLE 3
Mean percentages of correct responses for each reading task for the dyslexic subgroups and the CA comparison group

|  | Phonological dyslexics | Surface dyslexics | Severe dyslexics | Normal dyslexics | CA group |
|---|---|---|---|---|---|
| Lobrot L3 | 24.0 (18.1) | 27.5 (15.9) | 9.7 ( 5.9) | 47.9 (23.9) | 63.2 (16.3) |
| Pseudowords | 29.0 ( 6.9) | 56.5 (14.9) | 19.0 ( 2.8) | 58.4 (14.4) | 78.0 (13.0) |
| Irregular | 35.0 ( 8.9) | 32.7 (11.4) | 19.0 ( 2.8) | 57.9 (15.7) | 81.0 (14.6) |
| Regular | 45.7 (21.4) | 73.5 (20.7) | 45.5 (17.7) | 84.1 (14.7) | 96.6 ( 4.9) |

The mean percentage difference between regular and IW scores for the CA group was 15.6, while this difference for the surface dyslexics reached 40.8, reflecting poor lexical skills. The mean percentage difference between regular and IW reading scores for the phonological dyslexics was 10.7, suggesting that they are unable to use sublexical skills to assist their RW reading.

We used a 95% cutoff to carry out this analysis. A 90% cutoff is also usual and was indeed employed by Castles and Coltheart (1993). The choice of one or the other of these criteria is rather arbitrary. Interestingly, the proportion of surface and phonological dyslexics was not sensitive to choice of criterion. With cutoffs of 95%, 90% or 84% (1 SD), 56%, 60% and 63% of the sample, respectively, were categorized as surface dyslexics and 4%, 7% and 9% as phonological dyslexics.

As it was already noted for the previous analysis, the relative proportion of the two subtypes of dyslexia differs from those obtained in English, the incidence of surface dyslexia being much higher in the present study compared to phonological dyslexia. By contrast, the number of surface dyslexic children was lower than the number of phonological dyslexics in Castles & Coltheart's and Manis et al.'s studies (29% vs 33%, and 26% vs 55%, respectively, using a 95% cutoff).

*RL comparison on interrelated measures*

As discussed in the introduction, it is also interesting to compare the dyslexics' performance with that of younger children learning to read at a normal rate. The analyses described for the CA group were repeated, this time using the data from the RL comparison group. IW and PW reading show a strong linear relationship, $F(1,254) = 191.85$, $p < .001$, with 43% of the variance in one task accounted for by the other. For PW reading, the slope of the regression line is .59 and the intercept 39.8. For IW reading, the slope is .73 and the intercept .38. Standard deviations of the residuals are 14.7 for IW reading and 13.2 for PW reading, respectively. Figure 2 displays the distribution of dyslexics' performance together with the cutoff lines based on the RL data. Note that the classification indexed by the symbols is based on the CA analysis to permit direct comparison between the CA and RL outcomes. The results indicated that 6 out of the 75 dyslexics (i.e., symbols to the left of the PW line) had lower PW reading than reading-matched normals, given their performance on IWs. On the other hand, not a single subject had lower IW reading than RL normals, given their performance on PWs. Actually, numerous subjects (69 out of 75) were within the limits of normal variation for the RL group.

The comparison of the dyslexic subgroups with reading-matched children shows that all the dyslexics with the surface profile scored within the range of the RL group on both dimensions. The two severe cases performed within the RL range for IWs, but fell below the limit for PW reading. Similarly, all the children categorized as phonological dyslexics had lower performance than reading-matched younger readers on PWs, but not on IWs. These findings are in agreement with the results reported by Manis et al.

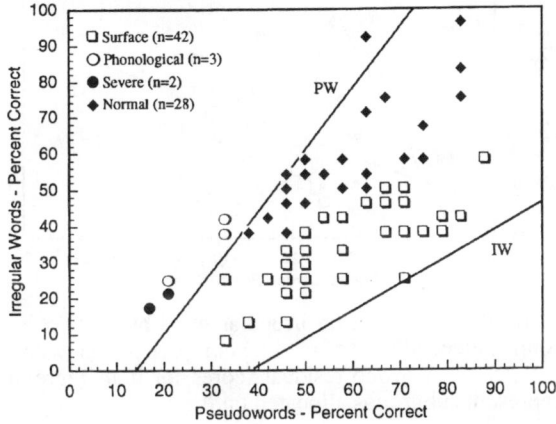

Fig. 2. Irregular word by pseudoword reading for dyslexic subgroups, with a cut-off score of 1.96 SD below the RL group scores for both regressions. Symbols in the legend represent subgroups allocated on the basis of CA group scores.

*CA comparison on interrelated measures adjusted for reading comprehension*

An alternative method to control for reading efficiency amounts to determining cutoff criteria on the residual scores for PWs and IWs, once the variance explained by the reading comprehension test has been partialled out. Thus, the residual scores indicate the level of efficiency of the dyslexics on the two dimensions, independently of reading comprehension, and by reference to normal reading children of the same age.

There are significant linear relationships between the Lobrot L3 performance and both PW and IW reading performances in the CA group (14% and 32% of variance explained, respectively). The parameter estimates for the two regression lines obtained on the CA group were used to compute residual scores for the CA group and the dyslexic group. For the CA group the relationship between the residual scores for IW reading and PW reading remains significant, $r = .44$, $p<.001$. For PW reading the slope of the regression line is .41 and the intercept —2.6, for IW reading the slope is .47 and the intercept 3.3. Standard deviations of the residuals are 11.7 for IW reading and 10.8 for PW reading. Cutoff values were based on a 95% probability level below the two regression lines.

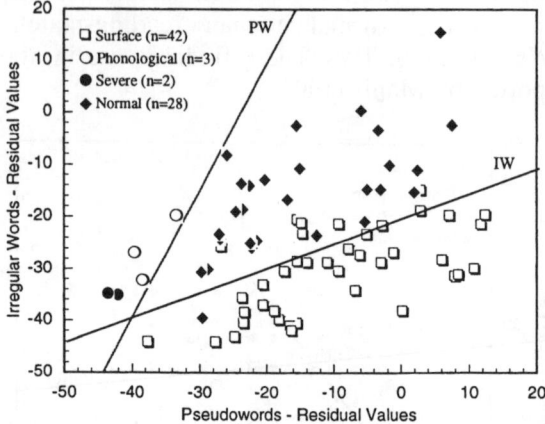

Fig. 3. Plot of residual values from irregular word by pseudoword reading for dyslexic subgroups independently of reading comprehension, with a cut-off score of 1.96 SD below the CA group residual scores for both regressions. Symbols in the legend represent subgroups allocated on the basis of CA group scores.

A plot of the dyslexics' residual scores is shown in Figure 3. Again, the classification indexed by the symbols is based on the CA analysis. The results reveal that the three phonological cases as well as the two severe cases had markedly lower PW reading than would be expected given their level of reading comprehension while falling within the limits for IW reading. Conversely, among the 42 surface dyslexics, 35 children showed the reverse pattern of results. About half of the subjects (34 out of 75) showed a normal IW and PW reading level when their reading comprehension performance was considered. In other words, they reveal a normal performance for both reading tasks when we consider a normal developing reading.

## DISCUSSION

The results of this study show that some developmental dyslexics exhibit a dissociation between their PW reading performance and their IW reading performance. Twenty-five cases out of 75 (33%) were found with a relatively "pure" form of dyslexia, that is, an important deficit in one task while their performance on the other fell within the normal range. At the same time, it is important to point out that the dyslexic sample as a whole tended to be impaired on both IW and PW reading. These results replicate Castles and Coltheart's (1993) and Manis et al.'s (1996) findings. The fact that most dyslexics tend to be impaired on both reading tasks seems to be in agreement with the notion of a dynamic articulation between the phonological and lexical abilities in the course of learning. According to this view, the development of the IW reading ability is somehow dependent on the PW reading ability. The decoding ability would aid in establishing detailed and precise orthographic representations in the lexicon.

On the other hand, the relative proportion of surface dyslexics was larger in our study than in the previous studies in English and conversely, less phonological dyslexics were observed. Using the regression procedure introduced by Castles an Coltheart (1993) in order to take into account the relationship between the two reading tasks, most of our dyslexic children (60%) were found to have larger than expected discrepancies between their IW and their PW reading, compared to the CA group. Among them, we also found a strong majority of surface dyslexic profiles (93%), and the proportion of the two dyslexic subtypes was relatively insensitive to the choice of a specified cut-off criterion (95%, 90% or 84%).

The fact that developmental phonological dyslexia is apparently less common in French than in English may be associated to the greater transparency of French orthography at the level of grapheme-phoneme correspondences. Moreover, it is worth noting that a strong emphasis on the learning of these correspondences characterizes the reading instruction of the children tested here. The French-speaking children may thus be in a better situation than the English-speaking children to overcome the difficulties associated with the acquisition of grapheme-phoneme correspondences. Our data do not allow us to differentiate the part played by the regularity of the grapheme-phoneme correspondences from the part played by the reading instruction, but it is likely that both are linked: since the use of grapheme-phoneme knowledge is highly reliable in the reading of French words, the "phonic" method would be preferred.

The fact that there were much more surface dyslexics in the present study than in the studies that examined English-speaking children is more surprising. In French, there are much less IWs than in English. Given that the French-speaking children have to learn only a very small number of irregularities, one might expect them to deal with these words rather easily. However, as suggested by Manis et al. (1996), developmental surface dyslexia may be related to a general lack of cognitive resources. The dominant utilization of grapheme-phoneme correspondences by the French-speaking surface dyslexics might leave insufficient resources for the encoding of word-specific orthographic knowledge.

A second issue concerns the validity and interpretation of the comparison between dyslexic children and reading-level matched controls. The reading-match design has been employed with different underlying objectives by different authors. It was employed by Manis et al. (1996) to tap the issue of delay vs deviance. They found that the surface dyslexics read in the same way as the RL controls. Such a result, although revealing a developmental delay, provides no clue about the cause(s) of this developmental subtype of dyslexia. Conversely, the phonological dyslexics showed a deviant pattern, supporting the notion of a causal phonological impairment. Our results clearly replicated those reported by Manis et al. (1996). There was a complete overlap between the performances of the surface dyslexics and of the RL group, confirming that surface dyslexics may suffer from a general delay in word recognition skills. Besides, the phonological dyslexics remained weaker in PW reading when compared to the RL group. These data are consistent with the view that the phonological dyslexic profile is associated with a specific deficit in phonological processing. However, phonological dyslexics appear able to build up a sight vocabulary larger than their phonological processing skills would predict.

On the other hand, Bryant & Impey (1986) argued that a reading-level-match comparison was required to extract causal inferences from performance patterns. Since word and PW reading performances may change as a consequence of reading experience and since dyslexic readers obviously differ from age-matched control in the quantity of material read, the deficits demonstrated by dyslexic children relative to normal readers of similar age can be consequential to their lack of reading experience, rather than a cause of their deficits. From the same viewpoint, Snowling, Bryant and Hulme (1996) took argument with Castles and Coltheart on the grounds that their typology was based on age-matched readers, rather than reading-matched readers and consequently, does not take into account the effects of reading experience on performance. In this framework, the PW deficit of phonological dyslexics might have causal status, whereas the surface dyslexic's impairment should be interpreted as an artefactual consequence of the difference in reading efficiency.

To assess the influence of reading efficiency in a different way, we compared the dyslexics to CA controls, after partialing out the effect of reading efficiency on PW and IW reading scores. By doing so, the variability between dyslexic children and the CA group in reading comprehension was controlled. The analysis revealed that all phonological dyslexics had poorer PW reading. They remain with a phonological impairment. This analysis thus corroborates the RL analysis for all the phonological dyslexics, and confirms the view that their deficit cannot be accounted for as a result of reading efficiency.

For surface dyslexics, however, the two analyses do not lead to the same results and confirm that it may be necessary to distinguish between the issue of delay vs deviance and the issue of the influence of reading efficiency. When compared to RL normal readers, the dyslexics classified as surface in the present study showed patterns of performance for IW and PW reading which did not differ from the normals, thus supporting the view that surface dyslexics may be considered as delayed readers. On the other hand, when reading efficiency was controlled by partialing out the variation in reading comprehension, most (83%) of the surface dyslexics still showed weaker performance than the CA controls on IW reading, suggesting that their difficulties do not result from reading efficiency differences.

This finding does not discount the delayed character of the surface profile. After all, it is a matter of fact that the surface dyslexics resemble younger normal readers as far as word and PW reading is concerned. However, the two analyses are inconsistent on the issue of causal relationships. Due to the limits of the RL match design, together with the important fact that the dyslexic children and the CA controls have the same age and consequently may also be better matched for general knowledge, we would tend to opt for the CA analysis. Nevertheless, the difference observed between the dyslexics and the CA controls on IW reading requires an explanation. One possible interpretation is that the weak performance on irregulars results from a lack of reading experience. Even though we controlled for reading efficiency, as indexed by the reading comprehension test, it may not reflect in the most accurate manner reading experience, the quantity of print materials a child has been effectively reading. Indeed, dyslexic children may be assumed to possess much less reading experience than normal readers of the same age, in spite of similar educational opportunities and exposure to print, because of differences in word recognition skills. Furthermore, reading experience, resulting from adequate and successful exposure to print, may be one of the major conditions favouring the gradual storage of orthographic word forms which presumably determine correct IW reading.

## ACKNOWLEDGEMENTS

This study was supported by the National Fund for Scientific Research (Loterie Nationale, convention 8.4513.95). We are grateful to the staff and children from the schools Ecole Joli-Bois Individualisé (Woluwé-Saint-Pierre) and Ecole la Charmille (Woluwé-Saint-Lambert).

## REFERENCES

Boder, E. (1973). Developmental dyslexia: a diagnostic approach based on three atypical reading-spelling patterns. *Developmental Medicine and Child Neurology, 15,* 663–687.

Bryant, P. E., & Impey, L. (1986). The similarities between normal readers and developmental and acquired dyslexics, *Cognition, 24,* 121–137.

Castles, A., & Coltheart, M. (1993). Varieties of developmental dyslexia. *Cognition, 47,* 149–180.

Ellis, A. W. (1985). The cognitive neuropsychology of developmental (and acquired) dyslexia: A critical survey. *Cognitive Neuropsychology, 2,* 169–205.

Ellis, A. W. (1993). *Reading, writing and dyslexia. A cognitive analysis.* Hove, UK: Lawrence Erlbaum.

Ellis, A. W., McDougall, S. J. P., & Monk, A. F. (1996). Are dyslexics different? II. Individual differences among dyslexics, reading age controls, poor readers and precocious readers. *Dyslexia, 2,* 31–58.

Frith, U. (1985). Beneath the surface of developmental dyslexia. In K. E. Patterson, J. C. Marshall, & M. Coltheart (Eds.), *Surface dyslexia : Neuropsychological and cognitive studies of phonological reading* (pp. 301–330). London: Erlbaum.

Leybaert, J., Alegria, J., Deltour, J. J., & Skinkel, R. (1994). Apprendre à lire, rôle du langage, de la conscience phonologique et de l'école [Learning to read: influence of language, phonological awareness and school]. In J. Grégoire & B. Piérart (Eds.), *Evaluer les troubles de la lecture. Les nouveaux modèles théoriques et leurs implications diagnostiques* (pp. 147–171). Bruxelles: De Boeck.

Lobrot, M. (1973). *Lire.* Paris: E.S.F.

Manis, F. R., Seidenberg, M. S., Doi, L. S., McBride-Chang, C., & Petersen, A. (1996). On the bases of two subtypes of development dyslexia. *Cognition, 58,* 157–195.

Mitterer, J. O. (1982). There are at least two kinds of poor readers: Whole word poor readers and recoding poor readers. *Canadian Journal of Psychology, 36,* 445–461.

Mousty, P., Leybaert, J., Alegria, J., Content, A., & Morais, J. (1994). Belec, une batterie d'évaluation du langage écrit et de ses troubles [Belec, an assessment battery of written language and of its disorders]. In J. Grégoire & B. Piérart (Eds.), *Evaluer les troubles de la lecture. Les nouveaux modèles théoriques et leurs implications diagnostiques* (pp. 127–145). Bruxelles: De Boeck.

Murphy, L., & Pollatsek, A. (1994). Developmental dyslexia: heterogeneity without discrete subgroups. *Annals of Dyslexia, 44,* 120–146.

Seymour, P. H. K. (1986). *Cognitive analysis of dyslexia.* London: Routledge and Kegan Paul.

Snowling, M. J., Bryant, P. E., & Hulme, C. (1996). Theoretical and methodological pitfalls in making comparisons between developmental and acquired dyslexia: some comments on A. Castles & M. Coltheart (1993). *Reading and Writing, 8,* 443–451.

Stanovich, K. E. (1980). Toward an interactive-compensatory model of individual differences in the development of reading fluency. *Reading Research Quarterly, 16,* 32–71.

Stanovich, K. E., Nathan, R. G., & Zolman, J. E. (1988). The developmental lag hypothesis in reading: Longitudinal and matched reading-level comparisons. *Child Development, 59,* 71–86.

Wilding, J. (1989). Developmental dyslexics do not fit in boxes: Evidence from the case studies. *European Journal of Cognitive Psychology, 1,* 105–127.

Wilding, J. (1990). Developmental dyslexics do not fit in boxes: Evidence from six case studies. *European Journal of Cognitive Psychology, 2,* 97–131.

Wimmer, H. (1996a). The nonword reading deficit in developmental dyslexia: evidence from children learning to read German. *Journal of Experimental Child Psychology, 61,* 80–90.

Wimmer, H. (1996b). The early manifestation of developmental dyslexia: evidence from German children. *Reading and Writing, 8,* 171–188.

JANE OAKHILL AND KATE CAIN

# PROBLEMS IN TEXT COMPREHENSION:
# CURRENT PERSPECTIVES AND RECENT RESEARCH

This chapter begins with an outline of the processes needed for effective text understanding in skilled readers, and the levels at which problems in text comprehension might arise. This overview provides some relevant background for later discussion of how children's comprehension can fail. We consider, in particular, the difficulties that children can have with reading, even when they are competent at single-word recognition. Although single word reading and comprehension skill are, in general, highly correlated, a substantial minority of children develop the former but not the latter skill.

Research has suggested that comprehension difficulties might arise in various ways. First, word recognition might be accurate, but not be sufficiently fast and automatic, for comprehension processes to operate smoothly. Second, poor comprehenders might have trouble at the level of sentences, because their syntactic knowledge is not well developed. Third, various aspects of memory might limit comprehension processes (perhaps because they limit some component processes). Fourth, higher-level processes, such as inference and integration skills, might be deficient in poor comprehenders. Thus, there are a number of views as to why a child who has adequate single-word reading skills and intelligence might, nevertheless, experience problems with text comprehension. The issue of why children have comprehension problems almost certainly does not have a single answer. Some children might experience difficulties in one area, some in another, and some in all of the areas outlined above.

In this chapter, we do not discuss all of the alternative theories of problems in text comprehension, and the evidence that support them (for a review, see e.g., Oakhill, Cain, & Yuill, 1998). Instead, we focus on our own research to illustrate the problems that children can have at the text level (i.e., beyond word and sentence level comprehension). We concentrate on three areas in particular: inference skills, ability to understand how stories are organized, and ability to monitor for comprehension problems. We also present work that suggests that the poor comprehenders' problem is not specific to reading, but extends to listening comprehension and to understanding of stories told in picture sequences. Possible underlying causes of comprehension difficulties will be considered, and in particular, some recent work on the role of working memory in children's text comprehension will be discussed.

*P.Reitsma, & L.Verhoeven (Eds.), Problems and Interventions in Literacy Development, 177—192.*
© *1998 Kluwer Academic Publishers. Printed in the Netherlands.*

*Processes in comprehension*

It is useful to consider briefly the wealth of processes that are needed for efficient comprehension. Our view is that understanding a text results in a mental representation of the state of affairs that the text describes. Such a representation is often termed a mental model.

To derive a model of a text, the reader needs not only to decode and understand the meanings of the individual words and sentences, but to integrate the meanings of the sentences and of the paragraphs into a coherent whole. Such integration will require some (at least implicit) identification of the main ideas and themes of the text. The reader will also need to make numerous inferences to fill in linking information that is left implicit by the author. The wealth of inferences and general knowledge that a reader makes even when reading a very short, apparently simple text can be illustrated by considering the following example, adapted from Charniak (1972):

> Jane was invited to Jack's birthday party. She wondered if he would like a kite. She went to her room and shook her piggy bank. It made no sound.

To understand this text, we need knowledge about birthday parties, and the conventions associated with them (buying presents). We need to know about the convention of saving money and the need for money to buy things. Someone who did not know about these things would find the story impossible to understand. Then, we have to make other inferences: for example, in the second sentence, Jane is not simply "wondering" if Jack would like a kite, she is thinking about buying him one and, in the last sentence, we make inferences about her ability to carry out her plans based on the information that the money box does not rattle.

In addition to the processes directly implicated in our understanding, we also need to employ meta-level processes to monitor our text processing and, if we perceive it to be going badly, to decide how to effect an improvement, or how to remedy some local problem.

## INDIVIDUAL DIFFERENCES IN TEXT COMPREHENSION

In this section, we discuss how factors beyond the word and sentence level might account for individual differences in text comprehension. We return to some of the processes that we mentioned above and, with reference to our own work, show how individual differences in these processes have been shown to differentiate between good and poor comprehenders. The research is discussed under three main headings: Inferences and integration, Understanding of text structure, and Comprehension monitoring. At the end of this section, we explore the role of working memory in regulating comprehension processes.

Before describing our own work in this area, we explain how the subjects were selected for our experiments. A small proportion of children in the early junior-school age range (7–10 years) are adequate or good at single word reading but, nevertheless, have difficulty understanding the core content of a text they have read. We have found that around 10% of children in mainstream schools can be classed as having a comprehension problem, that is, comprehension that is significantly behind what would be expected from their general reading ability. The children we have studied have a specific comprehension problem, in that their single-word reading and vocabulary is at least average for their age, but their ability to understand a text is considerably behind what would be predicted from their chronological age and word reading accuracy. We have compared the performance of such children with that of skilled comprehenders of the same age and word recognition ability.

Although different subjects participated in the different experiments, the criteria for selecting good and poor comprehenders were the same throughout, and are described here. The two groups are selected using the Neale Analysis of Reading Ability and the Gates-MacGinitie Vocabulary Test. The Neale Analysis provides measures both of reading Accuracy (word recognition in context) and Comprehension (assessed by ability to answer a series of questions about short passages). The Gates-MacGinitie test requires the child to select one of four written words to go with a picture. Thus, it acts as a measure of silent word recognition, out of context, and provides an index of the child's reading vocabulary. In all our studies, the groups of skilled and less-skilled comprehenders are matched for word recognition ability (Neale Accuracy and Gates-MacGinitie) and chronological age, but differ in Neale Comprehension scores. In summary, the children who participated in our experiments were all at or above average at word recognition; one group were also good comprehenders, while the other group were poor comprehenders, particularly with respect to their ability to recognize words. The characteristics of typical groups of subjects are shown in Table 1.

TABLE 1
Characteristics of groups of skilled and less-skilled comprehenders

|  | Chronol. age/yrs | Accuracy age/yrs | Compreh. age/yrs | Gates-MacGinitie (score / 48) |
|---|---|---|---|---|
| Less skilled | 7;9 | 8;4 | 7;3 | 38.0 |
| Skilled | 7;9 | 8;4 | 9;1 | 38.3 |

## INFERENCES AND INTEGRATION

There is now a wealth of evidence indicating that good and poor comprehenders differ in their ability to make inferences and to integrate information from different parts of a text. Poor comprehenders have difficulties in inferring information that is only implicit in a text, and also in making inferences to connect up propositions from different parts of a text. However, an important, and as yet unanswered, question is why poor comprehenders have difficulty with inferential processing. In an experiment to assess the relative importance of inference skill and memory in accounting for young children's comprehension problems, Oakhill (1984) tested children's ability to answer literal and inferential questions, both from memory, and when the text was available to refer back to. Poor comprehenders performed poorly on the inference questions, even when the text was available and they could re-read the passages and try to work out the answers. Those findings suggest that the poor comprehenders did not have a simple memory problem. Possible explanations for their difficulties with the inference questions are considered here, because they raise a number of interesting issues. First, poor comprehenders may lack the general knowledge needed to make the sorts of inferences required in the above experiment. Although this explanation seems unlikely, given the sorts of knowledge required, it was not explicitly tested by Oakhill (1984). However, in a more recent study, Cain (1994) found that poor comprehenders were unable or unwilling to make inferences even though they had the relevant knowledge to do so. Second, perhaps poor comprehenders don't realize that inferences are permissible, and have a very literal approach to text comprehension. Third, perhaps poor comprehenders do realize that inferences are not only permissible, but desirable, but are nevertheless restricted in their inferencing capabilities by processing limitations.

A further study explored the extent to which individual differences in inferential skills are dependent on differences in general knowledge (Oakhill, Cain, & Barnes, 1996). Because it is so difficult to assess and control for differences in children's general knowledge, a procedure, designed by Barnes to control for differences in background knowledge between the groups, was used. Barnes' idea (see Barnes, Dennis, & Haefele-Kalvaitis, 1996) was to teach children a new knowledge base (about a pretend planet, GAN). By teaching the children knowledge items to criterion, one can be sure that they all have the same knowledge base. Then, their ability to make inferences from this knowledge can be assessed. In the study we conducted, we also addressed a further issue: the direction of causality between inference making and comprehension skill. If there is a difference between good and poor comprehenders on some measure (such as inference making), the poor comprehenders' lower performance might be either a cause or a consequence of their poor comprehension. For instance, poor comprehenders might have trouble understanding a text adequately because they do not make the right inferences, or they might be poor at making appropriate inferences because they have had less experience of understanding connected text and less practice at inference making. One way to assess these different possibilities is to compare the performance of the poor comprehenders with that of a younger group of children who have the same absolute level of comprehension ability. If the poor comprehenders are worse on tasks tapping the skills of interest than younger children with the same comprehension skill, then we can infer that the observed deficits in the older group do not arise from less experience of reading, because the older poor comprehenders would be expected to have had more reading experience than the younger children. Thus, a causal link between the target skill and comprehension ability is a possibility (though not, of course, proven). In the present study, we used such a Comprehension Age Match (CAM). The three groups of subjects who participated in the study are shown in Table 2.

TABLE 2
Subject characteristics of the groups who participated in the GAN study

| group | age | gates | accuracy | compreh | no. of stories |
|---|---|---|---|---|---|
| less-skilled comprehenders | 8;0 | 41.3 | 8;10 | 6;9 | 3.9 |
| | (3 mths) | (2.01) | (12 mths) | (4 mths) | (.86) |
| skilled comprehenders | 8;1 | 41.7 | 8;8 | 9;2 | 4.1 |
| | (4 mths) | (1.88) | (7 mths) | (12 mths) | (.76) |
| comprehension age-match | 7;0 | 33.1 | 6;9 | 6;10 | 2.6 |
| | (3 mths) | (3.90) | (5 mths) | (4 mths) | (.51) |

Note. Number of subjects in each group is 13; standard deviations are shown in brackets.

The participants were taught a 12-item knowledge base (a shortened version of the one used by Barnes et. al.). The items, such as "The rivers and ponds on Gan are filled with **orange juice**"; "The shoes on Gan have **wings**" were read to them (with the wording in bold emphasized), and the children were tested both verbally and on a picture-recognition test. Any items from the knowledge base that they did not recall correctly first time were repeated until all children attained perfect performance. The poor comprehenders required slightly, but not significantly, more repetitions of the knowledge base to reach criterion. All children were then presented with a multi-episode story, which was read aloud to them by the experimenter. Each episode was followed by four questions, which tapped the following sorts of information:

One question required recall of *literal* information from the text, and one question required the explanation of a *simile*. The similes required integration of information in the text with information from general knowledge. One question required a *coherence inference*. Such inferences are necessary to maintain story coherence, and in this case, to understand a proposition which would be anomalous unless integrated with information from the knowledge base. For instance, in one episode, the statement that "Dack looked up at the ceiling and saw a squirrel on the roof" is anomalous unless the information from the knowledge base that houses on Gan are made of glass (and, therefore, have transparent ceilings) is brought to bear on its interpretation. Finally, there was a question that required an *elaborative inference*. Such inferences are not necessary for textual cohesion, but elaborate on the information in the text, leading to a richer interpretation.

The four sorts of questions were presented to the children. Finally, the children's retention of the knowledge base items was tested (both immediately and after a delay of one week) using the same verbal recall test as used in the knowledge base learning phase. Performance on the immediate recall of the knowledge base was taken into account in the subsequent scoring of the inference questions: only the responses to inference questions for which the relevant knowledge base items had been recalled were included in the analysis.

The results of the test of immediate retention showed near-perfect scores for all groups, and no significant differences between groups. However, after a delay of one week, the skilled comprehenders' memory for the knowledge base had not changed at all, whereas that of the less-skilled and CAM children had fallen off and was significantly lower than that of the skilled group.

The children's performance was analysed separately for the literal and simile questions. The skilled comprehenders were able to answer significantly more literal questions than the other two groups. There was also an overall significant effect of group on ability to answer the simile questions. However, this effect was mainly attributable to the younger children's poorer performance on these questions. The poor comprehenders performed slightly more poorly than the good comprehenders, but not significantly so. The two types of inference questions were analysed together, with type of inference as a factor in the analysis. The scores for the inference questions were conditionalised on memory for the relevant piece of information from the knowledge base, as explained above. The performance of the three groups for the two types of inference questions is shown in Table 3. Overall, the skilled comprehenders made more inferences than did the other two groups, and the children found it easier to make the coherence inferences than the elaborative inferences. The good comprehenders were significantly better than the poor comprehenders for both types of inference. The CAM group performed slightly, but not significantly, better than the poor comprehenders for both types of inference.

TABLE 3
GAN study: Scores for literal questions, similes, and mean proportional scores obtained by each skill group for the two types of inferences for all skill groups

|  | literal questions (max. = 18) | similes (max. = 18) | type of inference | |
|---|---|---|---|---|
|  |  |  | coherence | elaborative |
| Less-skilled comprehenders | 10.38 (3.52) | 12.31 (4.05) | 0.288 (.197) | 0.265 (.188) |
| Skilled comprehenders | 13.31 (1.84) | 14.92 (4.11) | 0.558 (.188) | 0.463 (.195) |
| Comprehension-age match group | 10.85 (3.13) | 10.77 (3.28) | 0.340 (.148) | 0.267 (.191) |

Note. Number of subjects in each group is 13; standard deviations in brackets.

Barnes et al.'s procedure also enabled us to explore the possible reasons for children's inference failures. There are a number of possibilities, but the results clearly pointed to "integration failure" as the major reason for inability to answer the inference questions in all groups, and for both types of inference. Integration failure was said to occur when a child both recalled the relevant premise information from the story in their response to the inference question, and recalled the relevant knowledge base information in the final test, but failed to integrate these two pieces of information. Such errors can be compared with, e.g., those in which the child fails to recall either the premise, or the knowledge base item, or both.

The results of this study demonstrated that, although the poor comprehenders were worse than same-age good comprehenders at answering both literal and inferential questions about texts, their failure to make as many inferences could not be attributed to failure to recall relevant information. Rather, the poor comprehenders failed to integrate relevant information on which an inference was based. The younger, CAM, group were not significantly better than the poor comprehenders on any of the measures, providing no specific evidence about the direction of the causal relation between inference skills and reading comprehension from this study. However, in another study (Cain & Oakhill, in press), we have found that poor comprehenders perform significantly more poorly than good comprehenders on text-connecting inferences, similar to the coherence inferences in the present study. Thus, a causal link between inference skill and comprehension ability remains a possibility which merits further exploration.

## UNDERSTANDING OF TEXT STRUCTURE

It is a reasonable hypothesis that children's knowledge about story structure and coherence will help them in understanding stories that they read or hear. There is now a good deal of research detailing how a child's concept of a story becomes refined with age (e.g., Applebee, 1978; Peterson & McCabe, 1983; Stein & Glenn, 1979; 1982), but little is known about how comprehension skill relates to such knowledge. In some earlier studies (Yuill & Oakhill, 1991), children were asked to retell stories prompted by picture sequences. A general finding from those studies was that less-skilled comprehenders did not seem to have an integrated idea of the stories as a whole: they tended to produce picture-by-picture accounts.

One major problem with these earlier studies was that we could not really tell whether the less-skilled comprehenders' problem was to do with story production, or with understanding of the picture sequence. Indeed, it is possible that they had problems with both, and were doubly disadvantaged. On the other hand, the differences that we found between good and poor comprehenders were fairly subtle and it may have been that, on the contrary, the poor comprehenders were advantaged by having the picture sequence present to cue their production. Furthermore, the previous studies did not enable us to differentiate between the problems that children might experience in making their productions cohere, as opposed to the problems they might have because of lack of basic knowledge about how stories are structured. Finally, the earlier studies provided no information about the possible direction of causality between comprehension skill and story knowledge.

A further experiment (Cain & Oakhill, 1996) set out to address these issues. In this study, a Comprehension Age Match group was again included. The three groups of subjects were very similar in characteristics to the children in the previous experiment on inferences described above. In order to address the issue of whether poor comprehenders are helped or hindered by picture sequences, we included two different ways of eliciting story productions. One was a sequence of six pictures, which "told a story" and the other was a topic title, e.g., "Pirates" about which the children were asked to tell a story. The children were asked to tell three stories using each prompt type.

Because we wanted to obtain separate assessments of the effects of story knowledge and ability to produce coherent text, we analysed the productions in two ways. One was to score them for conventional story information, such as setting information and stereotypical beginnings and endings. An analysis of these data showed no differences between the groups in their use of any of these conventional features:

they were used very frequently by the children in all three groups.

The other was to score the stories for "goodness" on a 3-point scale (non-stories, intermediate stories and complete stories). This classification reflected the overall coherence and causal structure of the stories, with non-stories tending to lack event structure and coherence, and complete stories, at the other extreme, showing a clear development of plot, a coherent series of events, and a clear outcome. Examples of a story at each level are shown in Table 4.

TABLE 4
Classification criteria and example stories from story production experiment.

---

1  *Non-stories*: these narratives were either totally incoherent, or lacked any obvious sequence of events. Some such non-stories comprised only an opening and character and/or scene setting information, but nothing else. For example: "Once upon a time there was a girl and she went on holiday" (topic prompt: The Holiday).

2  *Intermediate stories*: these narratives contained a sequence of events, but the main events were not causally linked to each other. "It was a lovely day. The family decided to go down to the seaside. They saw lots of people there. The baby was making a sandcastle, the older children were playing in the sea, the mum and dad had their last swim before they went home" (topic prompt: The Seaside)

3  *Complete stories*: narratives which related an integrated sequence of events, with the main events causally related. "There was once a girl who had scruffy hair. Her mum said she had to have her hair cut, but she didn't like to have her hair cut, she thought she might have the wrong haircut. So she went in mum's..... her mum's room and got her hair scissors and she cut her hair short so... and she looked in the mirror and she didn't like the hair cut she did, so her mum came in the room and gave her a hat, so it didn't show her fringe. The end". (picture sequence prompt: The Haircut).

---

The difference between the intermediate and complete stories is rather subtle, but interesting. The intermediate stories are coherent in that each sentence follows on from the last: there are appropriate anaphoric references and other cohesive devises. However, such stories lack overall coherence. In general, they comprise a rather boring string of events, with no "high point", and no resolution. The difference between these and the level 3 stories could be viewed as one of local vs. global coherence, a point to which we shall return later. The stories were scored by awarding points from 0–2 depending on the category to which the story was allocated. Thus, each child obtained a score out of 6 for each prompt type. The mean scores are shown in Table 5.

An analysis of these data showed that the poorer comprehenders produced less well-structured stories overall. There was also a main effect of prompt type: the picture prompts elicited better-structured stories. Although the interaction between comprehension skill and type of prompt did not reach significance, planned comparisons showed that in the title prompt condition the skilled comprehenders produced significantly better-structured stories than did the less-skilled group, and the CAM group also produced significantly better stories than the less-skilled comprehenders. In the picture-prompt condition, the skilled comprehenders were, once more, better than the less-skilled group, but the less-skilled group and CAM group did not differ significantly. In neither elicitation condition was there any difference between the performance of the skilled comprehenders and the CAM group.

TABLE 5
Mean scores for story structure in the narrative production task (the maximum possible for each prompt type is 6).

| Prompt condition | Less-skilled comprehenders | Skilled comprehenders | Comprehension-Age match group |
|---|---|---|---|
| Topic | 2.94 | 4.92 | 4.27 |
| Picture | 4.31 | 5.33 | 4.80 |
| Difference | 1.37 | 0.41 | 0.53 |

These results show no evidence of a relation between comprehension skill and knowledge of conventional features of stories. Thus, even poorer comprehenders and younger readers have this knowledge about story conventions. There were, however, differences amongst the groups in their ability to produce well-structured stories. The differences between groups were particularly marked in the topic prompt condition, where the poor comprehenders performed more poorly than either of the control groups. This result is especially interesting because it rules out the conclusion that the ability to produce a well-structured story is simply the result of extensive experience of reading (which the older children, and the older good comprehenders in particular, would be expected to have more of) and suggests, instead, an alternative explanation: that such knowledge might be causally linked to comprehension skill. There are two main reasons for coming to this conclusion. First, the less-skilled comprehenders produced less well structured stories than the CAM group in the generally-more-difficult title prompt condition. This result suggests that the ability to produce well-structured stories is not a consequence of reading comprehension skill, since the two groups are matched for comprehension. Second, the less-skilled comprehenders produced stories of equivalent quality to those of the CAM group when a picture sequence was provided as a prompt. This suggests that it was this structural framework that the poor comprehenders were lacking in the topic prompt condition, and that one of the reasons for poor story production and comprehension might be lack of ability to keep track of the event structure of a text. This inability to produce a well-structured and coherent event structure may be related to the children's working memory capacity, a point that we return to shortly.

## COMPREHENSION MONITORING

Readers need not only to attempt to understand a text, but also need to monitor their comprehension, and to know how to remedy comprehension failures. Poor comprehenders may not realize that they don't understand a particular text, or portion of text, and may not know what to do about their poor understanding, even if they do realize.

We mention one experiment in which we investigated the comprehension monitoring ability of good and poor comprehenders. The children were selected as described above, except that in this study they were a little older (9–10 years) and a CAM group was not included. We used a traditional error-detection paradigm (following Markman, 1977).

The errors were internal inconsistencies within the text, i.e., contradictory statements. This procedure had the advantage of allowing us to manipulate the intrinsic memory load of the task: the inconsistencies were either in adjacent sentences, or were separated by several sentences. An example passage is shown in Table 6. The children were presented with two passages in each of the memory load conditions. They were also asked to read and make judgements about two passages without any inconsistencies, so that we could make sure that they really could discriminate between passages with problems and those without.

TABLE 6
Example passage from comprehension monitoring experiment

---

Gorillas are clever animals that live together in groups in Africa.
*Gorillas sleep on the ground on a bed of leaves and they like to eat different types of fruit.*
They are shy and gentle and they hardly ever fight with each other.
Gorillas have flat noses and a very poor sense of smell but their eyesight is very good. They move about the ground on their hands and feet.
\*
Gorillas sleep in trees and they often build a shelter out of leaves above them, to keep the rain out.

\_\_\_\_ This passage makes sense, it does not need to be changed.
\_\_\_\_ This passage does not make sense, it needs to be changed.

---

*Note: in the adjacent condition, the italicized sentence occurred in this position.

The children read the passages aloud at their own pace, and were asked to identify any problems with them ("something that doesn't make sense") by underlining it. They were shown an example of the sort of blatant inconsistency that occurred in the test passages. At the end of each passage, they were asked to indicate their overall assessment of the passage (as shown in Table 6). If they had indicated a problem, they were asked to explain it. In the case of passages with inconsistencies, if the child did not immediately identify a problem, they were told that there was a problem, and were given another chance to find it. If they still failed to do so, the experimenter underlined the two inconsistent sentences, and asked the child if they made sense together.

For each of the inconsistent passages, each child obtained a minimum score of 0 (if they did not identify a problem, despite all prompting) and a maximum of 3 (if they ticked the correct option on first reading, and correctly identified the problem). The mean scores for the groups, in the two conditions, are shown in Table 7.

TABLE 7
Mean scores on detection task (max = 6)

| Condition | Adjacent | Distant |
|---|---|---|
| Less skilled | 4.3 | 3.2 |
| Skilled | 5.2 | 5.0 |

An analysis of these data showed that the skilled comprehenders were better overall, and that there was also an effect of distance: the inconsistencies were harder to detect when they were separated by several sentences. More interestingly, there was a significant interaction between the distance and the skill variables: the less-skilled comprehenders were more affected by the distance manipulation than were the skilled ones. Performance on the non-problematic passages was uniformly high.

WORKING MEMORY: CAUSE OF PROBLEMS IN TEXT PROCESSING?

Both these results, and those from an earlier study on anomaly detection (Yuill, Oakhill, & Parkin, 1989), suggest that the integration of information from different parts of a text is considerably harder for poor comprehenders. Such problems may well be related to working memory, which might perhaps be an underlying cause of other processing difficulties (we come back to the direction of the link between working memory and comprehension processes in more detail later). Although we did not find any differences between good and poor comprehenders on short-term memory tasks, the tests we used were primarily tests of storage capacity (see Oakhill, Yuill, & Parkin, 1986). Oakhill, Yuill, & Parkin (1988) suggested that good and poor comprehenders might differ on a task that makes heavier demands on working memory (i.e., a task that makes concurrent storage and processing demands). Indeed, many studies of adults have shown that comprehension skill is related to performance on tests of working memory (for a review, see Daneman, 1987). We developed a working memory span task suitable for young children. The children were presented with lists of numbers to read aloud (the processing requirement) and had to remember the final digit in each group (storage requirement). The memory load was varied by increasing the number of sets of digits (and, therefore, the number of final digits to be recalled): 2, 3 or 4. So, for example, in a two-digit case, the child might read the sets 7–4–2 and 1–3–9 and then have to recall 2 and 9. Although there was no difference between the groups in the easiest version (two-digit recall), there were differences in the three and four-digit versions of the task.

We have replicated this finding several times, with both 7 to 8-year-olds and 9– to 10–year-olds (including those who participated in the comprehension monitoring experiment, described above). So, one obvious way in which these findings might be married with those we presented earlier is to suggest that skilled comprehenders are better at making inferences, monitoring their understanding, producing and deriving the structure of stories because they have more efficient working memories. Indeed, the idea of a working memory deficit fits in nicely with our study of comprehension monitoring, described above, where we showed that it was only when the crucial pieces of information were non-adjacent in the text that the less-skilled comprehenders had particular difficulties.

This pattern of results—that the poor comprehenders are able to integrate information and detect inconsistencies at short distances, but not over longer distances—indicates that they are able to connect up information in text to some extent. The findings are consistent with the hypothesis that poor comprehenders are able to built adequate representations of parts of a text, but fail to relate and integrate these partial representations to produce a model of the text as a whole. Such a hypothesis would explain why they are able to appreciate anomalies and inconsistencies when the information on which this appreciation depends is not close together in the text, and why they are able to produce locally, but not globally, coherent stories. It can also explain why they have difficulty in making inferences that do not just depend on information that is locally available in the text, but on the integration of information from different parts, and perhaps the conjunction of that information with relevant background knowledge as well. We suggest that the poor comprehenders' more limited working memories are sufficient to support some local integration of text (whether in comprehension or production), but that they cannot support the integration of the text as a whole.

There are, however, at least three major problems with such a conclusion. First, as yet, we have no data that addresses the issue of the direction of the link. It may be the case, as Tunmer (1989) has suggested, that practice at reading with understanding increases working memory capacity, rather than the reverse.

Second, even if working memory were found to be causally linked to comprehension skill, it is very unlikely to be a complete explanation of individual differences in skill. We have found that even brief periods of training to raise children's awareness of the need to make inferences, and to go beyond the literal information in a text, were very successful in improving the poor group's performance on a standardized comprehension test, at least in the short term (for a review, see Oakhill and Yuill, 1991). This finding suggests that one reason for less inference making in poor comprehenders raised above -- that they do not realize that inferences are an integral part of text comprehension -- could well be plausible. It is highly unlikely that an incidental outcome of such training was that it also improved the children's working memory capacity. However, the two sets of findings—that the poor comprehenders have deficient working memories and that their comprehension can be improved by short periods of training—are not entirely incompatible. It may be the case that the training we gave the children provided them with strategies which helped them to circumvent their memory problems, rather than enabling them to process text as good comprehenders do.

Third, the conclusion from the training studies—that working memory deficits are unlikely to provide a complete explanation of comprehension problems—is supported by a very recent study in which we obtained measures of a number of skills and abilities in a large group of 7- to 8-year-olds, including measures of working memory, integration skill and comprehension monitoring. We found that, in regression analyses in which a number of control measures (verbal and non-verbal IQ, word recognition, reading rate, vocabulary and age) were entered at the first step, and working memory was entered at the second step, the specific comprehension measures (integration and monitoring) still predicted significant additional variance in comprehension skill when either one was entered at the third step. Thus, although working memory appears to be an important predictor of comprehension skill, it does not account for all the variance that these specific subskill measures have to contribute.

## CONCLUSIONS AND FUTURE DIRECTIONS

The text level comprehension processes discussed above all make demands on working memory resources, and it is reasonable to suppose that a child, or adult, who has a low working memory capacity might find them difficult. We have suggested that poor comprehenders' working memories may be sufficient to support models of parts of a text, but not to enable the integration of these sub-models into a coherent whole. Furthermore we have suggested that working memory deficits could contribute to the less-skilled comprehenders' problems in making inferences, understanding story structure and in monitoring and repairing their comprehension.

However, the precise patterns of causality between working memory skills and text comprehension have yet to be established, and as we have pointed out above, there are various reasons to suggest that working memory problems are unlikely to be a complete explanation of comprehension difficulties.

In a current project, we are exploring the possible patterns of causality between a number of skills and abilities, and reading comprehension. We intend to do address the issue of causality in two main ways. First by making further use of the "comprehension age match" (discussed above). Second, by exploring, in a longitudinal study, how well various skills that have been identified as problematic for poor comprehenders (e.g., inference-making, working memory, metacognitive skills) predict comprehension at a later age, and compare their predictive power with how well comprehension predicts performance on tasks that measure those skills at a later age. The relative strengths of these relations will throw light on the direction of causal links between comprehension skill and the other variables and, we hope, will enable us to develop a more complete model of comprehension skill and its breakdown.

## REFERENCES

Applebee, A. N. (1978) *The Child's Concept of Story: Ages Two to Seventeen.* Chicago: University of Chicago Press.

Barnes, M. A., Dennis, M., & Haefele-Kalvaitis, J. (1996). The effects of knowledge availability and knowledge accessibility on coherence and elaborative inferencing in children from six to fifteen years of age. *Journal of Experimental Child Psychology, 61,* 216–241.

Cain, K., & Oakhill, J. V. (1996) The nature of the relationship between comprehension skill and the ability to tell a story. *British Journal of Developmental Psychology, 14,* 187–201.

Cain, K., & Oakhill, J. V. (in press). Inference making ability and its relation to comprehension failure. Reading and Writing.

Charniak, E. (1972) *Toward a Model of Children's Story Comprehension.* Technical

Report A1-TR-266. Boston, Mass.: MIT.

Daneman, M. (1987). Reading and working memory. In J. R. Beech & A. M. Colley (Eds). *Cognitive Approaches to Reading*. Chichester: Wiley.

Markman, E. (1977). Realizing that you don't understand: A preliminary investigation. *Child Development, 48*, 986–992.

Oakhill, J. V. (1984). Inferential and memory skills in children's comprehension of stories. *British Journal of Educational Psychology, 54*, 31–39.

Oakhill, J. V., Cain, K., & Barnes, M. (1996). *Comprehension skill, inference making and their relation to knowledge*. Presented at the BPS Developmental Section Meeting, Oxford, September 1996.

Oakhill, J. V., Cain, K., & Yuill, N. M. (1998). Individual differences in young children's comprehension skill: Toward an integrated model. In C. Hulme & R. M. Joshi (Eds.), *Reading and Spelling: Development and Disorders* (pp. 343–367). Mahwah, NJ: Erlbaum.

Oakhill, J. V., Yuill, N. M., & Parkin, A. J. (1986). On the nature of the difference between skilled and less-skilled comprehenders. *Journal of Research in Reading, 9*, 80–91.

Oakhill, J. V, Yuill, N. M., & Parkin, A. J. (1988). Memory and inference in skilled and less-skilled comprehenders. In M. M. Gruneberg, P. E. Morris & R. N. Sykes (Eds), *Practical Aspects of Memory* (Vol. 2, pp. 315–320). Chichester: Wiley.

Peterson, C., & McCabe, A. (1983). *Developmental Psycholinguistics: Three ways of looking at a child's narrative*. New York: Plenum.

Stein, N. L., & Glenn, C. G. (1979). An analysis of story comprehension in elementary school children. In R. O. Freedle (Ed), *New Directions in Discourse Processing* (Vol 2, pp. 53–120). Norwood, NJ: Ablex.

Stein, N. L, & Glenn, C. G. (1982). Children's concept of time: the development of a story schema. In W. J. Friedman (Ed), *The Developmental Psychology of Time* (pp. 255–282). New York: Academic Press.

Tunmer, W. (1989). The role of language-related factors in reading disability. In D. Shankweiler & I. Y. Liberman (Eds), *Phonology and Reading Disability: Solving the Reading Puzzle* (pp.91–131). Ann Arbor, MI: University of Michigan Press.

Yuill, N. M., & Oakhill, J. V. (1991). *Children's Problems in Text Comprehension: An Experimental Investigation*. Cambridge: Cambridge University Press.

Yuill, N. M., Oakhill, J. V., & Parkin, A. J. (1989). Working memory, comprehension ability and the resolution of text anomaly. *British Journal of Psychology, 80*, 351–361.

MIENKE DROOP AND LUDO VERHOEVEN

# READING COMPREHENSION PROBLEMS IN SECOND LANGUAGE LEARNERS

The state of affairs concerning acquisition processes in reading in a second language (L2) is far from clear-cut. It is unclear what effect the linguistic and sociocultural characteristics of L2 learners have on the course of reading processes. From a linguistic point of view, two types of learning problems can be observed: interlingual and intralingual learning problems. Interlingual learning problems are caused by mother tongue influence; intralingual learning problems are caused by the structure of the second language. Traditionally, L2 learning problems were defined in terms of mother tongue interference. A contrastive analysis of similarities and differences which exist between two or more languages was taken as a starting point for the interpretation of L2 learning problems. However, the debate on the role of interference in L2 reading is far from conclusive (cf. Harris, 1992). In many cases L2 learning problems can be termed intralingual in that these relate to a specific interpretation of the target language.

A different way of looking at L2 learning problems is to refer to substantial similarities between the strategies employed in first language learning and those in second language learning. It can be assumed that the various processes of reading in a second language are a consequence of the difficulties learners have in grasping the linguistic patterns of the target language and in using (meta)linguistic cues in reading. Processes of learning to read in a first and second language can be different in many ways (see Verhoeven, 1990, 1994; Koda, 1994; Weber, 1991).

First, L1 and L2 learners may differ in their efficiency of word decoding. Due to a relatively small vocabulary, L2 learners may have trouble in filling their visual word representation system. There will only be a chance of constructing a visual representation of a word if its meaning is known. The most salient variable indicative of lexical accessibility is word frequency. It can be predicted that L2 learners will profit from word frequency in lexical access to a lesser degree. They may be relatively less efficient in decoding high frequency words as compared to low frequency or pseudowords.

Second, there may be differences between L1 and L2 readers as to higher order comprehension processes which follow the identification of words. Because of inefficient sentence processing, the storage capacity for retaining strings of words in short-term memory may fall short. At the same time, limited textual knowledge in L2 may give way to a poor understanding of discourse devices, such as coherence of sentences, anaphoric reference and inference.

Third, there may be differences between L1 and L2 learners in the interaction of the different subprocesses of word recognition and reading comprehension mentioned before. L2 learners may not attain the same degree of automaticity in comparable subprocesses as L1 learners. Thus, they will not be in a position to attend so closely to higher order processes. As a result, these processes can be inhibited.

The purpose of the present study, which was carried out in the Netherlands, was to investigate differences in reading comprehension processes between Dutch children learning to read in their native language and minority children learning to read in their second language. At schools in the Netherlands, Dutch is the only language of instruction. When entering primary school ethnic minority children start learning to read in Dutch as a second language while they are in the midst of the second language acquisition process. Several periodic assessments showed that already at the start, but also at the end of primary school the results of ethnic minority children are lower in comparison to their monolingual Dutch peers. From an educational point of view it is important to know which variables can explain the delay in reading comprehension development of the ethnic minority children.

In the present study the reading comprehension of native Dutch and ethnic minority (Turkish and Moroccan) students was monitored during the third and fourth grade of primary school in the Netherlands. An attempt was made to uncover the relation between linguistic knowledge and reading comprehension development. Problems in the early stages of reading comprehension development may relate to "bottom-up" word recognition processes, or "top-down" higher order processes. Children acquiring reading in a second language usually have greater problems with the latter type of processes, due to a restricted knowledge of the target language and restricted background knowledge. In the present study the role of oral language proficiency and decoding skills will be examined in the development of reading comprehension in children learning to read in Dutch as a first and second language. The aim of the study is to explore the relative influence of different aspects of language proficiency in L2 on reading comprehension, such as lexical knowledge, morpho-syntactic knowledge, oral text comprehension, and also decoding skills. Beside differences between first and second language learners we look at differences within these groups. Within the Dutch group we are interested in differences between children with a high and low SES background. Several studies showed low SES children to obtain lower scores at language proficiency tests than children from high SES background.

Following a longitudinal design, a componential analysis of first and second language reading was carried out. The study focused on answering the following main questions:
(1) Are there differences in the development of reading comprehension, decoding skills and oral language proficiency of first and second language learners. If so, do these differences remain constant over time or are they converging or diverging?
(2) Are there differences between the two ethnic groups, and between Dutch children with high and low ses?
(3) What interactions take place between oral language processes, word recognition processes and reading comprehension processes in first and second language learners?

DESIGN OF THE STUDY

*Subjects*

A total of 143 Dutch 62 Turkish and 60 Moroccan children of grade 3 from 21 primary schools in the Netherlands were selected to participate in the study. At the start of the third grade all children had gone through 2 years of formal reading instruction. All subjects came from mixed classes with 20 to 80 percent of the pupils belonging to ethnic minority groups. Though there is a rich variety of ethnic minority groups in the Netherlands we restricted ourselves to Turks and Moroccans, since these are the largest immigrant groups who came to the Netherlands during the seventies and eighties, and who have shown to have severe problems in Dutch education (Extra & Verhoeven, 1994). The first language of the Turkish children is Turkish. Among the Moroccan children there are children whose first language is either Moroccan Arabic or Berber. The children live in mother-tongue speaking homes. The early language input is restricted to the mother tongue, and the Dutch language enters into their lives only gradually, through Dutch playmates and school. The socio-economic status of both groups is low. The SES of Dutch children was based on the educational and vocational level of both parents.

Of the 143 Dutch children that participated in all measurement moments, there were 60 children with a high SES background. This group consisted of 20 girls and 40 boys with a mean age of 8;6 years. 8 children had once repeated a grade (13.3%) 83 Dutch children had a low SES background. This group included 46 girls, and 37 boys, with a mean age of 8;8 years. 22 children had once repeated a grade (26,5%). Of the 60 Moroccan children 32 were girls and 28 boys; mean age 8;10 years. 20 children had once repeated a grade (33.3%)

25 children have as their first language Moroccan Arabic, while 35 children are speakers of Berber. Of the 62 Turkish children 24 were girls and 38 boys; mean age 8;11 years. 28 children once repeated a grade (45.2%). It should be mentioned that the proportions of grade repetition among the Turkish and Moroccan children was high. however, in the vast majority of cases. It should be mentioned that the grade repetition included an extra year in Kindergarten.

*Materials*

Standardized tests were chosen originating from a battery constructed by the Dutch National Institute for Educational Measurement. The constructs to be measured were reading comprehension, word recognition and oral language proficiency. As components of oral language proficiency we distinguished lexical knowledge, morpho-syntactic knowledge and oral text comprehension. Oral tests were used to measure these linguistic aspects. With respect to reliability and validity, we used as much as possible two tests to measure each construct.

*Reading comprehension* was tested by means of three tests, each testing a different aspect of reading comprehension. The first one was a text coherence test in which children had to read short passages and had to answer 25 multiple-choice questions at the word, sentence, paragraph, and text level. In the second test, a reading vocabulary test, children had to read 50 sentences in which one word was underlined. The meaning of the word had to be chosen out of four alternatives. The third test aimed at measuring text cohesion. Children read two-texts and had to fill in connectives, such as *because, while*, in a multiple-choice format.

*Decoding skills* were tested by means of a test, consisting of three cards with lists of words differing in orthographic complexity: a first card with monosyllabic words of the type consonant-vowel-consonant, a second card with monosyllabic words with consonant clusters, and a third card with polysyllabic words. With all three cards children had to read as many words as they could in one minute. The child's score on each card was a combined score for speed and accuracy, consisting of the number of words read correctly in one minute.

*Lexical knowledge* was tested by means of a receptive vocabulary test and a productive, word definition test. In the receptive vocabulary test, a word was spoken as the child was shown four pictures, one of which corresponded to the correct meaning of the word. The child was asked to point to the picture that represented the word. The test comprised 98 items. In the word definition test the child was asked to give a definition of 25 words. According to a predefined scoring system the child's responses were rated with 1 (incomplete definition) or 2 points (complete definition).

In order to assess *morphological* knowledge we used a morphology test to test knowledge of plurals, conjugation of verbs and pronominal reference. Along with pictures the correct morphological elements were elicited. The test consisted of 42 items. *Syntactic knowledge* was measured by means of a sentence imitation test. In this test 20 sentences were offered that contained a rich variety of syntactic structures. The child was asked to reproduce each sentence as complete as possible. For each sentence the correct realization of two distinct grammatical structures was scored.

*Oral text comprehension* was tested by a listening comprehension test, consisting of short stories orally presented to the child with consecutive questions in a multiple choice format. The total number of questions was 33.

The children were tested at three moments in time: at the beginning of the third grade, at the end of the third grade and at the end of the fourth grade. The same tests were administered to the children at all three measurement moments. Oral tests were presented to the child by the researcher with help of research assistants. Test administration took about 45 minutes per child. The written tests were administered by the teachers themselves. There were no time limits or speed tests for the written tests.

*Procedure of analysis*

Multivariate analysis of variance with repeated measurements design (MANOVA) was used to analyse differences between groups and over time. For each test a 4 (Group) x 3 (Time) analysis of variance with repeated measurement on the last factor was performed. To compare differences between groups three contrasts were given in MANOVA. The first contrast compared the results of the Dutch low SES children with the ethnic minority children. Both groups have a low socio-economic background. In the second and third contrast differences within the Dutch group (low versus high SES) and within the ethnic minority group (Turkish versus Moroccan) were specified.

In order to analyse interactions among variables and causal relationships analyses by means of Linear Structural Relations Analysis analyses (LISREL) were performed. It was explored which linguistic components would predict the reading comprehension of first and second language learners. This analysis examined interactions between the various sub-processes and changes in their relative contribution to reading comprehension ability. LISREL was chosen because both cross-sectional and longitudinal relationships can be analyzed, a distinction between observed variables as well as latent variables can be made, and the fit of the model can be tested. The measurement model describes the relation between the measures taken and a latent variable. The structural model describes the underlying causal relationship among the latent variables.

The three reading comprehension tests were taken as observed variables of the construct Reading Comprehension, the three decoding tests as Decoding, the listening comprehension test as Oral Text Comprehension, morphology and sentence imitation as Morpho-Syntactic Knowledge, and the two vocabulary tests as Lexical Knowledge.

A series of LISREL models was conducted in order to clarify the constituent components of second language reading comprehension. In a model comprising all variables it was explored to what extent reading comprehension was explained by both decoding skills and oral Dutch. Analysis started with the data of the Dutch children. In a multi-sample analysis it was tested if the final model of the Dutch children fitted the data of the ethnic minority children.

## RESULTS

*Development of skills*

In Table 1 the means and standard deviations for each group at each measurement moment are given.

*Reading comprehension.* Table 1 shows a clear increase in scores over time for all groups on the three reading comprehension tests. Other than that, there were remarkable differences between the groups. On all tests the results of the ethnic minority children were lower than those of the Dutch children. Within the Dutch group, the high SES children obtained higher results than the low SES children. Within the ethnic minority group, the results of the Moroccan children were on all tests higher than the results of the Turkish children.

*Results MANOVA.* In the overall analysis of the total group the main effects Group and Time were significant for all three reading comprehension tests, indicating substantial differences between groups and substantial progress over time. (Group: Text coherence $F(3, 236)=28.29$, $p<.001$; Reading voc. $F(3, 239)=51.79$, $p<.001$; Text cohesion: $F(3, 253)=33.77$, $p<.001$; Time Text Coherence Wilks' $\lambda=.33$, $F=239$, $p<.001$; Reading voc. Wilks' $\lambda=28$, $F=307.65$, $p<.001$; Text Cohesion $F(1, 253)=191.11$, $p<.001$). A significant interaction Group by Time was found for Text coherence (Wilks' $\lambda=.95$, $F=2.21$, $p<.05$) as well as Reading vocabulary (Wilks' $\lambda=.75$, $F=12.44$, $p<.001$), indicating differences between groups in progress over time.

TABLE 1
Mean scores and standard deviations of Dutch and minority children on tests for reading comprehension, decoding, vocabulary knowledge, morpho-syntax and listening comprehension

|  |  | Dutch children | | | | Minority children | | | |
|---|---|---|---|---|---|---|---|---|---|
|  |  | High SES | | Low SES | | Moroccans | | Turks | |
|  |  | M | SD | M | SD | M | SD | M | SD |
| Text coherence | begin 3 | 17.1 | 5.3 | 15.1 | 5.5 | 12.7 | 4.9 | 10.4 | 4.2 |
| (25) | end 3 | 20.6 | 4.7 | 18.5 | 5.0 | 16.4 | 4.6 | 13.4 | 4.8 |
|  | end 4 | 23.1 | 2.1 | 20.9 | 4.1 | 19.1 | 4.2 | 17.7 | 4.7 |
| Reading vocabulary | begin 3 | 20.6 | 6.4 | 18.5 | 6.1 | 14.1 | 3.4 | 13.5 | 4.0 |
| (50) | end 3 | 27.2 | 7.6 | 22.4 | 7.5 | 18.0 | 4.7 | 14.7 | 3.8 |
|  | end 4 | 34.3 | 8.1 | 29.5 | 8.1 | 22.6 | 6.8 | 18.6 | 5.4 |
| Text cohesion (40) | end 3 | 30.5 | 6.7 | 26.4 | 7.0 | 22.5 | 6.4 | 19.6 | 5.7 |
|  | end 4 | 34.5 | 5.0 | 31.0 | 6.1 | 27.8 | 6.5 | 25.2 | 6.2 |
| Decoding 1 (CVC) | begin 3 | 75.0 | 17.5 | 64.7 | 16.7 | 69.3 | 18.2 | 69.3 | 17.7 |
|  | end 3 | 86.1 | 16.8 | 74.8 | 14.9 | 81.4 | 16.0 | 82.0 | 18.2 |
|  | end 4 | 94.7 | 15.8 | 84.3 | 15.2 | 92.2 | 16.6 | 97.2 | 18.0 |
| Decoding 2 (CCVCC) | begin 3 | 66.4 | 20.5 | 55.0 | 19.7 | 54.9 | 19.6 | 58.6 | 20.0 |
|  | end 3 | 79.1 | 18.2 | 66.6 | 16.7 | 71.3 | 18.4 | 72.3 | 21.2 |
|  | end 4 | 89.2 | 16.5 | 78.2 | 16.3 | 84.4 | 17.2 | 89.5 | 19.1 |
| Decoding 3 (polysyl) | begin 3 | 52.1 | 17.8 | 42.4 | 17.4 | 41.4 | 16.0 | 43.1 | 15.5 |
|  | end 3 | 65.8 | 16.4 | 54.1 | 16.5 | 57.1 | 16.5 | 55.3 | 16.8 |
|  | end 4 | 76.1 | 17.2 | 65.1 | 16.2 | 68.3 | 16.2 | 69.6 | 15.2 |
| Receptive vocabulary | begin 3 | 89.1 | 5.6 | 86.1 | 7.0 | 71.0 | 8.5 | 66.2 | 8.1 |
| (98) | end 3 | 92.4 | 3.6 | 89.8 | 4.8 | 79.6 | 6.4 | 72.3 | 8.9 |
| (40) | end 4 | 34.8 | 2.9 | 34.0 | 3.2 | 31.5 | 3.3 | 28.8 | 3.8 |
| Productive vocabulary | begin 3 | 19.5 | 8.4 | 14.9 | 8.4 | 5.6 | 4.4 | 3.0 | 3.5 |
| (50) | end 3 | 25.8 | 8.5 | 19.9 | 8.6 | 10.1 | 5.7 | 5.3 | 4.2 |
|  | end 4 | 32.4 | 7.5 | 27.9 | 10.6 | 15.8 | 7.3 | 11.4 | 6.8 |
| Morphology | begin 3 | 37.3 | 3.3 | 34.2 | 5.2 | 27.2 | 4.0 | 23.1 | 4.2 |
| (42) | end 3 | 39.2 | 2.7 | 36.6 | 4.7 | 30.8 | 5.0 | 25.6 | 4.2 |
|  | end 4 | 41.1 | 1.4 | 38.9 | 3.8 | 35.2 | 3.6 | 30.6 | 4.8 |
| Sentence imitation | begin 3 | 32.3 | 5.6 | 30.9 | 5.7 | 23.5 | 7.4 | 19.6 | 7.9 |
| (40) | end 3 | 34.1 | 5.2 | 32.2 | 5.2 | 27.2 | 6.6 | 22.6 | 7.0 |
|  | end 4 | 36.0 | 3.7 | 34.8 | 4.9 | 31.6 | 4.9 | 26.3 | 7.0 |
| Listening test | begin 3 | 23.9 | 4.5 | 21.4 | 4.5 | 17.7 | 4.4 | 15.5 | 3.2 |
| (33) | end 3 | 27.8 | 3.8 | 26.0 | 3.7 | 21.4 | 4.1 | 18.4 | 4.2 |
|  | end 4 | 28.8 | 3.1 | 27.8 | 3.3 | 24.7 | 4.1 | 21.8 | 6.8 |

Of more interest, are the results of the comparisons between groups. Of the three contrasts all main effects were significant. The observed differences between the ethnic minority children and the Dutch children, as well as within these groups are significant for all tests. (Dutch low SES versus minority: Text coherence $F(1,236)=30.26$, $p<.001$; Reading voc. $F(1,239)=57.03$, $p<.001$; Text cohesion: $F(1,253)=191.11$, $p<.001$; within Dutch group: Text coherence: $F(1,236)=8.64$, $p<.01$; Reading voc. $F(1,239)=19.37$, $p<.001$, Text cohesion: $F(1,253)=14.58$, $p<.001$; within minority group: Text coherence F(1, 236)=8.47, p<.001, Reading voc. F(1, 239)=5.35, p<.05, Text Cohesion: F(1, 253)=5.79, p<.05.)

The comparison of Dutch low SES versus ethnic minority children also revealed a significant interaction Group by Time for Text coherence (Wilks' $\lambda$=.97, F=3.92, p<.05). This means the differences between the Dutch low SES children and ethnic minority children are decreasing, while within the Dutch and ethnic minority group the differences remain constant over time.

For Reading vocabulary the interaction Group by Time turned out to be significant for all group comparisons, indicating increasing differences between the ethnic minority and the Dutch children (Wilks' $\lambda$=.95, F=6.57, p<.01), as well as increasing differences within these groups. (within Dutch group: Wilks' $\lambda$=.96, F=5.01, p<.01; within minority group: Wilks' $\lambda$=.95, F=6.57, p<.01)

For Text cohesion no significant interactions were found, which indicates constant differences between groups over time.

*Decoding*. The Table shows remarkable differences in the results of the Dutch high SES children versus low SES ones. The results of the latter group were lower on each card. There were only slight differences in results of the Turkish and Moroccan children. It is interesting that for the first card (CVC-words) the results of the ethnic minority children were at the same level as those of the Dutch children with high SES, while at the third card (polysyllabic words) the ethnic minority children dropped to the level of the Dutch children with low SES. The second card (CCVCC words) shows a clear interaction. At the beginning of grade three the ethnic minority children had a mean score comparable to the Dutch low SES children, while at the end of the fourth grade they came close to the level of the Dutch high SES.

*Results of MANOVA*. The overall analysis of the total group significant main effects were found for the factors Group (F(2,261)=6.28, p<.001), Time (Wilks' $\lambda$=.12, F=925.28, p<.001) and Task (Wilks' $\lambda$=.08, F=1610.99, p<.001). There are significant differences between groups; progress over time is substantial, and scores on the CVC cards are higher than scores on the CCVCC card which are in turn higher than scores on the polysyllabic words. Further, the significant interactions between the factors Group by Time (Wilks' $\lambda$=.91, F=4.02, p<.01), Group by Task (Wilks' $\lambda$=.81, F=9.94, p<.001), and Time by Task (Wilks' $\lambda$=.84, F=12.51, p<.001) indicate differences between groups over time, as well as differences between groups in scores on the three type of cards, and differences in growth over time on card type.

In the comparison of the ethnic minority children with the Dutch low SES children the effect for the factor Group (F(1,261)=5.58, p<.05) and the interaction Group by Time (Wilks' $\lambda$=.95, F=7.19, p<.01) and Group by Task (Wilks' λ=.87, F=18.86, p<.001) were significant. It can be concluded that the ethnic minority children are significantly faster decoders than the Dutch low SES children. In addition, it can be concluded that the ethnic minority children process short, mono-syllabic words faster than longer poly-syllabic words, while the Dutch children do not show much variation across card types.

The comparison of the two Dutch groups only revealed a clear significant main effect for the factor Group (F(1, 261)=28.29, p<.001), which means the Dutch high SES children are much faster decoders than the low SES children.

Of the comparison of the Turkish and Moroccan children the interaction Group by Task turned out to be significant (Wilks' λ=.96, F=4.85, p<.05) indicating differences between the two groups in scores for the card types.

*Oral Language proficiency.* For the measures of oral language proficiency the same ordering of groups was found as for the reading comprehension tests. On each test the scores increased over time. The receptive vocabulary test was given to the children at the beginning and at the end of the third grade. Already at the beginning of the first grade the Dutch children obtained high scores. The ethnic minority children also had relatively high scores. Because of this ceiling level another test was used at the end of the fourth grade. With respect to the productive vocabulary test the table indicates relative large differences between the Dutch and the ethnic minority children. The minority children obtained extreme low scores at the beginning of the third grade. For this test it seems the differences between groups are getting larger over time. On the morphology and sentence imitation test the Dutch children obtained high scores at the beginning of the third grade. At the end of the fourth grade it seems that they reached a ceiling: high means and small, decreasing standard deviations. The tested morpho-syntactic rules are known by most children. For the ethnic minority children we see a clear development over time on both tests.

*Results of MANOVA.* Vocabulary knowledge: The overall analysis of the total group revealed two significant main effects for the factors Group (receptive voc. F(3, 291)=182.77, p<.001; productive: F(3, 291)=105.63, p<.001) and Time (receptive: F(1, 291)=3811.71, p<.001; productive: Wilks' λ=.22, F=473.60, p<.001) as well as a significant interaction Group by Time (receptive vocabulary: F(3, 291)=19.20, p<.001); productive vocabulary: Wilks' lambda= .87, F=6.06, p<.001) indicating differences between groups in progress over time.

In the analysis of the Dutch low SES versus the ethnic minority children for both tests the main effect Group as well as the interaction Group by Time turned out to be significant (receptive vocabulary: Group $F(1, 291)=326.83$, $p<.001$; Group x Time: $F(1, 291)=34.07$, $p<.001$); productive vocabulary: Group: $F(1, 261)=160.82$, $p<.001$ Group x Time: Wilks' $\lambda=.94$, $F=8.88$, $p<.001$). With respect to the receptive vocabulary test it can be concluded that the differences between groups are decreasing over time. However, this might be due to the ceiling reached by the Dutch children. For the productive vocabulary test the interaction confirms the observation of increasing differences over time. The ethnic minority children lag behind the Dutch children in growth of productive vocabulary over time.

Comparison of the Dutch low SES and high SES children only revealed significant main effects for the factor Group (receptive voc. $F(1, 291)=7.36$, $p<.01$; productive voc: $F(1, 261)=17.16$, $p<.001$), but no significant interactions occurred. On both tests the differences between these groups remain stable over time.

Of the comparison of Moroccans and Turks significant main effects were found for both tests. (receptive voc. $F(1, 291)=30.38$, $p<.001$; productive voc.: $F(1, 261)=8.45$, $p<.001$). The significant interactions for both vocabulary tests indicate that on these tests the differences between these groups increase over time (receptive vocabulary: $F(1, 291)=9.72$, $p<.01$; productive vocabulary: Wilks' $\lambda=.97$, $F=3.48$, $p<.05$). The Moroccan children show relatively more progress over time than the Turkish children.

Morpho-syntax: The overall analysis of the total group revealed significant main effects for the factors Group and Time as well as significant interactions both tests (Morphology: Group: $F(3, 261)=159$, $p<.001$; Time: Wilks' $\lambda=.28$, $F=343.39$, $p<.001$; Group x Time: Wilks' $\lambda=.79$, $F=11.06$, $p<.001$; Sentence imitation: Group: $F(3, 261)=57.32$, $p<.001$), Time: Wilks' $\lambda= .45$, $F=158.69$, $p<.001$), Group x Time: Wilks' $\lambda=.87$, $F=6.20$, $p<.001$). Again, there are significant differences between groups. The interactions indicate differences between groups in progress over time.

With respect to the comparison of groups for the Morphology test all main effects group were significant, confirming the observed differences between groups in mean scores (Dutch low SES versus minority : $F(1,261)=233.53$, $p<.001$; within Dutch group: $F(1, 261)=17.64$, $p<.001$; within minority group: $F(1, 261)=53.88$, $p<.001$). The sentence imitation test showed two significant main effects. This time there are no significant differences between the Dutch high and low SES children. However, there were significant differences between the Dutch low SES children and ethnic minority children ($F(1,261)= 93.24$, $p<.001$) and between the Turks and Moroccans ($F(1, 261)=21.42$, $p<.001$). For both tests the interaction

Group by Time was only significant in the comparison of the Dutch low SES and ethnic minority children. (Morphology: Wilks' $\lambda=.86$, $F=20.72$, $p<.001$; Sentence imitation: Wilks' $\lambda=.92$, $F=12.04$, $p<.001$) These significant interactions might be due to the maximum level reached by the Dutch children. Already at the beginning of the third grade they showed high results on these tests and growth over time is relatively small compared to the ethnic minority children.

Listening Comprehension In the overall analysis of the total group significant main effects for the factors Group ($F(3, 229)=74.52$, $p<.001$) and Time ($F(2, 458)=324.01$, $p<.001$) were found, as well as a significant interaction Group by Time ($F(6, 458)=3.14$, $p<.01$), indicating differences between groups and differences in progress over time.

The group comparisons revealed three significant main effects. None of the interactions turned out to be significant. This means the observed differences between the Dutch and ethnic minority children ($F(1, 229)=111.65$, $p<.001$), between the Dutch high versus low SES ($F(1, 229)=8.20$, $p<.01$) and between the Turks and Moroccans ($F(1, 229)=14.96$, $p<.001$) are significant, and over time these differences remain stable.

In sum, we can state that on all tests, except decoding, the same ordering in groups was found. Dutch children obtained higher results than the ethnic minority children, while Dutch high SES outperformed low SES and Moroccans showed better results than Turks. Of the interactions we found most might be due to a performance at ceiling of the Dutch children (Text coherence, morphology, sentence imitation and listening comprehension). However, two interactions indicate that differences between the ethnic minority children and the Dutch low SES children are increasing over time (reading vocabulary, productive vocabulary). On these tests differences between Dutch high and low SES and between Moroccans and Turks are increasing as well.

*Interactions among oral language proficiency, decoding skills and reading comprehension*

In this section the results of the analysis of interactions among components are presented. A series of LISREL analyses was performed to explore to what extent reading comprehension of first and second language learners can be explained by their decoding skills and oral proficiency in Dutch. In designing the model several assumptions were considered. With respect to the different components of language proficiency, it was assumed that oral language proficiency is a construct which consists of several hierarchically related sub-processes. Knowledge of a process higher in the hierarchy assumes knowledge of the lower processes. Knowledge of words assumes knowledge of sounds, knowledge of sentences assumes knowledge of words, and knowledge of text assumes knowledge of sentences. Following from this model it was assumed that the comprehension of written text is dependent on comprehension of oral text. On the other hand reading comprehension was assumed to be dependent on decoding skills.

Furthermore, in designing the models the factor time was of great influence. In the first place for all constructs the longitudinal, auto-regressive causal effects were specified, since a construct measured earlier in time often is the strongest predictor of the same construct measured later in time. Exclusion of this effect would lead to over-estimated causal effects of other variables. With respect to relations among the various constructs causal effects were specified as cross-lagged relations between two constructs, taking into account the principle that causes take time to exert their effects. Bidirectional relations were specified between constructs at the first moment in time. Before a full model comprising all variables was set up, a submodel was tested in which the relations among the components of oral language proficiency were specified This was also done for the relations among decoding and reading comprehension. The data of the Dutch children was analyzed first, after which a multi-sample analysis was conducted to examine whether the best fitting model also fitted the data of the minority children. The final structural models of these analysis were taken as input to test the combined influence of oral proficiency, reading comprehension and decoding skills in a model comprising all variables. The final solutions of these last mentioned models are presented in this section.

*Dutch children*

The best fitting structural model of the Dutch children is depicted in Figure 1. The fit of the model is reasonable: $\chi^2(426)= 728.99$, p=.000, GFI=.77, AGFI=.72, SRMR=.07.

The circles in Figure 1 represent the latent variables. The structural model is displayed by the paths linking the latent variables. The values indicate path coefficients belonging to these relationships, which are standardized partial regression coefficients.

Strong longitudinal relations were found for decoding, lexical knowledge and morpho-syntactic knowledge. For reading comprehension the longitudinal relation was moderate and for oral text comprehension it was low. Furthermore, reading comprehension at the end of grade 3 was directly influenced by oral text comprehension, and indirectly -mediated through oral text comprehension- by morpho-syntactic knowledge. A small effect of decoding skill was found as well. At the end of the third grade 85% of the variance is explained by these factors. At the end of the fourth grade, no direct influence of decoding was found anymore, whereas also a direct relation from oral text comprehension was not significant. However, both morpho-syntactic knowledge and lexical knowledge turned out to have a direct effect on reading comprehension at this moment in time. The percentage of explained variance is high: 93%.

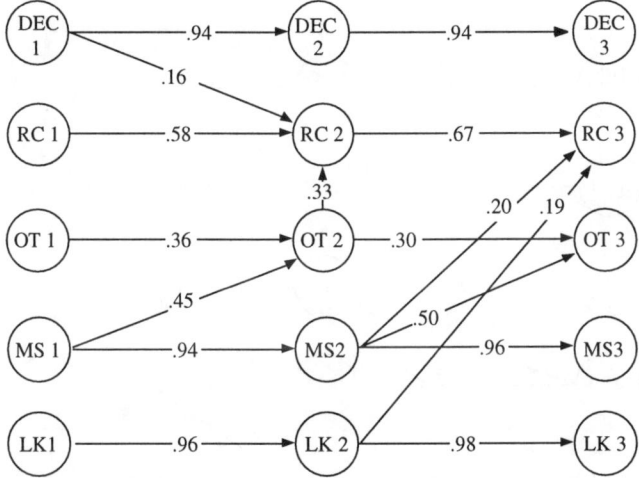

Fig. 1. Path diagram of the structural model specifying the relation between Lexical Knowledge (LK), Morpho-syntactic Knowledge (MS) and Oral Text Comprehension (OT), Reading comprehension (RC) and Decoding (DEC) of the Dutch children at the begin of the third grade (1), the end of the third grade (2) and at the end of the fourth grade (3).

## Ethnic minority children

The final model of the ethnic minority children is presented in Figure 2. The fit of the multi-sample analysis was reasonable: $\chi^2(850)=$ 1327.21, p=000, GFI=.78, SRMR=.06. Figure 2 shows that the longitudinal relations for most constructs are strong. For reading comprehension the relation is moderate and for oral text comprehension it is low. Beside the autoregressive effect, reading comprehension at the end of grade 3 is directly influenced by both decoding skills and oral text comprehension, while lexical knowledge and morpho-syntactic knowledge appeared to have an indirect effect through oral text comprehension. At the end of grade 3 these factors together explain 83% of the variance. At the end of the fourth grade there is no longer a direct influence of decoding. Beside the autoregressive effect and the effect of oral text comprehension, lexical knowledge also directly influences reading comprehension. An indirect effect of morpho-syntactic knowledge (and lexical knowledge) was found mediated through oral text comprehension. The percentage of explained variance is again 83%. Moreover, the model shows that lexical knowledge, besides morpho-syntactic knowledge, seems to be a critical factor in the explanation of oral text comprehension development.

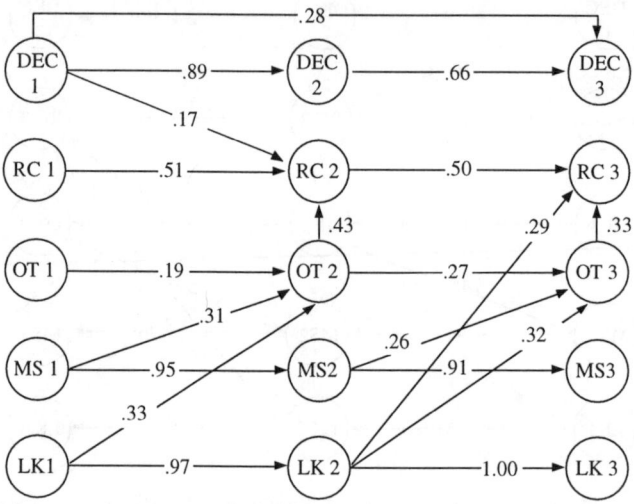

Fig. 2. Path diagram of the structural model specifying the relation between Lexical Knowledge (LK), Morpho-syntactic Knowledge (MS) and Oral Text Comprehension (OT), Reading comprehension (RC) and Decoding (DEC) of the ethnic minority children at the begin of the third grade (1), the end of the third grade (2) and at the end of the fourth grade (3).

## CONCLUSIONS AND DISCUSSION

Several conclusions can be drawn from the study. The analysis of the test results provides evidence that Turkish and Moroccan children, learning to read Dutch as a second language, are equally or even more efficient in word decoding, but less efficient in reading comprehension than their monolingual Dutch low SES peers. On three standardized reading comprehension tests the ethnic minority children showed a substantially lower level of achievement than the Dutch children. Given the fact that the ethnic minority students also lag behind their Dutch peers in the acquisition of oral Dutch, and show a slower development of lexical knowledge over time, it can tentatively be concluded that the differences in reading comprehension scores between first and second language learners are due to differences in knowledge of the target language.

Additionally, the study confirmed differences in language proficiency between high and low SES children. It can also be concluded that the Turkish children lag behind the Moroccan children. Their more frequent contact with Dutch might be the explanation for their higher proficiency in Dutch. These results are confirmed by Aarts et al. (1993) who found that at the end of primary school Turkish children were more focused on their home language and culture than were Moroccan children.

The componential analysis of oral language proficiency shows that for the second language learners lexical knowledge, and to a lesser degree morpho-syntactic knowledge turn out to be of crucial importance in explaining differences in oral text comprehension.

The componential analysis of reading comprehension shows that for both first and second language learners the development of reading comprehension tends to be more influenced by top-down, comprehension-based influences than by bottom-up processes of word decoding. This can be explained by the fact that in the course of the third grade decoding processes tend to get more or less automatized. However, for the ethnic minority children the development of reading comprehension is to a much higher degree influenced by the proficiency of oral Dutch than is the case for Dutch children. The larger influential role of top-down processes in second language reading can be explained from the fact that their lower level of Dutch oral proficiency becomes a more critical factor in reading comprehension than is the case in mother tongue reading. Moreover, for the group of second language learners a stronger effect from lower to higher linguistic skills is also evidenced. This result shows that the children's oral text comprehension in Dutch is highly influenced by their knowledge of lexical items and syntactic rules of the target language Dutch.

Practical implications for the educational field can be drawn from the study. The important role of oral language proficiency which was found in the componential models suggest that development of oral language proficiency in Dutch, and especially vocabulary knowledge should be stimulated in Kindergarten and the early years of primary school. Interactive story book reading in small groups has proven to be a good method in the education of second language learners in Kindergarten (Morrow, 1992). In reading education, activation of both linguistic knowledge and relevant conceptual knowledge in a thematically organized curriculum is considered to be extremely relevant. Prereading activities such as discussing the content and structure of a story, or explaining hard lexical items can be recommended to help children to develop or activate schemata relevant to their reading materials.

## REFERENCES

Aarts, R., De Ruiter, J. J., & Verhoeven, L. (1993). *Tweetaligheid en schoolsucces.* Studies in Meertaligheid 4. Tilburg: Tilburg University Press.
Extra, G., & Verhoeven, L. (Eds.). (1994). *Community languages in the Netherlands.* Lisse: Swets & Zeitlinger.
Harris, R. J. (Ed.) (1992). *Cognitive processing in bilinguals.* Amsterdam: Elsevier.
Koda, K. (1994). Second language reading research: Problems and possibilities. *Applied Psycholinguistics, 15,* 1–28.
Morrow, L. M. (1992). The impact of a literature-based program on literacy achievement, use of literature, and attitudes of children from minority backgrounds. *Reading Research Quarterly, 27,* 250–275.
Verhoeven, L. (1990). Acquisition of reading in Dutch as a second language. *Reading Research Quarterly, 25,* 90–114.
Verhoeven, L. (1994). Linguistic diversity and literacy development. In L. Verhoeven (Ed.), *Functional literacy: Theoretical issues and educational implications* (pp. 199-220). Amsterdam/Philadelphia: Benjamins.
Weber, R. (1991). Linguistic diversity and reading in American society. In R. Barr, M. L. Kamil, P. Mosenthal & P. D. Pearson. (Eds.), *Handbook of Reading Research* (pp. 97–119). New York: Longman

# PART 3

# TRAINING METALINGUISTIC AWARENESS

LEENA LAURINEN

# FOSTERING METALINGUISTIC AWARENESS DURING STORYBOOK READING

It is generally accepted that reading storybooks to young children improves their linguistic and literacy development. Read-aloud events involve social interaction between the adult reader and the child. According to Vygotsky (1978) children acquire higher mental functions by internalizing social relationships. In jointly processing the contents of a book, both the reader and the child are searching for meanings and messages on the pages. Reading is thus seen as a problem-solving process, the purpose of which is the search for meaning (see Clay, 1991, p. 14). When interacting repeatedly with storybooks and other written materials such as advertisements, street signs, and labels on food packaging, children go through a long and gradual process of becoming literate. In fact, literacy emerges for every child who lives in a culture with a rich tradition of written and spoken language (Teale & Sulzby, 1986). This notion has given the name to this approach: the study of emergent literacy, which can be further divided into emergent reading and writing.

Early storybook reading has mostly been studied from the point of view of school. Reading aloud to young children has been seen primarily as a way of improving their reading readiness and their later achievement at school (Morrow, 1983; Scarborough, Dobrich, & Hager, 1991; Teale, 1984; Wells 1985, 1986). Instead of asking whether early experiences of storybook reading promote the development of literacy in children, it might be most useful to ask how children proceed in their development when they get and share reading experiences.

Observation of children as readers when they cannot actually yet read, enables new insights to be gained into the relationship between reading development and metalinguistic awareness. Metalinguistic development consists of the following aspects of reading: *pragmatic awareness*, dealing with the meaning and functional use of written language, *word awareness*, that is the conception of words as meaningful units of language, and *phonological awareness*, concerning knowledge about the constituent sounds of words, such as syllables, onsets, rhymes, and phonemes.

From the point of view of teaching reading, it is useful try to find out properties which could foster incidental learning of metalinguistic awareness from interactive and informal reading situations. In informal reading situations adults usually adapt their behaviour to the children's needs, comments and questions. When the reader and the child spend plenty of time together, the adult reader is more willing to adjust her/his response according to the level of the child's development (Ninio & Bruner, 1978; Pellegrini & Galda, 1990).

In interactive reading situations perhaps the most prominent feature is that children like listening to stories and discussing them. Some children even attempt to "read" their story books to their parents and dolls long before they can actually read. Opportunities for "pretend reading" or "pseudoreading" represent an important step in the early acquisition of literacy of young children, especially if responsive and more competent adults are interested in taking advantage of them (Gallimore & Goldenberg, 1993). By participating in literacy practices such as situations around storybooks and pseudoreading, children acquire the forms of written language simultaneously with their search for the meaning of the text. It is thus reasonable to speak about the acquisition of literacy instead of the teaching of it.

In this study the acquisition of literacy in interactive storybook reading situations is approached from the point of view of metalinguistic development. Opportunities for metalinguistic development are revealed when reading is seen as a questioning and problem-solving process among the participants of a reading group. But when the purpose of reading is achieved and the meaning of the text has been constructed, the text itself can create new questions and problems. At this point, reading activities in particular can provide incentives for cognitive development in general.

The present study deals with the question of how children learn to elaborate their metalinguistic awareness during interactive storybook reading. Following a longitudinal design the storybook reading interaction of three Finnish children in private day-care is described and analysed. An attempt will be made to evaluate the nature of verbal interactions during the storybook reading from a qualitative point of view. This will be done both by classifying the initiating statements of discussions according to their relation to the texts, pictures or other properties of the storybooks and by analyzing the contents of discussions.

## METHOD

### Participants

Three monolingual Finnish boys, Sami, Anssi and Teemu, took part in this study. They all went to the same private home for daycare. At the beginning of the study Sami was 3 years and 2 months, Anssi 3 years and 10 months, and Teemu 5 years and 4 months old. Anssi and Teemu are brothers.

According to Sami's mother, Sami has about 30 books of his own, and books have been read to him each day for at least half an hour. Sami relates to himself and to his teddy bear what happens in his books. Sometimes he repeats literally phrases from the books such as "you're an old scrap heap" and "I'm in an excessively bad temper".

Anssi and Teemu have about 30 storybooks in their home and they visit the local library once a week. Books are read to the boys four days a week from half an hour to one hour. According to their mother, Teemu is able to save his questions and comments until the end of the book because he has been taught not to interrupt. The younger boy, Anssi, has not yet learnt to sit quietly and he often makes observations and comments during the reading. Sometimes Teemu uses words he has learnt from the books like "idler" and "foolhardy", whereas his mother has not yet noticed Anssi borrowing any words from the books.

At the beginning of the study all the boys were in the second stage of emergent reading when their pseudoreading of two storybooks was assessed by applying the classification scheme developed by Sulzby (1985). In this stage the independent reading attempts are picture-governed, the story is not formed between the pages of the books, and the child is able to follow the actions of the characters illustrated in the pictures in addition to only labeling and commenting on the things they see.

Emergent reading was also assessed by counting the number of structural elements the boys were able to recall from the two storybooks (cf. Morrow, 1985; Morrow & Smith, 1990). All the boys were able to recall the main properties of the settings of the stories and some plot episodes, and the order of the plot episodes was partially correct. Out of a maximum recall score of 11 Sami was scored 3.8, Anssi 3.6, and Teemu 4.2.

*Data collection*

The study lasted six months. Two university students visited the daycare home once a week. They read storybooks to the boys in turn. While one student was reading the other operated a tape recorder and tried to keep the situation as calm as possible. The caretaker herself was not present during the reading situations. The tapes were transcribed the same day as the recording.

The total number of recorded reading situations was 27. After measuring the level of emergent reading at the beginning of the study by using the favourite book of each boy and the book "Dragons do not exist" the reading situations were continued once a week. A new book was included in the reading visit each time, except during the last two weeks when only the favourite books and Dragons were reread. Altogether 23 different books were read. The length of the books varied from 17 to 32 pages, and from 2 to 15 sentences per page. Each book contained a coherent story which continued on successive pages. There was a picture on each page or double page. In the reading situations all three boys heard the books together 11 times (8 of which were tape recorded), two boys heard 7 story books together, and 12 of the book reading situations were shared by only one boy and the reader.

*Data analysis*

The verbal interaction between the three boys and the reader was analyzed by applying the insertion categories of Phillips and McNaughton (1990). In analysing the interaction, the focus was on any verbalization that constituted an insertion into or interruption of the reading. Such insertions which thus were not part of the actual text included questions, comments, statements, explanations and exclamations. The insertion categories were as follows:

*Narrative-related insertions*, which focus on information relevant to the events and goals of narratives, being further divided into:

- *clarifications,* which are attempts to clarify the narrative segment being read by paraphrasing, defining, illustrating or referring to personal experiences;

- *integrations*, in which the immediate narrative segment is joined to sections already read, and

- *anticipations*, which connect the immediate narrative segment to things or events that could conceivably follow.

*Print-and-Reading-related insertions*, which focus on concepts about print by referring to the activity of reading itself, such as attributes of the book and the print, references to letters, words and pages, and indications to read further by pointing to a certain place in a page.

*Other-book-related insertions*, which comment on all kinds of things which are neither related to narratives nor printing or reading; for example, personal responses to the pictures or to the text, discussion of attributes of characters, the counting of objects and the naming of animals.

In addition to these types of intrusions, an extra category was needed for *book-unrelated insertions*. A child may, for example, interrupt the reading for a while by starting some other activity, or the discussion may proceed to things far outside the contents of the book.

In Phillips and McNaughton (1990) the main distinction is between narrative-related and other-book related insertions. In the present study narrative-related insertions were divided into *text-based* and *picture-based insertions*. The latter completed narrative texts with elements presented only in pictures. The distinction was made because from the point of view of developing literacy it is important to concentrate on the text rather than pictures, or at least to pay attention mainly to the parts of the pictures relevant to the story. Furthermore, recognizing such details or facts from pictures that are related to the written information indicates that the story is being attended to.

The number of insertions in the different content categories was calculated separately for each boy and the reader. The insertions were coded according to the individual who had interrupted the reading and initiated the discussion. For this reason the two terms insertion and initiation are used interchangeably in this study. The measure of the length of discussions was the number of speech turns which belonged to the same series of exchanges (Sinclair & Coulthard, 1975). Speech acts other than initiations were not analyzed.

RESULTS

*Quantitative data*

During the 27 interactive reading situations the total number of insertions was 383, of which the boys contributed 64.5%. Thus the boys were fairly active participants in the reading situations.

The mean number of Sami's insertions during one reading situation was 3.6 (range 0–9). Sami often wanted to repeat some parts of the text after the reader. He also made comments on the characters in the stories, concentrated on the pictures and on the most exciting points in the narratives.

Anssi concentrated carefully on the pictures, he often wanted to check how things mentioned in the text were illustrated in them. Anssi made an average of 8.4 insertions, and his initiating activity varied from 1 to 17 between the reading situations.

Teemu did not usually interrupt the reading and produced 2.4 insertions on average (range 0–7). He often asked the reader to continue her reading when the smaller boys were talking about things unrelated to the story in question. Teemu liked to enumerate things that were either mentioned in the texts or presented in the pictures. He also liked to check whether the number of animals or other things was exactly the same in the pictures as in the text.

In some cases an insertion initiated a rather long discussion between the participants in the reading situation. The discussions were classified into four categories according to length. Discussion length was estimated by calculating the number of speech turns. The proportion of short discussions, which included only 3 speech turns at most, was 40.6%. This percentage is quite low, however, if we consider the fact that most of the teacher centered discussions during school lessons do not exceed this length (Stubbs, 1983).

When the discussions during the first and the last month of the study were compared, it was observed that the mean number of short discussions (which included 1–8 speech turns) decreased from 11.5 to 5.5 (means calculated to all groups irrespective of size), whereas the mean number of long discussions (including 9-50 turns) increased from 2 to 8.5.This difference was statistically significant ($\chi^2 = 6.15$, df=1, p<0.05). The boys were eager to make comments and ask questions right from the beginning of the study. During the first reading situations they were also willing to answer the reader's questions, although she had often to clarify them first. The first interactive discussions were very fragmentary compared to the last reading situations. For example, when Anssi asked questions at the beginning of the study, his big brother often had to elaborate the reader's answers. Sami put his questions directly to the reader and did not participate in the discussions held by the other boys. That was not the case at the end of the study.

*Nature of insertions*

Both the narrative texts and the pictures seemed to yield plenty of incentives for discussion. Most of the insertions (73.9%) were related to the narratives of the storybooks. The proportion of book-related insertions which were not related to the narratives was 13.6%. Only 6.0% of the insertions were unrelated to the books. The percentage of the print-and-reading-related insertions was 3.1%, and the remaining 3.3% of insertions were inaudible on the tape.

The distribution of the insertions in the different content categories is presented in Figure 1. Each column represents one individual. As there was only one adult in each reading situation the initiations of the two adults are combined. The height of each column illustrates the mean number of insertions made by that individual in one reading situation. The black section at the base of each column shows the proportion of text-based narrative-related insertions. Hence during one reading situation Sami made about 0.8, Anssi about 1.8, Teemu about 0.6, and the reader about 2.5 insertions of this sort. The next section of each column represents the number of picture-based narrative-related insertions. Most of the insertions belonged in this category. In particular, the boys responded to the things they saw in the storybooks, but the reader, too, utilized the pictures when she initiated the discussion. The proportion of print-and-reading-related insertions was rather low in this study. The reader made most of the insertions of this sort, Sami made none. All the boys made some insertions which were not related to the book at all. The proportion of book-unrelated insertions was small, however. The reader did not interrupt her reading with insertions of this sort.

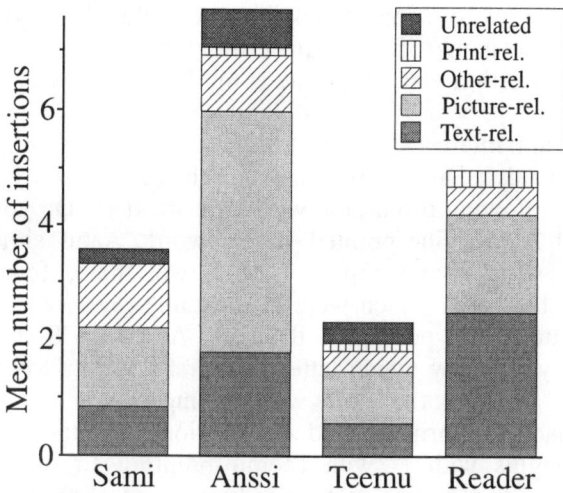

Fig. 1. Mean numbers of the insertions made by each boy and the reader in the different content categories. The categories are text-based narrative-related, picture-based narrative-related, other-book-related, print-and-reading-related and book-unrelated insertions.

The narrative-related insertions were further divided into clarifications, anticipations and integrations. The proportion of clarifications (84.1%, n=238) was rather high. The following discussion gives two examples of these. Sami's clarification is a definition, whereas Teemu gives a super-ordinate concept.

After reading the text, "there was a sign which said.....", the reader turns to Teemu. Teemu: "Nature preserve". Sami: "So that hunters and nasty dogs can't come, or else a police man will come and punish them". (The words on the sing were 'hunting forbidden').

The proportion of the anticipations and integrations was 15.9% (45 in total), and the boys made only 9 of them. Eight of these nine were integrations. Teemu, for example, noticed that the same action was performed repeatedly in one story. He verbalized his observation by saying "The same story twice".

Print-and-reading-related insertions were rarely made in this study. Sami was not aware that reading is based wholly on the text and not on the pictures. Teemu, on the other hand, was aware that a text is necessary for reading. The reader asked Sami at the end of the study, "Sami, show me the place where the reading happens in this double page!" When Sami pointed to one part of the picture Teemu immediately corrected his response by pointing to the text.

Anssi probably knew that reading is based on the text. He made two print-related insertions in total. At the beginning of the study he pointed to the word kana (chicken) and said, "It says Pesonen." Pesonen was the name of the main character of the story. The other print-related insertion was "That one is my letter!" On this occasion he was right.

Sami was not interested in print, either at the beginning or at the end of the study. During the last month of the study the reader initiated the following discussion with him: Reader: "Do you know the first letter of Aatu?" She pointed to the word "Aatu" simultaneously with her question. Sami replied, "one, two, three, four, five", by counting all the words which were in the same row. Reader: "Do You know that letter?" She pointed to the letter A. Sami: "Six!" Reader: "It is an A. Do you know which letter is yours?" Sami: "My name starts with A, S, A." He drew the letters with his fingers.

Teemu made two print-related observations in total. The first one was, "This begins with T" with Teemu pointing to the word Terve (Hello).The other insertion was an indication of phonological awareness. Teemu: "I'll show you where to read Mister OTSO. Look here, and here, too!" He pointed to the wrong words. Reader: "Could it be that it is printed only once on this page?" She pointed to the right word. Teemu: "Only once? But Mister OTSO could be made easily from these two words." He then pointed to the words ULOS and JOPA.

In the middle of the study the following discussion revealed that Teemu was able to recognize some parts of the text. This time the discussion was initiated by the reader after she had read the following words: "He could not even dream how LARGE the sea was." Reader: "Where is the word SUURI (LARGE)?" Teemu looked at the text for a while and pointed to the right word. Reader: "Very good, Teemu! I asked you because it is written in big letters." Teemu: "I know because I always take the first letter from the word." Reader: "That's a good idea." Teemu: "Look, sshh, then look, S." Reader: 'Oh, You take the first sound of the word.'

*Contents of discussions*

The actual interactive discussions and some of the pseudoreading attempts provided a better view of the developmental effects of the reading situations than the quantitative data. For example, when the Dragon book was read to Anssi at the beginning of the study, he interpreted the pictures without taking the story into account. To him the different sizes of the growing dragon meant different dragons: the mother, the father, and the child dragon. A half year later his responses were more adequate. When he was asked what happened to the dragon Anssi replied "it got smaller and smaller and then it got the size of a cat". This development could be considered as the first indication of pragmatic awareness or at least as a prerequisite for it.

In the reading situations the youngest boys in particular benefited from Teemu's comments and questions. Even the repetition of the words Teemu uttered provided effective practice for the small boys, given that the acquisition of vocabulary is largely based on repetition.

During the reading of his favourite book, Sami loved to play with words. That was not the case with books which he was not familiar with. The following example illustrates one type of word play which probably fosters the development of word awareness. Reader: "The fireworks are quite impossible." Sami: "Quite impossible, oh, quite impossible. Those chickens have played a possible trick because the other chicken does not speak."

In addition to words, the language of the storybooks provided the boys with plenty of new compounds and other verbal expressions. In the following example, Sami is pseudoreading the first page of his favourite book. He knew the page almost by heart. Had he continued in the same way, his reading attempt would have been classified as the seventh stage of emergent reading - reading a story verbatim-like. The growing awareness of the written form of the language is reflected in the manner in which Sami "reads" the phrases 'at the kitchen table' and 'in the wink of an eye'. Sami was, however, only at the second stage of emergent reading, but the well known and beloved page provided him with an occasion to practise a new verbal expression in a way which was far ahead of his usual cognitive operations with books.

| TEXT | SAMI'S READING ATTEMPT |
|---|---|
| It was autumn. Mr Pesonen was sitting at the kitchen table and drinking coffee in the morning. He sat there without saying a word and stared gloomily at the wet gray yard outside the window. | It was autumn. Mr Pesonen was sitting *at the kitchen* and drinking coffee in the morning. |
| Stripey Cat, instead, was more alert. He could not stay still at all. In the wink of an eye he jumped on the table and back down to the floor. | Stripey Cat, instead, was alert. He could not stay still at all. *In the wink of a cake....* Oh, it was in the wink of an eye, and not in the wink of a cake, did I make a little mistake? |

Group discussions and activities with books can be real incentives for cognitive development. Teemu was interested in exercising his memory by repeated efforts to memorize all the details which were mentioned in the texts. Animals, Christmas presents, the names of minor characters and the details in the pictures served this purpose well. In the following discussion, Teemu imagines a hypothetical problem and gives a creative solution to it. Reader (reading): "The witch gave a frozen sausage to the boy. Now the boy could change himself into a camel for a couple of hours simply by eating the magic sausage." Anssi: "It has to go to the zoo." Teemu: "What would happen if the boy eats only half the sausage?" Reader: "It's difficult to say, what do you think?" Teemu: "He would turn into half a camel." Anssi's elaboration is typical for children of his age (see Laurinen, 1985). He puts a new thing, a camel in this case, into its familiar context. Animals belong in a zoo, in spite of the fact that the plot of the story has nothing to do with a zoo.

An other example of Teemu's thinking is the following problem based on a careful observation of the picture. In the story Jason is going to get a lot of Christmas presents. The list of presents is presented in the text. The boys start guessing which presents belong to which parcels. Teemu interrupts the game and asks: "Are those two shoes similar?" Reader: "Oh, they seem to be slightly different in colour, but I'm not sure." Teemu: "Look! The lantern is shining on only one shoe." Reader: "Oh yes, the other one's in shadow. That explains the difference in colour."

The final example illustrates the first phase of the mechanism through which the sense of numeracy, the first necessary condition for calculation, is acquired. In the story a little man meets a philosopher, who has six sheep in his company. While Teemu counted the sheep aloud by pointing to each one in turn, Sami started to imitate Teemu by counting, "One three six two nine ten eight nine ten!" He simultaneously moved his forefinger from sheep to sheep occasionally pointing to the same sheep more than once. However, Sami seems to have recognized that only certain words are used for counting. Note that he did not include any letters in his list. Here, Teemu was working in Sami's *area of proximal development* (see Vygotsky, 1962). When Teemu consolidated his own learning by practising with details of pictures and narratives, he provided Sami at the same time with the possibility to discover the idea of counting.

## DISCUSSION

Each child seemed to use the storybooks in a manner that was most appropriate to his developmental state. The youngest boys were eager to repeat words and phrases immediately after they had been read or used as a replay to somebody's question. This is consistent with the earlier evidence that young children's vocabularies grow from listening to storybooks (Robbins & Ehri, 1994). In addition to vocabulary learning, the oldest boy tried to discover both some ideas about the Finnish writing system and some concrete operations by which the physical world becomes more comprehensible. The most prominent feature of his behavior was learning by discovery, irrespective of whether he was trying to find a certain word from the text or whether he was interested in the effect of a light on the colour of a shoe.

In this study the proportion of print-and-reading related insertions was low as compared to the insertions focusing on the meaning of the text. This result is consistent with Phillips and McNaughton (1990). This could be interpreted as an indication of well developed pragmatic awareness. However, the small number of print-and-reading related insertions have an important role in discovering the principles of the alphabetic writing system, which is fundamental in learning how to read (see Perfetti & Zhang, 1996, p. 40). When the oldest child in this study was trying to identify the word OTSO and confused it with the words ULOS and JOPA, he was spontaneously taking his first steps in an independent reading skill. He seemed to be in the first phase of the development of word-reading processes, in the visual cue phase, because he is trying to memorize visual or graphic features of words in order to remember how to read them (Ehri, 1994). In the second example in which he is able to identify the word SUURI by taking the first letter of the word, he is approaching the rudimentary alphabetic phase (Ehri, 1994). In this phase only some of the letters in printed words are processed. However, the child is looking for real words from the text. This suggests that he has well developed word awareness for spoken language but not for written words. These findings support the models in which the code for phonological representation in written text is discovered under the guidance of word awareness in spoken language prior to the identification of printed words.

Though phonological awareness is fundamental to an independent reading skill, children's basic literacy will probably not develop into functional literacy if they do not figure out that the purpose of reading is the search for meaning, and that the meaning they get from the text has some personal use and value for them. The examples of vivid discussions around the storybooks in this study indicate that both the children and the readers have enjoyed the reading sessions. Purcell-Gates (1996) has shown that in families where literate members read and wrote complex texts for their own entertainment, children knew more about the alphabetic principle and the specific forms of written language than in families where only simple texts were read. Moreover, Purcell-Gates emphasizes that children ought to attend to and personally experience many uses of written language. The children in this study got personal experiences from the reading situations especially when they created and solved cognitive problems. Their conversations indicate that the joined storybook reading is perhaps the best quarantee of learning how to enjoy reading.

The interactive reading situations provide incentives for discovery learning, especially if children are encouraged to interrupt the reading with their own observations and interpretations. In this study the reading groups in a private daycare home were small enough to allow each child to take an active role. This is not necessarily the case when storybooks are read to children in daycare centers. For example, Hurley (1992) found that in a daycare center the vast majority of interactions during storybook reading were caretaker initiated, and children participated in the reading by listening, looking at pictures and responding to literal-level questions.

The beliefs and reading habits of adult readers have also an effect on children's opportunities to discover and learn new things from storybooks. For example, some mothers tend to control the reading situation by establishing the purposes and expectations for story reading in such a way that their children's initiatives are extinguished (Neuman, 1995). Edwards (1995) reports that most of the parents who had been told to read storybooks to their children appeared not to know that they could stop before finishing the book. Even one of the boys in this study was taught to sit quiet during reading because his mother believed that the child will need that skill later at school. Fortunately, the truly interactive storybook reading behavior can be taught to parents and caretakers who are not familiar with it (Edwards & Garcia, 1994; Neuman, 1995; Whitehurst et al, 1994).

The qualitative analysis of the insertions and discussions which could foster the development of metalinguistic awareness is an alternative method for the experimental research in which different tests are used for measuring metalinguistic skills. Though the results of this study are only descriptive and hard to generalize, they demonstrate the complexity of verbal interaction during reading situations. Moreover, when the reading situations did not follow any strict plans, children's perspective's to the reading and to the contents of storybooks were revealed. When there was no formal goal to teach children in any way, the children got many possibilities to discover independently both some principles of reading and some properties of written stories.

In this study insertions were classified according to their relation to the book. In future studies other speech turns than initiations should be analyzed. Both a conversation analysis of speech turns and a functional analysis of speech acts and speaking strategies could shed more light on the nature of verbal interaction of small reading groups. Furthermore, the learning strategies through which children try to discover the alphabetic principles of their language when they participate in informal reading situations should be studied by using a longitudinal design in which the same children would be followed until they really learn to read.

REFERENCES

Clay, M. M (1991). *Becoming literate. The construction of inner control.* Portsmouth, NH: Heinemann.

Edwards, P. A. (1995). Combining parents' and teachers' thoughts about storybook reading at home and school. In L. M. Morrow (Ed.), *Family literacy connections in schools and communities* (pp. 54–69). Newark, DE: International Reading Association.

Edwards, P. A., & Garcia, G. E. (1994). The implications of Vygotskian theory for the development of home-school programs. A focus on storybook reading. In V. John-Steiner, C. P. Panofsky & L. W. Smith (Eds.), *Sociocultural approaches to language and literacy* (pp. 243–264). Cambridge, UK: Cambridge University Press.

Ehri, L. C. (1994). Development of the ability to read words: Update. In R. Ruddell, M. Ruddell, & H. Singer (Eds.), *Theoretical models and processes of reading* (4th ed., pp. 383–417). Newark, DE: International Reading Association.

Gallimore, R., & Goldenberg, C. (1993). Activity settings of early literacy: Home and school factors in children's emergent literacy. In E. Forman, N. Minick & C. A. Stone (Eds.), Contexts for learning. *Sociocultural dynamics in children's development* (pp. 315–335). New York, Oxford: Oxford University Press.

Hurley, F. K. (1992). Story reading in daycare: A help or hindrance? In N. D. Padak, T. V. Rasinski, & J. Logan (Eds.), *Literacy research and practice: Foundation for the year 2000* (pp. 17–25). Provo, UT: College Reading Association.

Laurinen, L. I. (1985). *Sentence elaboration and language understanding.* Helsinki, Finland: University of Helsinki, General Psychology Monographs, No. B6.

Morrow, L. M. (1983). Home and school correlates of early interest in literature. *Journal of Educational Research, 76,* 221–230.

Morrow, L. M. (1985). Retelling stories: Strategies for improving children's comprehension, concept of story structure, and oral language complexity. *Elementary School Journal, 85,* 647–661.

Morrow, L. M., & Smith, J. K. (1990). The effects of group size on interactive story bookreading. Reading Research Quarterly, 25, 213–231.

Neuman, S. B. (1995). Enchanging adolescent mothers' guided participation in literacy. In L. M. Morrow (Ed.), *Family literacy connections in schools and communities* (pp. 104–114). Newark, DE: International Reading Association.

Ninio, A., & Bruner, J. (1978). The achievement and antecedents of labeling. *Journal of Child Language, 5,* 1–15.

Pellegrini, A. D., & Galda, L. (1990). The joint construction of stories by preschool children and an experimenter. In B. K. Britton & A. D. Pellegrini (Eds.), *Narrative thought and narrative language* (pp. 113–130). NJ: Erlbaum.

Perfetti, C. A., & Zhang, S. (1996). What does it mean to learn to read. In M. F. Graves, P. van den Broek & B. M. Taylor (Eds.), *The first R: Every child's right to read* (pp. 37–61). Newark, DE: International Reading Association.

Phillips, G., & McNaughton, S. (1990). The practice of storybook reading to preschoolers in mainstream New Zealand families. *Reading Research Quarterly, 25,* 198–212.

Purcell-Gates, V. (1996). Stories, coupons and the TV guide: Relationships between home literacy experiences and emergent literacy knowledge. *Reading Research Quarterly, 31*, 406-428.
Robbins, C., & Ehri, L. C. (1994). Reading storybooks to kindergartners helps them learn new vocabulary words. *Journal of Educational Psychology, 86*, 54–64.
Scarborough, H. S., Dobrich, W., & Hager, M. (1991). Preschool literacy experience and later reading achievement. *Journal of learning Disabilities, 24*, 508–511.
Sinclair, J., & Coulthart, M. (1975). *Towards of an analysis of discourse.* London: Oxford University Press.
Stubbs, M. (1983). *Language, schools, and classrooms. Contemporary sociology of the school.* New York: Methuen.
Sulzby, E. (1985). Children's emergent reading of favorite storybooks: A developmental study. *Reading Research Quarterly, 20*, 458–481.
Teale, W. H. (1984). Reading to young children. Its significance for literary development. In H. Coleman, A. Oberg & F. Smith (Eds.), *Awakening to literacy* (pp. 110–121). Portsmouth, NH: Heinemann.
Teale, W. H., & Sulzby, E. (Eds.). (1986). *Emergent literacy: Writing and reading.* Norwood, NJ: Ablex.
Wells, G. (1985). Preschool literacy related activities and success in school. In D. Olson, N. Torrance, & A. Hilyard (Eds.), *Literacy, language, and learning* (pp. 229–255). Cambridge, MA: Harvard University Press.
Wells, G. (1986). *The meaning makers: Children learning language and using language to learn.* Portsmouth, NH: Heinemann.
Whitehurst, G. J., Epstein, J. N., Angell, A. L., Payne, A. C., Crone, D. A., & Fischel, J. E. (1994). Outcomes of an emergent literacy intervention in Head Start. *Journal of Educational Psychology, 86*, 542–555.
Vygotsky, L. S. (1962). *Thought and language.* Cambridge, MA: MIT Press.
Vygotsky, L. S. (1978). *Mind in society: The development of higher psychological processes.* Cambridge, MA: Harvard University Press.

ELLEN ROTH AND WOLFGANG SCHNEIDER

# TRAINING OF PHONOLOGICAL AWARENESS AND LETTER KNOWLEDGE IN CHILDREN-AT-RISK

Research on the acquisition of literacy conducted in the last few years has indicated that phonological awareness without a doubt plays an important role in the acquisition of reading and spelling. (e.g., Goswami & Bryant, 1990; Lundberg, Frost, & Petersen, 1988; Tornéus, 1984; Wagner & Torgesen, 1987). Phonological awareness involves the ability to segment speech into linguistic units such as syllables or phonemes. Available studies propose that it is important for the beginning reader to get insight into the sound structure of language in order to acquire the alphabetic principle.

Several longitudinal training studies have shown that phonological competencies can be taught successfully and that children's subsequent reading and spelling performance can be enhanced (e.g., Lundberg, Frost, & Peterson, 1988; Schneider, Visé, Reimers, & Blaesser, 1994). However, when one analyzes the results of this kind of literacy research closely, one easily realizes that the most impressive findings have been registered in intervention studies where children received a combined training program that emphasized the integration of phonological skills with letter knowledge (Ball & Blachman, 1991; Bradley & Bryant, 1985; Byrne & Fielding-Barnsley, 1989; Cunningham, 1990).

A classic intervention study was carried out by Bradley and Bryant (1985) who examined the effects of a training in sound categorization on reading and spelling performance. Sound categorization required the ability of detecting alliteration and rhyme. Preschool children who were poor at sound categorization participated in the study. There were two experimental conditions: The first group (N=13) was instructed in sound categorization only. The second group (N=13) categorized sounds by using plastic letters additionally in order to make clear the grapheme-phoneme correspondences. Moreover, there were two control groups: one group (N=26) receiving training in conceptual categorization and one group (N=13) without any training at all. Although the sound categorization group and the group with the combined training program performed significantly better in reading and spelling measures than the two control groups in posttests, only the children who received training in sound categorization and instruction in grapheme-phoneme correspondences outperformed all other children of the remaining groups on reading and spelling measures in the long-term analyses (Bradley, 1988).

Similar results were found in the training study of Ball and Blachman (1991), who evaluated the effects of an intervention connecting training in phoneme segmentation with instruction in letter-sound correspondences on kindergarten children's early reading and spelling skills. Preschool children participated in the study and were divided into three groups. The first group received training in segmenting words into phonemes and additionally instruction in letter-sound-correspondences (N=29). The second group was only instructed in correspondences between letter names and letter sounds (N=30). The third (control) group received no intervention (N=30). The training outcomes indicated that phonological awareness training connected with instruction in letter-sound correspondences significantly improved early reading and spelling skills of the preschool children. However, instruction in letter names and letter sounds alone did not significantly improve phonological skills, reading or spelling skills.

From these research findings the conclusion can be drawn that phonological awareness seems to be a necessary but no sufficient condition for reading and spelling acquisition. The knowledge of letter-sound correspondences may also not be sufficient. The most effective way to facilitate and improve children's literacy acquisition may be an integration of phonological training with letter-sound training. As a consequence, Hatcher, Hulme, and Ellis (1994) developed the phonological linkage hypothesis which suggests that an intervention involving a combination of phonological awareness training and letter-sound instruction (or more broadly reading instruction) should be more effective than an intervention involving either phonological awareness training or letter-sound instruction (respectively reading instruction) alone.

Hatcher et al. (1994) evaluated the phonological linkage hypothesis in a longitudinal intervention study. Subjects were 124 poor readers who were at the early stage of reading instruction. There were four groups. Children of the first group received a reading instruction combined with phonological awareness training (N=32), the second group was only instructed in reading (N=31), the third group was only instructed in phonological awareness (N=30), and finally a control group received no specific intervention (N=31). In accordance with the phonological linkage hypothesis, only children who received the combined training program that emphasized the connection between phonological awareness and reading skills significantly outperformed the control children in reading and spelling immediately after the intervention and in the follow-up analysis. These outcomes support the phonological linkage hypothesis. In order to obtain maximally training effects on reading and spelling, a training in phonological awareness ought to be explicitly connected with the teaching in literacy skills.

In the present study an attempt will be made to test the validity of the phonological-linkage hypothesis in the German language by means of a longitudinal training study. The question was whether the training results reported for the English language could be also transferred to the German language. A specific concern of our study was the early intervention for "at risk" children at kindergarten who would probably develop reading and/or spelling disorders in school. Like Hatcher et al. (1994), we chose three teaching conditions and one control condition: (1) training in phonological awareness alone, (2) training in phonological awareness and instruction in letter-sound correspondences, (3) training in letter-sound correspondences alone, and (4) no specific intervention. It is expected that a combination of phonological awareness and letter-sound training is the most effective way to improve literacy acquisition on long-term basis.

## METHOD

*Participants*

Participants in the experimental groups were 208 preliterate kindergartners with an average age of five years and eleven months who were identified as "at risk" children by a revised version of the Bielefeld Screening Battery (Marx, Jansen, Mannhaupt, & Skowronek, 1993). They attended 25 kindergartens in the south-east of Würzburg. The children-at-risk were assigned to one of three teaching conditions: 82 subjects participated in the phonological awareness training, 77 subjects received both training in phonological awareness and in letter-sound correspondences, and finally, 49 subjects were only taught letter-sound-correspondences. In addition, 146 unselected preschool children who attended six kindergartens in the north of Würzburg were recruited for the control group. Because of ethical reasons we decided to choose no "at risk" control sample. Care was taken to ensure that there was no opportunity for the kindergarten teachers of the training groups and the control group to get information about the different training programs and their purposes.

From pre- to posttests we lost a total of 22 subjects. Thus, only 193 of 208 children-at-risk and 139 of 146 control children participated in both pre- and posttests. Whereas nine children moved away from the Würzburg area, five children quit the training programs for various reasons (e.g., because of emotional or behavioural disorders). Eight children could not be posttested, because they were on holiday.

*Instruments*

The main purpose of the *Bielefeld Screening Battery* is the early identification of children-at-risk who will probably develop disorders in reading and spelling acquisition in school. Thus, the screening contains subtests assessing phonological information processing and visual attention skills that are significant for literacy acquisition. The subtests were constructed to produce ceiling effects in the sample in order to discriminate well in the lower third of the distribution (Marx, Jansen, Mannhaupt, & Skowronek, 1993).

Four subtests assessed *phonological awareness*: First, in the *rhyme production* task the child had to produce rhyming pairs finding a word or non-word that sounds similar to a given word (e.g., "What sounds similar to *ball?*"). Second, the *rhyme matching* task required to compare an orally given standard word with four pictorially represented words that are phonological or semantically comparable to the standard word. The child had to detect which pictorially represented word sounds similar to the orally given word. Third, a *syllable segmentation* task was given where the child had to break two-, three- and four-syllabic words into separate syllables by putting plastic coins down to mark each syllable. Fourth, the *phoneme-word matching* task was presented where the child had to decide whether an isolated vowel that was spoken out loud occurred in one of two pictorially and orally given words (e.g., "Can you hear an /a/ in *cake* or in *dog*?) Each subtest consisted of three practice and 12 test items. The number of correct answers was registered.

*Phonetic recoding in working memory* was assessed with the subtest *repeating pseudowords*. The child had to repeat a pseudoword that consisted of three to five syllables (e.g., "ki-blo-sa" or "wut-za-tri-no-was" ). This task tested the precision in articulating unknown words. There were three practice and 12 experimental trials. The number of correct repeated words was registered.

*Speed of access to phonological information* (in the sense of phonological recoding in accessing the semantic lexicon) was administered by subtests 6 and 7, called *rapid naming* of colours. In the first version the child had to name the colours of 24 uncoloured objects (e.g., plum, lemon, tomato, and salad) as quickly as possible. In the second version the objects were drawn in incorrect colours (e.g., a blue lemon) and the child had to name the correct colours of the objects. Both accuracy (number of errors) and speed of naming were registered.

Finally, *visual attention* was administered with the *word matching* task. The child was shown a series of cards (4 practice and 12 experimental trials). On top of each card a four-letter meaningful word (standard) was written and underneath four alternative words were written that corresponded in all, three, two or one letters with the standard word. The child's task was to detect the alternative word that was identical to the standard word. The number of correct answers was registered.

The screening lasted for about 30 minutes and was administered individually in a separate room of the kindergarten. Based on current research literature it was decided to classify children-at-risk as those who scored in the bottom 25% on the Bielefeld Screening Battery.

*Pre- and posttest* measures were conducted individually. The administration of the test took about 40 minutes (including a short break). Both phonological abilities and early literacy were assessed. Most subtests tapping phonological awareness were adopted from the training study by Lundberg et. al. (1988). In the first task, *phoneme blending,* the experimenter pronounced the phonemes of a word in isolation, one phoneme after another. The child's task was to blend the single phonemes and then to select the right word out of four pictures (e.g., "Combine these sounds to a word: /b/-/e/-/d/"). Eight items were presented. In the second task, *phoneme segmentation*, the child had to divide a simple word into the constituent phonemes and to mark each phoneme with a plastic coin (e.g., "What sounds do you hear in the word *car*?"). Pictures representing the words were shown simultaneously in order to reduce memory load. A total of eight items were presented. The third subtest required the *identification and deletion of initial phoneme* in a word. The child was first asked to identify the initial phoneme of the word that was represented in a picture. Then the child had to delete the initial phoneme and had to name the remaining part of the word (e.g., "What is the first sound in the word *man*?", "What word would be left if the first sound /m/ were taken away from the word *man*?"). These tasks also consisted of eight items. Finally, the *sound categorization task* of Bradley and Bryant (1985) that taps the ability to detect rhyme and alliteration was added to the pre- and posttest. Only the endsound and firstsound categorization task was used where the child had to find out which word differs from the others in the end sound or in the first sound (e.g., first sound: Tag, Tat, Tal, *Rad*; end sound: Saum, Baum, *Laut*, Raum). Each task consisted of 10 items.

Two tasks were given to assess *early literacy. Letter knowledge* was assessed by presenting a set of randomly arranged capital letters. The number of letters correctly identified was the dependent variable. A *word reading task* consisting of seven real words and non-words was given to those children who knew at least three letters. The total number of words read correctly was chosen as the dependent variable.

## Training programs

There were three experimental conditions and one control condition:

(1) training in phonological awareness alone, (2) training in phonological awareness and instruction in letter-sound correspondences, (3) training in letter-sound correspondences alone, and (4) no specific intervention. The training period of the phonological group and phonological linkage group was spread over 20 weeks. Exactly the same amount of time was spent for both training programs. The children were trained in groups and received daily training sessions of 10-15 minutes. After 10 weeks of the training period the instruction program in letter-sound correspondences started at the same time in both the phonological linkage group and in the letter-sound training group.

*Training in phonological awareness.* The phonological awareness training program, a translation of Lundberg et al. (1988), was evaluated in preceding intervention studies (Schneider, Visé, Reimers, & Blaesser, 1994; Schneider, Kuespert, Roth, & Visé, 1997). The goal of the training was to give children insight into the phonological structure of language. The program consisted of six metalinguistic exercise units. In the initial stages larger units of speech were presented in order to prepare children for smaller phonological units such as phonemes. The first training unit started with easy *listening games* where the children had to identify different verbal and nonverbal sounds. The second unit included *rhyming games*, using nursery rhymes, short stories for rhyme identification and production. Children had to complete sentences by finding rhyming word pairs, or pictures were presented to which rhyming words should be produced. In the next training periods the children were taught to recognize phonological units like *sentences and words*. Children were taught that a sentence consists of different words, and that words can be combined or divided to produce new words ("Snowman" consists of "snow" and "man"). This was followed by games that were focused on *syllable segmentation and blending.* Children segmented short and long words into syllables by clapping hands, dancing and marching around. Vice versa, they had to blend single syllables to a word, when a robot produced words in a fragmented, syllable-by-syllable mode (e.g., "kin-der-gar-ten").

In the next period, beginning with the 10th week of training, the smallest phonological unit, the phoneme, was introduced. At first the children were taught to identify and manipulate the *initial phoneme.* Children had to pay attention at the beginning of a given word to discriminate the first sound. They also learned that the initial phoneme could be omitted from a word or added to a word, in order to produce a new word with a different meaning. In the last training unit (at the beginning of the 12th week) games and exercises including *phoneme blending and segmentation* were presented. Children listened to a hobgoblin who spoke like a robot saying words phoneme by phoneme. The child's task was to blend the single phonemes into a word. Also, children themselves had to identify the single phonemes in a word by using coloured bricks to mark the different phonemes. Exercises started with simple vowel-consonant and consonant-vowel words and proceeded to more complex words with three and more phonemes.

*Training in phonological awareness and in letter-sound correspondences.* In this training condition, the training in phonological awareness described above was connected with the training in letter-sound correspondences. The instruction program in letter-sound correspondences was based on Ball and Blachman (1991). The children were taught 12 letter-sound correspondences that occur most frequently in the German language (A, E, M, I, O, R, U, S, L, B, T, N).

The letter-sound training program contained two steps. First, the children were told *letter-sound stories* where they had to produce a certain sound that occurs in the world around us and then they had to connect this acoustic sound with the corresponding visual symbol (grapheme-phoneme correspondences). For example, the children imagined a visit at the dentist where they had to articulate the sound "aaa" or children buzzed like a bee does: "sss" and afterwards they got to know the corresponding letter.

In the second step children learned to discriminate the first sound of a word in order to connect the initial sound with the corresponding letter. Picture cards were used to produce *initial sound associations*. Children played games where they had to relate the initial phoneme of a pictorially represented word to the corresponding grapheme, and vice versa (e.g., an apple for the letter *a*, or a moon for the letter *m*).

Children in the phonological linkage group first followed the training in phonological awareness as mentioned above. After ten weeks of training, at the time the training unit of identifying the initial phoneme began, the instruction in letter-sound correspondences started and was integrated into the phonological awareness program. From that moment on, children were taught both phonological awareness and grapheme-phoneme correspondences.

*Training in letter-sound correspondences.* Subjects of the letter-sound training group received the same instruction program in letter-sound correspondences as the phonological linkage group. The training program period was spread over 10 weeks.

It should be noted that it was difficult to persuade kindergarten teachers to implement the letter-sound training program, because in Germany kindergarten teachers normally refuse any kind of letter teaching in preschool children. In contrast to British or American kindergartens, any preparation for reading or spelling acquisition is strictly rejected in German kindergartens. Thus, only a comparably small number of 49 children-at-risk could be recruited for the letter-sound instruction program.

*Procedure*

At the beginning of the last kindergarten year a total of 726 preschool children were screened with the Bielefeld Screening Battery in order to identify the children-at-risk who were assigned to the experimental conditions. Later on, the children-at-risk of the experimental groups and the unselected children of the control group were pretested. After that, the training programs were conducted by the kindergarten teachers who were carefully instructed. The phonological linkage training program and the phonological awareness training program were spread over 20 weeks. After 10 weeks the letter-sound instruction began at the same time in the phonological linkage group and in the letter-sound training group. During the whole training period the kindergarten teachers were visited at least once a week by one of our specially trained research assistants in order to support and supervise the teachers. The control group followed the regular kindergarten program that emphasized social and emotional development and often contained fewer cognitive or specific metalinguistic aspects. After the completion of the training programs the posttest was conducted to assess short-term training effects. In order to assess the long-term training effects on phonological awareness a metalinguistic transfer test was provided at the beginning of first grade when reading and spelling instruction was in its initial stage. Finally, a reading and spelling test was administered at the end of first grade in order to examine long-term training effects on literacy acquisition.

RESULTS

*Results of the Bielefeld Screening Battery.* We expected no substantial differences between the experimental groups on the subtests of the Bielefeld Screening Battery. Table 1 contains means and standard deviations for the three training groups on the subtests. A visual inspection of Table 1 shows that the training groups did not differ on phonological processing and visual attention tasks. One-way analyses of variance with subsequent Student-Newman-Keuls tests yielded no significant differences between the experimental groups on the subtests. Although the subtests on general produced ceiling effects, the children classified as "at risk" children attained small results on most phonological tasks. Thus, the subjects of the training groups ranged below the average level of phonological awareness.

TABLE 1
Means and standard deviations (in parentheses) for the three training groups
(phonological awareness, phonological linkage, letter-sound training) on all
measures of the Bielefeld Screening Battery

| training group<br>variable | phonological<br>awareness<br>(N=82) | phonological<br>linkage<br>(N=77) | letter-sound<br>training<br>(N=49) |
|---|---|---|---|
| (A) Phonological awareness | | | |
| Rhyme production (12) | 4.22 (4.70) | 3.92 (4.54) | 5.25 (4.83) |
| Rhyme matching (12) | 5.13 (4.01) | 5.12 (3.54) | 5.44 (3.67) |
| Syllable segmentation (12) | 6.51 (3.03) | 6.51 (2.91) | 6.65 (3.20) |
| Phoneme word matching (12) | 8.09 (3.24) | 8.60 (2.65) | 7.88 (2.34) |
| (B) Phonetic recoding | | | |
| Repeating pseudowords (12) | 6.16 (2.77) | 5.67 (2.76) | 5.54 (3.35) |
| (C) Speed of access | | | |
| Rapid naming, uncoloured (sec) | 55.9 (22.4) | 59.9 (23.3) | 62.06 (23.1) |
| Rapid naming, coloured (sec) | 82.7 (29.9) | 86.6 (33.9) | 90.02 (37.3) |
| (D) Visual attention | | | |
| Word matching (12) | 7.96 (2.83) | 8.07 (2.72) | 8.85 (2.52) |

Note: Maximum score is given in parentheses after variable name.

*Results of pretest measures.* It was assumed that the children-at-risk of the experimental groups would be significantly inferior to the children of the control group in pretest measures assessing phonological awareness and letter knowledge. Table 2 presents means and standard deviations for the three experimental and the control groups on all measures of the pretest. The data shows that all children-at-risk had difficulties with mastering the phonological awareness tasks. No significant differences between the experimental groups could be found. There were significant group differences between the control children and the experimental children-at-risk on the phonological awareness tasks. One-way analyses of variance with subsequent Student-Newman-Keuls tests indicated that the control group significantly outperformed the experimental groups. The effects ranged between $F(3,350) = 4.44$, $p<.01$ for the end sound categorization task and $F(3,350) = 26.58$, $p<.01$ for the initial phoneme task. However, results on the end sound categorization task were an exception, because the control group differed significantly only from the phonological awareness group. The differences between the control group and the remaining experimental groups (phonological linkage group and letter-sound training group) did not reach statistical significance. Because of floor effects in the end sound categorization task, no group differences could be found.

Subtests tapping *early literacy* skills also yielded significant differences between the experimental groups and the control group. On average, control children identified three letters more than the children-at-risk on average. The results on the word reading task indicated that reading skills were almost non-existent in preschool children.

TABLE 2
Means and standard deviations (in parentheses) for the three experimental groups (phonological awareness, phonological linkage, letter-sound training) and the control group on all measures of the pretest

| Variable | phon. awareness (N=82) | phon. linkage (N=77) | letter-sound training (N=49) | control (N=146) |
|---|---|---|---|---|
| *(A) Phonological awareness* | | | | |
| Phoneme blending (8) | 3.48 | 3.34 | 3.12 | 4.02 |
| | (1.59) | (1.59) | (1.73) | (1.82) |
| Phoneme segmentation (8) | 0.29 | 0.18 | 0.35 | 1.61 |
| | (0.85) | (0.51) | (0.93) | (2.31) |
| Initial phoneme (8) | 0.70 | 0.44 | 0.84 | 2.69 |
| | (1.45) | (0.94) | (1.66) | (2.93) |
| Phoneme deletion (8) | 0.05 | 0.00 | 0.00 | 0.55 |
| | (0.35) | (0.00) | (0.00) | (1.51) |
| End sound categorization (10) | 1.73 | 2.23 | 2.67 | 3.05 |
| | (2.22) | (2.64) | (2.93) | (2.98) |
| First sound categorization (10) | 0.66 | 0.84 | 0.82 | 1.55 |
| | (1.30) | (1.68) | (1.63) | (2.12) |
| *(B) Early literacy* | | | | |
| Letter name (26) | 2.79 | 2.44 | 2.96 | 5.91 |
| | (4.31) | (3.89) | (3.66) | (7.17) |
| N of words read (7) | 0.05 | 0.00 | 0.02 | 0.26 |
| | (0.22) | (0.00) | (0.14) | (1.11) |

Note: Maximum score is given in parentheses after variable name.

*Results of posttest measures.* We assumed that the trained children-at-risk would be able to reach at posttest the control children's level of phonological awareness and letter knowledge in those tasks which were explicitly practised in the different training versions. Thus, the hypothesis was that no substantial differences between the experimental groups and the control group should be found after completion of the intervention programs. Table 3 presents means and standard deviations for the three experimental groups and the control group on all measures of the posttest. A visual inspection of the table shows that all three training groups improved more or less in their level of phonological awareness and letter knowledge after intervention. One-way analyses of variance with subsequent Student-Newman-Keuls tests were conducted to examine the group differences.

On the *phoneme blending task* no substantial differences were found between the phonological awareness and the phonological linkage group, both significantly outperformed the letter-sound training and the control group (F(3,328) = 10.26, p<.01). The control group was significantly ahead of the letter-sound training group, as was found in the pretest findings. A 4 (groups) x 2 (measurement point) repeated measures analysis of variance yielded significant main effects for group (F(3,328) = 5.94, p<.01), and measurement point (F(1,328) = 164.49, p<.01) qualified by a significant group x measurement point interaction (F(3,328) = 11.56, p<.01). Whereas the experimental groups were significantly worse than the control group at pretest, this pattern was dramatically changed after the training period. Although all groups made progress in blending phonemes, the greatest advances were made by the phonological awareness group and the phonological linkage group that could not only reach the control children's level but could surpass them.

TABLE 3
Means and standard deviations (in parentheses) for the three experimental groups and the control group on all measures of the posttest

| variable | phonol. awareness (N=73) | phonol. linkage (N=75) | letter-sound training (N=45) | control (N=139) |
|---|---|---|---|---|
| *(A) Phonological awareness* | | | | |
| Phoneme blending (8) | 5.68 | 5.31 | 3.96 | 4.77 |
| | (1.71) | (1.64) | (1.51) | (1.96) |
| Phoneme segmentation (8) | 4.23 | 3.05 | 1.38 | 1.89 |
| | (2.37) | (2.55) | (1.32) | (2.56) |
| Initial phoneme (8) | 6.56 | 5.88 | 5.27 | 3.79 |
| | (2.25) | (2.43) | (2.37) | (3.14) |
| Phoneme deletion (8) | 2.51 | 1.32 | 0.27 | 1.28 |
| | (2.57) | (1.80) | (0.69) | (2.31) |
| End sound categorization (10) | 5.16 | 4.41 | 4.07 | 4.68 |
| | (2.73) | (3.06) | (2.94) | (3.09) |
| First sound categorization (10) | 2.11 | 2.23 | 2.36 | 2.28 |
| | (2.42) | (2.40) | (2.38) | (2.62) |
| *(B) Early literacy* | | | | |
| Letter names (26) | 5.19 | 7.28 | 11.02 | 9.04 |
| | (5.32) | 5.85) | (3.53) | (8.11) |
| Letter sounds (26) | 3.56 | 6.18 | 9.09 | 5.2 |
| | (3.57) | (5.00) | (2.85) | (5.41) |
| N of words read (7) | 0.04 | 0.36 | 0.27 | 1.05 |
| | (0.20) | (1.08) | (0.84) | (2.06) |

Note: Maximum score is given in parentheses after variable name.

Results on the *phoneme segmentation task* showed that the phonological awareness group performed significantly better than the two remaining training groups and even than the control group. The phonological linkage group also significantly surpassed the letter-sound training group and the control group (F(3,328) = 20.30, p<.01). No substantial differences were found between the children-at-risk instructed in letter-sound correspondences and the control children. Because floor effects on the phoneme segmentation task were produced by both letter-sound training group and control group, these outcomes should be interpreted with caution.

An analysis of variance yielded significant main effects for group (F(3,328) = 6.30, p<.01), and measurement point (F(1,328) = 212.49, p<.01) qualified by a significant group x measurement point interaction (F(3,328) = 47.35, p<.01). All groups made a significant progress from pre- to posttests. The greatest progress was made by the phonological awareness group, followed by the phonological linkage group which both were significantly inferior of the control group at pretest, but significantly ahead of the control group at posttest.

The *initial phoneme task* showed that the trained children-at-risk were significantly superior to the control children (F(3,327) = 19.96, p<.01). Although the phonological awareness group performed significantly better than the letter-sound training group, there were no significant differences between the phonological linkage and the letter-sound training groups. The identification of the first sound was part of all training programs. An analysis of variance yielded significant main effects measurement point (F(1,327) = 630.38, p <.01) and a significant interaction (F(3,327) = 66.69, p<.01). No main effect was found for group. All children-at-risk in the experimental groups improved from pre- to posttests, in that they could not only reach the control children's level but could surpass them at posttest.

On the *phoneme deletion task*, floor effects were present in all groups. Thus, the results should be interpreted with caution. The phonological awareness group obtained significantly better results than the other training groups and the control group. No substantial differences were found between the phonological linkage group and the control group (F(3,327) = 11.07, p<.01). The children receiving letter-sound training were significantly surpassed by the other trained children and the control children. An analysis of variance yielded significant main effects for group (F(3,326) = 7.26, p<.01), and measurement point (F (1, 326) = 106.87, p<.01) and a significant interaction (F (3, 326) = 17.60, p<.01).

Similar to the results at pretest no significant group differences were found on the *end sound categorization task* at posttest. An analysis of variance showed significant effects for measurement point (F(1,328) = 147.20, p<.01), and a significant interaction (F(3,328) = 7.80, p<.01). The greatest increase was obtained by the phonological awareness group that reached the level of the control group at posttest. Somewhat surprisingly, the letter-sound training group in which rhyming games were not explicitly practised also made progress. Maybe the instruction in letter-sound correspondences made the children-at-risk more sensitive to sounds and words, so that they could more profit from the regular kindergarten program which also contains rhyming games.

On the *first sound categorization task*, there were also no substantial group effects. An analysis of variance yielded only significant effects for measurement point ($F(1,328) = 60.16$, $p<.01$). All children could improve their performance at this task. However, also floor effects were produced on this task at posttest, so the results should be interpreted with caution.

With regard to the *letter knowledge* the pattern had changed from pre- to posttests. An analysis of variance yielded significant main effects for group ($F(3,327) = 7.25$, $p<.01$), and measurement point ($F(1,327) = 336.20$, $p<.01$), qualified by a significant interaction ($F(3,327) = 5.77$, $p<.01$). The letter-knowledge of the phonological linkage group and the letter-sound training group was significantly improved, as expected. Children-at-risk of the letter-sound training group could identify significantly more *letter names and letter sounds* than the children-at-risk of the phonological awareness and also of the phonological linkage group. The letter-sound training group also outperformed the control group in the knowledge of letter-sound correspondences, but the difference in the correct identification of letter names did not reach statistical significance. The phonological linkage group did not differ significantly from the control group in the *identification of letter sounds,* but did significantly surpass the phonological awareness group (as demonstrated in a one-way variance analysis with subsequent Student-Newman-Keuls-test ($F(3,327) = 13.62$, $p<.01$).

On the *word reading task* the control group was significantly ahead of the training groups, similar to the outcomes on pretest ($F(3,327) = 9.23$, $p<.01$).

## CONCLUSIONS AND DISCUSSION

The training study was focused on two important aspects: First, children-at-risk's level of phonological awareness and letter knowledge should be significantly improved in order to prevent the development of difficulties in subsequent reading and spelling acquisition. Second, we evaluated the phonological linkage hypothesis for the German language, claiming that maximal long-term training effects on literacy acquisition can be obtained by using a combined intervention program emphasizing the integration of training in phonological awareness with training in letter-sound correspondences.

The screening results indicated that the children-at-risk had some difficulties with identifying and manipulating larger phonological units, such as rhymes or syllables. Pretest findings also showed that children-at-risk were hardly able to handle smaller phonological units like phonemes. They had great difficulties to blend, categorize or to segment. Therefore, the probability that these children would develop difficulties in reading and spelling at school would be very high (Marx, Jansen, Mannhaupt, & Skowronek, 1993).

The phonological awareness training program was conducted to enhance children-at-risk's insight into units of speech. In addition, the phonological awareness training was connected with a training in letter-sound correspondences. The combined training program was expected to have the greatest long-term effects on subsequent reading and spelling skills according to Hatcher et al. (1994).

Posttest measures indicated promising results. Children of the phonological awareness group did not only reach the control children's level, but also went beyond it for several tasks. However, they were not able to reach an average level in the identification of letter-sound correspondences. The greatest advance in the correct identification of letter-sound correspondences was made by the letter-sound training group who even outperformed the other training groups, but they made less progress in the phonological awareness tasks in comparison to the other training groups. Substantial improvements on both phonological awareness *and* knowledge of letter-sound correspondences was only gained by children-at-risk who received the phonological linkage training that emphasized the connection between grapheme-phoneme correspondences and phonological awareness.

In summary, with regard to the available results there is some cross-linguistic evidence for the phonological linkage hypothesis. Similar to Ball and Blachman (1991), Bradley and Bryant (1985), Hatcher et al. (1994), our findings indicated that phonological awareness and letter knowledge could be successfully enhanced in German children and that results obtained in previous English studies could easily be transferred to the German language.

REFERENCES

Ball, E. W., & Blachman, B. A. (1991). Does phoneme awareness training in kindergarten make a difference in early word recognition and developmental spelling? *Reading Research Quarterly, 26,* 49–66.

Bradley, L. L. (1988). Making connections in learning to read and spell. *Applied Cognitive Psychology, 2,* 3–18.

Bradley, L. L., & Bryant, P. E. (1985). *Rhyme and reason in reading and spelling.* Ann Arbor, MI: University of Michigan Press.

Byrne, B., & Fielding-Barnsley, R. (1989). Phonemic awareness and letter knowledge in the child's acquisition of the alphabetic principle. *Journal of Educational Psychology, 81,* 313–321.

Cunningham, A. E. (1990). Explicit versus implicit instruction in phonemic awareness. *Journal of Experimental Child Psychology, 42,* 49–72.

Goswami, U., & Bryant, P. (1990). *Phonological skills and learning to read.* London: Erlbaum.

Hatcher, P. J., Hulme, C., & Ellis, A. W. (1994). Ameliorating early reading failure by integrating the teaching of reading and phonological skills: The phonological linkage hypothesis. *Child Development, 65,* 41–57.

Lundberg, I., Frost, J., & Petersen, O. P. (1988). Effects of an extensive program for stimulating phonological awareness in preschool children. *Reading Research Quarterly, 23,* 263–284.

Marx, H., Jansen, H., Mannhaupt, G., & Skowronek, H. (1993). Predictions of difficulties in reading and spelling on the basis of the Bielefeld Screening. In H. Grimm & H. Skowronek (Eds.), *Language acquisition problems and reading disorders: Aspects of diagnosis and intervention* (pp. 219–242). Berlin: De Gruyter.

Schneider, W. (1989). Möglichkeiten zur frühen Vorhersage von Leseleistungen im Grundschulalter. *Zeitschrift für Pädagogische Psychologie, 3,* 157–168.

Schneider, W., Kuespert, P., Roth, E., & Visé, M. (1997). Short- and long-term effects of training phonological awareness in kindergarten: Evidence from two German studies. *Journal of Experimental Child Psychology, 66,* 311–340.

Schneider, W., Visé, M., Reimers, P., & Blaesser, B. (1994). Auswirkungen eines Trainings der sprachlichen Bewußtheit auf den Schriftspracherwerb in der Schule. *Zeitschrift für Pädagogische Psychologie, 8,* 177–188.

Tornéus, M. (1984). Phonological awareness and reading: A chicken and egg problem? *Journal of Educational Psychology, 76,* 1346–1358.

Wagner, R. K., & Torgesen, J. K. (1987). The nature of phonological processing and its causal role in the acquisition of reading skills. *Psychological Bulletin, 101,* 192–212.

PETRA KUESPERT AND WOLFGANG SCHNEIDER

# TRAINING PHONOLOGICAL AWARENESS VERSUS INDUCTIVE REASONING IN KINDERGARTEN

This chapter reports on a German longitudinal study in which we evaluated the effects of early phonological awareness training on both subsequent metalinguistic development and later reading and spelling success. Phonological awareness is defined as the ability to reflect on and manipulate the phonemic segments of speech. While speaking young children do not have much conscious control over these units of language. This lack of awareness of the phonological structure of speech is due to the complex nature of the acoustic signal, which offers no physical criterion for the segmentation of words, syllables, or phonemes. There is now a substantial body of evidence, that phonological awareness, verbal memory capacity, and verbal information processing speed are critical in the acquisition of literacy (cf. Bradley & Bryant, 1985; Goswami & Bryant, 1990; Wagner & Torgesen, 1987). In particular, the impact of early phonological awareness on subsequent reading and spelling has been demonstrated repeatedly on a variety of studies (e.g., Ball & Blachman, 1991; Marx, Jansen, Mannhaupt, & Skowronek, 1993; Schneider & Näslund, 1993; Wimmer, Landerl, & Schneider, 1994). Learning to read within an alphabetic system presupposes the capacity for explicit analysis of speech in terms of single phonemes.

The question whether phonological awareness emerges as a precursor or as a consequence of literacy has been discussed extensively (Bradley & Bryant, 1985; Lundberg & Høien, 1991; Morais, 1991; Wimmer, Landerl, Linortner, & Hummer, 1991). Training studies seem especially suited to clarify the issue concerning the causal link. In most of the training studies conducted in the last ten years, however, phonological awareness was taught while the children were learning to read, which made it difficult to interpret the effectiveness of the training program (Ball & Blachman, 1991; Bradley & Bryant, 1985; Olofsson & Lundberg, 1985). Only a few studies circumvented this confounding problem by teaching phonemic awareness before formal instruction in reading and spelling. One of the most sophisticated and thorough kindergarten training studies was conducted by Lundberg, Frost, and Petersen (1988). Lundberg et al. developed a comprehensive training program consisting of metalinguistic games and exercises which was evaluated in a longitudinal study with almost 400 Danish kindergarten children. The training was conducted during the last year of kindergarten and lasted for about 8 months. A control group did not receive any instruction in phonological awareness but participated in the regular kindergarten preschool program. Pre- and posttest measures taken immediately before and after the training program and tapping various metalinguistic abilities revealed significant treatment effects. Moreover, significant effects of the training program on subsequent reading and spelling skills were demonstrated for Grades 1 and 2. The training had a specific effect in that it did promote neither intelligence nor general language comprehension nor children's letter knowledge.

A first German study was conducted from 1991 to 1994 aiming at validating and extending Lundberg et al.'s finding for a different language (Schneider, Reimers, Visé, & Blaesser, 1994). Most of Lundberg et al.'s findings were replicated. It was shown again that phonological awareness can be developed before formal reading and spelling instruction and that this phonological awareness facilitates subsequent reading and spelling acquisition in Grade 1.

In a second study we planned to compare the effects of the phonological awareness training on metalinguistic abilities and later reading and spelling success with those of an alternative training program intending to stimulate inductive reasoning. In this study an attempt was made to test the following hypotheses: (1) Phonological awareness can be successfully trained in German kindergarten, (2) Effects of the training program are specific in that only phonological awareness skills are improved; other components of phonological processing, letter knowledge, and Children's general intellectual level will not be affected, (3) The training procedure has short- and long-term effects on subsequent reading and spelling, and (4) training inductive reasoning will neither stimulate metalinguistic abilities nor provide any advantages for learning to read and spell.

## METHOD

*Participants*

A total of 191 children (86 girls and 105 boys) were recruited for the training (phonological awareness) group. The control group consisted of 155 children (66 girls, 89 boys), and the control training (inductive reasoning) group consisted of 43 children (19 girls, 24 boys).

*Instruments*

*Kindergarten measures.*
All tests were administered individually in a separate kindergarten room. The tasks chosen tapped phonological processing skills, such as phonological awareness, phonological memory, and verbal information processing speed (phonological recoding in lexical access).

Furthermore, indicators of (nonverbal and verbal) intelligence and measures assessing early literacy (i.e., letter knowledge, reading of real words and pseudowords) were included in the test battery.

Most measures tapping *phonological awareness* were adopted from the study by Lundberg et al. (1988). In the first subtest, *deletion of initial phoneme*, children were first asked to identify the initial sound of the word depicted on a line drawing. They were then asked to give the remaining part of the word after deleting the first sound. A total of eight words of increasing length were presented to the children. One point was given for each correct response. In the second subtest, *phoneme synthesis*, the experimenter presented a word slowly phoneme-by-phoneme. The child was then asked to select from two pictures the one that represented the word. In the third subtest, *phoneme analysis*, children were asked to divide eight simple words into phonemes and to mark each phoneme with a plastic marker. Pictures representing the words were shown simultaneously to reduce memory load. Finally, the *sound categorization* task developed by Bradley and Bryant (1985) was used to assess rhyming skills. Here, the children's task was to identify the one word (out of four words) that did not rhyme with the others. Because of time constraints only the subtests alliteration and end sound were used.

To assess *phonological memory*, the *word span task* developed by Case, Kurland, and Goldberg (1982) was used. Children had to reproduce a series of words and the number of words within a series gradually increased. Testing stopped after two sets of the same size could not be reproduced correctly. Children's word span was defined as the maximum number of words correctly reproduced. *Articulation speed* was assessed as an additional indicator of verbal information processing speed. In this task, children were given word triples (e.g., hat – bear – tea) which they should repeat as quickly as possible over a total of 10 trials. The amount of time needed for the articulation task was chosen as dependent variable.

Verbal information processing speed in the sense of phonological recoding in accessing the semantic lexicon was assessed using the *rapid naming* task developed by Skowronek and Marx (1989). In the first task version, children had to name the colors of uncolored objects (e.g., plum, lemon, tomato) as quickly as possible. The second version consisted of sets of objects drawn in a wrong color. Again, children had to name the correct colors of the objects. Naming speed was used as the dependent variable.

Two tasks were given to assess *early literacy*. First, in order to assess *letter knowledge*, children were confronted with a set of randomly arranged uppercase letters. The number of letters correctly identified was used as dependent variable. A *reading* task consisting of seven real words and nonwords was given to all those children who knew at least three and more letters. The total number of words read correctly was used as dependent variable. To control for the impact of verbal intelligence we used the *vocabulary* subtest of the Hannover-Wechsler Intelligence Scale for Preschool Children (HAWIVA; Eggert, 1978). The vocabulary subtest consisted of 20 words that had to be defined by the children. Depending on the quality of Children's responses, between zero and two points could be obtained per item.

*Nonverbal intelligence* was assessed by the Grundintelligenztest CFT 1 (Weiß & Osterland, 1977). This standardized intelligence scale includes six subtests assessing children's abilities concerning visual perception (subtests 1 and 2) and inductive reasoning (subtests 3, 4, and 5). The IQ is taken as dependent variable.

*School measures.*
A battery of *metalinguistic* tasks adopted from Lundberg et al. (1988), Näslund (1990), and Wimmer, Linortner, and Hummer (1991) was administered at the beginning of elementary school. It was ensured that none of the tasks had been practiced in the kindergarten training program. The first three tasks were translations and adoptions of measures used by Lundberg et al. (1988). In the first subtest, *initial sound analysis*, children had to draw lines between objects with the same initial sounds. A similar task, *identification of end sounds*, required children to draw lines between objects that shared the same end sound. In the new *phoneme analysis* task, children had to segment words into their constituent phonemes by using a plastic marker. The words were represented by line drawings in order to reduce memory load. In the fourth subtest, *word length analysis*, the children were asked to mark the object whose word had the largest number of sounds from a set of four pictures. The subtest *phoneme reversal* was adopted from Näslund (1990). Children were first asked to repeat a word presented by the experimenter, and were then instructed to reverse the first and second phonemes of the word (e.g., to convert "lion" into "ilon"). The number of correct reversals (max = 10) was chosen as the dependent variable. Finally, the subtest *vowel substitution* was adopted from Wimmer et al. (1992). The children's task was to replace the vowel "a" by the vowel "i" in a total of ten words (e.g., the word "hand" had to be reproduced as "hind"). Whereas the first five words required the substitution of one vowel, two vowels had to replaced in the remaining five words.

Due to organizational constraints, *reading and spelling* skills had to be assessed in group sessions. A standardized test (Hamburger Schreibprobe für erste Klassen; HSP 1) developed by May (1995) was used to assess children's spelling performance at the end of Grade 1.

In this test, children are asked to write 8 words and a sentence. The number of words spelled correctly and the total number of grapheme hits (correctly spelled graphemes) were chosen as dependent variables. The children's reading skills were assessed by using the Würzburger Leise Leseprobe (Kuespert & Schneider, 1998), which is constructed similarly as the Scandinavian reading test OS400 used by Lundberg et al. In this test, children are asked to read each word from a list of 120 words on the left side as quickly as possible and select one out of four pictures on the right side. In order to increase task difficulty, the distractors are similar to the target in different ways. The total number of correct answers in five minutes was used as dependent variable.

*Training programs*
*Phonological awareness training program.* The kindergarten teachers were carefully instructed in the procedure of the phonological awareness training program, before it started in January, 1994. The slightly modified German translation of the program used by Lundberg et al. which had been adopted for the first German study was – except for some additional modifications – replicated in this study. The program consisted of six metalinguistic exercise units. It started with easy listening games that included verbal and nonverbal sounds. The second unit comprised games that emphasized on the identification of rhymes. This was followed by a period in which sentences and words were introduced by means of games and exercises. The next unit focused on syllable segmentation and analysis. In the next period, phonemes were introduced. One of the first tasks was to identify the initial phonemes. Children also learned that new words resulted when the initial phoneme was omitted or when a new initial phoneme was added to an existing word. In the last training unit, phoneme analysis and synthesis proceeded to phonemes within words, with slow progression from simple vowel-consonant and consonant-vowel words to more complex words. Each of these training units included about six to nine different metalinguistic games. Some of these games required children to listen carefully and give verbal responses to the teachers, whereas others were designed to teach children elements of oral language processing by moving their bodies and clapping their hands.

*Inductive reasoning training program.* The 120 tasks of the Denk-training I developed by Klauer (1989) can be assigned to the following types of problems: generalization (discover common features of different objects, e.g., butterflies, kites, and planes have one common feature: they all can fly), discrimination (discover the features in which objects differ, e.g., a tomato, an onion, a cucumber, and an apple are depicted; children have to find out that the apple is misplaced as it is a fruit, not a vegetable), cross-classification (discover different and common features), relations (discover common relations), different relations (discover different relations), and system construction (discover common and different relations). Children are trained individually. First a problem type is introduced, then the solution is worked out together with the child. When a problem is solved and the child has understood the strategy, the same problem is presented in a more abstract setting.

*Procedure*

Three months after the beginning of the last kindergarten year, the children in the training group and the control group were pretested on general intellectual ability, phonological processing skills (phonological awareness, verbal memory capacity, and verbal information processing speed), and early literacy. During the following six months the children of the training group participated in the training program on phonological awareness which included daily sessions of about 10 min of metalinguistic exercises and games. The children of the control group participated in the regular kindergarten program. Due to organizational constraints, pretesting in the control training group started two months later. The training on inductive reasoning was implemented immediately after the pretest. The children were trained individually and took part in 20 training sessions over a total of about two weeks. At the end of the school year, all three groups were posttested on the same tasks used at pretest. A metalinguistic transfer test using new materials was given at the beginning of the first school year. Reading and spelling skills were assessed, respectively, at the end of Grade 1 and at the beginning of Grade 2.

In the training group 178 of the 190 children, in the control group 151 out of 155 children, and in the control training group 41 out of 43 children, participated in both pre- and posttests. In the metalinguistic transfer test 146 children (training group), 131 children (control group), and 33 children (control training group) participated. Spelling and reading scores could be assessed from 143 children (training group), 143 children (control group), and 31 children (control training group).

RESULTS

*Kindergarten measures*

Table 1 gives an overview of the pretest data of all three groups. It should be noted that the control training group was pretested three months later than the other two groups.

## TABLE 1
Means and standard deviations (in parentheses) for the metaphonological and the other subtests during pretesting, as a function of group

| Variable | Training N=190 | Control N=155 | Control Training N=43 |
|---|---|---|---|
| *Metaphonological subtests* | | | |
| Phoneme synthesis (8) | 5.82 | 5.96 | 6.14 |
| | (1.60) | (1.67) | (1.54) |
| Phoneme analysis (8) | 0.98 | 1.45 | 1.51 |
| | (1.84) | (1.95) | (2.48) |
| Initial Phoneme (8) | 2.06 | 2.34 | 3.00 |
| | (2.80) | (2.79) | (3.23) |
| Phoneme Deletion (8) | 0.31 | 0.47 | 0.63 |
| | (1.26) | (1.47) | (2.07) |
| Endsound (10) | 3.52 | 4.18 | 4.53 |
| | (3.22) | (3.36) | (3.23) |
| Alliteration (10) | 2.32 | 2.43 | 3.07 |
| | (2.61) | (2.36) | (2.82) |
| Total combined metaphonological (52) | 14.96 | 16.83 | 18.88 |
| | (8.89) | (9.52) | (11.34) |
| *Other subtests* | | | |
| Word span | 3.86 | 3.95 | 4.02 |
| | (0.75) | (0.82) | (0.74) |
| Articulation speed | 19.36 | 19.70 | 16.06 |
| | (7.36) | (7.93) | (4.92) |
| Rapid naming (uncoloured) | 54.51 | 50.78 | 49.02 |
| | (17.15) | (21.51) | (11.87) |
| Rapid naming (coloured) | 74.17 | 73.77 | 63.84 |
| | (23.14) | (27.97) | (14.33) |
| Letter knowledge (26) | 4.72 | 5.77 | 8.37 |
| | (6.30) | (7.31) | (7.62) |
| Reading (7) | 0.44 | 0.54 | 0.81 |
| | (1.26) | (1.40) | (1.97) |
| Vocabulary (40) | 18.03 | 18.20 | 23.56 |
| | (5.37) | (4.97) | (5.27) |
| Nonverbal intelligence | 107.19 | 109.15 | 116.70 |
| | (14.93) | (14.35) | (14.96) |

Note: Maximum score is given in parenthesis after variable name

There is no significant difference between the training group and the control group except for the phoneme analyses with the control group outperforming the training group. However, there are significant differences between the control training group and both the training group and the control group. Analysis of covariance using group (training vs. control vs. control training) as the independent variable and the age at pretest as the covariate yielded significant effects for nonverbal intelligence ($F(2,295)=5.85$, $p<.01$), vocabulary ($F(2,374)=19.90$, $p<.01$), and articulation speed ($F(2,367)=4.15$, $p<.05$), indicating the control training group surpassing both other groups. Moreover, the control training group outperformed the training group in two scores: letter knowledge ($F(2,375)=3.83$, $p<.05$) and the total combined metaphonological score ($F(2,374)=3.04$, $p<.05$).

TABLE 2
Means and standard deviations (in parentheses) for the metaphonological and the other subtests during posttesting, as a function of group

| Variable | Training N=178 | Control N=146 | Control Training N=41 |
|---|---|---|---|
| *Metaphonological subtests* | | | |
| Phoneme synthesis (8) | 7.32 | 6.48 | 6.71 |
| | (1.04) | (1.55) | (1.52) |
| Phoneme analysis (8) | 4.16 | 1.58 | 2.49 |
| | (2.81) | (2.25) | (2.79) |
| Initial Phoneme (8) | 6.03 | 2.43 | 4.39 |
| | (2.56) | (2.82) | (3.05) |
| Phoneme Deletion (8) | 2.27 | 0.79 | 1.27 |
| | (2.79) | (1.82) | (2.47) |
| Endsound (10) | 5.44 | 4.77 | 5.85 |
| | (3.17) | (3.52) | (2.98) |
| Alliteration (10) | 3.52 | 2.52 | 3.24 |
| | (2.67) | (2.70) | (3.02) |
| Total combined metaphonological (52) | 28.74 | 18.58 | 23.95 |
| | (11.10) | (10.78) | (11.90) |
| *Other subtest* | | | |
| Word span | 4.17 | 4.16 | 4.44 |
| | (0.86) | (0.95) | (1.00) |
| Articulation speed | 15.76 | 15.54 | 13.05 |
| | (5.90) | (4.87) | (3.56) |
| Rapid naming (uncoloured) | 44.82 | 43.04 | 43.51 |
| | (12.19) | (13.53) | (12.64) |
| Rapid naming (coloured) | 57.63 | 58.01 | 55.98 |
| | (14.32) | (18.67) | (14.23) |
| Letter knowledge (26) | 8.05 | 7.65 | 10.12 |
| | (7.18) | (7.88) | (8.48) |
| Reading (7) | 0.93 | 0.84 | 1.12 |
| | (1.88) | (1.88) | (2.16) |
| Vocabulary (40) | 21.50 | 21.12 | 24.90 |
| | (5.41) | (5.13) | (4.87) |

Note: Maximum score is given in parenthesis after variable name

Table 2 gives an overview of the posttest data for the metaphonological subtests. The question of most interest was whether training phonological awareness would provide specific effects on the various phonological measures, and no effects on the remaining kindergarten measures. Therefore we will first focus on the comparison of the results of the training group with those of the control group. The tables also contain the results of the control training group, which will be discussed later. The effects of phonological awareness training and inductive reasoning training will be compared separately later on.

A visual inspection of Table 2 indicates that the training group performed better on all of the metalinguistic subtests. According to a one-way analysis of variance the differences between training group and control group turned out to be significant for all metaphonological variables, F-values ranging from 11.03 (alliteration) to 145.10 (initial phoneme), except for endsound (p=.07). A 2 (group) x 2 (measurement point) repeated measures analysis of variance yielded significant group x measurement point interactions for each subtest, which indicated the effectiveness of the phonological awareness training. The interaction effect was smallest for alliteration (F(1,321)= 8.17, p<.01), and largest for initial phoneme (F(1,321)= 133.44, p<.01). Additionally, the effect size measure $d$ was used to assess training effects. The strongest effects were found for the initial phoneme identification task (d=1.34), followed by that for the phoneme analysis task (d=1.00). Whereas the results for the phoneme deletion (d=0.62) and phoneme synthesis (d=0.64) indicate moderately large training effects, the effect sizes found for the alliteration and end sound components (d´s = 0.37 and 0.20) indicate only small to moderate training effects. When the outcomes for the various phonological awareness tests were linearly combined to establish a total score indicating the general level of metaphonological skills, a pattern similar to that found by Lundberg et al. (1988) emerged (see also Figure 1). That is, whereas the control group slightly outperformed the training group at pretest, this finding was dramatically reversed at the posttest.

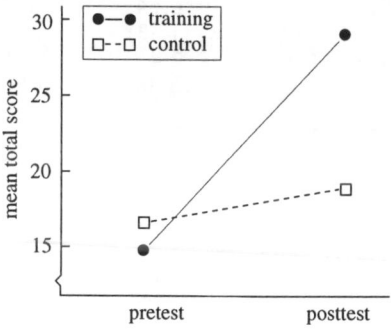

Fig. 1. Pretest to posttest combined scores for the six metalinguistic tests as a function of training condition.

Table 2 also shows that there are no major group differences for the non-metalinguistic variables. This was confirmed by the results of analyses of variance that did not reveal any training effects (all p's > .05). These findings replicate those of Lundberg et al. and confirm our claim that the training program has specific effects on phonological awareness. The remaining components of phonological information processing (i.e., phonological memory and verbal information processing speed) were not affected by the training procedure.

*Metalinguistic transfer test*

The group differences obtained for the metalinguistic transfer test at the beginning of Grade 1 are given in the upper part of Table 3. The data show that the training group outperformed the control group on most variables. One-way analyses of variance using group membership as the independent factor yielded significant main effects for all but one of the variables.

TABLE 3
Means and standard deviations (in parentheses) for the various measures of the metalinguistic transfer test, and for spelling and reading.

| Variable | Training<br>N=146 | Control<br>N=131 | Control<br>Training<br>N=33 |
|---|---|---|---|
| Initial phoneme (10) | 7.01 | 3.71 | 4.82 |
| | (2.55) | (2.90) | (3.12) |
| End sound (10) | 5.79 | 2.95 | 4.16 |
| | (2.83) | (2.64) | (2.87) |
| Word length (10) | 5.68 | 3.89 | 5.06 |
| | (2.36) | (2.26) | (2.41) |
| Phoneme analysis (10) | 3.62 | 1.57 | 2.59 |
| | (2.89) | (2.21) | (3.14) |
| Phoneme reversal (10) | 0.64 | 0.35 | 0.72 |
| | (1.43) | (1.42) | (2.26) |
| Vowel substitution (10) | 2.45 | 1.57 | 2.13 |
| | (3.38) | (3.06) | (3.82) |
| | N=143 | N=143 | N=31 |
| *Spelling:* | | | |
| Grapheme hits (63) | 49.32 | 47.13 | 47.63 |
| | (4.51) | (7.61) | (8.71) |
| Words correct (15) | 6.65 | 5.77 | 6.22 |
| | (1.92) | (2.38) | (2.21) |
| *Reading:* | | | |
| Items correct | 57.48 | 50.14 | 56.52 |
| | (16.20) | (16.32) | (22.29) |

Note: Maximum score is given in parenthesis after variable name

The most impressive effect was obtained for identification of initial phoneme (F(1,275)=101.57, p<.01). The effect size (d=1.21) indicates that the mean difference between the training and control groups is more than one standard deviation. A similar effect was found for the identification of end sounds (F(1,275)=74.09, p<.01, d=1.04). The effect sizes for the word length analysis and phoneme analysis were smaller (d=.77 and .79, respectively), but they still indicate moderately large training effects.

Whereas the difference between the two groups was still significant for the vowel substitution (F(1,273)= 5.08, p<.05, d=0.27) nonsignificant findings for the vowel reversal task were due to floor effects. Altogether, the results of the metalinguistic transfer test indicated substantial long-term effects of the phonological awareness training program.

*Spelling and reading measures*

Sum scores representing both the total number of correctly written graphemes and the number of words written correctly were calculated (see lower part of Table 3). In both dependent variables the training group was ahead of the control group. According to one-way analyses of variance these differences turned out to be significant (grapheme hits: F(1, 265)=8.59, p<.01, d=0.36; words correct: F(1,265)=11.21, p<.01, d=0.41). The findings obtained in the reading test also indicated the training group outperforming the control group. The difference was significant: F(1,284)= 14.58, p<.01, d=0.45). These results indicate additional long-term effects of the training program on spelling skills.

*Comparison with the training of inductive reasoning*

The control training (inductive reasoning) group outperformed both other groups in the pretest in five variables (i.e., nonverbal intelligence, vocabulary, total combined metaphonological score, letter knowledge, and articulation speed) even if the influence of age was controlled in analyses of covariance. Visual inspection of the posttest data in Table 3 shows that the mean scores of the three groups follow the same pattern for all metaphonological variables with the training (phonological awareness) group scoring highest, the control group scoring lowest and the control training group in between.

One-way analyses of variance yielded significant group effects indicating the significant superiority of the training group over the two other groups in phoneme synthesis (F(2,362)=16.77, p<.01), phoneme analysis (F(2,362)=40.10, p<.01), and deletion of the initial phoneme (F(2,362)=15.54, p<.01). In the subtest demanding the identification of the initial phoneme the significant group effect

($F(2,362)=70.26$, $p<.01$) indicated that the training group surpassed both other groups significantly and that the control training group also outperformed the control group significantly. The different effect sizes (phonological awareness training: $d=1.34$; inductive reasoning training: $d=0.24$) indicate that the effect of the inductive reasoning training was comparably small. The results concerning the phonological awareness in a broader sense were less clear. Whereas the one-way analysis of variance did not yield any significant group effect for the endsound task, the training group significantly outperformed the control group in the alliteration task, and the control training group did not differ significantly from any other group. The significant superiority of the control training group compared with he two other groups in vocabulary and articulation speed could also be demonstrated in the posttest by means of one-way analyses of variance.

*Metaphonological transfer test*

Table 3 gives an overview of the transfer test data of all three groups. One-way analyses of variance yielded the significant superiority of the training group over the control group in all subtests. For some subtests, the analyses of variance also indicated the significant superiority of the control training group over the control group. So, we additionally conducted analyses of covariance using group as the independent variable and verbal intelligence (assessed by the vocabulary test) as the covariate to find out, whether the superiority of the control training group could be due to their superiority in verbal intelligence. The analyses of covariance indicated that the training group outperformed the two other groups (which did not differ significantly from each other) in almost 2 variables, namely initial phoneme (($F(2,298)=49.0$, $p<.01$) and end sound ($F(2,297)=36.16$, $p<.01$). In the subtests phoneme analysis and vowel substitution the training group significantly outperformed the control group, whereas the control training group did not differ significantly from one of the two other groups. In the subtest word length the training group significantly outperformed the control group and the control training group, and also the control training group surpassed the control group significantly. Again, the phonological awareness training produced a larger effect size ($d=0.77$) compared with the inductive reasoning training ($d=0.51$).

*Spelling and reading measures*

Table 3 gives an overview of the spelling and reading data for the three groups. Analyses of variance indicated that the training group outperformed the control group significantly in reading (decoding speed) and spelling (grapheme hits, words written correctly). There was no significant difference between the control training group and one of the two other groups.

## CONCLUSIONS AND DISCUSSION

The findings of this training study indicate that phonological awareness in the broad and narrow senses can be taught effectively to German kindergarten children. So we can state that Lundberg et al's findings for a fairly regular language such as Danish could be generalized to a less transparent language such as German.

Additionally, this study confirmed Lundberg et al.'s result that the training only improved metaphonological skills. The training effects on rhyming skills were less impressive than those on phonological awareness in the narrow sense. Training phonological awareness had no effects on nonverbal intelligence, vocabulary, early literacy, and theoretically related phonological information processing skills, such as phonological memory and verbal information processing speed.

Like Lundberg and colleagues we were able to show that phonological awareness can be developed before children are formally instructed in reading and spelling, and that this phonological awareness facilitates the acquisition of subsequent reading and spelling. Thus our empirical findings support the view that phonological awareness is causally linked to the acquisition of literacy.

It should be noted that the available evidence showing systematic effects of temporarily preceding metalinguistic skills on subsequent reading and spelling performances does not imply a deterministic view of causality in the sense that phonological awareness is the only cause of successful reading and spelling. The only moderate effect sizes found for the reading and spelling tests given at the end of grade one seem to indicate that phonological awareness is necessary but not sufficient for explaining the variance in spelling and reading tests (for a similar view, see Byrne & Fielding-Barnsley, 1993, 1995; Hatcher, Hulme, & Ellis, 1994).

A comparison of the effects of training phonological awareness and training inductive reasoning shows that training inductive reasoning cannot provide similar effects on metalinguistic abilities and subsequent reading and spelling achievement. These findings indicate that literacy acquisition can not be facilitated by training general cognitive abilities; the implementation of a specific training, such as the phonological awareness training program, is necessary.

Of course, this study does not raise the claim to present a full-fledged comparison of the effects of training phonological awareness vs inductive reasoning. Our main interest was to evaluate the phonological awareness training program; the inductive reasoning training was simply added to a design which clearly focused on the metalinguistic training. So, one shortcoming of the present study is the lack of testing nonverbal intelligence after the implementation of the training programs.

A second shortcoming of this study is that the teacher factor has not been controlled for. Student's progress is naturally influenced by context factors, such as the general intellectual level of their classrooms and the abilities of their teachers. Although we realize that this is a complicated issue, future research on training effects of interventions implemented in preschool children should try to take these important context factors into account.

## REFERENCES

Ball, E. W., & Blachman, B. A. (1991). Does phoneme awareness training in kindergarten make a difference in early word recognition and developmental spelling? *Reading Research Quarterly, 26,* 49–66.

Bradley, L. L., & Bryant, P. E. (1985). *Rhyme and reason in reading and spelling.* Ann Arbor, MI: University of Michigan Press.

Byrne, B., & Fielding-Barnsley, R. (1993). Evaluation of a program to teach phonemic awareness to young children: A 1-year follow-up. *Journal of Educational Psychology, 85,* 104–111.

Byrne, B., & Fielding-Barnsley, R. (1995). Evaluation of a program to teach phonemic awareness to young children: A 2- and 3-year follow-up and a new preschool trial. *Journal of Educational Psychology, 87,* 488–503.

Goswami, U. ,& Bryant, P. E. (1990). *Phonological skills and learning to read.* London: Erlbaum.

Hatcher, P. J., Hulme, C., & Ellis, A. W. (1994). Ameliorating early reading failure by integrating the teaching of reading and phonological skills: The phonological linkage hypothesis. *Child Development, 65,* 41–57.

Klauer, K. J. (1989). *Denktraining für Kinder I. Ein Programm zu intellektuellen Förderung.* Göttingen: Hogrefe.

Lundberg, I., Frost, J., & Petersen, O. P. (1988). Effects of an extensive program for stimulating phonological awareness in preschool children. *Reading Research Quarterly, 23,* 263–284.

Lundberg, I., & Høien, T. (1991). Initial enabling knowledge and skills in reading acquisition: Print awareness and phonological segmentation. In D. J. Sawyer & B. J. Fox (Eds.), *Phonological awareness in reading: The evolution of current perspectives* (pp. 73–96). New York: Springer Verlag.

Marx, H., Jansen, H., Mannhaupt, G., & Skowronek, H. (1993). Predictions of difficulties in reading and spelling on the basis of the Bielefeld screening. In H. Grimm & H. Skowronek (Eds.), *Language acquisition problems and reading disorders: Aspects of diagnosis and intervention* (pp. 219–242). Berlin: De Gruyter.

May, P. (1995). *Hamburger Schreibprobe für die erste Klasse* (HSP 1) [Hamburg spelling test for first grade]. Hamburg: Verlag für pädagogische Medien.

Morais, J. (1991). Constraints on the development of phonemic awareness. In S. A. Brady and D. P. Shankweiler (Eds.), *Phonological processes in literacy - A tribute to Isabelle Y. Liberman* (pp. 5–27). Hillsdale, NJ: Erlbaum.

Olofsson, A., & Lundberg, I. (1985). Evaluation of long-term effects of phonemic awareness training in kindergarten: Illustration of some methodological problems in evaluation research. *Scandinavian Journal of Psychology*, 26, 21–34.
Kuespert, P., & Schneider, W. (1998). *Würzburger Leise Leseprobe.* Göttingen: Hogrefe.
Schneider, W., & Näslund, J. C. (1993). The impact of early metalinguistic competencies and memory capacity on reading and spelling in elementary school: Results of the Munich Longitudinal Study on the Genesis of Individual Competencies (LOGIC). *European Journal of Psychology of Education*, 8, 273–288.
Schneider, W., Visé, M., Reimers, P., & Blaesser, B. (1994). Auswirkungen eines Trainings der sprachlichen Bewußtheit auf den Schriftspracherwerb in der Schule [Effects of training in phonemic awareness on learning to read and write in elementary school]. *Zeitschrift für Pädagogische Psychologie*, 8, 177–188.
Wagner, R. K., & Torgesen, J. K. (1987). The nature of phonological processing and its causal role in the acquisition of reading skills. *Psychological Bulletin, 101*, 192–212.
Wimmer, H., Landerl, K., Linortner, R., & Hummer, P. (1991). The relationship of phonemic awareness to reading acquisition: More consequence than precondition but still important. *Cognition*, 40, 219–249.
Wimmer, H., Landerl, K., & Schneider, W. (1994). The role of rhyme awareness in learning to read a regular orthography. *British Journal of Developmental Psychology, 12*, 469–484.

HANNEKE WENTINK,
INGE DRENT, WIM VAN BON, AND ROBERT SCHREUDER

# THE EFFECTS OF A FLASH CARD TRAINING PROGRAM ON NORMAL AND POOR READERS' PHONOLOGICAL DECODING SKILLS

Numerous studies that investigated the reading problems of poor readers have centered on whether or not poor readers employ the same strategies in word reading as do normally developing readers. These studies showed that both normal and poor readers are able to employ a grapheme-phoneme conversion strategy, but that poor readers are less skillful in using this strategy (e.g., Beech & Awaida, 1992; Holligan & Johnston, 1988). Poor readers are slower and less efficient in grapheme-phoneme decoding than normal readers with a comparable reading level. As a consequence, poor readers and reading-level-matched normal controls differ most in reading pseudowords (Rack, Snowling, & Olson, 1992). Pseudowords (orthographically regular and phonologically legal letter strings that do not form existing words), in contrast to words, do not have a representation in the mental lexicon, and therefore, place heavy demands on phonological decoding. Thus, a deficit in phonological decoding manifests itself most clearly in pseudoword reading.

There is considerable evidence that a deficit in phonological decoding causes severe problems with rapid, automatic processing of words (e.g., Badian, 1994; Rack et al., 1992; Vellutino, Scanlon, & Spearing, 1995), and consequently, with reading in general (Adams, 1990; Perfetti, 1985). Therefore, many reading programs for the poor reader are directed at improving phonological decoding skills (e.g., Olson & Wise, 1992; Van den Bosch, 1991; Wentink, Van Bon, & Schreuder, 1997; Yap, 1993). These decoding programs often contain pseudowords as training materials, because pseudowords are useful for training grapheme-phoneme conversion rules.

This chapter presents the results of a computer-based training program that emphasizes improvement in decoding speed. Normal second-grade readers and poor readers with comparable reading levels were trained in reading aloud multisyllabic pseudowords. The effects of the training on normal and poor readers' decoding skills were compared. A comparison between poor and normal reading performance during a training program might give more insight in the poor reader's difficulties in processing printed reading materials. We employed the flash card method developed by Van den Bosch (1991) in which words or pseudowords are presented briefly on a computer screen. The exposure duration (the time that a pseudoword is presented) of word materials is controlled on-line, for each child and for each orthographic structure separately, so that the accuracy rate of each child remains at a minimum level of 67% (see the method section for further details). This specific flash card method seems to be effective in improving poor readers' decoding speed (Van den Bosch, 1991; Wentink et al., 1997).

An important issue in the present study was whether normal and poor readers with a second-grade reading level use syllable-bound decoding strategies in reading pseudowords. In the past, decoding has been described as a process in which the reader segments words and pseudowords into graphemes, translates each grapheme into its corresponding phoneme, and then blends the phonemes to pronounce the word (Coltheart, 1978). However, there is a consensus view nowadays that higher order units like subsyllabic units or syllables also play a role in word processing. For instance, Treiman, Fowler, Gross, Berch, and Weatherston (1995) showed that onsets (the first consonant or consonant cluster of a syllable) and rimes (the vowel and any consonants coming after the onset) are functional orthographic units in English. In Dutch, however, these units do not seem to play a role in reading (Van Daal, Reitsma, & Van der Leij, 1994; Van den Bosch, 1991). An explanation for these differences in onset-rime effects between languages might be related to the difference in orthographic depth between English (which has a opaque orthography) and Dutch (which has a rather transparent orthography; cf. Reitsma, 1990).

Another linguistic structure that seems to play a role in word identification is the syllable (Scheerer-Neumann, 1981; Tousman & Inhoff, 1992; Wentink, 1997). For instance, Wentink found in a Dutch cross-sectional study with elementary-school students and adults, that beginning readers use grapheme-phoneme conversion rules during phonological decoding, whereas proficient readers also use processes at the syllabic level. Furthermore, Wentink et al. (1997) found indications for a syllabic role in reading Dutch in a training study with poor readers. The children in this study were at least one year behind in the development of word reading skills. Their reading level was comparable to the reading level of normal readers in grade two. The goal of the training was to improve poor readers' decoding skills through extensive practice in reading aloud pseudowords. Pseudowords that differ in number of graphemes and/or in number of syllables were presented by using Van den Bosch's flash card method. The syllable boundaries within the pseudowords were marked in order to stimulate the children to process the letter strings in syllabic units. The results of the study of indicated, that poor readers benefit from a training program in which the individual syllables of words or pseudowords are highlighted (see Olson & Wise, 1992, and Scheerer-Neumann,

1981, for a comparable finding). It helps the poor reader to segment (pseudo)words into larger functional orthographic units, which consequently leads to a progress in phonological decoding skills.

The current study further investigated the role of the syllable in phonological decoding in Dutch beginning readers. The following two questions were addressed: 1) Do normal and poor readers, who have a comparable level of word identification skills, both improve their decoding skills during the flash card training?, and 2) Do normal and poor readers both use syllable-bound processes in phonological decoding as a result of the flash card training program? Normal and poor readers were trained in reading aloud pseudowords that differ in number of graphemes (5 or 7 graphemes) and/or in number of syllables (2 or 3 syllables). The children in the two training groups (normal versus poor) received reading practice twice a week for a period of four weeks. Naming latency, i.e., the time between the onset of pseudoword presentation and the onset of the verbal response of the child, was the dependent measure. The transfer effects of the flash card training to other untrained conditions and materials were tested in four pre- and posttests. The control groups participated in the pre- and posttests only. As a result of restricted availability of poor readers at the participating schools, the reading level of the poor readers was three months below that of the normal readers. We, therefore, analysed the data of the normal and poor readers separately by using a pretest-training-posttest control group design (instead of a reading-level-matched design), to investigate the two research questions.

To find an answer to the first research question, we investigated the naming latencies over the training sessions for the normal and the poor readers. We expected to find an increase in decoding speed over the training sessions in both normal and poor readers. However, since normal second-grade readers develop phonological decoding skills faster than poor readers with a comparable reading level (e.g., Ehri & Wilce, 1983; Yap, 1993), and poor readers are decidedly worse at decoding pseudowords than reading-level-matched peers (Rack et al., 1992), we expected shorter overall naming latencies of pseudowords and larger improvements in decoding speed in the normal readers during the flash card training compared to the poor readers.

The second topic of research was, whether the flash card training stimulates normal and poor readers to use syllabic information in the processing of word materials. There is evidence that normal readers use syllable-bound strategies in reading words when they are in second grade (Marmurek & Rinaldo, 1992). In reading pseudowords, however, they do not use these strategies before approximately the fourth grade (Katz & Feldman, 1981; Wentink, 1997). They process pseudowords letter-by-letter.

On the other hand, poor readers with a second-grade reading level are, despite the fact that they are more often exposed to multisyllabic words than their reading-level-matched peers, less sensitive to intraword structures, such as syllables, than normal readers (Scheerer-Neumann, 1981; Butler, Jared, & Hains, 1984). Only after an extensive training program that emphasizes syllable-bound decoding, poor readers learn to use syllabic information in reading aloud (pseudo)-words (e.g., Olson & Wise, 1992; Wentink et al., 1997). Based on these findings, we assumed that the second-grade normal readers and the poor readers would both learn to use syllabic information in decoding letter strings by our flash card training, which would result in an improvement in decoding speed. To investigate this assumption, we compared naming latencies of pseudowords that differ in number of syllables (two- versus three-syllable pseudowords with seven graphemes). Naming latencies were predicted to be longer for pseudowords with more syllables in both normal and poor readers (see Wentink et al., 1997, for a comparable finding in poor readers; see Das & Siu, 1989, for a comparable result for words in poor and normal readers). In addition, we compared naming latencies of pseudowords with a different number of graphemes (two-syllable pseudowords with five versus seven graphemes) to investigate the effect of number of graphemes. Naming latencies were predicted to be longer for pseudowords with more graphemes over all training sessions for both the normal and the poor readers (see Van den Bosch, 1991, and Wentink et al., 1997, for comparable findings in poor readers). Because of the severe decoding problems in most poor readers, we expected larger grapheme and syllable effects in the poor than in the normal readers.

The pseudowords that were presented in the training consisted of low-frequency (LF) syllables or of high-frequency (HF) syllables. If syllables are retrieved from a mental syllabary (Levelt & Wheeldon, 1994) during reading, naming latencies should be shorter for pseudowords containing HF syllables than for those containing LF syllables, since HF syllables are more often processed by children.

## METHOD

### Participants

Participants were 20 normal readers from elementary school and 20 poor readers from a school for children with learning disabilities, ranging in age from 7;8 years to 11;5 years. All children spoke Dutch as a first language. The reading methods used by the schools were primarily based on a phonics approach of reading instruction. The poor readers were at least one year behind in the development of word reading skills. The reading level of all children was comparable with the reading level of normal readers in grade two. This was established by a standardized reading test of isolated words (DMT; see below for a description of this test). The mean score on the DMT was 75.20 words per minute (SD = 15.27) for the normal readers, and 56.35 (SD = 9.32) for the poor readers. These mean scores indicate that there was no successful match between the normal and the poor readers. The mean score of the normal readers was equal to the standard DMT-score of normally achieving readers at the end of second grade (May); the reading level of the poor readers was three months lower (March second grade).

The two reading-level groups (normal vs. poor readers) were divided into a training group and a no-training control group. The training and the control groups were matched on mean DMT score (see Table 1) and age (normal readers' training group: 97.6 months (SD = 4.9), and control group: 98.8 months (SD = 4.5); poor readers' training group: 117.8 (SD = 10.2), and control group: 117.5 (SD = 8.7))

## Apparatus

The training program and two pre- and posttests (a word naming task and a pseudoword naming task) were presented by a Macintosh Plus ED computer. Word materials were presented in black lowercase letters on a white background in the center of the screen. A letter font used in many Dutch educational textbooks was chosen. Letter strings had a height of approximately 0.6 cm and ranged from 2 to 5.5 cm in length. Each child was tested and trained individually in a quiet room at school. The children were seated in front of the computer screen, at a distance of approximately 60 cm. Headphones were used for the acoustic warning signal that preceded stimulus presentation. The microphone was attached to the headphones to keep a constant distance between the microphone and the mouth of the child during the experimental sessions. Naming latencies were measured to millisecond accuracy by a voice-activated relay attached to the computer. The correctness of the verbal responses of the participants was recorded by the experimenter.

## Materials and procedure for the flash card training

The set of pseudowords contained the following three orthographic structures: 1. Two-syllable pseudowords with five graphemes (CVCVC, e.g., *bafijt*), 2. two-syllable pseudowords with seven graphemes (CCVCCVC, CVCCVCC, and CCVCVCC, e.g., *branpor*), and 3. three-syllable pseudowords with seven graphemes (CVCVCVC, e.g., *gofijmor*). For each orthographic structure 120 pseudowords consisting of low-frequency syllables and 120 pseudowords consisting of high-frequency syllables were constructed. Syllable frequencies were obtained from the computer database CELEX[1], containing a Dutch lexicon based on 42 million word tokens. The syllable frequencies were calculated from the database using the number of word form occurrences per million. The frequency of occurrence of each syllable in a particular ordinal word position was calculated (i.e., first, second or third syllable position). Low-frequency syllables (counts less than 100) and high-frequency syllables (counts over 100) were randomly selected. Each syllable occurred at most five times in the list of training materials to reduce the effect of repeated presentations. In case of pseudowords with more than one legal pronunciation, all legal pronunciations were accepted. All pseudowords were orthographically and phonologically legal.

The training program consisted of eight training sessions of approximately 30 min. Participants were trained individually twice a week. In each training session 90 pseudowords (30 per orthographic structure, 15 containing HF syllables and 15 containing LF syllables) were presented, one-by-one, and in a random order. The pseudowords were randomly extracted from the six lists of 120 pseudowords. The first and the third syllable of each pseudoword were presented in bold letters, and the second syllable was presented in a standard font (e.g., '**pau**teu**kaat**'). This was done to clarify the syllabic structure of the pseudowords for the children and to stimulate them to process the presented letter strings in syllabic units.

The exposure duration of the pseudowords was controlled on-line for each child and for each orthographic structure separately. It varied as a function of the child's naming accuracy. After each trial, accuracy of the current pseudoword and the previous two pseudowords of the same orthographic structure was evaluated. The exposure duration of the next pseudoword increased with 17 ms when two or more incorrect responses were given and decreased with 17 ms after three correct responses. The exposure duration remained unchanged, when two out of three pseudowords had been named correctly.

Five hundred milliseconds before stimulus presentation an acoustic warning signal was given via headphones and, simultaneously, a fixation asterisk appeared in the center of the screen for a period of 500 ms. The target stimulus appeared immediately after the asterisk at the same location. Participants were asked to read the presented pseudoword aloud as accurately as possible. The instruction did not emphasize speed, since the flash card method itself appears to put implicit time pressure on responding (Van den Bosch, 1991). The time-out for a naming response was set to 9.5 s after pseudoword presentation. Immediately after presentation of the pseudoword a

---

[1] The Centre for Lexical Information, University of Nijmegen, The Netherlands.

cross-hatched mask appeared which remained on the screen for 1.5 s. Naming latencies were recorded by a voice-activated relay for each trial. By pushing one of three buttons on a button box the experimenter recorded whether the stimulus was identified correctly, and whether the voice-activated relay was triggered by the verbal response of the child or by a sound other than the name of the stimulus (such as "um"). The participants received positive feedback by the computer after each correct response (a picture of a smiling face). There was a short break after each set of approximately 30 trials. Each training session started with the final exposure duration's (one for each orthographic structure) of the previous session.

A practice session was held prior to the first training session to familiarize the children with the task format, and to determine the initial exposure duration for each orthographic structure, for each individual child.

We presented a digit naming task at the beginning of each training session to test whether or not a possible decrease in naming latencies was the result of a progress in the execution of response production processes. If naming latencies of digits decrease during the training, this progress in naming latency should be the result of improved response production processes. A set of nine different digits (1–9) were presented, one-by-one, in a random order. Participants were asked to name the digits as accurately as possible. Positive feedback was given by the computer immediately after a correct response and the children received no explicit feedback after an incorrect response. Naming latency and accuracy were measured.

*Materials and procedure for the pre- and posttests*

*DMT - Drie-Minuten-Toets [Three-Minutes-Test].* The DMT is a Dutch standardized single word reading test (Verhoeven, 1992). The test consists of three cards containing several columns of words of increasing difficulty: Card 1 consists of 150 regularly spelled VC, CV and CVC words, card 2 of 150 monosyllabic words with consonant clusters and card 3 of 120 multisyllabic words. The children were instructed to read aloud the words of each card, column-by-column, as quickly and accurately as possible in 1 min. Errors were recorded by the experimenter. In our study, the mean score of the three cards was used as a measure of reading performance. The DMT consists of three versions (version A, B and C) that contain the same words, but in a different order. Version B was used for selecting the children for the experiment (the scores were also used as pretest scores) and version C was used as posttest. The pre- and posttest scores were used to assess the transfer effects of the flash card training on the ability to read isolated words.

*Lexical Decision Task.* A lexical decision task was presented by means of a paper-and-pencil procedure to determine whether the flash card training affected the speed of lexical processing. In this task, 72 high-frequency words and 18 pseudowords of the same orthographic structures as the ones that were used in the training, were presented on a sheet of paper in a pseudo-random order. One out of every five items was a pseudoword. The pseudowords were orthographically legal and pronounceable letter strings. Participants were instructed to cross out as many pseudowords as possible in one minute. The number of false positives (real words crossed out) and false negatives (pseudowords not crossed out) subtracted from the number of items read in 1 min was used as a measure. The pre- and posttest contained the same items, but in a different order. Prior to the experimental items, 10 practice trials were given. The children received no feedback about their performance.

*Word Reading Task.* A computerized word reading task was used to assess whether training in pseudoword decoding affected the processing of existing words. The pre- and posttest consisted of 30 high-frequency words each. The orthographic structures of the words were the same as those that were presented in the training. None of the words were presented in the DMT, nor in the Lexical Decision Task.

The items were presented, one-by-one, on a computer screen. Syllables were not highlighted; all items were printed in bold. The participants were instructed to read the words aloud, as quickly and accurately as possible. Each child received a different randomization of the trials. The words remained on the screen for 2 s after the response onset. A maximum of 8 s was allowed for responding. Naming latency and accuracy were measured. The children received no feedback about their performance. The child was familiarized with the task format by a series of 10 practice trials.

*Pseudoword Reading Task.* A computerized reading task was used to assess whether the flash card training affected naming latency and accuracy of untrained pseudowords. The pre- and posttest consisted of 30 items each. The pseudowords had the same orthographic structures as the ones that were used in training. None of the pseudowords were presented in the training, nor in the Lexical Decision Task. The procedure was the same as in the Word Reading Task.

RESULTS OF THE NORMAL READERS

*Results of the flash card training*

The naming of the pseudowords with an equal number of syllables and a different number of graphemes (two-syllable pseudowords with five versus seven graphemes) were compared to investigate the effects of number of graphemes. In addition, naming latencies of pseudowords with an equal number of graphemes and a different number of syllables (two- versus three-syllable pseudowords with seven graphemes) were compared to examine the effects of number of syllables. The two planned comparisons between different orthographic structures for naming latencies are discussed separately below.

The first five trials of each training session served as starting trials and were, therefore, excluded from the analyses. Latencies for incorrect responses (12.7%) and for responses with voice key errors (2.8%) were also not used. For each participant, the median naming latency for each orthographic structure per training session was calculated. The eight training sessions were divided into four training blocks, in which the data of two consecutive training sessions were collapsed. These data were entered into two repeated measures analyses of variance (one for each planned comparison of orthographic structures). Orthographic Structure (three levels), Frequency (pseudowords containing HF versus LF syllables) and Training Block (four levels) served as the within-subjects factors. The mean naming latencies for the three orthographic structures, split by syllable frequency, are displayed in Figure 1.

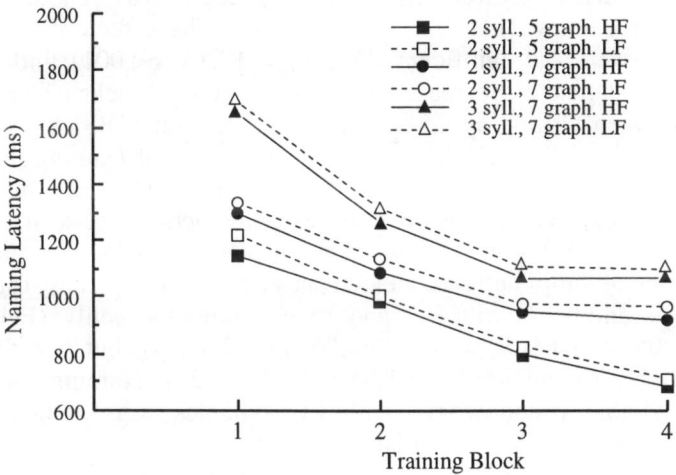

Fig. 1. Mean naming latencies for the three orthographic structures, split by syllable frequency, over the training blocks in normal readers

*Two-syllable pseudowords.* To test the effects of number of graphemes, naming latencies of two-syllable pseudowords with five vs. seven graphemes were compared. The analysis yielded a significant main effect of Orthographic Structure ($F(1,9) = 33.36$, $p<.001$), reflecting a grapheme effect. Naming latencies were on average 165 ms longer for two-syllable pseudowords with seven graphemes. There was also a main effect of Frequency: $F(1,9) = 8.64$, $p<.05$. Naming latencies were on average 40 ms longer for pseudowords that contained LF syllables. In addition, we found a main effect of Training Block: $F(3, 27) = 43.93$, $p<.001$. Participants improved in naming latency over the training blocks. There was an interaction between Orthographic Structure and Training Block ($F(3,27) = 5.87$, $p<.01$). The improvement in naming latency was largest for two-syllable pseudowords with five graphemes (with a latency decrease of 485 ms over the training blocks; naming latency of two-syllable pseudowords with seven graphemes decreased with 368 ms). The differences in naming latency between the pseudowords with LF and with HF syllables remained constant over the training blocks, indicated by the absence of a three-way interaction between Orthographic Structure, Frequency and Training Block ($F<1$).

*Two– versus three–syllable pseudowords.* To test the effects of number of syllables, we compared naming latencies of two- versus three-syllable pseudowords with seven graphemes. The results of the analysis showed a main effect of Orthographic Structure ($F(1,9) = 15.29$, $p<.01$), reflecting a syllable effect. Naming latencies were on average 200 ms longer for three-syllable pseudowords. There was no effect of Frequency ($F(1,9) = 3.56$, $p=.09$). The effect of Training Block, however, was significant ($F(3,27) = 17.16$, $p<.001$), indicating that naming latencies decreased over the training blocks. The interaction between Orthographic Structure and Training Block was also significant: $F(3,27) = 3.08$, $p<.05$. The decrease of naming latency was largest for the three-syllable pseudowords (viz., 593 ms over training blocks). There was no three-way interaction between Orthographic Structure, Frequency, and Training Block ($F<1$).

Analyses of simple effects yielded an effect of Frequency for two-syllable pseudowords with five and seven graphemes only ($F(1,9) = 4.94$, $p=.05$, and $F(1,9) = 5.15$, $p=.05$, respectively), but not for the three-syllable pseudowords ($F(1,9) = 1.72$, $p=.22$). Naming latencies of two-syllable pseudowords with LF syllables were longer than naming latencies of those with HF syllables.

In sum, the results of the analyses indicate that the normal readers improved in decoding speed during the flash card training. Both the number of graphemes and the number of syllables seem to play a role in phonological decoding: We found a grapheme effect in pseudowords that only differed in number of graphemes and a syllable effect in pseudowords that only differed in number of syllables. A syllable frequency effect was found in the two-syllable pseudowords only, with longer latencies for pseudowords containing LF syllables.

*Results of the digit task*

Incorrect responses and responses with voice key errors were eliminated (2.6%). Means of the subject median digit naming latencies were calculated for each training block. These data were entered into a repeated measures analysis of variance with Training Block (four levels) as the within-subjects factor to test whether training affected digit naming latency. The analysis yielded a significant main effect of Training Block ($F(3,27)= 6.89$, $p=.001$), indicating that digit naming latencies decreased over the training blocks (the mean digit naming latencies were 716 ms (SD = 47 ms) for block 1, 665 ms (SD = 78 ms) for block 2, 644 ms (SD = 71 ms) for block 3 and 633 ms (SD = 71 ms) for block 4).

TABLE 1
The results of the pre- and posttests of the normal readers (N), and of the poor readers (P) with SD in parentheses, and F-tests of differences between the training and control conditions.

| Test | Group | Training Pretest | Training Posttest | Control Pretest | Control Posttest | F(1, 18) |
|---|---|---|---|---|---|---|
| DMT (max=140) | N | 74.0 | 82.2 | 76.4 | 79.4 | |
| | | (15.4) | (14.4) | (15.9) | (15.0) | 4.94 ** |
| | P | 56.0 | 64.0 | 55.8 | 64.3 | |
| | | (9.7) | (10.1) | (9.6) | (9.8) | < 1 ns* |
| LDT (max=90) | N | 36.5 | 41.7 | 31.9 | 40.1 | |
| | | (10.4) | (9.1) | (7.0) | (6.8) | 1.92 ns |
| | P | 26.1 | 32.7 | 32.1 | 34.8 | |
| | | (5.3) | (8.5) | (6.1) | (7.9) | < 1 ns* |
| WRT latency (ms) | N | 935 | 754 | 1015 | 901 | |
| | | (279) | (139) | (355) | (312) | 1.07 ns |
| | P | 1191 | 1183 | 1132 | 1009 | |
| | | (297) | (373) | (183) | (181) | < 1 ns |
| accuracy (max=30) | N | 30.0 | 29.7 | 28.5 | 29.7 | |
| | | (0.0) | (0.7) | (1.8) | (0.5) | 5.67 ** |
| | P | 26.8 | 29.2 | 28.2 | 29.5 | |
| | | (2.6) | (1.3) | (0.9) | (0.7) | 1.39 ns |
| PRT latency (ms) | N | 1749 | 977 | 1566 | 1294 | |
| | | (912) | (154) | (744) | (609) | < 1 ns |
| | P | 2329 | 2008 | 1762 | 1772 | |
| | | (753) | (772) | (706) | (722) | < 1 ns |
| accuracy (max=30) | N | 27.2 | 28.1 | 24.7 | 26.8 | |
| | | (2.2) | (1.9) | (3.6) | (2.2) | < 1 ns |
| | P | 19.6 | 27.6 | 18.5 | 23.7 | |
| | | (5.7) | (1.3) | (4.3) | (2.6) | < 1 ns |

Note. DMT = Three-Minutes-Test, LDT = Lexical Decision Task, WRT = Word Reading Task, PRT = Pseudoword Reading Task; *$df=$ (1, 17), ** = $p < .01$.

*Results of the pre- and posttests*

Group means of the training and the control group on the four pre- and posttests are presented in Table 1. The data of the pre- and posttests were submitted to separate repeated measures analyses of variance, with Group (training versus control) as the between-subjects factor and Test (pre versus post) as the within-subjects factor.

Naming latency and accuracy data of the two computerized naming tasks (the Word Reading Task and the Pseudoword Reading Task) were analysed separately. The median latency (based on at least 5 observations) and accuracy scores were calculated for each pre- and posttest, for each child. Incorrect responses and responses with voice key errors were eliminated in the latency analyses. The F-values of the Group by Test interactions from the repeated measures analyses of variance are presented in Table 1.

There was a significant difference between the training and the control group on the standardized reading test (DMT) only. Analyses of simple effects showed that the reading of isolated words improved in the training group ($F(1,9) = 45.75$, $p<.001$), and remained unchanged in the control group ($F(1,9) = 2.21$, ns). The training group read on average eight words per minute more on the posttest, indicating a transfer effect of the flash card training on the ability to read isolated words.

The significant difference in accuracy between the training and the control group on the Word Reading Test was the result of a slight improvement in word reading accuracy in the control group ($F(1,9) = 4.10$, $p=.07$), whereas there was a ceiling effect in the training group. In all other cases, the training and the control group improved to an equal extent from pre- to posttesting. Thus, in normal readers, the flash card training seemed to have an effect only on the standardized reading test.

As was mentioned in the introduction of this chapter, it was assumed that normal readers in second grade use syllabic information in reading words. To test this assumption, we further analysed the data of the Word Reading Task by comparing naming latencies of words with a different number of syllables. These analyses yielded no significant syllable effects (training group: $F(1,9) = 3.02$, ns for the pretest, and $F<1$ for the posttest; control group: $F<1$ for the pretest, and $F(1,9) = 1.45$, ns for the posttest), indicating that the normal readers did not use syllable-bound processing strategies in reading words before or after the flash card training.

## RESULTS OF THE POOR READERS

*Results of the flash card training*
Means of subject median naming latencies were computed for each orthographic structure, for each training block, and analysed in the same way as the naming latencies of the normal readers. Incorrect responses (19.8%) and responses with voice key errors (4.7%) were excluded. The mean naming latencies for the three orthographic structures, split by syllable frequency, are presented in Figure 2.

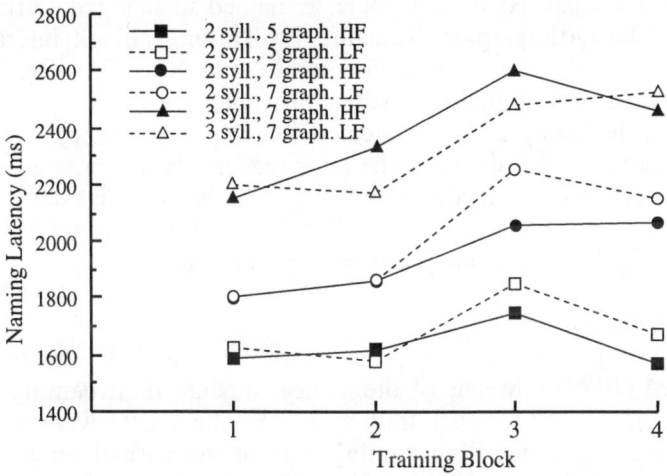

Fig. 2. Mean naming latencies (in milliseconds) for the three orthographic structures, split by syllable frequency, over the training blocks in poor readers.

*Two-syllable pseudowords.* The analysis on naming latencies of two-syllable pseudowords with five versus seven graphemes yielded a main effect of Orthographic Structure ($F(1,9) = 12.22$, $p<.01$), indicating a grapheme effect. Naming latencies were on average 326 ms longer for two-syllable pseudowords with seven graphemes than for those with five graphemes. There was a marginal effect of Frequency ($F(1, 9) = 4.23$, $p=.07$), but simple effects did not show frequency effects for either of the two orthographic structures (for two-syllable pseudowords with five graphemes: $F(1,9) = 2.58$, ns; for two-syllable pseudowords with seven graphemes: $F(1,9) = 3.12$, ns). Overall, naming latencies did not change during the training, indicated by the absence of an effect of Training Block ($F < 1$). There was a marginal interaction between Orthographic Structure and Training Block ($F(3,27) = 2.51$, $p=.08$). Naming latencies, collapsed over syllable frequency, slightly increased over the training blocks for two-syllable pseudowords with seven graphemes, whereas naming latencies for two-syllable pseudowords with five graphemes did not change significantly over the training blocks. There was no three-way interaction between Orthographic Structure, Training Block, and Frequency.

*Two- versus three-syllable pseudowords.* The analysis on naming latencies of two- versus three-syllable pseudowords with seven graphemes yielded a significant main effect of Orthographic Structure ($F(1,9) = 8.16$, $p<.05$), indicating a syllable effect. Naming latencies were on average 383 ms longer for three-syllable pseudowords. There was no significant effect of Frequency ($F<1$) or Training Block ($F(1,9) = 1.19$, ns). Naming latencies remained unchanged during the training. The Orthographic Structure by Training Block interaction, and the interaction between Orthographic Structure, Training Block, and Frequency also failed to reach significance (Fs <1).

In sum, the training data indicated that naming latency remained constant during the training in the poor readers. However, we found a grapheme effect as well as a syllable effect, indicating that the number of graphemes and the number of syllables play a role in phonological decoding. Syllable frequency effects were not obtained.

### Results of the digit task

Incorrect responses and responses with voice key errors were eliminated (10.4%). Means of the subject median digit naming latencies were calculated for each training block. These data were analysed in the same way as the digit naming data of the normal readers. The analysis revealed a significant effect of Training Block ($F(3,27) = 4.15$, $p<.05$). Digit naming latencies decreased over the training blocks (mean digit naming latencies were 759 ms (SD = 96 ms) for Block 1, 696 ms (SD = 59 ms) for Block 2, 684 ms (SD = 61 ms) for Block 3, and 660 ms (SD = 99 ms) for Block 4).

### Results of the pre- and posttests

The means of the training and the control group on the pre- and posttests are shown in Table 1. One child in the control group was not at school when the posttest of the DMT and the Lexical Decision Task were administered and was, therefore, excluded from the analyses on these two tests. Data of the pre- and posttests were submitted to separate repeated measures analyses of variance. Group (training versus control) served as the between-subjects factor and Test (pre versus post) as the within-subjects factor.

Naming latency and accuracy data of the two computerized naming tasks were analysed in the same way as the data of the normal readers. Incorrect responses (5.3% for words and 24.3% for pseudowords) and responses with voice key errors were eliminated in the latency analyses

(3.3% for the words and 5.2% for the pseudowords). The F-values of the Group by Test interactions are presented in Table 1.

Table 1 shows that there were no transfer effects of the flash card training on either of the four tests. The training and the control group improved to an equal extent on the DMT and on the Lexical Decision Task. In addition, both groups became more accurate in reading words and pseudowords from pre- to posttesting, and naming latency of words and pseudowords did not change in either group.

As in the normal readers, we further analysed the data of the Word Reading Task to test for possible syllable effects on the pre- and posttest in the training and the control group. The results of this analysis showed a marginal syllable effect between two- versus three-syllable words in the training group on the posttest (training group: $F(1,9) = 1.57$, ns, for the pretest, and $F(1,9) = 4.80$, $p=.06$ for the posttest; control group: $F<1$ for the pretest, and $F(1,9) = 2.28$, ns, for the posttest). The size of this syllable effect was 233 ms.

## DISCUSSION

The main purpose of this study was to investigate whether second grade normal readers and (older) poor readers with approximately the same reading level improve in decoding speed by means of a computer-based flash card training that emphasizes syllable-bound decoding. The results of the training showed that the normal readers improved in decoding speed during the training, while decoding speed in the poor readers remained unchanged. Both the normal and the poor readers improved in digit naming latency, but inspection of the data indicates that this improvement was the result of a relatively large decrease in digit naming latency in the first training block. In addition, the large difference in improvement between the digit naming task (a progress of 12%) and the flash card training (a progress of 35%) indicates that the normal readers improved at least to some extent in phonological decoding speed. This progress was largest on pseudowords that did not contain consonant clusters. Transfer effects of the training program to other (untrained) reading materials and conditions were only found on the standardized reading test in the normal readers.

Comparisons between naming latencies of different orthographic structures showed grapheme effects in both the poor and the normal readers: Over all training blocks naming latencies were significantly longer for pseudowords with more graphemes. Most importantly, we also found a syllable effect in both groups: Naming latencies were significantly longer for pseudowords with more syllables. Thus, it seems that processes at both the grapheme-phoneme level and the syllabic level play a role in phonological decoding in second grade normal readers and in poor readers with a comparable reading level. Although the poor readers did not improve in decoding speed during the flash card training, it seems that they used, like the normal readers, syllabic information in processing pseudowords. Syllable frequency did not seem to play an important role in the naming latency of pseudowords.

It was rather surprising that the poor readers did not show any progress in naming latency during the flash card training. A comparable study of Wentink et al. (1997), in which exactly the same flash card method was used and which was conducted with poor readers with a comparable reading level as the poor readers in the present study, showed a remarkable improvement of poor readers' decoding skills during the training. However, there were two important differences between these two studies that might explain these contradictory findings. First, the training program in the Wentink et al. study was twice as long as the one presented here. We suspect that more lengthy training would have greater benefit for poor readers. The second difference has to do with the orthographic transparency of the pseudowords. In the Wentink et al. study, all pseudowords were orthographically transparent, implying that each grapheme in the pseudowords had only one possible pronunciation. As a consequence of the fact that we used existing syllables, that differed in degree of regularity, in the present study, 40 per cent of the pseudowords were less transparent than the pseudowords in the Wentink et al. study. This implies that the children had to use contextual information in addition to the decoding rules to produce the correct pronunciation of the pseudowords. It is possible that the pseudowords in the present study therefore required longer processing time in poor readers than the pseudowords in the Wentink et al. study. If this assumption is correct, it is reasonable to assume that the poor readers spent much time on producing the correct responses and, as a result, could not improve their decoding speed.

A comparison between the naming latencies of the normal and the poor readers, indicated that the poor readers had more difficulty in decoding pseudowords than the normal readers. The poor readers had much longer naming latencies during the training than the normal readers, as was reflected by the results of an additional analysis of variance on overall naming latencies of the poor and normal readers ($F(1,18) = 19.08$, $p<.001$). The overall naming latencies were on average 904 ms shorter in the normal readers. In addition, the poor readers had overall a smaller number of correct responses than the normal readers (on average 87% for the normal readers vs. 80% for the poor readers). These differences between normal and poor readers' decoding skills are in line with the literature (Rack et al., 1992). Although the word reading level of the poor readers was three months behind the level of the normal readers, it is unlikely that, in the view of the large differences in naming latency between the two groups, these differences would not exist if the poor readers had the same word reading level as the normal readers.

As was mentioned earlier, it is plausible that the poor readers needed quite some time to produce the correct pronunciations of the pseudowords, and could, therefore, not yet improve in speed. In addition, the height of the accuracy rate (viz., 80%) indicates that the exposure duration of the training materials was longer than was intended in view of the adopted exposure duration procedure. This implies that the children had more time to process the presented letter strings and to read them out correctly, and were not stimulated by the flash card method to respond as quickly as possible. The long exposure duration's had no effect on the accuracy rate of the normal readers, since their accuracy level was already high from the beginning of the training (viz., 87%). As a result of the training, they improved in decoding speed. To test whether the poor readers indeed improved their naming accuracy as a result of the flash card training, whereas the normal readers did not, we analysed the accuracy data of both reading level groups.

The analysis of variance on mean numbers of correct responses per training block, collapsed over orthographic structures, yielded no main effect of the factor Training Block ($F<1$) in the normal readers, indicating that the overall accuracy rate remained constant over the training blocks (viz., 87%). The poor readers, however, improved in accuracy (viz., from 74% to 86%), as shown by a significant main effect of Training Block ($F(3,27) = 20.40$, $p<.001$). An interesting result is that the poor readers had approximately the same accuracy rate at the end of the training as the normal readers had during the whole training period. Based on these findings, it is reasonable to posit that the poor readers would have improved their naming latency if the training had contained more training sessions.

Thus, it seems that during the flash card training the normal readers improved in naming latency while the accuracy rate remained unchanged, whereas the poor readers improved in accuracy, while their naming latencies remained unchanged. The results of the Word Reading Task and the Pseudoword Reading Task support this conclusion: Only the normal readers improved in naming latency on these tasks. The poor readers training and control group improved in accuracy from pre- to posttest, but not in naming latency. These results imply that children first improve in decoding accuracy, before they improve in decoding speed (Adams, 1990; Ehri & Wilce, 1983).

A surprising finding emerged in the additional analyses on the data of the Word Reading Task in which naming latencies of words with a different number of syllables were compared. These analyses yielded no syllable effects in the normal readers, indicating that they did not use syllabic information before or after the training. This finding conflicts with a study of Marmurek and Rinaldo (1992), who found that normally achieving readers use syllabic information in reading words when they are in second grade. Thus, although the flash card training seemed to stimulate normal readers to process pseudowords in syllabic units, they did not use syllable-bound processes in reading words after the training.

For the poor readers, the additional analyses on the data of the Word Reading Task yielded a marginal syllable effect in the training group. This suggests that the poor readers, in contrast to the normal readers, learned to use syllabic information in processing pseudowords during the training and were able to use this skill in processing words after the training. Thus, although there were no transfer effects of the flash card training on the Word Reading Task, there are some indications that the poor readers acquired syllable-bound decoding skills during the flash card training, while the normal readers did not.

A final interesting result was the transfer effect from the flash card training in the normal readers to their performance on the standardized reading test (the DMT), in contrast to the lack of transfer effects in the poor readers. This difference in generalization effects between poor and normal readers indicates that second grade normal readers are more sensitive to a training in decoding skills than poor readers with approximately the same reading level. Poor readers need much more intensive training than normal readers, to improve their decoding skills. This supports the claim that the poor readers' difficulties with phonological decoding are very persistent and hard to remediate by training. The flash card method we used in the current study seems to be a helpful tool for improving poor readers decoding skills, but it is evident from earlier studies (Van den Bosch, 1991; Wentink et al., 1997) that poor readers need to practise intensively, and over long periods of time before they will show improvement in decoding speed.

To conclude, the results of the present study are in accordance with earlier findings (see, for instance, Beech & Awaida, 1992; Szeszulski & Manis, 1987), indicating that normal and poor readers are able to employ comparable decoding processes in reading aloud, but differ in their efficiency in using these processes. The flash card program used in the current study had an effect on accuracy in the poor readers and on naming latency in the normal readers, who had a high accuracy rate prior to the training already. The lack of generalization effects of the training on decoding skills in the poor readers implies that poor readers need a much more lengthy and intensive training in decoding skills than normal readers.

## ACKNOWLEDGEMENTS

This study was conducted by the second author for her master's thesis, and formed a part of the dissertation project of the first author. We are most grateful to the staff and children of the Juliana School and the Wilhelmina School in Doetinchem and the Meginhard School in Arnhem for their co-operation.

## REFERENCES

Adams, M. J. (1990). *Beginning to read: Thinking and learning about print.* Cambridge, MA: MIT Press.

Badian, N. A. (1994). Do dyslexic and other poor readers differ in reading-related cognitive skills? *Reading and Writing: An Interdisciplinary Journal, 6,* 45–63.

Beech, J. R. & Awaida, M. (1992). Lexical and nonlexical routes: A comparison between normally achieving and poor readers. *Journal of Learning Disabilities, 25,* 196–206.

Butler, B. E., Jared, D., & Hains, S. (1984). Reading skill and the use of orthographic knowledge by mature readers. *Psychological Research, 46,* 337–353.

Coltheart, M. (1978). Lexical access in simple reading tasks. In G. Underwood (Ed.), *Strategies of information processing* (pp. 151–216). New York: Academic Press.

Das, J. P., & Siu, I. (1989). Good and poor readers' word naming time, memory span, and story recall. *Journal of Experimental Education, 57,* 101–114.

Ehri, L. C., & Wilce, L. S. (1983). Development of word identification speed in skilled and less skilled beginning readers. *Journal of Educational Psychology, 75,* 3–18.

Holligan, C., & Johnston, R. S. (1988). The use of phonological information by good and poor readers in memory and reading tasks. *Memory & Cognition, 16,* 522–532.

Katz, L., & Feldman, L. B. (1981). Linguistic coding in word recognition: Comparisons between a deep and a shallow orthography. In A. M. Lesgold & C. A. Perfetti (Eds.), *Interactive Processes in Reading* (pp. 85–106). New Jersey: Lawrence Erlbaum.

Levelt, W. J. M., & Wheeldon, L. (1994). Do speakers have access to a mental syllabary? *Cognition, 50,* 239–269.

Marmurek, H. H. C., & Rinaldo, R. (1992). The development of letter and syllable effects in categorization, reading aloud, and picture naming. *Journal of Experimental Child Psychology, 53,* 277–299.

Olson, R. K., & Wise, B. W. (1992). Reading on the computer with orthographic and speech feedback: An overview of the Colorado remediation project. *Reading and Writing, 4,* 107–144.

Perfetti, C. A. (1985). *Reading Ability.* New York: Oxford University Press.

Rack, J. P., Snowling, M. J., & Olson, R. K. (1992). The nonword reading deficit in developmental dyslexia: A review. *Reading Research Quarterly, 27,* 29–53.

Reitsma, P. (1990). Development of orthographic knowledge. In P. Reitsma & L. Verhoeven (Eds.), *Acquisition of Reading in Dutch* (pp. 43–64). Dordrecht: Foris Publications.

Scheerer-Neumann, G. (1981). The utilization of intraword structure in poor readers: Experimental evidence and a training program. *Psychological Research, 43*, 155–178.
Szeszulski, P. A., & Manis, F. R. (1987). A comparison of word recognition processing in dyslexic and normal readers at two reading-age levels. *Journal of Experimental Child Psychology, 44*, 364–376.
Tousman, S., & Inhoff, A. (1992). Phonology in multisyllabic word recognition. *Journal of Psycholinguistic Research, 21*, 525–544.
Treiman, R., Fowler, C. A., Gross, J., Berch, D., & Weatherston, S. (1995). Syllable structure or word structure? Evidence for onset and rime units with disyllabic and trisyllabic stimuli. *Journal of Memory and Language, 34*, 132–155.
Van Daal, V. H. P., Reitsma, P., & Van der Leij, A. (1994). Processing units in word reading by disabled readers. *Journal of Experimental Child Psychology, 57*, 180–210.
Van den Bosch, K. (1991). *Poor Readers' Decoding Skills: Effects of Training, Task, and Word Characteristics.* Unpublished doctoral dissertation, University of Nijmegen, The Netherlands.
Vellutino, F. R., Scanlon, D. M., & Spearing, D. (1995), Semantic and phonological coding in poor and normal readers. *Journal of Experimental Child Psychology, 59*, 76–123.
Verhoeven, L. (1992). *Drie-Minuten-Toets* [Three-Minutes-Test]. Arnhem: Cito.
Wentink, H. (1997). *From graphemes to syllables: The development of phonological decoding skills in poor and normal readers.* Doctoral dissertation, University of Nijmegen, The Netherlands.
Wentink, H., Van Bon, W. H. J., & Schreuder, R. (1997). Training of Poor Readers' Phonological Decoding Skills: Evidence for Syllable-bound Processing. *Reading and Writing, 9*, 163–192.
Yap, R. (1993). *Automatic Word Processing Deficits in Dyslexia: Qualitative Differences and Specific Remediation.* Doctoral dissertation, Free University of Amsterdam, The Netherlands.

ELISABETH ARNBAK AND CARSTEN ELBRO

# TEACHING MORPHOLOGICAL AWARENESS TO DYSLEXIC STUDENTS

Morphemes are the smallest meaningful units of language. In the word *babysitter* there are three morphemes: baby-sitt-er, and in the word *unforgetfulness* there are five: un-for-get-ful-ness. The meaning of a word is, more or less clearly, the combined meanings of the morphemes of that particular word. Four different types of morphemes are used in the formation of words: root morphemes, prefixes, suffixes, and inflections. Root morphemes may be words in themselves; there are at least one root in every word (sleeping, dreamed, cats, a reader, brownish). The other three types of morphemes are bound morphemes, meaningful units of words, but never words in themselves. Prefixes change the meaning of a root, but not its grammatical class (unhappy, forgiving, behold). Suffixes change both the meaning and the grammatical class of a root (a reader, forgetful, unforgettable, sweeten), and inflections add information about, for example, number, gender, and tense (cars, helped, loving, larger).

The compounding, derivation, and inflection of a root morpheme often results in a phonological change of the root morpheme. As a consequence of this, the morphological relation between words sharing the same root may be rather intransparent in spoken language. The term transparency refers the degree of which the sound and the meaning of a complex word is predictable from its constituent morphemes. Thus, the morphological structure of words like fourth (in analogy with four) and easily (easy) is phonologically transparent in contrast to words like fifth (five) and length (long). Likewise, the morphological structure of words, such as *mean, meaning* (of a word), and *meaningless* is quite semantically transparent, in contrast to words such as *motherboard* (part of a computer) and *customer* (related to custom). Both the phonological and the semantic transparency of the morphological structure of words is reported to be of importance to the development of morphological awareness, the ability to become aware of and to manipulate the morphological structure of words, (Carlisle, 1988; Tyler & Nagy, 1989).

Even though the compounding, derivation, and inflection of a root morpheme often results in a phonological change, the root morpheme often holds the same spelling in the different complex words of which it is a part (e.g., nature / natural, divide / division). Because of this, knowledge of the morphological relations between words may ease the reading and spelling of many complex words.

IMPORTANCE OF MORPHOLOGY TO READING AND SPELLING

Because morphology is important to orthographies such as Danish and English, it may also play a part in the development of reading and spelling skills. Elbro and Arnbak (1996) list several arguments of the importance of morphology to reading and spelling skills:

1. Alphabetic orthographies are morpho-phonemic constructions. Many irregularities from a phonemic point of view are often regularities from a morphemic point of view. This is the case for some of the words containing silent letters, e.g., bomb (bombardment), and for the spelling of ambiguous letters, e.g., the c in ecstacy (ecstatic).

2. Morphemes are meaningful units of words, and it is possible to understand many new words by analysing their morpheme constituents. For example, the new kind of rollerskates is called inliners, because the wheels are placed in one line. Nagy & Anderson (1984) reported that most of the new words students are expected to learn are morphologically complex, but at the same time morphologically transparent. Therefore, it is quite possible that the large growth in students' vocabulary which is seen during the school years is made possible by the students' morphological analysis of such new words (White, Power, & White, 1989).

3. An orthographic lexicon organized in morpheme units rather than whole word representations would be economical as the root morpheme would only have to be stored once: e.g., read + -s, -ing, -er, -able and ready + -made, -ness, -ly.

4. Error analyses are thought to be a productive way of studying students' reading and spelling strategies. Some reading and spelling errors are evidently morphologically based errors (e.g., proceedure in analogy with proceed).

5. Finally, the existence of non-alphabetic writing systems which are morphologically based like Chinese and Japanese provides a strong argument in favour of the importance of morphology to reading and spelling.

*Morphological skills and reading and spelling abilities*

A number of studies have in fact reported a relation between good reading and spelling skills and the use of morphological rules in oral and written language tasks (Carlisle, 1987, 1995; Fischer, Shankweiler, & Liberman, 1985; Leong 1989; Rubin, 1991). Based on these studies, it seems evident that morphological analysis skills are important to the development of reading and spelling skills.

What is left to demonstrate, however, is the actual nature of this relation. At least three different hypotheses about the relation between morphological skills and reading and spelling abilities have been presented in reading research. One hypothesis deals with morphological awareness as a cause of development of reading skills, another hypothesis holds the opposite causal direction between morphological awareness and reading skills to be true, namely that written language experience is a causal factor in the development of morphological awareness. A third hypothesis is one in which the development of both morphological awareness and reading and spelling skills is influenced by phonological skills in spoken language.

Evidence of morphological awareness as a predictor of reading abilities comes from at least two longitudinal studies. Tornéus (1987) found that the morphological awareness of kindergartners as measured by a morphological analysis test (explain the meaning of bee grass and grass bee) predicted their reading ability in the second grade. Likewise, Carlisle (1995) found that the morphological awareness of kindergartners measured by a morphological production test (farm: my uncle is a _____, farmer) predicted reading comprehension in the second grade. A few correlational studies report data that may point in the same direction. In these studies, differences in reading and spelling skills in groups of both normal and poor readers were explained by individual differences in morphological awareness of spoken language (Brittain, 1970; Rubin, 1991).

The opposite causal relation between orthographic experience and the development of morphological awareness may be just as likely. Many complex words are semantically and phonologically intransparent (difficult to analyse in their morpheme constituents). Exposure to print, seeing the same morpheme unit in many different words, might be necessary in order to become aware of the morphological structure of such words. Fowler and Liberman (1995) examined the relation between morphological awareness and reading ability of young students in the second to fourth grade. Morphological awareness was measured by a morphological production test modeled after Carlisle (1987). There were two tasks: one requiring production of a derived form on the basis of the base form (Four. The big racehorse came in ____, fourth) and one to produce the base form from the derived form (Fourth. When he counted the poppies, there were ___, four). Half of the stems underwent a phonological change from base to derived form (complex); the other half did not (simple). Fowler and Liberman (1995) found no differences in awareness of derivations between poor and good readers differing in age but of similar reading ability (reading-level match), suggesting that differences in the morphological awareness of poor and good readers might be caused by differences in knowledge of written language.

The third relation between morphological awareness and reading development is one in which the two are connected via a third underlying factor – phonological awareness. The main part of the study of Fowler and Liberman dealt with the importance of phonological factors to the development of morphological awareness. The results of the study indicated that only ability to solve phonologically complex items divided poor readers from good. Fowler and Liberman suggest that differences in morphological awareness depend on differences in the phonological domain.

*Morphological awareness and dyslexia*

A number of studies of morphological skills in good and poor readers have documented that poor readers lag behind their normal peers in the acquisitions of morphological skills in both oral and written language. Elbro (1990) has presented data from a study of the reading and spelling skills and strategies of 15-year old dyslexics. Elbro found that the dyslexics relied more on the morphological structure of words in word decoding than did the younger reading level matched controls, and that the dyslexics had a greater tendency to use a meaning oriented reading strategy. These results might suggest that the dyslexics were using an alternative decoding strategy based on morpheme units. However, when examining the dyslexic students´ awareness of morphemes in spoken language, Elbro found that the 15-year old dyslexics were less aware of morphemes in spoken language in 3 of 5 tests of morphological awareness than both their normal peers and the reading level matched younger controls (a test of segmenting words into their morpheme constituents and reversing them, a test of morpheme completion, and a test of counting words in sentences). Thus, the dyslexics might not possess a sufficient level of morphological awareness for them to be able to efficiently employ an alternative decoding strategy based on morphemes.

The results of the above mentioned study further suggest that morphological awareness does not develop by itself over time or in the course of reading instruction. This possibility alone calls for a further examination of the causal relation between morphological awareness and reading and spelling. Furthermore, it seemed interesting to see whether it was possible to help develop the morphological awareness of dyslexics.

We conducted a morphological awareness training study to see whether it was at all possible to improve dyslexic students' awareness of morphemes through an oral training and further to examine the causality of morphological awareness to the reading and spelling abilities of young dyslexics. We expected the experimental students to gain more than the controls in awareness of all types of morphemes in spoken language, in the reading and spelling of morphologically complex words, and in reading comprehension.

## METHOD

### Participants

The experimental group consisted of 33 students from Grade 4 and 5 (23 boys and 10 girls) with severe reading and writing problems selected from 9 schools in the area of Copenhagen. The students were identified in the second term of Grade 3 or 4 by remedial teachers as reading at least 2 years below expected reading level in spite of an otherwise normal development of oral language and cognitive skills. At the onset of the experiment, the students were between 10 and 12 years old. The students had already received remedial teaching for some time and were receiving remedial teaching during the whole experiment as well.

Twenty-seven students (17 boys and 10 girls) were selected by the same criteria to form a control group. They attended 8 different schools in the area of Copenhagen. The two groups were matched on age, gender, and Raven's Progressive Matrices IQ (see Table 1).

TABLE 1
Experimental group (N=33) and matched control group (N=27).

|  | Experimental group | | | Control group | | |
|---|---|---|---|---|---|---|
|  | M | SD | Range | M | SD | Range |
| Age (yrs.) | 11.0 | 0.11 | 9.9-12.11 | 11.2 | 0.11 | 10.0-12.9 |
| Raven raw score | 33.8 | 7.4 | 12-48 | 31.3 | 7.5 | 20-47 |
| Raven percentile | 47 | 20.0 | 4-92 | 40 | 24.7 | 9-96 |

### Teaching procedures

The teaching of the students was carried out by the remedial teachers of the dyslexic students. Prior to the training period, the remedial teachers had participated in a 12 hr course on morphology and dyslexia. The experimental students received morphological awareness training for 15 min three times a week over a three month period. The morphological awareness training was part of the remedial training of the experimental group, which for the rest of the time consisted of traditional reading and spelling instruction (in Denmark morphological instruction is not traditionally a part of remedial training; remedial training would deal with various silent and oral reading tasks, instruction in letter to sound correspondences, syllable segmentation, phonological awareness training, and spelling to dictation). The control group received the same kind of traditional remedial training for the same period of time. As the morphological awareness training was predominantly oral, the experimental students spent less time on reading and spelling activities than the controls did.

### The morphological awareness training programme

The morphological awareness training was primarily oral and the focus was on the semantics of morphemes (Arnbak, 1993). The type of morpheme trained and the individual words used in the programme was ordered according to semantic transparency.

Part 1 of the programme dealt with root morphemes. The following are examples of tasks: *(1) Stationmaster - what does a stationmaster do? (2) Name the two morphemes of the word. (3) Switch the two morphemes around - what does the new word mean?* An example of a more open ended task is the following: *A candy factory does not sell enough bon bons. They sell bon bons of four different flavours: Orange slices, liquorice bon bons, caramel balls, chocolate chips. Help the candy factory sell more candy: make up more interesting and fun names for the four types of bon bons. The names of the candy should be compounds.*

In Part 2 (affixes) of the training programme, prefixes were trained first as this morpheme type changes only the meaning of the root morpheme, but not its grammatical class. After that, suffixes were trained. The students segmented words into morpheme units, analysed the semantic relationship between affixes and roots, and made up many new word forms by changing or adding different affixes to the roots. For example: *Segment the words into prefix and root: fore - forewarn, foreshow, foreclose, forego, foresee, or un - unaware, uncertain, unknown, untamed. Add a suffix and change the word to something you are or might be (an adjective): To love, to hate, to eat, to talk, to recommend.*

In Part 3 (inflections) only inflections of nouns, verbs, and adjectives were trained. Inflections were trained in two different ways: first the students analysed the meaning of the inflections in question and then they segmented inflected words into root and inflection, focusing on the semantic, as well as the phonological and orthographic identity of the inflections. This last part of the morphological training was the only part of the programme that involved written language. For example, *Listen to the following sentences: does the present tense always mean "now"? He works from 9 to 5 every week. He goes to Copenhagen tomorrow. He loves candy. What is the difference between 'a killing man' and 'a killed man' - who is doing what to whom?*

In order to further qualify the students' understanding of morpheme units in words the students were taught about pseudo-morphemes in words (the unit car in carpet or ab in abdomen). Tasks involving pseudo-morphemes were part of the whole programme e.g., *If pet is a morpheme in the word carpet – what would the word mean?*

*Procedure and tests*

The same set of language, reading and spelling tests were administered before and after the training period. Several oral language measures were included as control measures.

*Oral language measures*

*Morpheme Subtraction and Identification.* The students were first asked to identify and name the first root of a compound, e.g., "What is left in hand-grenade if you take away grenade?" Then they were asked to name the free variant of the same roots (hand). The test had 20 items of varying phonological and semantic transparency. The scores were number of correctly named free variants of the first roots.

*Morphological Analogy.* The students were asked to name the base morpheme of a derived or inflected word following a pattern from another set of words: reading relates to read as writing relates to ...... The test had 20 items; these were inflections and derivations of nouns, verbs, and adjectives. The score was number of correct analogies.

*Compounding and Inflecting New Words.* A Danish version of Berko's Wug test ("Here's a wug, here's another. Now, there are two ......?"). There were 18 items, 13 inflections and 5 compounds. The number of correctly named inflections and compounds were scored.

*Phoneme Identification* (Nielsen & Petersen, 1992). Two tests of phoneme identification were used: (1) "The word mouth begins with the sound /m/. Find the word with an /m/." (2) "The word hat contains the sound /a/ find the word which has an /a/ in the same position as in hat". Each test had 10 items. The score was a total number of correct of all 20 items.

*Phoneme Discrimination* (Elbro, 1990). The task was to discriminate between minimal pairs of words, i.e., sat–fat. The students were presented with pairs of pictures and asked to point to the picture matching a spoken word embedded in white noise. The test consisted of 34 word pairs. The score was number of correctly identified items.

*Receptive Vocabulary.* The Peabody Picture Vocabulary Test (Dunn & Dunn, 1981) was used.

*Non-verbal Cognitive Ability.* The Raven progressive matrices, series a, b, c, and d (Raven, 1960) were used.

*Reading Measures*

*Passage Comprehension* (SL 60, Nielsen, Kreiner, Søgård, & Poulsen, 1986). A standard silent reading test with picture selection (60 sentences of varying length and complexity; about half of the words in the sentences are morphologically complex). The scores were number of correct in 5 min and within a 15 min limit.

*Nonword Reading* (Elbro, 1990). Forty nonwords matched real words as to number of letters and word structure. The score was number of correctly read nonwords.

*Morpheme Reading*. The students read 80 words aloud. The words were 20 quartets of words. The words of each quartet shared the same root morpheme (e.g., mouse, mousetrap, mousy, mice). Half of the roots had conventional spellings, the other half had more unconventional spellings in terms of phoneme-grapheme predictability. Reading accuracy was computed for each of the four word types (20 free roots, 20 compounds, 20 derived words, and 20 inflected words).

In addition to the analyses performed on correctly read words, we carried out some analyses of misread words: percentage of preserved 1st roots in misread words, preserved 2nd roots in misread compounds, preserved derivations in misread derived words, preserved inflections of misread inflected words, and phonetic (letter-preserving) misreadings.

## Spelling Measures

*Morpheme Spelling*. The same 80 words were used as in the Morpheme Reading Test. Each word was presented in a context and then repeated by the experimenter. For each of the four word types total sum scores of all correctly spelled words were computed.

Furthermore, we did the following analyses of the misspelled words: percentage of preserved first roots of all misspelled words, percentage of preserved endings of all misspelled words, and percentage of phonetic spelling errors of all misspelled words.

## RESULTS

We hypothesized that training morphological awareness with young dyslexics would improve their general level of awareness of all types of morphemes. The individual schools (teaching groups) were chosen as units for analyses because the teachers of each school planned the training sessions together. We performed a series of Reader Group (2) x Test Occasions (2) MANOVAs with repeated measures on schools (teaching groups) for each measure of morphological awareness.

The experimental group gained significantly more than the controls on the test of morphological analogies. Pretest mean scores (SD in parenthesis) for the experimental group were 9.3 (5.1); for the control group 7.8 (5.0). Post-test mean scores (SD in parenthesis) for the former group were 12.4 (3.2); for the latter group 10.4 (4.7), $F = 4.7$, $p<.05$. The experimental group also gained more than the controls on a measure of compound formation; this result, however, was not significant. The experimental group showed no effect of the training on a measure of morpheme subtraction. In a post hoc analysis of the items of the morpheme subtraction test, 20 university students judged the items of the morpheme subtraction test according to phonological and semantic transparency. The analysis revealed that the dyslexic students had great difficulties dealing with the intransparent items at pretest, and neither the experimental group nor the controls made any progress with these items during the training period. On the other hand, there was a near ceiling effect on the transparent items at pretest. Thus, a training effect on transparent words would hardly show in the data because of ceiling effects for these easy items. Finally, the experimental group did not gain more than the controls on measures of phonemic awareness or in receptive vocabulary.

The following tables with data from the morphological awareness training study were first presented in Elbro and Arnbak (1996).

TABLE 2
Pre- and posttest performance on measures of reading skills and strategies. Standard deviations are given in parentheses. Significance levels of interactions between groups and time of testing are added in the last column

| Measure | Teaching Condition | Pretest Mean | (SD) | Posttest Mean | (SD) | Significance of interaction F (1.15), p |
|---|---|---|---|---|---|---|
| Total number correct | Morph. | 29.4 | (16.4) | 37.1 | (20.0) | 1.7, n.s. |
| Words (max = 80) | Control | 27.8 | (13.3) | 38.5 | (17.8) | |
| Real word responses | Morph. | 55.6 | (15.8) | 61.7 | (13.5) | 7.2, <.05 |
| of misreadings (%) | Control | 56.0 | (19.4) | 52.3 | (19.7) | |
| Nonwords | Morph. | 17.0 | (8.2) | 17.8 | (9.2) | 1.9, n.s. |
| correct (of 40) | Control | 16.6 | (8.5) | 19.8 | (9.6) | |
| Passage comprehension | Morph. | 3.3 | (1.4) | 4.4 | (1.9) | 5.6, <.05 |
| (correct/min.) | Control | 3.3 | (1.4) | 4.1 | (1.7) | |

We expected the experimental group to gain more than the controls in reading of complex words. As it turned out, the experimental group did not improve their decoding of words (neither simple nor complex words) more than the controls did (see Table 2). There was a tendency for the experimental group to improve more in reading of derived and inflected words than the controls, but these results did not reach significance.

However, error analyses revealed that when misreading a word, the experimental students significantly more often replied with a real word than the controls did. Furthermore, when reading a derived word the experimental group made significantly larger gains on a measure of preserved derivations than the controls. Mean pre- and posttest scores for the experimental group were 20.9 (16.4) and 37.4 (29.7);

mean pre- and posttest scores for the controls were 33.8 (28.9) and 31.1 (21.9) (F(1,15) = 6.11, p<.05). A similar tendency could be seen for inflected words; the experimental group made larger gains on a measure of preserved inflections than the controls, but this difference was statistically not significant.

We expected the experimental group to gain more than the controls in reading comprehension. As seen in Table 2, the experimental group did have a marginally higher gain in passage comprehension than the control group. As expected, there was no significant effect of the morphological awareness training on the reading of non-words.

The experimental group gained more than the controls in the spelling of all 78 words The result was significant by subjects, F(1,58) = 5.3, p<.05; however, the difference was not significant by schools. As seen in Table 3, the gain in spelling was primarily due to the experimental group's gain in spelling of compounds.

TABLE 3

Pretest and posttest performance on measures of spelling skills and strategies. Standard deviations are given in parentheses. Significance levels of interactions between groups and time of testing are added in the last column

| Measure | Teaching Condition | Pretest Mean (SD) | Posttest Mean (SD) | Significance of interaction $F (1.5), p$ |
|---|---|---|---|---|
| Simple words | Morph. | 7.7 (4.2) | 10.4 (4.9) | <1 n.s. |
| correct(max 20) | Control | 7.4 (5.3) | 9.1 (4.9) | |
| Compounds | Morph. | 4.4 (3.4) | 7.4 (4.5) | 6.8 <.05 |
| correct(max 20) | Control | 5.2 (4.0) | 6.3 (4.6) | |
| Derived words | Morph. | 2.6 (2.6) | 5.1 (4.3) | 1.7 n.s. |
| correct(max 20) | Control | 2.8 (2.6) | 4.1 (3.9) | |
| Derivations preserved | Morph. | 26.8 (18.2) | 45.3 (25.1) | 16.9 <.01 |
| (% of misspelled words) | Control | 27.5 (14.1) | 30.7 (17.5) | |
| Inflected words correct | Morph. | 2.8 (2.5) | 4.5 (3.3) | <1 n.s. |
| (max 19) | Control | 3.0 (2.3) | 3.6 (3.6) | |
| Inflections preserved | Morph. | 33.5 (20.3) | 39.4 (20.3) | <1 n.s. |
| (% of misspelled words) | Control | 33.9 (23.6) | 35.2 (20.7) | |
| Total number correct | Morph. | 17.2 (12.3) | 27.6 (16.3) | 1.4 n.s. |
| (max 78) | Control | 18.6 (13.9) | 23.4 (16.4) | |
| Sound-preserving errors | Morph. | 19.0 (14.5) | 29.1 (18.8) | 11.9 <.01 |
| (% of misspelled words) | Control | 20.4 (17.7) | 21.8 (16.1) | |

An error analysis showed the same tendency as the measure of correctly spelled words. The experimental group gained significantly more than the controls on a measure of the proportion of preserved derivations. The same (nonsignificant) trend could be seen in misspelled inflected words and in preserved inflections. Thus, the morphological awareness training did seem to have an overall positive effect on the experimental students' ability to spell morphemes of complex words. Somewhat surprisingly, the experimental group gained significantly more on a measure of phonetically acceptable misspelling than the control group did.

## DISCUSSION

The morphological training did have a small, but positive effect on the level of morphological awareness of the experimental group compared to that of the controls. In contrast to this, the experimental group did not gain more than the controls on tests of phonological awareness or in receptive vocabulary. It seems that the larger gains of the experimental group on the one test of morphological awareness compared to the controls were not a result of a higher level of overall linguistic awareness. Based on these results it seems that awareness of morphemes *can* be trained independently of awareness of phonological units.

The morphological awareness training programme was an orally presented training programme. The students were trained to segment and analyse complex but transparent words and to produce complex words. The experimental group only gained more than the controls on one of three morphological awareness measures. They did not gain more than the controls on a test of morpheme subtraction. This test included items of various degrees of phonological and semantic transparency. The post hoc analysis of the items of the morpheme subtraction test indicated that the dyslexics experienced great difficulties with the intransparent items at pretest, and neither the experimental group nor the controls made any progress with these items during the training period. Apparently, there was no transfer effect from training awareness of phonologically and semantically transparent words to more intransparent items. The poor result of the dyslexics on the phonologically intransparent items might be interpreted along the lines of the phonological deficit hypothesis of Fowler and Liberman even though the present study did not allow us to neither verify or falsify this.

However, another explanation might be just as likely. Perhaps it is not possible to become aware of the morphological structure of intransparent words through an oral training. Awareness of the morphological structure of intransparent words possibly develop as a consequence of orthographic knowledge, through seeing the same morphological unit as part of many different words. Thus, the above mentioned results of the morpheme subtraction test might just as well be interpreted along the lines of the importance of written language skills to the development of morphological awareness.

We expected the experimental group to gain more than the controls in the reading of morphologically complex words. This, however, was not the case although the experimental group gained more than the controls in preserving the bound morphemes of misread words. Thus, the basic problem of the experimental group was to decode the root morpheme of the words. It seems likely that being aware of the morphological structure of words does not support the decoding of words if the student is not able at least to identify the root morpheme. When reading a word, one does not know if a candidate morpheme, e.g., read is part of the word before the whole word is identified (e.g., in words such as reader and ready). An increased morphological awareness in spoken language may not *per se* lead to better word decoding skills in reading.

The experimental group gained more on percentage of real word replies in attempting to read the words of the morpheme reading test. This result might indicate that the experimental group improved their understanding of words as meaningful units. In contrast to word decoding and as predicted, the experimental group did show a small gain in reading comprehension compared to the controls. Knowledge of the morphological structure of words seems to some extent to boost reading based on a meaning oriented strategy. The participants in the experimental group seem to have become better at identifying (guessing at) the base morphemes of the words in order to extract the meaning of the sentences. A morpheme identification strategy in single word reading poses great demands on the accuracy of the morpheme recognition, whereas a meaning oriented strategy in the reading of coherent text may be less demanding with regards to a precise identification of the root morphemes of words. This may at least be the case when demands on precise decoding and comprehension are low—as in the silent reading test employed.

The morphological awareness training seems to have had a positive effect on the spelling ability of the dyslexics. The experimental group gained significantly more than the controls in the spelling of complex words. In contrast to reading, the meaning of a word is fully available to a student from the beginning of the spelling process. The result in spelling suggests that awareness of morpheme units in words enabled dyslexic students to segment complex words into linguistic units they knew how to spell.

The results in spelling might also be an indication of an ease of the load on working memory. The dyslexic students with some morphological analysis skills might be better at maintaining meaningful units of words (morphemes) in working memory while spelling.

The experimental group gained also more in terms of phonetically acceptable misspellings. This is interesting since the control group was better at reading non-words at posttest than the experimental group, and because there was no difference between the two groups on tests of phonological skills in oral language. Again, it seems that being able to segment words into morpheme units is supportive to the development of dyslexics' written language skills. The results of the spelling measures seem to suggest that the experimental students were in the process of developing an alternative encoding strategy based on morpheme units.

Based on both former research on the development of morphological awareness and morphological skills and data from this morphological training study, chances increase that dyslexic students improve in morphological awareness and in reading and spelling when morphological awareness training includes written language as well as oral language tasks. Furthermore, it might be necessary to point out the morphological structure of semantically and phonologically intransparent words as well. Further studies of the relation between morphological awareness and reading and spelling skills are clearly needed.

### REFERENCES

Arnbak, E. (1993). *Er mor-femdeling mord?* Herning, Denmark: Specialpædagogisk forlag.
Ball, E. W. (1993). Phonological awareness: what's important and to whom? *Reading and Writing: An interdisciplinary Journal, 5,* 141–159.
Berko, J. (1958). The child's learning of English morphology. *Word, 14,* 150–177.
Brittain, M. M. (1970). Inflectional performance and early reading achievement. *Reading Research Quarterly, 6,* 34-48.
Bowey, J. A., & Francis, J. (1991). Phonological analysis as a function of age and exposure to reading instruction. *Applied Psycholinguistics, 12,* 91–121.
Byrne, B., & Freebody, P. (1992). Longitudinal data on the relations of word-reading strategies to comprehension, reading time, and phonetic awareness. *Reading Research Quarterly, 27,* 141–151.
Carlisle, J. F. (1987). The use of morphological knowledge in spelling derived forms by learning-disabled and normal students. *Annals of Dyslexia, 39,* 90–108.
Carlisle, J. F. (1988). Knowledge of derivational morphology and spelling ability in fourth, sixth, and eight graders. *Applied Psycholinguistics, 9,* 247–266.
Carlisle, J. F. (1995). Morphological awareness and early reading achievement. In L. B. Feldman (Ed.), *Morphological Aspects of Language Processing.* Hillsdale, NJ: Erlbaum.
Clark, E.V., & Hecht, B. F. (1982). Learning to coin agent and instrument nouns. *Cognition, 12,* 1–24.
Dunn, L. M., & Dunn, L. M. (1981). *Peabody Picture Vocabulary Test - Revised.* Circle Pins, MN: American Guidance.
Elbro, C. (1990). *Differences in Dyslexia. A Study of Reading Strategies and Deficits in a Linguistic Perspective.* Copenhagen: Munksgaard.
Elbro, C., & Arnbak, E. (1996). The role of morpheme recognition and morphological awareness in dyslexia. *Annals of Dyslexia, 46,* 209–240.
Elbro, C., & Petersen, T. (1993). *Udviklingsarbejde om undersøgelse af ordblinde*

*elevers læsestrategier* ('A study of reading strategies in dyslexic students'. In Danish). Copenhagen: Det tværkommunale projektsamvirke.

Fischer, F. W., Shankweiler, D. P., & Liberman, I. Y. (1985). Spelling proficiency and sensitivity to word structure. *Journal of Memory and Language, 24,* 423–441.

Fowler, A. E., & Liberman, I. Y. (1995). The role of phonology and orthography in morphological awareness. In L. B. Feldman (Ed.), *Morphological Aspects of Language Processing.* Hillsdale, N.J: Erlbaum.

Henry, M. K. (1989). Children´s word structure knowledge: Implications for decoding and spelling instruction. *Reading and Writing: An Interdisciplinary Journal, 2,* 135–152.

Henry, M. K. (1990). *Words: Integrated Decoding and Spelling Instruction Based on Word Origin and Structure.* Los Gatos, CA: Lex Press.

Leong, C. K. (1989). The effects of morphological structure on reading proficiency - a developmental study. *Reading and Writing: An Interdisciplinary Journal, 1,* 357–379.

Lyster, S. A. H. (submitted). The effects of metalinguistic training in kindergarten on reading development. Paper submitted to *Reading and Writing: An Interdisciplinary Journal.*

Nagy, W., & Anderson, R. C. (1984). How many words are there in printed school English? *Reading Research Quarterly, 19,* 304–330.

Nielsen, J. C., Kreiner, S., Poulsen, A., & Søegård, A. (1986). *Sætningslæseprøverne SL60 og SL40. SL-håndbog* [The sentence reading tests SL60 and SL40. SL-handbook]. Copenhagen: Dansk Psykologisk Forlag.

Nielsen, I. & Petersen, D. K. (1992) *DIAVOK. Et materiale der afdækker eventuelle læse- og stavevanskeligheder* [DIAVOK. A screening test for reading and spelling disabilities in adults]. Copenhagen: Workers Educational Association (AOF).

Olson, R. K. (1989). Specific deficits in component reading and language skills: genetic and environmental influences. *Journal of Learning Disabilities, 22,* 339–348.

Raven, J. C. (1960). *Guide to the Standard Progressive Matrices, Sets a, b, c, d, and e.* London: Lewis.

Rubin, H. (1991). Morphological knowledge and writing ability. In R. M. Joshi (Ed.), *Written language disorders* (pp. 43–69). Boston: Kluwer Academic Publishers.

Tornéus, M. (1987). *The importance of metaphonological and metamorphological abilities for different phases of reading development.* Paper presented at the Third World Congress of Dyslexia, Crete.

Tyler, A. & Nagy, W. (1989). The acquisition of English morphology. *Journal of Memory & Language, 28,* 649–668.

Wechsler, D. (1974). *Wechsler Intelligence Scale for Children - revised.* New York: Psychological Corporation.

White, T. G., Power, M. A., & White, S. (1989). Morphological analysis: Implications for teaching and understanding of vocabulary growth. *Reading Research Quarterly, 24,* 283–304.

# PART 4

# INTERVENTIONS AT THE WORD LEVEL AND BEYOND

ARYAN VAN DER LEIJ

# READING DISABILITIES AND COGNITIVE COMPETENCE

Quite a few students fail to develop reading skills necessary to meet the demands of the school and in the long run of the society. Within the broad category of reading difficulties, dyslexia has received more attention from researchers than any of the other subcategories (Vellutino, 1979). The phenomenon of dyslexia is intriguing because of the fact that individuals who otherwise are able to learn and perform like normal peers, have so much trouble when it comes to mastery of the alphabetic system.

To indicate the cognitive characteristics of reading difficulties, it is relevant to subdivide reading skills in word decoding skills and reading comprehension. Although mastery of the reading skills involves the interaction between a variety of cognitive processes, it is clear that the acquisition of word decoding skills relies heavily on lower level automatization processes (bottom-up). However, after the first stage of reading acquisition, the development of reading comprehension is decreasingly explained by competency in decoding skills and increasingly by the influence of higher level language competence (Perfetti, 1985; Aaron, 1991).

Reading difficulties may be caused by factors like low IQ, impairments of higher level processes and/or poor motivation, sometimes correlated with environmental factors like poor quality of education at home, low SES or ethnic background. According to the traditional definition, dyslexic students are not affected by these more or less general factors. They are students within the middle and upper parts of the intelligence distribution, stemming from environments which stimulate language, metacognition and motivation for learning at school. Dyslexia is, in contrast to other reading difficulties, associated with the existence of specific lower level deficits (Rutter, 1978; Spear & Sternberg, 1987). For decades, the diagnosis 'dyslexia' has been based on exclusionary criteria: a specific cause but no involvement of general factors.

However, the assumptions which lead to exclusion have met serious criticism. For one thing, most dyslexics suffer from developmental dyslexia, originated by a genetic factor (Olson, Wise, & Rack, 1989). If the cause is hereditary the question may be raised why nature would be so selective to protect children with lower IQ's and lower SES backgrounds from lower level deficits. It is hard - if not impossible - to find a reason other than an arbitrary decision. For instance, Rutter (1978) already noted that there is no reason to assume that "... social disadvantage protects children from dyslexia." Furthermore, empirical evidence shows that specific reading disability associated with a lower level deficit is not correlated to IQ level (see for a review Stanovich & Siegel, 1994). Therefore, the restriction of lower level deficits to relatively intelligent students of higher SES and, more importantly, the suggestion that they suffer from exclusive deficits, does not seem to be a valid one. Students who show reading backwardness and are in the lower regions of the IQ-distribution, may suffer from the same kind of lower level deficits as the dyslexic students do. Stanovich (1988) has proposed the 'phonological core variable difference' model which states that students with poorly developed instrumental reading skills and varying general intellectual levels, will show the same deficits when task demands rely heavily on phonological processing. This is the case in phonological awareness tasks or in tasks that involve phonological decoding like the reading of unfamiliar or pseudo-words. In contrast, differences between subgroups of poor readers emerge when task demands allow for the use of top-down, time-consuming processing that relates to reading comprehension. Evidence has been put forward to suggest that very poor readers of different intellectual levels are comparable in tasks that involve phonological processing and phonological decoding, but differ in tasks that allow for the use of verbal competence and of metacognitive processes. In tasks that rely on top-down processing, students who belong to the traditionally specified category of dyslexics outperform students who belong to the so-called Garden Variety readers, characterized by lower IQ's.

As a consequence of the critical appraisal of the exclusionary definition of dyslexia, it may be hypothesized that students who share a severe reading disability but show varying degrees of general intellectual ability are comparable in 1) the core of their reading deficit: phonological processing and phonological decoding (in contrast, they are expected to differ from each other in tasks which involve top-down processes), 2) effects of treatment aimed at remediation of the core of their disability (improvement of phonological decoding), and 3) development of their phonological decoding (dis)ability over a period of time. In this chapter, data are presented to test the three parts of the hypothesis.

STUDY 1: READING DISABILITIES AND GENERAL INTELLIGENCE.

Some years ago, the (in)comparability of categories of students with reading difficulties was the topic of a study which focused on the first two issues, mentioned in the former section: the core of the deficit and the effects of treatment (Van der Leij, 1983). Students with severe reading disabilities and varying levels of general intellectual competence took part in the study. According to traditional definitions, students in the normal range were labeled as dyslexic (DYS), whereas students with lower than normal IQ's served as the Garden Variety group (GV). The selection test was a standardized decoding test (Brus & Voeten, 1973), that consists of a list of 116 unrelated words in progressive order of difficulty. The student is asked to read the words aloud, as fast as possible. The score is the number of accurately read words within one minute, so it indicates both accuracy and speed.

The groups were matched in age and severity of reading backwardness as is shown in Table 1. A reading age of 1.9 means a performance of the DYS group at the level which is normally reached at the end of grade two (for simplicity, a grade is divided in 10 subgrades). A reading backwardness of 3.5 indicates that the subjects lag three and a half years behind normal performance at their age. Both groups visited schools for special education; the DYS students were at the school for primary learning disabled students, the Garden Variety group at the school for educable retarded students (for a brief review of the Dutch system of special education see Van der Leij, 1987).

TABLE 1
Subjects of the first study

|  | n | mean age (months) | mean reading age (grades) | reading backwardness (grades) |
|---|---|---|---|---|
| DYS | 14 | 127 | 1.9 | 3.5 |
| GV | 14 | 130 | 1.8 | 3.8 |

After selection and matching, the students were tested on a variety of reading and reading-related tasks. For the present purposes, the results of three tests are given. They all represent the instrumental part of reading aloud, but differ in information sources that may be used. The Story Reading test consisted of a story of 110 words. In the Word Reading test 36 one- and two-syllable words of different frequency were presented in short lists for which the total accuracy score will be used. The Words test was designed as a more or less pure phonological decoding measure because there was no context. Four lists of eight words containing the same letter cluster (*grap, groen, greep*) comprised the third test. The idea behind the test was that the performance of the students would reveal whether they were able to use letter cluster information to shorten their process of word recognition.

We assumed that the latter two tasks would be directly related to the phonological core of the disability, while the story reading would be farther away from that core, because it allows for the top-down use of semantic and context information. As a consequence of the matching procedure based on phonological decoding disability, we hypothesized that the groups would not differ on the words and lists, while the DYS group would profit from their superiority in general intelligence, more specifically their greater verbal competence, in the story reading task. The results are shown in Table 2.

TABLE 2
Performance of dyslexic and Garden Variety students on three reading tasks

|  | n | stories | | words | | lists | |
|---|---|---|---|---|---|---|---|
|  |  | mean | SD | mean | SD | mean | SD |
| DYS | 14 | 74 | 9 | 17 | 10 | 8 | 7 |
| GV | 14 | 70 | 12 | 14 | 12 | 7 | 6 |

None of the differences between the dyslexic and Garden Variety groups was significant. The results with the more or less pure phonological decoding tasks support the hypothesis that severely reading disabled students are comparable, independent of their intellectual level. However, contextual information did not help the students who had better top-down resources when they were asked to read aloud.

The second question was whether the two groups were still comparable when the instruction conditions were improved by an experimental treatment program. After the period of initial testing, the groups were divided at random in an experimental and a no-training control group. In both control groups one student had to be removed from the analysis because of missing data. In the experimental groups the method of presenting text simultaneously to eye and ear was used (Van der Leij, 1981). Essentially, the children listened silently and repeatedly to a tape while following the text with their eyes. Short and easy books, containing 400–500 words each, were used. Before and after the training they read the same text out loud. In a period of 11 weeks they read seven to nine books with an average of eight repetitions per book (twice a day, four times a week). They did their (silent) practice of reading and listening alone in their classrooms. Every week they were tested individually with short lists of words, taken from the texts. Besides, content of the stories and issues of particular interest were discussed. Difficult words were selected for further practice. Obviously, this kind of intervention program involved both top-down and bottom-up processing because phonological decoding (and spelling) and the use of contextual cues were triggered. Scores on parallel versions of the reading tests described above were obtained to determine transfer effects.

Gain scores between pre and posttest are presented in Table 3. Again, we expected comparable progress on the measures for phonological decoding, but more progress of the DYS group on the story reading task. The results did not confirm our expectations with regard to the experimental dyslexic group because it did not gain more than their controls on any of the tasks. The experimental Garden Variety group did better. Although they did not progress more in reading stories, the difference with their control group in reading words was marginally significant and the difference in reading lists was significant. Furthermore, the experimental Garden Variety group progressed more than the experimental dyslexic group in the word reading task.

TABLE 3
The effect of intervention on three reading tasks (gain scores).

|  | n | stories mean | SD | words mean | SD | lists mean | SD |
|---|---|---|---|---|---|---|---|
| DYS-E | 7 | 5 | 7 | 5 | 5 | 5 | 5 |
| DYS-C | 6 | 3 | 4 | 7 | 5 | 7 | 3 |
| GV-E | 7 | 4 | 11 | 11 | 6 | 7 | 6 |
| GV-C | 6 | 6 | 7 | 6 | 5 | -2 | 3 |

Gain scores between pre and posttest are presented in Table 3. Again, we expected comparable progress on the measures for phonological decoding, but more progress of the DYS group on the story reading task. The results did not confirm our expectations with regard to the experimental dyslexic group because it did not gain more than their controls on any of the tasks. The experimental Garden Variety group did better. Although they did not progress more in reading stories, the difference with their control group in reading words was marginally significant and the difference in reading lists was significant. Furthermore, the experimental Garden Variety group progressed more than the experimental dyslexic group in the word reading task.

The findings of this small-scaled study suggested that 1) the core of the deficit was indeed comparable in both groups, and 2) the Garden Variety students showed more progress after a period of intensive treatment. While the first conclusion confirmed our expectations, the second did not. However, the samples were small and the findings could have been caused by the selection of one or two groups. For example, one or two late-bloomers in the Garden Variety group could have made the difference.

STUDY 2: READING DISABILITIES AND VERBAL COMPETENCE.

Recently, we returned to the issue of comparability of students with varying intellectual levels in a larger scaled study (Van der Leij, Hoeksma, & Smeets, 1994; Smeets & Van der Leij, 1995 Smeets, 1997). To the questions of the core of the deficit and the effects of treatment we added the question whether over a substantial period of time, the development of phonological decoding would differ. This question is related to the old controversy between lag or deficit as a main characteristic of reading difficulties (Rutter, 1978). As was tentatively suggested above, in the long run some the students with lower levels of general cognitive functioning might turn out to be late-bloomers with continuous and increasing progress, indicating a developmental lag instead of a deficit. In contrast, the development of students with higher levels of cognitive functioning could be slower and less increasing, indicating that they were approaching the asymptote of their performance.

To start with the last question, we followed severely reading disabled students of about ten years of age longitudinally to be able to describe their reading development. We were interested in the differences between a group with a verbal competence at an average level (DYS) and a group with a significantly lower level of verbal functioning (GV). The reason to take verbal competence and not general cognitive level as the dividing measure was that we considered the contrast between the development of different abilities within the verbal domain to be the most striking characteristic of traditional dyslexia. According to their average scores on verbal tasks, they have learned how to use language as a means to reasoning, and have gained adequate knowledge of words and concepts. Still they fail to learn the writing system that essentially is a reflection of words and language in visual symbols. Non-verbal intelligence like spatial ability was not selected because it is a more independent domain of intellectual functioning. Because of the contribution of non-verbal intelligence, total IQ was not used either. In contrast to their extreme differences in verbal competence, DYS en GV were matched on chronological age and reading age.

Verbal competence was measured by the Peabody Picture Vocabulary Test (PPVT; Dunn & Lloyd, 1965), because this task correlates fairly high with more general verbal competence and is easy to apply. Raw scores were translated into a verbal IQ score. Reading development was measured with the standard decoding test described before (Brus & Voeten, 1973)

Table 4 shows the characteristics of the subjects selected in the second study. According to statistical analysis the matching procedure was successful. The groups were of the same reading age and chronological age, but extremely different in verbal IQ. The students were tested four times in a period of 15 months. In comparison to the first study, the students were on the average less backward. However, the average reading backwardness was two and a half years and the students were extremely poor readers (lowest 5%).

TABLE 4
Subjects of the second study.

|  | n | age (months) mean | age (months) SD | reading age mean (grades) | reading backwardness (grades) | verbal IQ mean | verbal IQ SD |
|---|---|---|---|---|---|---|---|
| DYS | 25 | 120 | 11 | 2.3 | 2.5 | 117 | 13 |
| GV | 29 | 123 | 9 | 2.4 | 2.6 | 79 | 20 |

The analysis showed that the Dyslexic group developed worse than the Garden Variety readers ($\chi^2$ (df=3)=9.35; p<.01, see Figure 1[1]). When the demands on phonological decoding ability were heavy – reading aloud single words under time pressure – dyslexic readers increasingly lagged behind in comparison to Garden Variety readers. This suggests that the results do not support the idea that phonological decoding disability is independent from general cognitive ability. In that case the development of groups with severe reading backwardness but different verbal competence, would be comparable. Instead, the students with the greater verbal competence seemed to have a more defective learning mechanism for phonological decoding, while the students with less verbal competence were more characterized by a developmental lag.

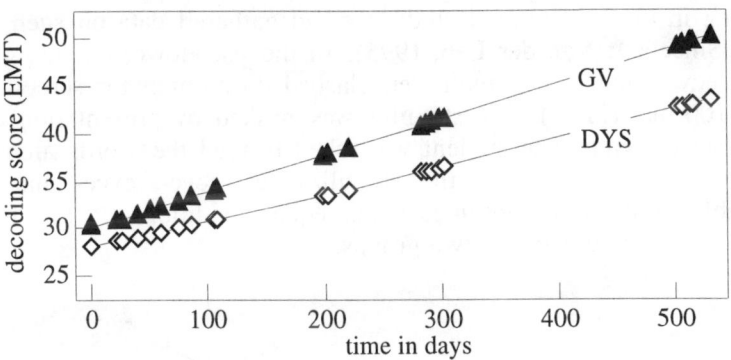

Fig. 1. Progress of dyslexic and Garden Variety students in word identification over a period of 15 months.

## The phonological decoding deficit

According to current theories, a phonological deficit accounts for delays in development of decoding ability. More specific, dyslexics

---

[1] The analysis of the EMT-scores resulted in a polynome model of the second degree. For calculations the age scale was centered on 250 days and intercept and differences related to the point in time of 250 days after the start of the study (for details see Van der Leij, Hoeksma, & Smeets, 1994).

have trouble with reading words that are unfamiliar to them, most dramatically shown by their difficulty with reading pseudowords (Rack, Snowling, & Olson, 1992). On the other hand, they may possess relatively better ability to learn wordspecific knowledge and therefore be able to develop some kind of orthographic compensation, indicated by the way they recognize high-frequency words (Lovett, Borden, DeLuca, Lacerenza, Benson, & Brackstone, 1994; Yap & Van der Leij, 1994). We reasoned that, if the deficit vs. lag interpretation of the difference between DYS and GV was a valid one, the contrast between the phonological deficit on the one hand and orthographical compensation on the other would be more pronounced in the DYS group than in the GV group. Specifically, the dyslexics would show a greater discrepancy than the Garden Variety group between the performance on words versus pseudowords in the period before the longitudinal study started.

In another study, it had become clear that the contrast between phonological decoding and word recognition was triggered best by presenting (well-pronounceable but unknown) pseudowords and (overlearned) high-frequency words in a speeded condition (Yap & Van der Leij, 1993). In the period when all groups were nicely matched on general reading achievement, i.e., the period of the first testing in the longitudinal study, we had gathered data on such tasks (see Smeets & Van der Leij, 1995). In the pseudoword reading task cvc-, ccvc-, and cvcc-stimuli were flashed on a computer screen (200 and 100 ms) (Fl ps). The stimulus was masked by presentation of an abstract drawing. The student was asked to read the words aloud. In the high-frequency task, the stimuli (cvc-, ccvc-, cvcc- and two-syllable words) were presented under equal conditions (Fl hf). Figure 2 shows the results of the two groups.

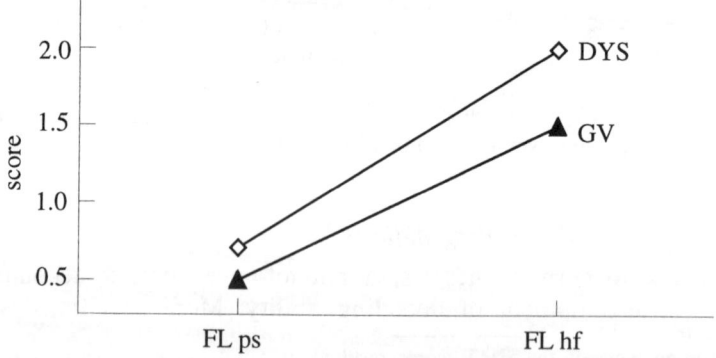

Fig. 2. Flashed pseudoword and word reading of dyslexic and Garden Variety students.

Although the dyslexic group showed the expected profile (a sharp contrast between pseudoword and high-frequency word reading) more clearly than the Garden Variety group, the interaction between groups and tasks proved not to be significant. The differences fitted well into the ideas of a phonological deficit and orthographical compensation, but for both groups equally. The Garden Variety group showed more or less the same kind of profile as the dyslexics. The conclusion was drawn that the difference in progress (Figure 1) was not predicted by a difference in word/pseudoword contrast (Figure 2) at the start of the period of progress.

*The effect of intervention.*

Their was a parallel in the findings of the developmental study and the intervention study of 1983. Both studies suggested that the students with lesser verbal competence progressed more than the dyslexic students. In an extension of the longitudinal study the question was explored whether intensive instruction would affect the reading ability of the two groups differently and whether the results of the 1983 study could be replicated. In the experiment, a pretest-posttest group design was used with an experimental group and a no-training group randomly selected from the sample of dyslexic and Garden Variety readers described in Table 4.

Interactive computer-assisted instruction was used. The advantages of computers are obvious. Control over input and output is large. Activity is secured by asking the student to respond to stimuli and by giving immediate feedback. Especially when students require many repetitions and drill-and-practice, computer programs are very useful (Torgesen, 1986; Van der Leij, 1994).

The program consisted of nine tasks. Words or parts of words were presented on screen and/or by headphones. The tasks ranged from matching tasks (e.g., "fill in the right consonant or vowel that is missing") to typing tasks (e.g., "type the word you just heard"). Speed was involved in some of the tasks by flashing the words on the screen. The students received direct feedback on accuracy. Task conditions were regularly adapted by the teacher to the progress of the students, e.g., moving on to more complex words when easy words were mastered or selecting more difficult tasks when easier tasks were mastered. This multicompoential remedial program is aimed at stimulating word decoding and spelling. Different parts of the program have been tested in earlier experiments and have shown positive results (e.g., Van Daal, 1993). During a period of five months, the students practiced individually, ten minutes a day. On the average, they received 70 sessions, adding up to 700 minutes of individual training.

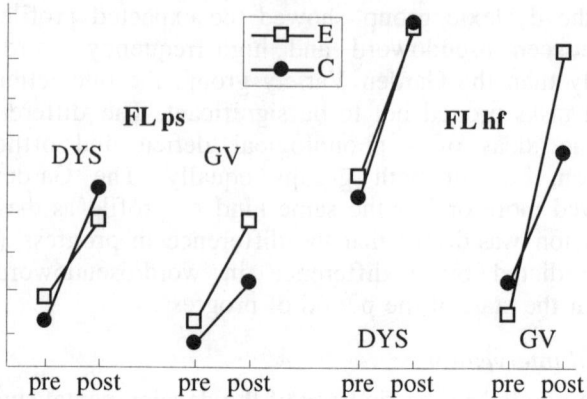

Fig. 3. Effects of computer-assisted practice on flashed pseudoword and word reading of dyslexic and Garden Variety students.

The two experimental tasks described in the former section are selected to illustrate the results (Figure 3). Dyslexic and Garden Variety readers did not gain more than their control groups in flashed pseudoword reading (Fl ps). However, in the condition of high-frequency word reading (Fl hf) Garden Variety readers progressed more than their controls, while DYS did not. Again, the Garden Variety group seemed to have a slightly better prognosis than the dyslexic readers, as also was indicated by the 1983 study and, more convincingly, by the longitudinal part of the second study.

## GENERAL DISCUSSION

It was hypothesized that students with severe reading disabilities but varying degrees of general intellectual ability, are similar in 1) the core of their reading deficit: phonological processing and decoding (in contrast, they are expected to differ in tasks which involve 'top-down' processes), 2) effects of treatment aimed at remediation of the core of their disability (improvement of phonological decoding), and 3) development of their phonological decoding (dis)ability over a period of time.

The two studies reviewed in this chapter confirm the first hypothesis (Table 2 and Figure 3). In addition, the combination with the factor of speed of processing was stressed again, supporting the idea of an automatic decoding deficit (Yap & Van der Leij, 1993). However, no sign was found in the first study of a relatively better performance of the students with greater intellectual competence when story reading allowed for the use of 'top-down' processes. We replicated this finding in the second study (data are not presented in this chapter).

Apparently, the validity of the verbal efficiency theory of Perfetti (1985) is demonstrated in both studies: as long as most (or even all) attention is absorbed by lower level decoding, there is little (or even no) attention left for higher order processes to be used.

With regard to the second and third hypothesis, the studies had confusing results. Both in the condition when development was influenced by some form of intensive treatment (Table 3 and Figure 3) and in the condition when development was followed over a period of time (Figure 1), the group with a lower level of intellectual functioning had some advantage over the other group. The results of the first intervention study were thus replicated in the recent study, using more subjects and a better controlled and more specific kind of treatment. Furthermore, the results shown in Figure 1 are a strong indicator for differential development, because the data were based on repeated testing over a period of 15 months. However, the differences in development were not related to different contrasts between familiar and unfamiliar word reading (Figure 2), measured at the start of the period in which development was followed or the intervention was executed.

One possible explanation may be that we did not select the right predictors. It should be noted that the complete series of tasks used in the second study included quite a few experimental conditions which have been shown to correlate with severe reading disability: unspeeded oral (pseudo) word reading, story reading, auditory-visual matching, spelling and typing of dictated words. None of these tasks revealed a difference between the groups, neither did tasks outside the domain of reading, such as tasks that tap working memory capability like a nonword repetition task. Possibly, predictability is reduced in extreme groups of the normal distribution of achievement because of restriction of range. An additional source of complication may be that the variation across tasks within subjects and within groups is always large in extreme groups. An illustration of this point are the standard deviations in the first study. Especially, when groups are not large, a few outliers of some sort or other can disrupt differences between groups.

Although the fact that the recent study replicated the finding of the 1983 study is intriguing, it may be suggested that the evidence of large-scaled studies (Stanovich & Siegel, 1994; Stanovich, 1994; Fletcher, Stuebing, Shaywitz, Shaywitz, Rourke, & Francis, 1994; Francis, Shaywitz, Stuebing, Shaywitz, & Fletcher, 1996) should be taken as caution against overinterpretation of results of studies that are relatively small-scaled. Even when some significant results are found, they may be more the consequence of sheer coincidence than of any reliable factor. When students with severe deficits in phonological decoding are selected, the 'rule' seems to be that their decoding skills develop very slowly and that the transfer effects of interventions aimed at the core of their deficits are small, independent of general intellectual level or verbal competence. This idea is supported by the size of the effects we have found. The differences were small. Furthermore, although the growth curves differed on the decoding test (Figure 1), there was considerable overlap in scores. To illustrate, we calculated that the mean progress of the total group of Figure 1 with complete data (21 DYS and 28 GV) was 16 words per minute in the period of 15 months. The group above this mean consisted of 9 students of the dyslexic group and 16 students of the Garden Variety group, while 12 students of the dyslexic group and 12 students of the Garden Variety group progressed below the mean. The difference of Figure 1 can be attributed to the fact that an extra four of the Garden Variety students appeared in the upper half and an extra three of the dyslexic group were in the lower half. The vast majority of the total group (86 %) overlapped in development.

However, one could argue that we should dig deeper into specific reading processes to find the key to differential prediction of reading development of groups with different levels of intellectual competence. Possibly, we selected more 'late-bloomers' who showed slightly more sensitivity to individual treatment and special instruction in the Garden Variety group than in the dyslexic group, for reasons not covered by our data. The only clue in our data of both groups that correlated with larger progress was a significantly higher general reading score at the time of first testing. Apparently even in extreme groups, reading itself may be the best and only predictor of differential development.

## REFERENCES

Aaron, P. G. (1991). Can reading disabilities be diagnosed without using intelligence tests? *Journal of Learning disabilities, 24*, 178–186.

Brus, B. T., & Voeten, M. J. M. (1973). *Een-minuuttest* [One-minute-test]. Nijmegen: Berkhout.

Dunn, D., & Lloyd, M. (1965). *Peabody Picture Vocabulary Test.* Washington: American Guidance Service.

Fletcher, J. M., Stuebing, K. K., Shaywitz, B. A., Shaywitz, S. E., Rourke, B. P., & Francis, D. J. (1994). Validity of the concept of dyslexia: alternative approaches to definition and classification. In K. P. Van den Bos, L. S. Siegel, D. J. Bakker, & D. L. Share (Eds.), *Current directions in dyslexia research* (pp. 31–44). Lisse, The Netherlands: Swets & Zeitlinger.

Francis, D. J., Shaywitz, S. E., Stuebing, K., Shaywitz, B. A., & Fletcher, J. (1996). Developmental lag versus deficit models of reading disability: a longitudinal, individual growth curve analysis. *Journal of Educational Psychology, 88*, 3–17.

Lovett, M. W., Borden, S. L., DeLuca, T., Lacerenza, L., Benson, N. J., & Brackstone, D. (1994). Treating the core deficits of developmental dyslexia: evidence of transfer of learning after phonologically- and strategically-based

reading training programs. *Developmental Psychology, 30,* 805–822.
Olson, R. K., Wise, B. W., & Rack, J.P. (1989). Dyslexia: deficits, genetic aetiology and computer-based remediation. *The Irish Journal of Psychology, 10,* 494–508.
Perfetti, C. A. (1985). *Reading ability.* New York: Oxford University Press.
Rack, J. P., Snowling, M. J., & Olson, R. K. (1992). The nonword reading deficit in developmental dyslexia: a review. *Reading Research Quarterly, 27,* 28–53.
Rutter, M. (1978). Prevalence and types of dyslexia. In A. L. Benton, & D. Pearl (Eds.), *Dyslexia. An appraisal of current knowledge.* New York: Oxford University Press.
Smeets, H. (1997). *Dyslexie en leesproblemen* [Dyslexia and reading difficulties]. Amsterdam: Vrije Universiteit (unpublished doctoral dissertation).
Smeets, H., & Van der Leij, A. (1995). Effecten van een multicomponentieel computergestuurd programma op technisch lezen [Effects of a multi-componential computerassisted program on decoding ability]. *Tijdschrift voor Orthopedagogiek, 34,* 128–149.
Spear, L. C., & Sternberg, R. J. (1987). An information-processing framework for understanding reading disability. In S. J. Ceci (Ed.), *Handbook of cognitive, social, and neuropsychological aspects of learning disabilities* (pp. 3–31). Hillsdale, N.J: Lawrence Erlbaum.
Stanovich, K. E. (1988). The right and wrong places to look for the cognitive locus of reading disability. *Annals of Dyslexia, 38,* 154–177.
Stanovich, K. E. (1994). Are discrepancy-based definitions of dyslexia empirically defensible? In K. P. Van den Bos, L. S. Siegel, D. J. Bakker, & D. L. Share (Eds.), *Current directions in dyslexia research* (pp. 15–30). Lisse: Swets & Zeitlinger.
Stanovich, K. E., & Siegel, L. S. (1994). Phenotypic performance profile of children with reading disabilities: a regression-based test of the phonological-core variable-difference model. *Journal of Educational Psychology, 86,* 24–53.
Torgesen, J. K. (1986). Computer-assisted instruction with learning-disabled children. In J. K. Torgesen, & B. L. Wong (Eds.), *Psychological and educational perspectives on learning disabilities.* (pp. 417–435). New York: Academic Press.
Van Daal, V. H. P. (1993). *Computer-based Reading and Spelling Practice for Young Dyslexics* (doctoral dissertation). Amsterdam: Vrije Universiteit.
Van der Leij, A. (1981). Remediation of reading-disabled children by presenting text simultaneously to eye and ear. *Bulletin of the Orton Society, 31,* 229–243.
Van der Leij, A. (1983). *Ernstige leesproblemen* [Severe reading difficulties], (doctoral dissertation). Lisse, The Netherlands: Swets & Zeitlinger.
Van der Leij, A. (1987). Netherlands, Special Education in the. In C. R. Reynolds, & L. Mann (Eds.), *Encyclopedia of Special Education.* Vol. 2. (pp. 1094–1095). New York: Wiley & Sons.
Van der Leij, A. (1994). Effects of computer-assisted instruction on word and pseudoword reading of reading-disabled students. In K. P. Van den Bos, L. S. Siegel, D. J. Bakker, & D. L. Share (Eds.), *Current directions in dyslexia research* (pp. 251–267). Lisse, The Netherlands: Swets & Zeitlinger.
Van der Leij, A., Hoeksma, J. B., & Smeets, H. (1994). *The development of reading achievement of dyslexics.* Poster presented at the Conference of the Rodin Society, Malta.
Vellutino, F. R. (1979). *Dyslexia: Theory and Research.* Cambridge: MIT Press.
Yap, R. L., & Van der Leij, A. (1993). Word processing in dyslexics. An automatic decoding deficit? *Reading and Writing: An Interdisciplinary Journal, 5,* 261–279.
Yap, R. L., & Van der Leij, A. (1994). Automaticity deficits in word reading. In A. Fawcett, & R. Nicolson (Eds.), *Dyslexia and children. The acquisition and development of skills* (pp. 77–107). Hemel Hempstead: Harvester Wheatsheaf.

MARTIN VAN LEERDAM,
ANNA M. T. BOSMAN, AND GUY C. VAN ORDEN

# THE ECOLOGY OF SPELLING INSTRUCTION: EFFECTIVE TRAINING IN FIRST GRADE

Since Huey (1908), reading and reading pedagogy have been popular topics among psycholinguists and educational researchers. Spelling and learning to spell, however, never reached the popularity of reading research. Yet, in most alphabetic languages spelling is more difficult than reading. Therefore, increased attention to beginning spelling is warranted. Our objectives with this chapter are both practical and theoretical. Our practical goal is to review what contributes to effective spelling instruction. Theoretically, we present a perspective on reading and spelling that helps us understand the basis of effective spelling-instruction. We also describe an empirical study that illustrates different outcomes of several instruction methods. After that, we discuss why some instruction methods are more successful than others and discuss some educational implications. This final section also broadly describes a theoretical framework within which to understand spelling and reading performance.

Reading and spelling are closely related, as suggested by moderate to high correlation's between scores on reading and spelling tests (see Frith, 1980; Mommers, 1987). However, reading and spelling are not each other's inverse (Frith, 1979; Read, 1981; Treiman, 1993). An asymmetry develops as children learn to read and spell. Not only is learning to spell more difficult than learning to read, spelling problems are also more persistent than reading problems (for a review see Bosman & Van Orden, 1997; Mushinski Fulk, & Stormont-Spurgin, 1995). Results from experimental studies show that merely reading words does not contribute greatly to spelling ability (Bosman & De Groot, 1992; Bosman & Van Leerdam, 1993).

If reading is not very effective for learning about words' spellings, how should spelling be taught? Various methods have been used to investigate this question. Next, we review four aspects of spelling instruction that have shown to contribute to enhanced spelling performance.

*Kinematic aspect.* A common and fairly straightforward method to teach spelling is having children copy words into a notebook. The effectiveness of this procedure has been studied experimentally. Results indicate that copying is a great deal more effective than reading (Bosman & De Groot, 1992; Bosman & Van Leerdam, 1993; Van Doorn-van Eijsden, 1984). One reason why children learn the spelling of words more effectively through copying may be because the actual kinematics of writing inculcates precise mnemonic constraints for writing movements of correct spellings.

To our knowledge, only one study has failed to find enhanced spelling performance after a copying training. Sears and Johnson (1986) tested a group of children from grades four to six, but did not find superior spelling performance in a copying condition as compared to a condition that involved visualizing the word and using the computer keyboard. Yet, it must be noted that in the condition using the computer keyboard, a correct response was followed by the request to spell the word by heart. Spelling from memory is itself an effective aspect of instruction, which may mask the effect of copying. As indicated by the studies above, when spelling from memory is not part of the training, the advantage for copying emerges.

For example, Cunningham and Stanovich (1990) assigned children from first grade to three different kinds of spelling training. In all three conditions, words printed on cards were presented to the child. After the experimenter named the word the child repeated it, and then reproduced the word either with a pencil on paper, or using letter tiles, or using a computer keyboard. The word remained visible throughout the training procedure. Spelling performance was assessed through a writing-to-dictation test. Children in the copying condition performed better than those in the letter-tile condition or in the computer condition. Thus, the precise motor activity of writing appears to benefit learning to spell.

*From memory.* People usually produce the spelling of words from memory when they write. Thus, training in which the spelling of words are produced from memory may differ in its effect from training in which spellings remain visible (see above, Sears & Johnson, 1986). Roberts and Ehri (1983) had second grade children rehearse the spelling of pseudowords, which they had seen several times before. One group of children were instructed to make visual images of the spellings of these pseudowords, followed by letter-analysis tasks requiring the use of those images. Another group performed the same letter-analysis tasks without the imaging instructions, but with the correct spellings in view. Subsequent spelling tests revealed that visualizing from memory led to superior spelling performance (see also Bosman & De Groot, 1992; Bosman & Van Leerdam, 1993; but see Van Daal & Van der Leij, 1992).

*Immediate feedback.* The importance of immediate feedback has been shown by Harward, Allred, and Sudweeks (1994). Spelling performance of fourth graders who received immediate visual feedback on the spellings they produced was better than that of children who received delayed visual feedback (Gettinger, 1993; but see Ormrod, 1986, in a study with college students).

Visual feedback that included imitation of children's spelling errors followed by immediate presentation of the correct spelling improved spelling performance of two mildly retarded children and one 12-year old with learning disabilities. Moreover, the contrast provided by error imitation benefited subsequent spelling performance more than just showing the correct spelling (Kauffman, Hallahan, Haas, Brame, & Boren, 1978; Gerber, 1984).

The effectiveness of on-line visual support was also investigated by Farnham-Diggory and Simon (1975). Third graders who learned the spelling of words by consecutive visual presentation of each letter of the word performed better on a spelling test than children who learned the words by consecutive oral presentation of each letter. Conversely, saying each letter while writing the word down appeared to be an effective way to improve spelling performance in children with learning disabilities (Kearney & Drabman, 1993; Bradley, 1981; but see Cunningham & Stanovich, 1990).

*Whole word.* Learning the spelling of a word is often a matter of learning to remember an ambiguous phoneme-to-grapheme relation. For example, in spelling the word Feel the phoneme [i:] presents the greatest difficulty. The letters F and L are relatively unambiguous, but for the vowel [i:], the phoneme can be spelled two different ways, either with EA as in DEAL, or with EE as in PEEL.

Bosman and De Groot (1992) tested a spelling training (i.e., problem naming) that involved practicing the ambiguous part of the word exclusively. Words were presented on a piece of paper with the ambiguous part, the target problem, underlined. The children who practiced the words in this condition were instructed to explicate the ambiguity in each word. Although this method was more effective than learning the spelling through reading, it was less effective than a condition in which the whole word was practiced, i.e., oral spelling. In this condition, children were instructed to read the word aloud and then spell it orally from memory. The superiority of the oral-spelling condition, requiring reconstruction of the whole word, was clear both in a test assessing the correctness of the entire word, as well as one in which target errors (i.e., ambiguous part) were assessed. Note, however, that oral-spelling also required that children practiced the spelling from memory, which was not the case in the problem-naming training.

*Summary.* This brief review of the literature on spelling-instruction methods provides insights concerning the effectiveness of spelling training. Reconstructing the spelling from memory appears more beneficial than having the spelling of the word available. Practicing the entire word may be more helpful than exclusively focusing on the ambiguous phoneme-grapheme part of the word. Both immediate feedback and the involvement of the kinematic modality may provide additional learning benefits.

In the study that follows, we illustrate the previous points by contrasting four different spelling-instruction methods comprising some or all four aspects. Young Dutch-speaking children learned the spellings of words by means of copying, grapheme selection, oral spelling, or visual dictation. We used reading, effectively, an implicit spelling training, as a baseline condition to assess four explicit spelling-instruction methods. The copying condition involves the motor aspect, it requires reconstructing the entire word, but not from memory. Visual feedback is provided to some extent in the form of a child's own hand-written spelling. Grapheme-selection training focuses on the ambiguous phoneme-grapheme relation in a word. It does not require the reconstruction of the entire word, but the ambiguous part is practiced from memory. Visual feedback and some motor movement is involved in the training. Oral spelling training does not involve handwriting, nor is visual feedback provided, but the spelling of the whole word must be reconstructed from memory. Finally, the visual-dictation training involves all four aspects, children must write whole words from memory. It is expected that the visual-dictation training that combines the four beneficial aspects will be the most successful spelling training. Another aspect we will investigate is the differential effectiveness of instruction methods for more advanced spellers and less advanced spellers.

## METHOD

### Participants

Seventy children, five groups of 14 children each, from regular primary schools participated in the experiment. All children attended first grade. Their mean age was 88 months at the time the experiment was conducted. The experiment took place in June, ten months after formal reading and spelling instruction had started.

All children were instructed according to the reading curriculum *Veilig Leren Lezen* (Caesar, 1979). The emphasis in this method is on phonics. Initially, only regular words are used. After four months of instruction, children are familiar with the main grapheme-phoneme relations. Assessment of reading and spelling levels is straightforward and reliable because the curriculum imposes a strict day-by-day and week-by-week program.

About one week prior to the experiment, we assessed spelling and reading levels of all children (see Table 1). Spelling level was estimated with a word-dictation test developed by the second author. The test consists of 20 words, and their orthographic complexity resembles those of the words from the curriculum. The score on the spelling test is the number of correctly spelled words in a dictation task. Each of the five groups of children was composed of seven more advanced spellers and seven less advanced spellers. The mean spelling scores of the five groups did not differ significantly from each other (p > .30), but the more advanced spellers scored higher on the spelling test than the less advanced spellers.

TABLE 1
Gender ratio, mean age (in months), mean word-reading level and mean spelling levels of children who participated in the study

| Spelling Training | Girl/Boy | Age | Reading[a] | Spelling[b] More advanced | Less advanced | N |
|---|---|---|---|---|---|---|
| reading | 9/5 | 87 | 38.6 (16.7) | 19.1 (0.4) | 16.6 (2.1) | 14 |
| copying | 6/8 | 89 | 39.9 (15.2) | 19.1 (0.4) | 15.9 (2.0) | 14 |
| grapheme selection | 7/7 | 89 | 38.7 (10.6) | 19.3 (0.5) | 17.3 (0.8) | 14 |
| oral spelling | 5/9 | 89 | 43.4 (13.2) | 19.3 (0.5) | 17.0 (1.0) | 14 |
| visual dictation | 6/8 | 88 | 46.9 (14.1) | 19.3 (0.5) | 17.1 (0.9) | 14 |
| total | 33/37 | 88 | 41.5 (14.1) | 19.2 (0.4) | 16.8 (1.5) | 70 |

Note. [a] Maximum score is 100. [b] Maximum score is 20. Standard deviations in parentheses.

Reading level was assessed by means of a standardized test for reading-decoding. This test consists of a list of unrelated words. The score on the test is the number of words read correctly in one minute. The reading test scores of the five participant groups did not differ significantly from each other (F < 1).

## Materials

Twelve words with at least one grapheme likely to be a spelling problem constituted the set of training words. All words were semantically familiar (see Krom, 1990), but orthographically unfamiliar to the children. All words were multi-syllabic, and their mean length in letters was 6.7 (SD = 1.37), with the shortest word having five letters and the longest nine. One grapheme in each word was assigned the target spelling problem. The target spelling problems are known to be causing difficulties for the beginning speller. Appendix A lists the words and their target spelling problems.

## Procedure

The experiment consisted of a training and a test session. During individual training the children practiced spelling of the 12 training words three times each, making a total of 36 trials. A child practiced the training words according to one of four explicit spelling-instruction methods (copying, grapheme selection, oral spelling, and visual dictation) or practiced the words through reading. We describe each method, in turn, next.

*Reading:* children in this condition simply read the training words aloud. Each reading error was pointed out by the experimenter, and the child was asked to read the word again.

*Copying:* children assigned to this condition copied a printed list of the training words into a notebook. The experimenter encouraged the children to consult the list of target words throughout the training.

*Grapheme selection:* in this condition, children focused on the target spelling problem in each training word. The child was asked to read the word first. Subsequently, the experimenter covered the word, and presented one of the graphemes that occurred in the word and a possible (incorrect) alternative grapheme. The child circled the correct grapheme. Finally, the word was shown without the target grapheme, and the child filled in the missing grapheme.

*Oral spelling:* children in this condition read the training word from a list, and subsequently named each letter of the word without consulting its written form. Generally, children at this age use letter sounds to name the letters that constitute the word. In cases where letter-sound naming led to ambiguity concerning the letter, the experimenter asked the child for clarification.

*Visual dictation:* children in this condition were presented with each training word separately. The word was presented on a card for about 4 seconds. The children were encouraged to observe the word carefully. After the card was removed, the children wrote the word into a notebook.

The test session took place shortly after the training session was completed. Spelling knowledge of all target words was assessed individually in a writing-to-dictation task.

RESULTS

*Training results.* During the training, the experimenter kept note of the spelling errors made by the children, and the time it took each child to complete the training. Table 2 presents the mean number of spelling errors during training and the mean time-on-task.

A 5 (spelling training: reading vs. copying vs. grapheme selection vs. oral spelling vs. visual dictation) by 2 (spelling level: more advanced vs. less advanced) ANOVA on the mean number of spelling errors during training revealed significant main effects and a non-significant interaction effect. A significant difference in number of errors among spelling training conditions was apparent, $F(4, 60) = 2.83$, $p < .05$. The mean number of errors made by the children in the visual-dictation condition was significantly higher than those in the copying condition (Newman-Keuls, p < .05). None of the other conditions differed significantly from each other. More advanced spellers made fewer errors (M = 5.5; SD = 4.3) than less advanced spellers (M = 8.0; SD = 5.6), F(1, 60) = 5.21, p < .05. The maximum number of errors possible is 36.

TABLE 2
Mean number of spelling errors during training and the time it took the children to complete the training

| Training results | Reading | Copying | Grapheme selection | Oral spelling | Visual dictation |
|---|---|---|---|---|---|
| Mean error rate [a] | 5.3 (5.4) | 4.1 (4.0) | 6.9 (3.9) | 8.4 (6.5) | 9.1 (4.3) |
| Time on task [b] | 3.1 (2.1) | 18.2 (4.4) | 13.5 (4.5) | 12.4 (4.4) | 23.5 (3.1) |

Note. [a] Maximum is 36. [b] In minutes and seconds. Standard deviations in parentheses.

The same analysis of variance on the mean time-on-task variable also yielded significant main effects and a non-significant interaction effect. The children in the visual-dictation took longest to complete the training, followed by those in the copying condition. The children in the oral-spelling and the grapheme-selection training required statistically similar amounts of time, but needed more time than the children who participated in the reading condition, F(4, 60) = 59.35, p < .001. All differences of the time-on task variable, except the one between oral-spelling and grapheme-selection, were significant (Newman-Keuls, p < .01). Finally, the more advanced spellers (M = 13.0; SD = 7.5) took less time to complete the training than the less advanced spellers (M = 15.44; SD = 7.5), F(1, 60) = 9.50, p < .01.

Thus, both the results of the analysis on the number of spelling errors made during the training, and the results of the time-on-task variable indicate that the spelling training appeared somewhat easier for the more advanced than for the less advanced spellers. The results also indicate that there was no speed-accuracy trade-off between time-on-task and the number of errors made during training. After all, those children who took part in the visual-dictation condition needed more time to complete the training than any of the children in the other conditions, and they also had more trouble getting the spelling correct during the training. Keeping the spelling mentally available, as is required in the visual-dictation training, does not seem an easy task.

*Test results.* Two analyses of variance were conducted on the data of the dictation test: A 5 (spelling training: reading vs. copying vs. grapheme selection vs. oral spelling vs. visual dictation) by 2 (spelling level: more advanced vs. less advanced) ANOVA on the mean proportion of target errors, and the same analysis on the mean proportion of wrongly spelled words. Figure 1 presents the mean proportions of target errors of the more and less advanced spellers in all five spelling-training conditions.

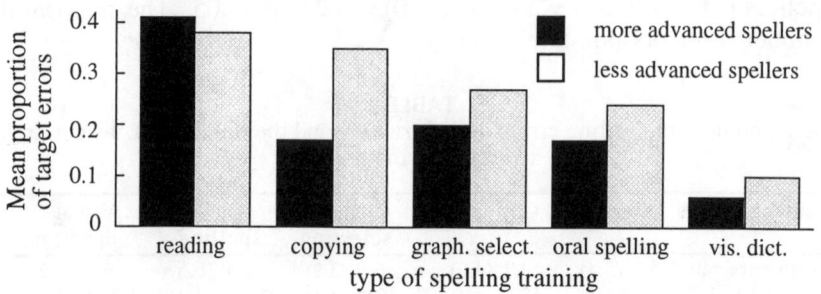

Fig. 1. Mean proportion of target errors on the dictation test for all five experimental groups. Standard deviations are presented in the text.

The analysis on the mean proportion of target errors yielded a significant main effect of spelling training, $F(4, 60) = 7.19$, $p < .001$, by subjects, and $F(4, 44) = 8.00$, $p < .001$, by items. Children in the visual-dictation condition ($M = .08$; $SD = .08$) made significantly fewer errors than the children in the remaining groups (Newman-Keuls, $p < .05$), and the children in the reading condition ($M = .40$; $SD = .12$) made significantly more errors than those in the other groups (Newman-Keuls, $p < .05$). The differences between the copying ($M = .26$; $SD = .22$), grapheme selection ($M = .24$; $SD = .18$) and oral-spelling ($M = .21$; $SD = .16$) conditions did not reach significant levels.

The main effect of spelling level was marginally significant, $F(1, 60) = 3.10$, $p = .08$, by subjects, and $F(1, 11) = 4.48$, $p = .06$, by items. More advanced spellers ($M = .20$; $SD = .18$) made fewer errors on the dictation test than the less advanced spellers ($M = .27$; $SD = .19$). However, the marginally significant interaction effect between spelling level and instruction level qualifies this result ($F < 1$, by subjects, and $F(4, 44) = 2.33$, $p = .07$, by items). Simple effects indicate that in the copying condition more advanced spellers benefited disproportionately as compared to less advanced spellers, $F(1, 11) = 5.10$, $p < .05$.

The same analysis on the mean proportion of wrongly spelled words revealed a similar pattern. The children in the visual-dictation condition made fewer errors than those in any of the other conditions, whereas children in the reading condition made more errors than children in the other conditions, $F(4, 60) = 6.89$, $p < .001$, by subjects, and $F(4, 44) = 19.43$, $p < .001$, by items. More advanced spellers ($M = .39$; $SD = .25$) made fewer errors on the dictation test than the less advanced spellers (M = .57; SD = .31), $F(1, 60) = 9.24$, $p < .01$, by subjects, and $F(1, 11) = 25.28$, $p < .001$, by items. Again, the interaction effect qualifies this result, $F(4, 44) = 7.12$, $p < .001$, by items, and $p > .25$ by subjects. In both the copying condition $F(1, 11) = 34.71$, $p < .001$ and the oral-spelling condition $F(1, 11) = 4.71$, $p < .05$ more advanced spellers benefited more than the less advanced spellers, whereas in the other conditions no significant differences emerged between the two groups.

Thus, both more advanced and less advanced spellers in the visual-dictation condition benefited most from the training. They outperformed their peers in all other conditions. The results suggest that more advanced spellers benefit more and from a greater variety of instruction methods than less advanced spellers. Less advanced spellers in the copying and in the oral-spelling condition did not benefit to the same extent as the more advanced spellers. Bosman and De Groot (1992) also found that less advanced readers/spellers in a copying condition were less effected by training than the more advanced children. Our finding that reading is not a very effective way to learn the spelling of words is supported by the results of earlier studies (Bosman & De Groot, 1992; Van Doorn-van Eijsden, 1984).

One explanation of why visual dictation is so successful might be that the children spent more time doing the training. However, this is not supported by the results of a correlational analysis. For most conditions, the longer children took to complete the training, the more errors they made in the dictation test. The values for the correlations between the time-on-task variable and the number of target errors was positive in all five conditions, reading: $r = .17$; copying: $r = .77$; grapheme selection: $r = .53$; oral spelling: $r = .74$, except the visual-dictation condition in which it was $r = -.04$ (significance is reached when $r < -.43$, or $r > .43$).

## DISCUSSION

The results of our experiment corroborates the superiority of the visual-dictation training. This is not surprising. After all, visual-dictation includes all of the beneficial key aspects that we reviewed in the introduction, that is, practicing the whole word from memory, with immediate feedback and kinematics supporting the learning process. In this final section, we discuss the broad theoretical implications of these four aspects of spelling training. The point we want to emphasize is that instruction must include ecologically informative relations. Stated differently, we believe that training methods best reflecting the natural demands of spelling lead to the best subsequent spelling performance.

Most contemporary accounts of reading and spelling are information-processing-type theories, the most successful being Coltheart's Dual-route theory (1978). Spelling and reading are assumed to have a common basis in orthographic representations (e.g., Brown & Ellis, 1994; Hanley & McDonnell, 1997; Rapp, Benzing, & Caramazza, 1997). In such accounts, "inputs" (stimulus forms, e.g., spoken and written words) and "outputs" (the language functions they serve) have arbitrary relationships to the mental representations and processes that are proposed. Mental representations are symbols representing an abstraction of a stimulus or response, and are independent of the environment that initiate their activation. Consequently, with respect to our topic, any training method that "activates" orthographic representations should be as good as any other. However, the results of our study indicate that training methods do differ in their effectiveness. Conventional accounts thus require ad hoc ways of accounting for the demonstrated differences. Such ad hoc theorizing could be made very plausible, and our point is not to discredit these models with the present data. Rather, we wish to motivate an alternative framework in which the effects obtained in our study are more naturally expected.

The theoretical perspective we present is rooted in dynamic systems theory, which provides an alternative metaphor for cognitive systems (e.g., Thelen & Smith, 1994; Van Orden, Bosman, Goldinger & Farrar, 1997; Van Orden & Goldinger, 1994). Van Orden and colleagues framed reading and spelling in terms of a recurrent network. Recurrent networks are connectionist models in which activation flows from input to output and back again, creating feedback loops. The assumed dynamics approximate those of the interactive-activation model of McClelland and Rumelhart (1981). Behavior is modeled in self-organizing patterns of activation, but activation in any part of the network is always reflected throughout the network. Bi-directional flow of activation binds activation at each part to activation at every other part. Consequently, input (stimulus) and output (perceiver) become an irreducible whole, and the patterns of interrelation between input and output become the essential basis of theorizing. In contrast to information-processing theories, there is a meaningful or non-arbitrary relationship between the environment or the input (here, printed words) and the perceiver or the output (here, language functions of printed words). Accordingly, the behavior of a system (it being a network or cognizant organism) is determined by the history of the bi-directional correlations between a stimulus forms and their functions.

At this point, we need not concern ourselves with the details of the proposed network (cf. Bosman & Van Orden, 1997; Van Orden &

Goldinger, 1994; Van Orden, Pennington, & Stone, 1990). Three properties of the framework that we adhere to are relevant for our discussion here, namely, all parts of the network are interdependent, the type of input affects the output, and the history of the input-output relations is crucial for predicting future performance. Assuming that input and output have meaningful relationships explains why a spelling training that mimics natural spelling will be more beneficial than one that mimics natural spelling to a lesser degree. Natural spelling usually involves both writing whole words and writing them for memory. These aspects are combined in the visual-dictation training.

The benefits of training whole-word spellings also agrees with the claimed interdependency of input and output. For example, all letters and all phonemes of a word are intertwined through recurrent feedback. Each letter and each phoneme of a word contribute to the production of each letter in spelling (and to the production of each phoneme in reading). Training of just the ambiguous phoneme-grapheme relation (as in the grapheme-selection training) disregards an essential property of our account.

Immediate feedback is not usually provided during natural spelling. It makes a natural sense that it would be an important aspect of spelling training, however. For example, any account that includes associative learning, as is the case in a recurrent network, would work best when correct spellings are appropriately available to be associated. After all, it is important to prevent erroneous spellings to consolidate.

To conclude, the way we understand differential effects of various spelling-instruction methods comes less from the details of models than from the larger assumptions of the modeling framework. As we argued above, it matters that instruction includes ecologically informative relations. Once a child is viewed as a person situated in an environment (rather than as an information processing device) we expect factors like the kinematic modality to be important. The ecology of spelling is the production of written words to function properly in written language (e.g., to usefully reflect phonology and meaning). The ecology is relatively well represented in training that includes production of words from memory, actual writing of words, and immediate feedback so that errors are not perpetuated. This is precisely the collective message of studies reviewed here, and it is illustrated as well in the outcome of our study.

Finally, we wish to note a further entailment of our claims. In our study we found a differential effect of spelling level on the effectiveness of spelling training; the less advanced spellers hardly benefited from the copying training, whereas the more advanced spellers did.

Thus, there is unlikely to be one solution to teaching spelling across languages and cultures. Not only do languages have different functional relations with their printed forms, but cultures have different relations to literacy, both in perceived importance and material support. Thus, the ecology of natural spelling may change in a language that is not more ambiguous from phonology to spelling (e.g., Hebrew; Berent, Frost, & Perfetti, 1997) or in a culture in which literacy must be taught without notebooks (see Verhoeven, 1994). A focus on organism-environment relations may escape the attractive simplicity of one-size-fits-all educational programs. To be most effective, instructional methods must evolve to fit the ecology of literate cultures and the functional relations of print to language.

NOTE

We are greatly indebted to all teachers and children from primary schools in Alkmaar, The Netherlands: In den Bongerd, De Meerpaal, De Middelburg, De Rank, Tesselschade, and De Vogelboom. Thanks to Charles Perfetti who helped us thinking up a name for the training method 'grapheme selection'. The research reported here was carried out while the second author was appointed at the Department of Psychology of the University of Amsterdam. Preparation of this article was partly supported by an Independent Scientist Award (1 K02 NS01905-01) of the National Institute of Neurological Disorders and Stroke awarded to Guy C. Van Orden.

REFERENCES

Berent, I., & Frost, R., (1997). The inhibition of polygraphic consonants in spelling Hebrew: Evidence for recurrent assembly of spelling and phonology in visual word recognition. In C. A. Perfetti, M. Fayol, & L. Rieben (Eds.), *Learning to spell* (pp. 195–219). Mahwah, NJ.: Lawrence Erlbaum.

Bosman, A. M. T., & De Groot, A. M. B. (1991). De ontwikkeling van woordbeelden bij beginnende lezers en spellers [The development of orthographic images in beginning readers and spellers]. *Pedagogische Studiën, 68*, 199–215.

Bosman, A. M. T., & De Groot, A. M. B. (1992). Differential effectiveness of reading and non-reading tasks in learning to spell. In F. Satow & B. Gatherer (Eds.), *Literacy without frontiers* (pp. 279–289). Widnes: UK Reading Association.

Bosman, A. M. T., & Van Leerdam M. (1993). Aanvankelijk spellen: de dominantie van de verklankende spelwijze en de geringe effectiviteit van lezen als spelling-instructie-methode [Beginning spelling: Prevalence of the phonological strategy in spelling and the scant effectivity of reading as a spelling instruction method]. *Pedagogische Studiën, 70*, 28–45.

Bosman, A. M. T., & Van Orden, G. C. (1997). Why spelling is more difficult than reading. In C. A. Perfetti, M. Fayol, & L. Rieben (Eds.), *Learning to spell* (pp.173–194). Mahwah, NJ: Erlbaum.

Bradley, L. L. (1981). The organization of motor patterns for spelling: An effective remedial strategy for backward readers. *Developmental Medicine and Child Neurology, 23*, 83–91.

Brown, G. D. A., & Ellis, N. C. (1994). Issues in spelling research: An overview. In G. D. A. Brown & N. C. Ellis (Eds.), *Handbook of spelling: Theory, process and intervention* (pp. 3–25). New York: John Wiley.

Caesar, F. B. (1979). *Veilig leren lezen* [Learning to read safely]. Tilburg, The Netherlands: Zwijsen.

Coltheart, M. (1978). Lexical access in simple reading tasks. In G. Underwood (Ed.), *Strategies of information processing* (pp. 151–216). New York: Academic Press.

Cunningham, A. E., & Stanovich, K. E. (1990). Early spelling acquisition: Writing beats the computer. *Journal of Educational Psychology, 82,* 159–162.

Farnham-Diggory, S., & Simon, H. A. (1975). Retention of visually presented information in children's spelling. *Memory & Cognition, 3,* 599–608.

Frith, U. (1979). Reading by eye and writing by ear. In P. A. Kolers, M. Wrolstad, & H. Bouma (Eds.), *Processing of Visible Language, vol. 1* (pp. 379–390). New York: Plenum Press.

Frith, U. (1980). Unexpected spelling problems. In U. Frith (Ed.), *Cognitive Processes in Spelling* (pp. 495–515). London: Academic Press.

Gerber, M. M. (1984). Techniques to teach generalizable spelling skills. *Academic Therapy, 20,* 49–58.

Gettinger, M. (1993). Effects of error correction in third graders' spelling. *Journal of Educational Research, 87,* 39–45.

Hanley, J. R., & McDonnell, V. (1997). Are reading and spelling phonologically mediated? Evidence from a patient with a speech production impairment. *Cognitive Neuropsychology, 14,* 3–33.

Harward. S. V., Allred, R. A., & Sudweeks, R. S. (1994). The effectiveness of four self-corrected spelling test methods. *Reading Psychology: An International Quarterly, 15,* 245–271

Huey, E. B. (1908). *The psychology and pedagogy of reading.* Cambridge, MA: MIT Press (reprinted in 1968).

Kauffman, J. M., Hallahan, D. P., Haas, K., Brame, T., & Boren, R. (1978). Imitating children's errors to improve spelling performance. *Journal of Learning Disabilities, 11,* 217–222.

Kearncy, C. A., & Drabman, R. S. (1993). The write-say method for improving spelling accuracy in children with learning disabilities. *Journal of Learning Disabilities, 26,* 52–56.

Krom, R. S. H. (1990). *Wenselijke woordenschat en feitelijke frequenties* [Target vocabulary and observed frequencies]. Arnhem, The Netherlands: Cito.

McClelland, J. L., & Rumelhart, D. E. (1981). An interactive-activation model of context effects in letter perception: Part 1: An account of basic findings. *Psychological Review, 88,* 375–407

Mommers, M. J. C. (1987). An investigation into the relation between word recognition skills, reading comprehension and spelling skills in the first two years of primary school. *Journal of Research in Reading, 10,* 122–143.

Mushinski Fulk, B., & Stormont-Spurgin, M. (1995). Spelling interventions for students with disabilities: A review. *The Journal of Special Education, 28,* 488–513.

Ormrod, J. E. (1986). Effects of feedback and mandatory practice on learning to spell during computer-assisted instruction. *Perceptual and Motor Skills, 63,* 487–494.

Rapp, B., Benzing, L., & Caramazza, A. (1997). The autonomy of lexical orthography. *Cognitive Neuropsychology, 14,* 71–104.

Read, C. (1981). Writing is not the inverse of reading for young children. In C. H. Frederiksen & J. F Dominic (Eds.), *Writing: Process, development and communication* (pp. 105–118). Hillsdale, NJ: Erlbaum.

Roberts, K. T., & Ehri, L. C. (1983). Effects of two types of letter rehearsal on word memory in skilled and less skilled beginning readers. *Contemporary Educational Psychology, 8,* 375–390.

Sears, N. C., & Johnson, D. M. (1986). The effects of visual imagery on spelling performance and retention among elementary students. *Journal of Educational Research, 79,* 230–233.

Thelen, E., & Smith, L. B. (1994). *A dynamic systems approach to the development of cognition and action.* Cambridge, MA: MIT Press.

Treiman, R. (1993). *Beginning to spell: a study of first-grade children.* New York: Oxford University Press.

Van Daal, V. H. P., & van der Leij, A. (1992). Computer-based reading and spelling practice for children with learning disabilities. *Journal of Learning Disabilities, 25,* 186–195.

Van Doorn-van Eijsden, M. (1984). Leer je spellen door veel te lezen? [Do you learn to spell by reading a lot?] *Tijdschrift voor Taalbeheersing, 6,* 252–263.

Van Orden, G. C., Bosman, A. M. T., Goldinger, B. F., & Farrar, W. T. IV. (1997). A recurrent network account of reading, spelling and dyslexia. In J. Donahoe (Ed.), *Neural network models of complex behavior: A biobehavioral foundation.* Amsterdam, The Netherlands: Elsevier.

Van Orden, G. C., & Goldinger, S. D. (1994). Interdependence of form and function in cognitive systems explains perception of printed words. *Journal of Experimental Psychology: Human Perception and Performance, 20,* 1269–1291.

Van Orden, G. C., Pennington, B. F., & Stone, G. O. (1990). Word identification in reading and the promise of subsymbolic psycholinguistics. *Psychological Review, 97,* 488–522.

Verhoeven, L. (1994). *Functional literacy: Theoretical issues and educational implications.* Amsterdam, The Netherlands: John Benjamins.

## APPENDIX A

Stimuli used in this experiment with English translations in parentheses and means of the target errors per item; Target spelling problem is italicized.

| Stimulus | Reading | Copying | Graph.Select | Oral Sp | Vis.Dict. |
|---|---|---|---|---|---|
| Pale*i*s (palace) | .50 | .21 | .36 | .36 | .00 |
| Sto*u*terd (naughty boy/girl) | .21 | .29 | .14 | .29 | .07 |
| Ka*ch*el (stove/heater) | .79 | .43 | .57 | .14 | .14 |
| Ron*dj*e (round/lap) | .57 | .43 | .29 | .21 | .07 |
| *V*uilnis (garbage) | .07 | .00 | .00 | .00 | .00 |
| Mo*dd*er (mud/dirt) | .64 | .36 | .50 | .29 | .21 |
| Schilder*ij* (painting) | .07 | .14 | .00 | .07 | .14 |
| Mi*au*wen (miaow) | .64 | .43 | .36 | .29 | .00 |
| Na*g*el (nail) | .07 | .00 | .00 | .14 | .14 |
| Bloo*t* ( nude) | .14 | .14 | .14 | .00 | .00 |
| Panto*ff*el (slipper/house shoe) | .86 | .29 | .36 | .43 | .00 |
| He*n*gel (fishing rod) | .14 | .36 | .14 | .21 | .14 |

MONIQUE COENEN,
WIM VAN BON, AND ROBERT SCHREUDER

# THE EFFECT OF READING AND SPELLING PRACTICE ON READING SKILL

Dual-route models of both reading (Coltheart, Curtis, Atkins, & Haller, 1993) and spelling (Kreiner & Gough, 1990) assume that a phonological route and a lexical route are available. However, no model specifies the relationship between reading and spelling processes. In this study we try to gain more insight into this relationship by examining the effect of spelling practice on reading skill as compared with the effect of reading practice on reading skill. First, we look at the relationship between the phonological route in reading and spelling.

In reading, the phonological route involves the application of Grapheme-to-Phoneme Correspondence (GPC) rules and the blending of phonemes into words. In spelling, the phonological route involves segmenting words into phonemes and application of Phoneme-to-Grapheme Correspondence (PGC) rules. Phonological decoding (in reading) and phonological encoding (in spelling) involve similar but reverse processes. The question arises how these processes relate to each other. Yopp (1988) showed that blending and segmenting are significantly correlated, but that phoneme segmentation is more difficult than phoneme blending. Waters, Bruck, and Seidenberg (1985) argue that "ease of spelling a particular word is determined by the number of possible spellings for a given pronunciation, while ease of reading a word is determined by the number of possible pronunciations for a given spelling pattern" (p. 525). In most alphabetic orthographies phoneme-to-grapheme relations are less consistent than grapheme-to-phoneme relations. The foregoing suggests that phonological encoding (in spelling) is more difficult than phonological decoding (in reading), but does not provide an insight into the relationship between these skills.

In this study we examine whether training in phonological encoding improves phonological decoding skill. There is some evidence to support this idea. Training children to segment words into phonemes and represent the phonemes with letters--more than training children to read words--is found to improve their ability to read pseudowords (O'Connor & Jenkins, 1995, Uhry & Shepherd, 1993). Ability to read pseudowords is believed to reflect phonological decoding skill. In both studies spelling training included explicit segmentation instruction. Training in phonemic segmentation may, by itself, improve reading skill. Indicative of this, kindergarten children who had been taught to segment words into phonemes required fewer trials to learn to read new words in a paired associate learning task (Torgesen, Morgan, & Davis, 1992) and read more words correctly (Davidson & Jenkins, 1994) than controls. In the present study, spelling training did not include explicit segmentation instruction. Children were simply required to spell unfamiliar words. For these words no orthographic representation is stored in the mental lexicon and therefore must be spelled by application of PGC rules. We examine the effect of this training in phonological encoding (i.e., spelling unfamiliar words) on decoding skill as compared with the effect of training in phonological decoding (i.e., reading unfamiliar words) on decoding skill. Decoding skill was assessed by children's reading performance on nonpractised, unfamiliar words. We assume that the children read these words by application of GPC rules. Words containing a consonant cluster were used, because beginning readers are known to have difficulty decoding printed consonant clusters (Treiman, 1985). Some of the consonant clusters were practised during the training and some were not.

Next, we look at the relationship between the lexical route in reading and spelling. The lexical route involves access to the orthographic representation of a word in the mental lexicon. In reading, a direct match is made between the printed word and its stored orthographic representation. In spelling, the orthographic representation is read out from the lexicon. Coltheart and Funnell (1987) and Friedman and Hadley (1992) argue in favour of a single orthographic representation that is used in both reading and spelling. Availability and utility of orthographic representations for reading and spelling, however, may differ because access routes are different and because different demands are made upon the quality of the representations. As Frith (1985) points out, the orthographic representations that children construct from their experience with written language will at first not be precise enough to be useful for spelling, but may be sufficient to be used in recognising written words. Another factor that may affect the utility of the representation is the means through which the word-specific orthographic knowledge is acquired, by reading a word repeatedly or by spelling it a number of times.

In Ehri's (1992) conceptualization of the acquisition of word-specific orthographic knowledge readers form systematic connections between graphemes seen in the printed word and phonemes detected in the pronunciation of the word. Knowledge of grapheme-phoneme correspondences is used to form these connections. Also, the whole spelling is connected to the whole pronunciation in that the sequence of graphemes corresponds to the sequence of blended phonemes. Analogously, we assume that spellers establish connections between phonemes heard in the spoken word and graphemes used in its spelling and, eventually, between the pronunciation of a word and its spelling. If the direction of the connection affects the utility of the representation for reading, it can be expected that reading practice improves lexical reading skill more than spelling practice. If the direction of the connection has no effect, no differential effect of reading and spelling practice on reading performance is expected.

To our knowledge only one training study reports data relevant to this question. Van Daal and Van der Leij (1992) found that words that had been read or spelled repeatedly during training were read correctly more often and were read faster than words that had not been practised. The advantage of practised words over nonpractised words indicates that lexical knowledge was acquired during the training. No differences between practice conditions were found. Reading practice and spelling practice improved to the same degree both the accuracy and fluency of reading practised words aloud. This suggests that lexical representations acquired through reading and through spelling are equally available for reading. However, since in the reading practice condition no overt response to the written word (e.g., reading aloud, matching words to pictures, etc.) was required, we cannot be certain that the children actually read the words. Assuming that they did, our interpretation of the Van Daal and Van der Leij (1992) results is still somewhat premature. In the spelling practice condition a written word was presented and then the child had to copy the word or write the word from memory. Spelling practice thus also involved reading. The effect of spelling practice on reading skill may actually be caused by the reading component in the spelling training.

In the present experiment reading practice and spelling practice were designed to try to get round these confounding factors in the Van Daal and Van der Leij study. In the reading condition a written word and three spoken words were presented to the child, who then had to indicate which one of the three alternatives was represented by the written word. In the spelling condition a spoken word was presented to the child, who then had to spell the word by selecting the correct graphemes from a given set and putting them in the correct order. The written word was presented—by way of providing feedback—only after the child had spelled the word. We believe that by doing so the reading component is reduced to a minimum in our spelling condition.

We examine whether the means through which lexical knowledge is acquired—by reading a word repeatedly or by spelling it a number of times—affects the utility of the representation for reading. Words were practised 8, 4, or 0 times during the training. If accuracy and speed improve more from pretest to posttest for words practised more often, this is taken as evidence that word-specific knowledge is acquired during training and is used for reading. We examine whether the effect of the number of times words have been practised is equally large for children who practised reading the words and for children who practised spelling the words. Two types of words were used: words containing a consonant cluster and words containing an ambiguous phoneme.

## METHOD

### Participants

Thirty-four children (23 boys and 11 girls; mean age 9;3 years) who were classified by their teachers as poor readers were selected from three schools for special education. The children performed at least one year below age expectancy on a standardized reading achievement test. All children were native speakers of Dutch.

### Materials

All words selected for this experiment were familiar in meaning to the children who participated. The words probably were not familiar in print to the children, as they are relatively low in frequency. The mean frequency count of the test words is 6 in a corpus of 202,526 printed words from Dutch books and textbooks for children from 7 to 13 years old (Staphorsius, Krom & De Geus, 1988).

*Words containing a consonant cluster.* We selected 113 CCVC and CVCC words (C = consonant / V = vowel). About half of these words were practised during training. About half of the words that were not practised during training contained a consonant cluster that was practised. We also selected 14 CCVCC words. These words were not practised during training. All words can be read and spelled through straightforward application of GPC rules and PGC rules.

For each training word, two words were selected that were to be presented as distractors in reading practice. Three or four phonemes of the training word--one or both of the consonants of the cluster, the vowel, and the single consonant--correspond to phonemes of the distractor words (e.g., klok -> blok, kok; kans -> kast, knal).

The set of graphemes the child had to choose from in spelling practice contained the vowel, the three consonants of the training word, and two other consonants. Each of the additional consonants can make up an orthographically legal cluster with one of the consonants of the target cluster.

*Words containing an ambiguous phoneme.* We selected 24 words containing the ambiguous phoneme /ɛi/, which in Dutch is most often represented by the grapheme 'ij', but also by 'ei'. In 16 words /ɛi/ was represented by 'ij', and in 8 words by 'ei'. We selected 15 words containing the ambiguous phoneme /au/, which in Dutch most often is represented by the grapheme 'ou', but also by 'au'. In 10 words /au/ was represented by 'ou', and in 5 words by 'au'. All words were practised during training. The words were of simple orthographic structure (CVC, CV or VC). The words can be read through straightforward application of GPC rules, but cannot be spelled unequivocally.

For each training word, two words were selected that were to be presented as distractors in reading practice. One distractor word contained the same vowel as the training word and different initial and final consonants (e.g., vouw -> hout; reis -> pijp). The other distractor word contained a vowel which is represented by one of the letters of the digraph representing the vowel of the training word (e.g., vouw -> vos) or by a digraph in which the letters are transposed (e.g., reis -> riem). The initial consonant was the same.

The set of graphemes the child had to choose from in spelling practice contained the two graphemes that can be used to represent the ambiguous phoneme and the consonant(s) of the training word.

*Design*

Half of the children received a reading training, and the other half a spelling training. In both conditions, words were practised 8, 4, or 0 times during 16 training sessions (see Table 1). Note that the words that are spelled with 'ei' or 'au' were all practised 8 times.

In each session 20 or 21 words containing a consonant cluster and 16 or 17 words containing an ambiguous phoneme were practised. Words were presented in a random order. Words practised eight times were presented once every two sessions; words practised four times were presented once every four sessions.

TABLE 1
Number of words practised 8, 4 or 0 times

| Words containing a consonant cluster | | | |
|---|---|---|---|
| Orthographic Structure  CCVC | CVCC | Times Practised | |
| 13 | 14 | 8 | |
| 13 | 14 | 4 | |
| 16 | 16 | 0 [1] | |
| 12 | 15 | 0 [2] | |
| Words containing an ambiguous phoneme | | | |
| Grapheme    ij | ei | ou | au | Times Practised |
| 8 | 8 | 5 | 5 | 8 |
| 8 | | 5 | | 4 |

Notes. [1] CCVC / CVCC words containing practised consonant clusters
[2] CCVC / CVCC words containing nonpractised consonant clusters

## Procedure

The experiment was conducted in a four-month period starting at the end of January. In the first three weeks pretests were carried out. Three weeks later the training started. During eight or nine weeks 16 training sessions were held. In the last three weeks posttests were carried out.

In the *reading pre- and posttest* the practised and nonpractised words were presented one by one on the screen of a computer. The child was asked to read the words as fast and as accurately as possible. Naming times were measured accurately to the millisecond by a voice-activated relay. The experimenter registered whether the word was read correctly and whether the clock was stopped by the verbal response of the participant. No feedback was given.

The *training* comprised 16 sessions. Two sessions were held each week. Both the reading and the spelling training were implemented on a computer. The program enabled the children to practice without supervisor.

In the reading condition each trial started by presenting the word on the computer screen. A row of boxes was located at the top of the screen. Each grapheme of the word was placed in a separate box. The word disappeared when the child clicked on *Klaar* [ready]; the word reappeared when the child clicked on *Woord* [word]. The child listened to one, two or all three of the words (the intended word plus two distractor words) by clicking on any of three pictures (a juggler with one, two, or three balls). The child was allowed to look at the word and listen to the words as often as desired, but not simultaneously. The child indicated which one of the three spoken words he thought was represented by the printed word by marking the relevant picture. The position of the intended word was varied. The computer provided feedback by presenting the printed word, stating whether or not the child had made the correct choice, and pronouncing the intended word. The next word was presented when the child clicked on *Verder* [next].

In the spelling condition three rows of six boxes were located one below the other on the screen. Each trial started by presenting the set of graphemes the child had to choose from. Each grapheme was placed in a separate box in the top row. Correct and incorrect graphemes were presented in random order. The word was dictated by the computer when the child clicked on the picture of a stave. The child was allowed to listen to the word as often as desired. The child spelled the word by selecting the correct graphemes and putting them in the correct order in the middle row. The child could correct any error detected in his own spelling until he clicked on *Klaar* [ready]. The computer provided feedback by stating whether or not the child had spelled the word correctly, pronouncing the word again, and in case the word had been spelled incorrectly by presenting the correct spelling in the bottom row. The next word was presented when the child clicked on *Verder* [next].

## RESULTS

The data of six participants were excluded from the analyses. Records kept during training suggested that four children were poorly motivated to perform the task. Following a series of sessions in which they performed quite well, they appeared to give incorrect responses deliberately. One child completed only twelve training sessions, because of a technical failure of the apparatus. And finally, of one child no data were available on the posttest. Of the remaining 28 participants, 13 took part in the reading condition and 15 took part in the spelling condition. The children in the two conditions were matched for reading ability as measured by the standardized reading achievement test.

We examine the effect of training in phonological encoding (i.e., spelling unfamiliar words) on decoding skill as compared with the effect of training in phonological decoding (i.e., reading unfamiliar words) on decoding skill. Decoding skill was assessed by children's reading performance on nonpractised, unfamiliar words.

Words were practised 0, 4, or 8 times during the training. If reading accuracy and speed have improved more from pretest to posttest for words practised more often, this is taken as evidence that lexical knowledge has been acquired during training and was used for reading. We examine whether the effect of the number of times words had been practised was equally large for children who had practised reading the words and for children who had practised spelling the words. We are mainly interested in the effect of the training on reading skill. Therefore, we focus on interaction effects involving the factor test (pretest vs. posttest). In order to improve readability, we only report significant effects ($p<.05$) and marginally significant effects ($p<.10$).

*Nonpractised CCVCC words.* Error percentages and median naming times were calculated. Naming times for words that were read incorrectly (16.2%) and times recorded when the clock had not been stopped by the verbal response of the participant, but by another sound (6.9%), were discarded. Median naming times were calculated only if at least 50% of the relevant observations were valid. As a consequence the data of three more participants were excluded from the analysis of naming times besides the data of six participants excluded at the outset. Table 2 presents mean error percentages and means of median naming times of nonpractised words.

A two (test: pretest vs. posttest) by two (practice form: reading vs. spelling) analysis of variance was performed on subjects' error percentages and on subjects' median naming times. Test is a within-subjects factor. Practice form is a between-subjects factor. The main effect of test was significant in the analysis of naming times ($F(1,23) = 4.11$, $p=.05$). Naming latency decreased from pretest to posttest, similarly for children in both practice conditions. Error percentages did not decrease.

TABLE 2
Mean error percentages and means of median naming times on pretest and posttest of nonpractised words containing practised or nonpractised consonant clusters (standard deviations in parentheses)

| Word Type Consonant cluster Practice condition | CCVC / CVCC practised | | nonpractised | | CCVCC | | |
|---|---|---|---|---|---|---|---|
| | n | | | | n | | |
| *Error percentages* | | | | | | | |
| Reading Pretest | 13 | 18.3 (8.4) | 16.8 | (9.4) | 13 | 14.8 | (11.5) |
| Posttest | 13 | 16.1 (7.5) | 14.0 | (8.2) | 13 | 18.1 | (14.2) |
| Effect | | 2.2 | 2.8 | | | −3.3 | |
| Spelling Pretest | 15 | 19.4 (9.8) | 19.0 | (7.1) | 15 | 17.1 | (15.2) |
| Posttest | 15 | 15.8 (10.0) | 19.8 | (12.4) | 15 | 14.8 | (16.3) |
| Effect | | 3.6 | −0.8 | | | 2.3 | |
| *Naming times* | | | | | | | |
| Reading Pretest | 12 | 2566 (762) | 2318 | (780) | 12 | 2731 | (1082) |
| Posttest | 12 | 2186 (1113) | 2141 | (999) | 12 | 2358 | (1323) |
| Effect | | 380 | 177 | | | 373 | |
| Spelling Pretest | 15 | 2045 (1081) | 2219 | (1125) | 13 | 2470 | (1448) |
| Posttest | 15 | 1895 (999) | 1874 | (1120) | 13 | 2184 | (1178) |
| Effect | | 150 | 345 | | | 286 | |

*Nonpractised CCVC / CVCC words.* These words contained either a practised consonant cluster or a nonpractised consonant cluster. Error percentages and median naming times were calculated. Naming times for words that were read incorrectly (17.5%) and times recorded when the clock had not been stopped by the verbal response of the participant, but by another sound (4.1%), were discarded. Median naming times were calculated only if at least 50% of the relevant observations were valid. As a consequence the data of one more participant were excluded from the analysis of naming times besides the data of six participants excluded at the outset. Table 2 presents mean error percentages and means of median naming times of nonpractised words.

A two (test: pretest vs. posttest) by two (practice form: reading vs. spelling) by two (consonant cluster: practised vs. nonpractised) analysis of variance was performed on subjects' error percentages and on subjects' median naming times. Test and consonant cluster are within-subjects factors. Practice form is a between-subjects factor. The main effect of test was significant in the analysis of naming times ($F(1,25) = 14.82$, $p < .01$). Naming latency decreased from pretest to posttest, similarly for children in both practice conditions and similarly for words containing practised consonant clusters and words containing nonpractised consonant clusters. Error percentages did not decrease.

*CCVC / CVCC words practised 8, 4, or 0 times.* In this analysis the words that were practised 0 times contained practised consonant clusters. Error percentages and median naming times were calculated. Naming times for words that were read incorrectly (14.8%) and times recorded when the clock had not been stopped by the verbal response of the participant, but by another sound (3.4%), were discarded. Median naming times were calculated only if at least 50% of the relevant observations were valid. As a consequence the data of one more participant were excluded from the analysis of naming times besides the data of six participants excluded at the outset. Table 3 presents mean error percentages and means of median naming times of CCVC / CVCC words practised 8, 4, or 0 times during training.

TABLE 3
Mean error percentages and means of median naming times on pretest and posttest of CCVC / CVCC words as a function of practice form and number of times practised (standard deviations in parentheses)

| Practice condition | n | Number of times practised | | | | | |
|---|---|---|---|---|---|---|---|
| | | 8 | | 4 | | 0 | |
| *Error percentages* | | | | | | | |
| Reading Pretest | 13 | 19.4 | (9.7) | 16.8 | (8.5) | 18.3 | (8.4) |
| Posttest | 13 | 8.0 | (7.2) | 12.3 | (8.7) | 16.1 | (7.5) |
| Effect | | 11.4 | | 4.5 | | 2.2 | |
| Spelling Pretest | 15 | 14.6 | (6.3) | 13.6 | (8.5) | 19.4 | (9.8) |
| Posttest | 15 | 11.6 | (8.0) | 10.1 | (7.2) | 15.8 | (10.0) |
| Effect | | 3.0 | | 3.5 | | 3.6 | |
| *Naming times* | | | | | | | |
| Reading Pretest | 12 | 2241 | (841) | 2309 | (973) | 2566 | (762) |
| Posttest | 12 | 1597 | (914) | 1734 | (849) | 2186 | (1113) |
| Effect | | 644 | | 575 | | 380 | |
| Spelling Pretest | 15 | 2077 | (1123) | 2083 | (1311) | 2045 | (1081) |
| Posttest | 15 | 1732 | (899) | 1689 | (925) | 1895 | (999) |
| Effect | | 345 | | 394 | | 150 | |

A two (test: pretest vs. posttest) by two (practice form: reading vs. spelling) by three (times practised: 8 vs. 4 vs. 0) analysis of variance was performed on subjects' error percentages and on subjects' median naming times. Test and times practised are within-subjects factors.

Practice form is a between-subjects factor.

First, we discuss the results of the analysis of error percentages. The main effect of test was significant ($F(1,26) = 10.91$, $p<.01$), and the interaction between test and times practised approached significance (Wilks' Lambda = .80, $F(2,25) = 3.07$, $p=.06$). Separate analyses were carried out, which revealed that the interaction was significant when comparing words practised 8 times and words practised 4 times ($F(1,26) = 4.46$, $p<.05$), but was not significant when comparing words practised 4 times and words practised 0 times. Error percentages decreased from pretest to posttest, and decreased more for words practised 8 times than for words practised 4 times, but did not decrease more for words practised 4 times than for words practised 0 times.

The interaction between test, times practised, and practice form was significant (Wilks' Lambda = .76, $F(2,25) = 3.95$, $p<.05$). Additional analyses were carried out, which revealed an interaction between test and times practised for subjects in the reading practice condition (Wilks' Lambda = .40; $F(2,11) = 8.18$, $p<.01$), but not for subjects in the spelling practice condition. In the reading practice condition error percentages decreased more for words practised more often; in the spelling practice condition error percentages decreased to the same degree for words practised 8, 4, or 0 times.

Next, we discuss the results of the analysis of naming times. The main effect of test was significant ($F(1,25) = 21.44$, $p<.01$), but the interaction between test and times practised was not significant. Separate analyses were carried out, which revealed that the interaction approached significance when comparing words practised 4 times and words practised 0 times ($F(1,25) = 3.62$, $p=.07$), but was not significant when comparing words practised 8 times and words practised 4 times. Naming latency decreased from pretest to posttest, and decreased more for words practised 4 times than for words practised 0 times, but did not decrease more for words practised 8 times than for words practised 4 times. In contrast with the error analysis no differential effect of reading and spelling practice was found.

*CVC words practised 8 or 4 times.* These words are spelled with 'ij' or 'ou'. Recall that the words that are spelled with 'ei' or 'au' were all practised 8 times. Error percentages and median naming times were calculated. Naming times for words that were read incorrectly (7.6%) and times recorded when the clock had not been stopped by the verbal response of the participant, but by another sound (3.0%), were discarded. Median naming times were calculated only if at least 70% of the relevant observations were valid. As a consequence the data of three more participants were excluded from the analysis of naming times besides the data of six participants excluded at the outset. Table 4 presents mean error percentages and means of median naming times of words spelled with 'ij' or 'ou'.

TABLE 4

Mean error percentages and means of median naming times on pretest and posttest of words spelled with IJ or OU as a function of practice form and number of times practised (standard deviations in parentheses)

| Practice condition | | n | Number of times practised | | | |
|---|---|---|---|---|---|---|
| | | | 8 | | 4 | |
| *Error percentages* | | | | | | |
| Reading | Pretest | 13 | 6.5 | (6.2) | 11.2 | (7.4) |
| | Posttest | 13 | 7.7 | (12.6) | 5.3 | (5.8) |
| | Effect | | - 1.2 | | 5.9 | |
| Spelling | Pretest | 15 | 9.2 | (8.8) | 9.7 | (8.5) |
| | Posttest | 15 | 5.1 | (5.6) | 5.6 | (7.4) |
| | Effect | | 4.1 | | 4.1 | |
| *Naming times* | | | | | | |
| Reading | Pretest | 11 | 1343 | (545) | 1349 | (582) |
| | Posttest | 11 | 1127 | (375) | 1246 | (572) |
| | Effect | | 216 | | 103 | |
| Spelling | Pretest | 14 | 1432 | (674) | 1417 | (622) |
| | Posttest | 14 | 1112 | (394) | 1167 | (448) |
| | Effect | | 320 | | 250 | |

A two (test: pretest vs. posttest) by two (practice form: reading vs. spelling) by two (times practised: 8 vs. 4) analysis of variance was performed on subjects' error percentages and on subjects' median naming times. Test and times practised are within-subjects factors. Practice form is a between-subjects factor. The main effect of test was significant in the error analysis ($F(1,26) = 4.83$, $p<.05$) and in the analysis of naming times ($F(1,23) = 16.28$, $p<.01$). Error percentages and naming latency decreased from pretest to posttest, similarly for children in both practice conditions and similarly for words practised 8 times and words practised 4 times.

## DISCUSSION

Our objective was to gain more insight into the relationship between reading and spelling, by examining the effect of spelling practice on reading skill. As for the phonological route, we examined the effect of training in phonological encoding (i.e., spelling unfamiliar words) on decoding skill as compared with the effect of training in phonological decoding (i.e., reading unfamiliar words) on decoding skill. Decoding skill was assessed by children's reading performance on nonpractised, unfamiliar words (CCVC / CVCC or CCVCC). On the pretest the children read already over 80% of the words correctly, suggesting that they can read by application of GPC rules--but it took them over two seconds to name the words. Accuracy did not improve. Naming speed did improve, similarly for children in both practice conditions and similarly for words containing nonpractised consonant clusters and words containing practised consonant clusters. Since no effect was found of either manipulated factor, practice form (reading vs. spelling) and consonant cluster (practised vs. nonpractised), we cannot be certain that the higher decoding speed on the posttest is solely attributable to the training. The fact that the children had three more months of reading experience probably also contributed to their improved reading performance.

As our training did not require the children to respond quickly, it may be the case that the training did not affect decoding speed. This appears plausible, considering the results of Van den Bosch, Van Bon, and Schreuder (1995). Poor readers received training in decoding monosyllabic pseudowords. In one group the pseudowords were presented only briefly; in another group exposure duration was unlimited. The children who had practised under time pressure faster named practised pseudowords and nonpractised words than the children who had practised without time pressure. Training without time pressure even appeared to slow down word processing speed.

We also examined whether the means through which lexical knowledge is acquired--by reading a word repeatedly or by spelling it a number of times--affects the utility of the representation for reading. Are lexical representations that are constructed during spelling practice available for reading and, if so, are they equally useful for reading as representations that are constructed during reading practice? Naming speed increased more from pretest to posttest for CCVC / CVCC words practised 4 times than for the same type of words practised 0 times, indicating that lexical knowledge was acquired during the training. Practising the words 8 times did not further increase naming speed. This corresponds with the results of Bosman and De Groot (1991), who found that naming speed increased most between the first and second presentation of a word.

No differential effect of reading practice and spelling practice on speed of reading practised words was found. This suggests that lexical representations that are constructed during spelling are equally useful for reading as representations that are constructed during reading. Bosman (1994, chapter 7), on the other hand, did not find (oral) spelling training to benefit reading. In one experiment beginning readers / spellers were instructed in the spelling of words they had not seen in print before. In another experiment advanced readers / spellers were instructed in the spelling of pseudowords containing at least one ambiguous phoneme. During the spelling training the (pseudo)words were practised orally, and consequently were not encountered in written form. Words that had been practised during training were spelled correctly more often than words that had not been practised. On a naming task, however, the beginning and advanced readers did not seem to profit from the newly acquired spelling knowledge. Words they had learned to spell were not named faster than words they did not know the spelling of. The fact that they were never visually presented with the words probably was crucial. In our spelling training the children did see the correct spelling of the words, either produced by themselves or presented by the computer after an incorrect spelling attempt. The effect of spelling training on reading skill probably is caused by the reading component in spelling.

We found spelling practice to increase the naming speed of practised words as much as reading practice did. With regard to accuracy, however, reading practice and spelling practice were found to have different effects. In the reading practice condition accuracy improved more for words practised more often; error percentages decreased more from pretest to posttest for CCVC / CVCC words practised 8 times (11.4%) than for the same type of words practised 4 times (4.5%). In the spelling practice condition no differential effect was found of the number of times the words had been practised on accuracy of reading practised words; error percentages decreased 3.0% and 3.5% on average for CCVC / CVCC words practised 8 times and 4 times respectively. The accuracy results suggest that lexical representations that are constructed during reading are more useful for reading than representations that are constructed during spelling.

Error percentages for the CVC words spelled with 'ij' or 'ou' decreased from pretest to posttest, similarly for children in both practice conditions and similarly for words practised 8 times and words practised 4 times. Error percentages for these words--which were of simple orthographic structure--were already very low on the pretest. This may have prohibited differential progress.

## REFERENCES

Bosman, A. M. T. (1994). *Reading and spelling in children and adults: evidence for a single-route model.* Doctoral dissertation. University of Amsterdam, The Netherlands.

Bosman, A. M. T., & De Groot, A. M. B. (1991). De ontwikkeling van woordbeelden bij beginnende lezers en spellers. [The development of orthographic images in beginning readers and spellers.] *Pedagogische Studiën, 68,* 199–215.

Coltheart, M., Curtis, B., Atkins, P., & Haller, M. (1993). Models of reading aloud: dual-route and parallel-distributed processing approaches. *Psychological Review, 100,* 589–608.

Coltheart, M., & Funnell, E. (1987). Reading and writing: one lexicon or two? In A.

Allport, D. MacKay, W. Prinz, & E. Scheerer (Eds.), *Language perception and production: Relationships between listening, speaking, reading, and writing.* (pp. 313-339). Harcourt Brace Jovanovich.

Davidson, M. & Jenkins, J. R. (1994). Effects of phonemic processes on word reading and spelling. *Journal of Educational Research, 87*, 148-157.

Ehri, L. C. (1992). Reconceptualizing the development of sight word reading and its relationship to recoding. In P. B. Gough, L. C. Ehri, & R. Treiman (Eds.), *Reading Acquisition* (pp. 107-143). Hillsdale, NJ: Erlbaum.

Friedman, R. B. & Hadley, J. A. (1992). Letter-by-letter surface alexia. *Cognitive Neuropsychology, 9*, 185-208.

Frith, U. (1985). Beneath the surface of developmental dyslexia. In K. E. Patterson, J. C. Marshall, & M. Coltheart (Eds.), *Surface dyslexia* (pp. 301-330). London: Erlbaum.

Kreiner, D. S., & Gough, P. B. (1990). Two ideas about spelling: rules and word-specific memory. *Journal of Memory and Language, 29*, 103-118.

O'Connor, R. E., & Jenkins, J. R. (1995). Improving the generalization of sound/symbol knowledge: teaching spelling to kindergarten children with disabilities. *Journal of Special Education, 29*, 255-275.

Staphorsius, G., Krom, R. S. H., & De Geus, K. (1988). *Frequenties van woordvormen en letterposities in jeugdlectuur* [Word frequencies and frequencies of letter positions in reading matter for the youth]. Arnhem: CITO.

Torgesen, J. K., Morgan, S. T., & Davis, C. (1992). Effects of two types of phonological awareness training on word learning in kindergarten children. *Journal of Educational Psychology, 84*, 364-370.

Treiman, R. (1985). Onsets and rimes as units of spoken syllables: Evidence from children. *Journal of Experimental Child Psychology, 39*, 161-181.

Uhry, J. K., & Shepherd, M.J. (1993). Segmentation/spelling instruction as part of a first-grade reading program: effects on several measures of reading. *Reading Research Quarterly, 28*, 218-233.

Van Daal, V. H. P., & Van der Leij, A. (1992). Computer-based reading and spelling practice for children with learning disabilities. *Journal of Learning Disabilities, 25*, 186-195.

Van den Bosch, K., Van Bon, W. H. J., & Schreuder, R. (1995). Poor readers' decoding skills: effects of training with limited exposure duration. *Reading Research Quarterly, 30*, 110-125.

Waters, G., Bruck, M., & Seidenberg, M. (1985). Do children use similar processes to read and spell words? *Journal of Experimental Child Psychology, 39*, 511-530.

Yopp, H. K. (1988). The validity and reliability of phonemic awareness tests. *Reading Research Quarterly, 23*, 159-177.

ELISA POSKIPARTA,
MARJA VAURAS, AND PEKKA NIEMI

# PROMOTING READING SKILLS IN A COMPUTER-BASED TRAINING PROGRAM

The best guarantee to become a fast and accurate reader is to read a lot. According to Reitsma (1988), practice in reading is needed to refine and extend knowledge of letter-sound correspondences and to increase familiarity with printed words so that they can be identified quickly and without phonemic decoding. Stanovich (1990) goes even a step further, arguing that reading comprehension, general knowledge, vocabulary, and syntactic knowledge all develop through reading. Although a majority of children seem to acquire basic reading skills with some facility in the course of the first school years, some children find the task very difficult. According to Stanovich (1990), there are developmental changes in to what extent the reading deficits display cognitive specificity. The performance of reading-disabled children is characterised by a relatively high degree of specificity upon entering school with the specificity being located in the phonological domain. But the specificity eventually breaks down, in part because of the consequences of reading failure. Motivational and emotional side effects enter the picture. When the reading is halting and when comprehension - the ultimate goal of reading - is disturbed by uncertainty and insecurity, then children tend to lose their interest in reading and spend less time on it (see Allington 1977, 1980, 1984; Gambrell, Wilson, & Gant 1981; Juel 1988). Hence, it is important to ask: Is it possible to get poor readers to read more? What kind of practice is most beneficial for a slowly progressing reader?

Ehri (Ehri & Roberts 1979; Ehri & Wilce 1980) found advantages in learning to recognize words in the context of whole text instead of learning them separately. On the other hand, specific decoding programs often tend to dissociate between decoding and comprehension, which may negatively affect the reader's motivation (Fleisher, Jenkins, & Pany, 1979). Therefore, it is important that even decoding exercises are embedded in a continuous text. In many countries, computer-based teaching programs have been created for children with decoding problems (Elbro, Rasmussen, & Spelling 1996; Lundberg & Olofsson 1993; Olofsson 1992; Olson & Wise 1992). In these programs, poor readers read stories presented on the computer screen. They request synthetic-speech feedback for difficult words by targeting them with a mouse. The results from these longitudinal studies indicate that children working with synthetic-speech feedback improved more in reading ability than children who were given about the same amount of traditional special education instruction. However, Reitsma (1988) found that guided-reading practice and independent reading with self-selected speech feedback are equally effective in promoting word recognition skill in grade one. Guided-reading is an often used classroom practice in which children take turns in reading aloud a story while the teacher comments on their performance. A detail worth noting is that the subjects in Reitsma's (1988) study were normal first graders whose motivation to learn to read was probably still high.

Computer-based programs with synthetic-speech feedback have also proved to be a suitable tool to promote the spelling skills of poor writers (Van Daal & Van der Leij 1992; Wise & Olson 1992). Auditory feedback on written text, by means of which one may listen to what one is typing, will expose errors that are typical for poor writers, such as, the omission of letters, reversals or exchanged letters. Compared to ordinary proof-reading, auditory feedback offers an extended possibility to use an internal control to decide whether or not the result corresponds to the intention. Poor readers and writers often have great problems in detecting their own misspellings and decoding errors. Therefore, much support and external control is required. External control of one's own production demands less concentration and endurance than an internal control. Pupils receiving much external aid may very soon learn to depend on the other person. However, self-regulation is the key word in the way toward effective learning (cf. Brown, 1987).

In Finland, compulsory education starts at the age of seven. Most teachers use a modern version of phonics in beginning reading instruction. Due to its nearly perfect grapheme-to-phoneme correspondence, the Finnish language favours this approach. Syllables are used as an aid both in reading and spelling instruction. In most schools, the autumn term of grade one is a period of intensive and systematic decoding and spelling instruction during which all letters and syllable constructions are taught. In spring in grade one, most of them are already able to read whole stories (100 words) and write short passages at moderate speed and with remarkable accuracy. However, there are pupils whose reading and writing skills are far from fluent and accurate when they enter grade two. They are especially troubled by long words. Those pupils who have problems with reading and/or writing are given extra help by the special education teacher and sometimes also by their classroom teacher. The special education instruction mostly revises classroom instruction. The major difference from the classroom curriculum is that children are taught in small-groups. Those pupils who have the most serious problems are sometimes taught individually. A common way to promote reading fluency and accuracy is so called guided-reading practice. The pupils take turns reading aloud a couple of lines of a story while the teacher monitors their word identification skill and presents corrective feedback when errors are made. In writing lessons the children write their own short stories and then the teacher gives them feedback on their misspellings and syntactic errors. Independent exercises on spelling, handwriting and syntactically correct sentence formation are also included in the instruction.

The purpose of the present study was to design a new kind of special education practise for Finnish second graders. In particular, the aim was to compare the effects of a computer-based program with the traditional special education instruction on word recognition, spelling, and reading comprehension skills. In contrast to the traditional special education practice, in the computer-based program, the use of synthetic-speech feedback made it possible for the pupils to overcome decoding and spelling problems independently, without external help. Furthermore, reading and writing skills were practised within the same task. The case of Finland provides an interesting test at this point. In the second grade, even poor readers compare quite well with the world average (Elley, 1992). According to Reitsma (1988), normally reading Dutch first graders did not have a selective advantage due to a computer-assisted reading program. Would the poorly reading Finnish second graders display such a gain or would they follow the pattern suggested by Reitsma's (1988) Dutch first graders? If there were a gain, it would probably be due to the more advanced metacognitive skills possessed by the older Finnish pupils (mean ages 8 years 3 months and 7 years 2 months, respectively).

## METHOD

*Subjects*

The participants were 236 children who entered the second grade in four primary schools in the town of Turku. Two of the schools were designated as experimental schools (n=119) and the other two as control schools (n=117). Both the experimental group and control schools had 6 classes with 16–25 pupils in each class. No major differences in the regular or remedial teaching practices were found between the schools.

Twenty children were selected for the training program, with 2–5 pupils from each experimental school class. There were 11 girls and 9 boys. Their mean age was 8 years, 3 months. All children in the experimental schools with specific and marked difficulties in decoding (n=6), spelling (n=4) or listening and reading comprehension (n=4) were included in the training program. Furthermore, there were

2 pupils with marked difficulties in both decoding and spelling and 2 pupils with marked difficulties in both spelling and comprehension skills. Their decoding, spelling and/or comprehension skills were about 1.5 SD below the average performance of Finnish second graders. The remaining 2 pupils included in the training program had moderate difficulties in decoding, spelling and comprehension skills.

The experimental children had pair-wise matched controls from six control school classes, 1–7 pupils from each class. There were 7 girls and 13 boys in the control group. Their mean age was 8 years, 1 month. Matching was based on decoding, spelling, listening comprehension, reading comprehension and text production skills. The group means of these variables are given in Table 1. A MANOVA showed that experimental and control pupils did not differ from each other statistically, F<1.

TABLE 1
Mean performance scores (and SD in brackets) of the experimental (N = 20) and control groups (N = 20) before the intervention.

| Task | Experimental group | | Control group | |
| --- | --- | --- | --- | --- |
| Word recognition (max 400) | 114.3 | (53.4) | 119.6 | (40.9) |
| Spelling (max 10) | 4.8 | (3.2) | 4.5 | (2.8) |
| Reading comprehension (% correct) | 29.0 | (12.5) | 25.4 | (16.3) |
| Listening comprehension (% correct) | 48.8 | (22.7) | 40.4 | (20.5) |
| Text production (number of propositions) | 2.0 | (1.2) | 2.7 | (1.7) |

## Procedure

The children in the experimental group participated on an individual basis in the computer-assisted training program during the autumn term in grade 2. The training was carried out during the school day, 20 minutes at a time, twice a week, during 15 weeks. The pupils were supervised by the first author.

The control pupils were taught according to the regular curriculum, except that 12 of them received more intensive instruction from their classroom teacher and/or special education teacher. These 12 pupils were selected for the traditional special education instruction by their teachers with no influence from the researchers. The special education instruction revised the classroom instruction in order to fill in gaps in the pupils' knowledge of reading and spelling. The major difference from the classroom curriculum was that the children were taught individually or in small groups. Computer-assisted learning was not included in the instruction.

## Purpose and content of the training program

A computer-based training program with synthetic-speech feedback was devised. The program was developed for the IBM-PC with a hard-disk and VGA graphic card. A standard mouse was used as pointing device. The synthetic-speech system Mikropuhe 3.0 (Time House Oy) was used.

In the training the child read short stories, reread the most difficult words in them, and answered questions about the content of the stories. There were both two-choice and open- ended questions. In the latter case, the child wrote down the answers with the computer and corrected his/her misspellings. The child used synthetic-speech feedback as an aid both in decoding and spelling. Furthermore, the first steps of reading comprehension and text production instruction were included in the program. The goal was to create a training program in which both reading and writing skills could be promoted within one coherent task.

The content of the training program was as follows:

1. In every training session (sessions 1–29), the child read aloud one short story, 41 to 132 words long, presented on the screen. Half of them were expository texts on history, biology etc, and the other half consisted of narratives such as detective stories. In the beginning of the story reading, all the letter spaces in the words were hidden under a row of zeros. The words appeared on the screen one at a time when the child clicked the mouse and the words stayed there until the end of the story reading. The child was trained to request synthetic-speech feedback for difficult words (i.e., long words with difficult syllables, words of low frequency) by targeting the word with the mouse. In eight sessions, the child was asked what the title brought to his/her mind and what s/he believed the forthcoming text to be about. In 14 sessions, before reading the story, the computer always asked the child, both orally and in writing, to pause at the end of each sentence and to think about the message of the sentence just read. Afterwards the computer asked him/her if s/he had remembered to do that.

2. In every training session, the computer presented, both orally and in writing, two questions about the content of the stories. There was also a third voluntary question, the so- called joker. The child answered the questions by pressing a yes/no button and received immediate feedback on his/her performance from the computer. The child received +1 for a correct answer and −1 for an incorrect answer. For the joker question, the corresponding points were +2 and −2. Feedback was given both numerically and pictorially. In the latter, facial expressions told the child of his or her success or failure.

3. In sessions 1–19, the program asked the child to reread aloud the five words in the stories that had resulted in the longest reading times. The words were presented one at a time by the computer. The three first words stayed on the screen a little longer (5%) than the time the

child had needed for reading them for the first time. After that, the child him/herself chose how long the words would stay on the screen: the same as, 20% longer or 20% shorter than the time needed for the first reading. Two seconds after the word had disappeared from the screen, the computer pronounced it and the child judged the correctness of his/her own reading by pressing a yes/no button. If the child did not have time to read the word s/he was instructed to press a no-button.

4. In sessions 9–29, the computer asked the child, both orally and in writing, 1–3 questions about the content of the stories and the child wrote down the answers with the computer. S/he was instructed to produce whole sentences in his/her written answers instead of single words. If the child was not able to give any answer to a question, the supervisor helped him/her with cues. Furthermore, in the last 8 sessions, the child practised producing longer answers by writing a proper end to the narrative or a short essay about the expository text. In sessions 9–29, the child was also instructed to correct his/her misspellings in the sentences by first asking the computer to "read" what s/he had written and then listening carefully to whether there were any misspellings. If his/her spelling ability was very poor, the child was asked to check the spelling after every word or even after every syllable.

The role of the supervisor was active when a new task or sub-skill was introduced to the child, but as soon as possible the child was encouraged to engage in self-regulated work while getting feedback from the computer instead of the supervisor. However, if the child had great difficulties in some sub-skill, the supervisor actively helped him/her in improving that specific sub-skill, such as spelling. In other tasks, this child was encouraged to work independently.

*Assessment*

*Word recognition.* The word recognition test was a Finnish version of the Danish OS–400 (Lundberg, Frost, & Petersen, 1988). It includes 400 words written in a column and four pictorial alternatives for each word. The subject identifies as many correct word-picture pairs as possible during 15 min. The test was given as pre- and post-test to the experimental and control groups.

*Spelling.* The spelling test consisted of 10 sentences. These were 2 to 6 words long and were read aloud by the experimenter. The score was equal to the number of correctly written sentences. The test was given as pre- and post-test to the experimental and control groups.

*Comprehension.* Parallel versions of a reading comprehension task were prepared for the pre-, post- and delayed tests. The delayed test was given 3 months after the training had ended. On every testing occasion, one narrative and one expository text were given. They were 88–93 words long, depicting familiar animals. The linguistic properties and macrostructures were made comparable across the texts. The children were asked to read the text at their own pace, carefully enough to be able to answer questions about the message afterwards. Mutually comparable recall tasks were prepared for each text. The comprehension test for main ideas consisted of five questions. The experimenter asked one question at a time and the child gave his/her answer verbally. All answers were both written down and tape-recorded. Answers were scored on a 2 pt scale, from 0 to 2 (questions demanding one to two words to answer), or on a 3 pt scale, from 0 to 3 (questions demanding more complex answers). The score indicates the accuracy of understanding of the specific main idea. Answers were rated twice by two independent judges. Disputes were resolved by discussion. A composite score, that is, a sum of points for the story, was computed for each subject whose final score was expressed as a percentage of the maximum score.

One further reading comprehension task was presented three months after the intervention. In this task the child wrote down the answers to the questions instead of giving them orally.

Listening comprehension was measured in spring in grade 1 with texts and recall tasks parallel to those used to test reading comprehension. The texts were read aloud twice in a neutral tone by the experimenter. The children were instructed to listen carefully so that they would be able to answer questions about the contents afterwards.

*Text production.* Text production ability was assessed before the intervention by showing the children pictures of animal activities (e.g., "Two foxes fighting") and asking them to write a story on the basis of the picture. The score was the number of written propositions.

The first 8 sessions of the experimental group during the intervention were considered practice sessions during which the child learned to use the mouse, to request synthetic-speech feedback for difficult words etc. In the last 2 sessions, only those pupils were involved who had serious spelling and text production problems

The following data were gathered and scored from each of the 19 sessions. The computer recorded the reading time for a text. The clock was activated when the first word of the text appeared on the screen and stopped when the child targeted the "go to the next task" - area on the screen with the mouse. The score was the average time the child spent reading one word. The child was given 1-3 questions about the content of the text and s/he was asked to write down the answers with the computer. The misspelling scores were equal to the mean number of errors per word. The number of targeted words for sound feedback in reading the story was computed. The child was asked about his/her motivational and emotional tendencies toward the training program. At the beginning of each session, the child was asked: "How do you feel as you start to do the tasks today?" At the end of each session a similar question was asked. The child gave his/her answer by ticking the appropriate facial expression from a five point scale. Furthermore, the child was asked to choose the most pleasant task and the most unpleasant one from among the tasks. The possible tasks were: reading the story, rereading the individually presented words, answering the two-choice questions, writing down answers to the questions and producing a continuation to the story.

For data analyses, 19 sessions (i.e., sessions 9–27) were divided into 5 blocks with 3–4 sessions in each block. For each block (1–5), a composite score of the performance on each task was computed.

## RESULTS

To find out the effects of computer-based instruction compared with traditional special education instruction, the 12 control pupils who were given traditional special education instruction were identified. Their 12 matched counterparts in the experimental group formed a corresponding subgroup. Compared to the remaining 8 control children, the 12 control pupils who participated in the special education instruction had significantly lower scores in reading comprehension (m=18.5 vs m=35.4) and IQ (m=79.1 vs m=87.0), and symptomatically lower scores in word recognition (m=106.7 vs m=138.9).

The effects of computer-based instruction compared with traditional special education instruction on word recognition, and spelling were analysed with a MANCOVA (CSS: Statistica, 1991). The between-subject variable was computer-based instruction vs. traditional special education instruction. The word recognition and spelling skills in the pre-test and the listening comprehension skill in Grade 1 were used as covariates. The relevant group means of the computer-based instruction and traditional special education are given in Table 2.

The MANCOVA proved significant $F(2,18) = 4.21$, $p=.032$. Univariate analysis involving spelling revealed a significant main effect of training $F(1,19) = 5.27$, $p=.033$. A parallel result was obtained for word recognition $F(1,19) = 4.81$, $p=.041$.

The development of reading comprehension skills in the two groups was analysed with an ANCOVA. The reading comprehension skill in the pretest and the listening comprehension skill in Grade 1 were used as covariates. Separate ANCOVAs were performed for the post-test and delayed test. No significant differences in reading comprehension skill could be found between the experimental and the control groups in the post-test with oral answers, or in the delayed test with oral answers (F's<1), or with written answers F(1,20) = 1.14, ns.

TABLE 2
Mean performance scores (and SD in brackets) of the children receiving computer-based instruction vs traditional special education instruction before and after the intervention

| Task | Computer-based | | Traditional Special Ed | |
|---|---|---|---|---|
| *Word recognition (max 400)* | | | | |
| Pretest | 106.3 | (42.7) | 106.7 | (35.9) |
| Posttest | 181.8 | (26.7) | 157.8 | (42.3) |
| *Spelling (max 10)* | | | | |
| Pretest | 4.0 | (3.3) | 4.1 | (2.6) |
| Posttest | 7.0 | (2.4) | 5.3 | (3.1) |
| *Reading comprehension (% correct)* | | | | |
| Pretest (oral) | 25.4 | (12.1) | 18.8 | (12.9) |
| Posttest (oral) | 29.2 | (14.2) | 23.1 | (17.2) |
| 3 mths after (oral) | 42.7 | (14.1) | 31.6 | (13.9) |
| 3 mths after (written) | 30.3 | (16.2) | 20.5 | (16.1) |
| *Listening comprehension (% correct)* | | | | |
| 6 mths before | 54.5 | (21.3) | 37.8 | (20.8) |

The effect size measure was used to assess instruction effects in the computer-based training and the traditional special education instruction groups. The effect sizes for word recognition, spelling and reading comprehension were calculated separately for both groups in the following way: $ES_{Effect\ size} = (m_{Post-test} - m_{Pre-test}) / SD_{Pre-test}$ (Castro 1987). The effect sizes of the word recognition were 1.77 in the experimental group and 1.43 in the control group. For spelling, the effect sizes were 0.90 and 0.45, respectively. The results indicate a steady development of word recognition and spelling skills from pre- to post-test for both groups, although the improvement was more profound among the computed-based training group. The effect sizes of reading comprehension from pre- to post-test test were 0.31 in the experimental group and 0.33 in the control group. The two teaching methods seemed to be equally ineffective in promoting reading comprehension.

During the intervention, the development of the reading time of the texts and the misspellings of the written answers among the experimental group (n=12) were analysed using individual growth curves analysis (see Fletcher et al., 1991). The growth of decoding and spelling abilities from block 1 to block 5 was computed for each child using a linear regression analysis (CSS: Statistica 1991). The standardized regression weight (beta), that is, the slope of the straight line, was used as the score for the development of these skills. All children except one (beta = .11) showed a marked development in the speed of reading during the intervention. Their beta weights varied from .68 to .95. The development of spelling during the intervention did not look quite as clear. Three children produced almost no misspellings in the computer-assisted learning situation and five children showed a clear improvement from block 1 to 5. Their beta weights varied from .44 to .87. However, there were three children whose misspelling scores remained about the same (beta weights varied from .29 to .03) and one child whose misspellings even increased from block 1 to block 5 (beta = –.62). He had also the most serious problems in spelling before the intervention.

The number of words targeted for sound feedback in blocks 1–5 was analysed with ANOVA. There was a significant decrease in targeted words from block 1 to 5, $F(4,44) = 7.07$, p=.00). In block one the children targeted an average of 4.8 words per story. In blocks 2–5, the corresponding scores were 2.1, 1.8, 1.2 and 1.3. According to observations of the supervisor, the decrease in the amount of the targeted words did not happen at the expense of reading accuracy. There were clear differences in the amount of targeted words among the children. Half of the children hardly ever asked for sound feedback while the other half targeted an average of 4.3 words per story. The children were seemingly selective. The words they targeted for sound feedback were usually long words, words with uncommon case endings or low frequency words.

Rereading the five words from the stories that had resulted in the longest reading times did not work well. The reread words were not relatively the most difficult words in the stories. The children had no difficulties in rereading the words quickly and accurately. Probably they did not benefit much from this part of the training program.

The children's feelings toward the training at the beginning and at the end of each session were analysed with an ANOVA. One within-subject variable was the child's feeling at the beginning vs. at the end of the session, and the other within-subject variable was time of testing (blocks 1–5). There was a significant main effect associated with feelings at the beginning vs. at the end of the session $F(1,11) = 6.04$, p =.03, and a significant main effect of the time (blocks 1–5), $F(4,44) = 2.87$, p =.03, but no interaction between these two variables. The children seemed to have a better feeling at the end of the session (m = 4.03) after finishing the tasks than at the beginning of the session (m = 3.91). Furthermore, their positive attitude toward the training even increased from block 1 (m = 3.83) to block 5 (m = 4.21).

The children's preferences for the various tasks performed during the intervention are given in Table 3. The children had no difficulties in choosing the most pleasant task of each session, while they were able to pinpoint up the most unpleasant one in less than half the cases.

As much as 15% of the choices fell into the category "All tasks are equally pleasant" and no one found all tasks equally unpleasant. The children did not like the reading tasks but rather preferred the comprehension questions, writing down the answers and correcting their misspellings.

TABLE 3
The relative pleasantness of the various tasks during the intervention among the experimental group. Raw frequencies are given within brackets

| Task | most pleasant | most unpleasant |
|---|---|---|
| Comprehension (answering two-choice questions) | 34% (76) | 18% (16) |
| Reading (the story or rereading individually presented words) | 13% (30) | 58% (53) |
| Writing (an answer to questions / a continuation to the story) | 33% (86) | 22% (22) |
| All tasks (equally pleasant or equally unpleasant) | 15% (27) | – |
| Total | 100% (219) | 100% (91) |

## DISCUSSION

The present study showed that the computer-based training program with synthetic-speech feedback had beneficial effects on the word recognition and spelling skills of children whose performance lags behind their classmates in the beginning of grade 2. The superiority of the computer-based training program over traditional special education instruction was reasonably clear. The 12 children receiving computer-based training with synthetic-speech feedback outperformed their pair-wise matched controls who received traditional special education instruction. This happened both in word recognition and spelling. The results coincide with other longitudinal studies (Elbro, Rasmussen, & Spelling 1996; Lundberg & Olofsson 1993, Olofsson 1992; Olson & Wise 1992). The children working with synthetic-speech feedback improve more in reading and writing ability than children who are given about the same amount of traditional special education instruction. In the Olofsson (1992) study, the older disabled children with better metacognitive skills benefited more from the computer-aided reading than the younger ones. The results from this study showed that the program is also suitable for poorly achieving second graders. What was also worth noting was the marked development of word recognition skill during the four months of the intervention in both the experimental and control children. In this respect, our poorly reading second graders seem to have been a bit more advanced, after all, than the normally achieving Dutch first graders in Reitsma's (1988) study. In other words, there was a basic skill, albeit shaky, to build upon. Hence, our conclusion is that, in grade 2, the computer-aided instruction with synthetic speech-feedback is a suitable tool in preventing cumulative learning problems.

However, the two teaching methods were equally ineffective in promoting reading comprehension during the intervention in grade 2. Promoting reading comprehension appears to demand more than was included in the present program. Recent training studies on comprehension suggest that it takes a lot of time and particularly explicit instruction on how to use comprehension strategies efficiently and how to develop metacognitive reflection (e.g., Vauras, Lehtinen, Kinnunen, & Salonen, 1992).

The results concerning the decrease in targeted words for sound feedback without decrease in reading accuracy suggest that the pupils started to monitor their decoding more carefully and behave in a self-regulated way. The ability of 8-year-old Finnish subjects to monitor their decoding is probably an additional factor contributing to the finding that they benefited from the computer-aided program in contrast to the 7-year-old Dutch subjects of Reitsma (1988). The observations showed that, instead of asking for sound feedback, the children wanted to try to decode the words by themselves. The fact that the presentation mode permits them to proceed only word by word stresses the importance of accurate word recognition. All this happened in parallel with the development of reading speed.

The marked development of word recognition observed in the pre-post-test comparison in the experimental group occurred also in their performance during the training sessions. All the children except one showed a strong development in the speed of reading. The poor spellers of the experimental group improved their spelling skills with varying success during the training sessions. It seems that the training program was not suitable for children with the most severe spelling problems. For them, a computer-based training program in which the child writes individual words from dictation might have been a better solution. For instance, Wise & Olson (1992) have successfully used this type of computerized spelling program with children.

The children's mood ratings showed that they enjoyed the training sessions. Most children used only the upper part of the scale in their ratings. The positive attitude towards the training was also observed in the children's difficulty in choosing the most unpleasant task in the session compared with the ease of finding the most pleasant one. They preferred the comprehension and writing tasks to the reading tasks. The result suggests that it is worthwhile to link the training of decoding to something goal-directed and even pleasant like the comprehension of a text in order to get points or to be able to answer the questions. We are not reading the detective stories because we like decoding, but because we sometimes like to be in an exciting fantasy world.

## REFERENCES

Allington, R. L. (1977). If they don't read much, how they ever gonna get good? *Journal of Reading, 21,* 57–61.
Allington, R. L. (1980). Poor readers don't get to read much in reading groups. *Language Arts, 57,* 872–876.
Allington, R. L. (1984). Content coverage and contextual reading in reading groups. *Journal of Reading Behavior, 16,* 85–96.
Brown, A. L. (1987). Metacognition, executive control, self-regulation, and other more mysterious mechanisms. In F. Weinert & R. Kluwe (Eds.), *Metacognition, motivation and understanding.* Hillsdale, New York: Erlbaum.
Castro, G. (1987). Plasticity and the handicapped child. A review of efficacy research. In J. J. Gallagher & C. T. Ramey (Eds.) *The Malleability of Children.* Baltimore, Paul H. Brookes Publishing Co.
Ehri, L. C., & Roberts, K. (1979). Do beginners learn printed words better in context or in isolation? *Child Development, 50,* 675–685.
Ehri, L. C., & Wilce, L. S. (1980). Do beginners learn to read function words better in sentences or in lists? *Reading Research Quarterly, 15,* 451–476.
Elbro, C., Rasmussen, I., & Spelling, B. (1996). Teaching reading to disabled readers with language disorders: A controlled evaluation of synthetic speech feedback. *Scandinavian Journal of Psychology, 37,* 140–155.
Elley, W. (1992). *How in the world do students read? IEA study of reading literacy.* Hamburg: International Association for the Evaluation of Reading Achievement.
Fleisher, L. S., Jenkins, J. R., & Pany, D. (1979). Effects on poor readers' *comprehension* of training in rapid decoding. *Reading Research Quarterly, 15,* 30–48.
Fletcher, J. M., Francis, D. J., Pequegnat, W., Raudenbush, S. W., Bornstein, M. H., Schmitt, F., Brouwers, P, & Stover, E. (1992). Neurobehavioral outcomes in diseases of childhood. Individual change models for pediatric human immunodeficiency viruses. *American Psychologist, 46,* 1267–1277.
Gambrell, L. B., & Wilson, R. M., & Gant, W. N. (1981). Classroom observations of task-attending behaviors in good and poor readers. *Journal of Educational Research, 74,* 400–404.
Juel, C. (1988). Learning to read and write: A longitudinal study of 54 children from first through fourth grades. *Journal of Educational Psychology, 80,* 437–447.
Lundberg, I, Frost, J., & Petersen, O. P. (1988). Effects of extensive program for stimulating phonological awareness in preschool children. *Reading Research Quarterly, 23,* 263–283.
Lundberg, I., & Olofsson, Å. (1993). Can computer speech support comprehension? Special issue: Swedish research on learning and instruction with computers. *Computers in Human Behavior, 9,* 283–293.
Olofsson, Å. (1992). Synthetic speech and computer aided reading for reading disabled children. *Reading and Writing: An Interdisciplinary Journal, 4,* 165–178.
Olson, R. K., & Wise, B. (1992). Reading on the computer with orthographic and speech feedback. An overview of the Colorado remediation project. *Reading and Writing: An Interdisciplinary Journal, 4,* 107–144.
Reitsma, P. (1988). Reading practice for beginners: Effects of guided reading, reading-while-listening, and independent reading with computer-based speech feedback. *Reading Research Quarterly, 23,* 219–235.

Stanovich, K. E. (1992). Speculations on the causes and consequences of individual differences in early reading acquisition. In P. B. Gough & L. C. Ehri, & R. Treiman (Eds.), *Reading acquisition* (pp. 307–342). Hillsdale, NJ: Erlbaum.

Van Daal, V. H. P. & Van der Leij, A. (1992). Computer-based reading and spelling practice for children with learning disabilities. *Journal of Learning Disabilities, 25,* 186–195.

Vauras, M., Lehtinen, E., Kinnunen, R., & Salonen, P. (1992). Socioemotional coping and cognitive processes in training learning-disabled children. In B. Y. L. Wong (Ed.), *Contemporary intervention research in learning disabilities.* An international perspective. New York: Springer-Verlag .

Wise, B. W., & Olson, R. K. (1992). How poor readers and spellers use interactive speech in a computerized spelling program. *Reading and Writing. An Interdisciplinary Journal, 4,* 145–163.

PETER AFFLERBACH

# HELPING STUDENTS BECOME CONSTRUCTIVELY RESPONSIVE READERS

Literacy acquisition is a life long process. When literacy acquisition is viewed as a lifelong process, the 'basics' necessary for successful reading change. For example, young children listening to a story read by an adult need basic abilities that differ from the basics that are needed by children who are reading independently. These basics are different still than those needed by students who are reading text contained in books and on computer screens to create a multimedia report to present to a history class. A student developing the basic abilities to decode a printed word to sound and match it with a familiar word in listening vocabulary still requires basic abilities to comprehend and synthesize information from different texts.

In this chapter I propose that all acts of reading have situational variables that determine the basics needed for success at the reading tasks in which individuals find themselves, or place themselves. This distinction is a critical one, for accomplished readers often place themselves in reading situations that are meaningful, rewarding, and motivating. In contrast, readers lacking the basic abilities to succeed at particular reading tasks may also lack the sense of agency to use reading in a wide array of contexts, and for different purposes. These readers will have a restricted use for reading and may actively avoid reading. A goal of this chapter is to propose a reconsideration of what, exactly, are the basics of literacy, based on the model of constructively responsive reading (Pressley & Afflerbach, 1995). A related goal is to describe the curriculum and instruction that contribute to students' acquisition of a wide array of basics of literacy, leading them towards constructively responsive reading.

### USING VERBAL REPORT DATA TO DEVELOP THE MODEL OF CONSTRUCTIVELY RESPONSIVE READING

The model of constructively responsive reading provides a context for discussing the basics that are necessary for success with demanding reading (Pressley & Afflerbach, 1995). The model was developed through the analysis and synthesis of think-aloud protocol data of expert readers. Protocol analysis data reveal that accomplished readers use basics of constructively responsive reading, including strategies for identifying important text content, monitoring comprehension, and evaluating text and author. A hallmark of the accomplished reader, constructively responsive reading resides on one end of the continuum of reading development. At the other end are the 'traditional' aspects of reading acquisition, including the basic skills of decoding and literal comprehension. Readers' progression along this continuum from relatively simple to relatively sophisticated reading allows us to envision a series of literacy acquisitions through which people may progress across their careers as readers.

The model of constructively responsive reading was developed, in part, through the analysis of 38 primary studies which used think-aloud protocols to investigate reading processes and strategies. A synthesis of this data involved the conversion of each reported reading process in each study into a data point. In turn, these data points became the information which was used in a grounded analysis (Strauss & Corbin, 1990) to build a theory of the data. The intent was to identify meaningful dimensions in the data and how these dimensions related to one another.

A DESCRIPTION OF CONSTRUCTIVELY RESPONSIVE READING

Constructively responsive reading is overwhelmingly strategic and it requires specific, 'basic' reading abilities. There are three major categories of reader strategy within constructively responsive reading: Identifying and learning text content, monitoring, and evaluating. It is reductionist to portray constructively responsive reading as consisting of three general categories of strategy that are easily separated, for one of the truly grand accomplishments of constructively responsive readers is that they are able to orchestrate many types of strategies while processing text. The sheer quantity of reader strategies that comprise constructively responsive reading prohibits a full accounting of the strategies within the format of this chapter. Readers who are interested in exploring more fully the strategies are referred to Pressley and Afflerbach (1995). However, it is possible to provide a thumbnail sketch of constructively responsive reading which provides detail about the diversity of reader strategies.

Constructively responsive readers:
– Overview text before reading, determining what is there and deciding which parts to process. These readers establish clear goals and plans for reaching their goals.
– Look for important information in text and pay greater attention to it than other information, adjusting reading speed and concentration depending on the perceived importance of text to reading goals.
– Attempt to relate important points in text to one another in order to understand the text as a whole. Such readers constantly look for

connections between the parts of the text they read to build summaries, main ideas, and synopses of the text.
- Activate and use prior knowledge to interpret text, generate hypotheses about text, and predict text content. Constructively responsive readers understand the value of their prior knowledge, and they seek to use it when appropriate.
- Reconsider and/or revise hypotheses about the meaning of text based on text content. Although constructively responsive readers are markedly proactive, initial hypotheses about text may be refined and revised by information encountered in the ongoing reading of text.
- Reconsider and/or revise prior knowledge based on text content. Constructively responsive readers closely monitor their prior knowledge and ongoing knowledge construction. This provides them with the ability to modify their understanding when information in the text is deemed important to remember.
- Attempt to infer information not explicitly stated in text when the information is critical to comprehension of text. Expert readers make copious inferences that are central to the accurate and appropriate construction of meaning.
- Attempt to determine the meaning of words not understood or recognized, especially when a word seems critical to meaning construction. Once this distinction is made, constructively responsive readers employ an array of strategies to determine word meaning.
- Use strategies to remember text such as underlining, repeating words and phrases, making notes, visualizing, summarizing, paraphrasing, and self-questioning. As constructively responsive readers progress through the text, they are aware of the importance of holding onto the meaning they have constructed.
- Change reading strategies when comprehension is perceived not to be proceeding smoothly. The flexibility of constructively responsive reading allows readers to change the means to the end of understanding text.
- Evaluate the qualities of text, with these evaluations in part affecting whether text has impact on reader's knowledge, attitudes, and behavior. Expert readers may employ criteria of accuracy, truthfulness, relevance, and importance during reading to evaluate their understanding as it occurs, and to evaluate the text after meaning is constructed.
- Reflect on and process text additionally after a part of text has been read, or after reading alternative interpretations and possibly deciding between them. These readers consider how to process the text additionally if there is a feeling it has not been understood as

much as it needs to be understood.
- Carry on responsive conversation with the author. Constructively responsive readers know that texts are written by people, and they may converse with an hypothesized or imagined reader for a number of purposes.
- Anticipate or plan for the use of knowledge gained from the reading. Constructively responsive readers' strategic nature is demonstrated by their proactive planning for how knowledge gained from reading might be used in future situations, be it a discussion, a lecture, a work task, or recreation.

As demonstrated by the preceding sketch, constructively responsive readers have made exceptional progress along the continuum of reading basics. These readers require word identification skills, literal comprehension ability, and vocabulary knowledge. Yet these basics are not nearly sufficient to facilitate the complex strategy use and reading dispositions sketched above. Traditional basics are foundations for ensuing, more complex skills, strategies, and their orchestration.

In summary, constructively responsive reading is strategic, knowledgeable, motivated, and reflective. Constructively responsive readers are in control of the act of reading, aware of the possible benefits of reading, flexible and strategic in approaches to reading and understanding, and empowered through the act of reading. While it was not possible to study the evolution of the novice reader into the constructively responsive reader using existing think-aloud protocol data, it appears that such readers become so through frequent and varied reading experiences. We may infer from the verbal report data that constructively responsive reading builds on basic foundational abilities including decoding and word recognition.

## THE RELATIONSHIP OF CONSTRUCTIVELY RESPONSIVE READING WITH EXISTING THEORIES OF TEXT PROCESSING AND TEXT COMPREHENSION

Pressley & Afflerbach's (1995) analysis of think-aloud protocol data was informed not only by their prior experience with the methodology, but also by theories that have shaped much of the research related to understanding text. Research that uses the think-aloud methodology has also been informed by these theories. For example, the examination of readers' metacognitive strategies reported in verbal report data was informed by the work of Flavell (1977) and Markman (1979). Using such theories to guide think-aloud investigations, there has been a reciprocal influence in that the data from protocol studies then serve to modify or refine theory. The analysis of think-aloud protocols provides the opportunity to sample and draw from the influential text processing models, and to build connections between them. Theories of reader transaction with text (Rosenblatt, 1978), metacognition in reading (Baker & Brown, 1984), schema theory and prior knowledge (Anderson & Pearson, 1984), discourse comprehension (Van Dijk & Kintsch, 1983), and text inferencing (Graesser & Bower, 1990) are briefly considered in this section. Each contributed to the development of the model of constructively responsive reading, and each is a basic in the repertoire of constructively responsive readers.

Transactional theory and reader response (Rosenblatt, 1978) provide a broad framework for understanding interactions between readers and text, although the specifics of the model are vague. Central to reader response theory is the proposition that reading involves a transaction between the text and the individual reader, each of whom brings different knowledge, perspectives, and beliefs to the act of reading. Reader response theory proposes that the meaning of text will vary from reader to reader based on a unique transaction between the reader and text. The meaning of text is not entirely subjective, for there are better and worse interpretations made by different readers. Reports of this transaction between reader and text are quite common in expert readers' think-aloud protocols.

Successful readers use strategies that are basic to successful comprehension monitoring. These strategies allow readers to set goals and monitor progress towards those goals. Metacognition also allows readers to monitor their prior knowledge, their cognitive resources, availability of memory, and probability of completing the reading task. The role of metacognition in successful reading is well established in the reading research literature (Baker & Brown, 1984), and 'going meta' is essential for expert reading and for expert performance of all kinds. Knowing that we know or don't know is a critical skill. In protocol analysis studies, constructively responsive readers actively monitor and evaluate their comprehension of the text and initiate corrective actions (often called 'fix it' strategies) to remain on task and focused on the goals of reading. Schema theory (Anderson & Pearson, 1984) describes the basic role that readers' prior knowledge plays in constructing meaning from text. It permits the reader to make inferences, default assumptions, and hypotheses about text content and structure, and author purpose and intention (Afflerbach, 1990). Schemata inform the process of selective attention, and schemata also provide information that may affirm or refute information that is encountered in text.

Van Dijk and Kintsch's model of discourse comprehension (1983) describes the microprocesses and macroprocesses that help readers pay attention to words and propositions, determine the microstructure and build the macrostructure of text, and use knowledge of text structure and syntax to construct meaning. Verbal reports of expert readers contain the macroprocesses and microprocesses described by van Dijk and Kintsch. There are detailed accounts of building meaning at the word level and clause level, especially when constructively responsive readers read challenging text. Readers also give detailed descriptions of the macroprocess of assigning importance, generalization of redundant information, the deletion of unimportant information, and the synthesis and retention of information deemed important. The ability to make accurate inferences during reading is a basic skill for successful reading (Graesser & Bower, 1990; Van den Broek, Fletcher, & Risden, 1993). Inferential processes may help readers determine pronoun referents, superordinate goals, and causal antecedents that are absent in the printed text. The ability of readers to make accurate inferences makes the acts of reading and writing more efficient.

Each of the text processing models described above has provided much to guide our understanding of how people read. However, none of the single theories is sufficient to fully explain the strategies for identifying and remembering text information, monitoring the act of reading, and evaluation of aspects of reading that are reported in the aggregate of think-aloud protocols and that comprise constructively responsive reading. Thus, constructively responsive reading has roots in existing models of text processing and comprehension, each of which provides important information about the different basics that are necessary for expert reading. The sketch of constructively responsive reading and the comparison to popular models and conceptions of reading helps us anticipate the argument that we should help students develop into constructively responsive readers. Constructively responsive readers succeed at varied acts of reading. They use reading to pursue goals in their academic, social, and professional worlds. Becoming a constructively responsive reader is a critical aspect of literacy acquisition, for it helps individuals shape their world and their work. Constructively responsive reading provides individuals increased personal fulfillment, empowerment, and participation in school and society through critical literacy. Constructively responsive readers move beyond literal comprehension of text to more fully construct a situated understanding of text. These readers may challenge the authority of the text and author, detect propaganda, read for a subtext that is embedded in the literal text, and relish the author's ability to use language. Constructively responsive readers may be motivated to read by reading. Ultimately, this provides students with the means to use reading to achieve goals in varied reading situations, be they self-selected or imposed, in school or out.

## HOW DO STUDENTS MEASURE UP TO THE MODEL OF CONSTRUCTIVELY RESPONSIVE READING?

Are students around the world developing into constructively responsive readers? Do developing readers possess the foundations, or basics that will allow them to progress on a path to constructively responsive reading? Data from international studies such as the IEA Study of Reading Literacy (Elley, 1992) and national large-scale assessments of reading in the United States (National Assessment of Educational Progress, 1995) demonstrate that many students do not develop into constructively responsive readers. Nor do they develop early and consistent reading habits that would provide the considerable experience that is needed to become full-fledged constructively responsive readers. For example, the 1994 National Assessment of Educational Progress of reading ability of United States' students found that there is a distinct "plateau" effect for middle school and high school students (National Assessment of Educational Progress, 1995). Many students have skills and strategies for constructing meaning of fairly easy texts written at an elementary or middle school level of difficulty. These results also clearly demonstrate that students are lacking in the ability to be constructively responsive when they read, despite the fact that the majority of students develop the basic literacy skills of word decoding and literal comprehension. Thus, while students may face increasingly demanding texts and tasks, few will actually possess the basic abilities needed to succeed at these reading challenges. The assessment of students in countries participating in the IEA Reading Literacy Study (Elley, 1992), the most recent international assessment of students' reading ability, also provides relevant data. Particularly, students in 3rd and 4th grades read a variety of materials, and mean response levels indicated that students could read expository, narrative, and document texts and answer related questions which were rated as intermediate in difficulty. However, the majority of readers in each of the participating IEA countries was not able to respond to very difficult items. This indicated difficulty with reading strategies, including comprehending complex stories and complicated figures, and making inferences about major themes and the motives of story characters. Thus, current indices of reading ability demonstrate that large numbers of students are not capable of constructively responsive reading. Few students reaching levels of advanced reading, and many student readers never progress beyond the level of basic, literal comprehension. It appears that many readers develop one set of basics, but many more readers fail to move along the continuum of reading development towards constructively responsive reading.

## HOW MIGHT DEVELOPING READERS ACQUIRE THE BASICS OF CONSTRUCTIVELY RESPONSIVE READING?

Constructively responsive student readers require basic abilities to identify and learn information in text, monitor their progress, and evaluate various aspects of the act of reading. Readers must be able to do so with different types of texts and in different contexts and situations. What promotes students' development as constructively responsive readers? An obvious answer is ongoing opportunities for students to further develop their reading ability. This answer challenges us to examine the factors that impact students' development as readers. Students need to build mastery in the 'traditional' basics for success in early reading, including phonemic awareness, decoding ability, word recognition, and the ability to construct understanding from relatively simple text. As important are the literacy experiences, competencies, and prior knowledge that students bring to reading instruction, and the influences of home and community on literacy practices. Further, the reading strategies and skills instruction that students receive in school, and the reading materials, contexts, and tasks that comprise the reading curriculum will influence student movement from basic to constructively responsive reading. It is noted that each of these broad categories discussed in this section may be influenced by another. For example, particular types of literacy learning in different households may familiarize students with the content and strategies needed for success at particular school reading tasks, but not prepare others.

Helping students develop as constructively responsive readers should be a primary goal of schooling. Full-blown, constructively responsive reading is not possible for readers lacking numerous and diverse reading experiences. Students lacking the basic ability to process and comprehend simple text will also encounter difficulties. In contrast, students who bring practiced and polished skills of decoding and cognitive strategies, and students who bring habits of mind of questioning, clarifying, challenging, monitoring, and evaluating may be best prepared to develop as constructively responsive readers. Thus, a challenge is developing curriculum that anticipates all students' needs and paths towards constructively responsive reading. Students who are encouraged to be persistent in attempting to read, to be mindful while reading, and to be knowledgeable of the social uses of reading may have a path to constructively responsive reading that is considerably shorter than for students who lack these opportunities.

A key to establishing successful reading curricula that will encourage student progress towards constructively responsive reading is to understand and use the knowledge and experiences that students bring to reading instruction. Students may have considerable knowledge related to content areas and the content of texts (Chi, Glazer, & Farr, 1988). In such cases, the student's developing reading ability may be positively influenced by well-developed vocabulary and conceptual knowledge in particular content domains (e.g., ballet, dinosaurs, football). Rich prior knowledge may support the acquisition of traditional basics, as when vocabulary knowledge of familiar content domain words helps students understand general sound/-symbol correspondences. In addition, the "expert" status of a student who knows much about a particular content area can fuel student motivation for speaking and listening in academic and social situations within and outside the classroom. These experiences emanate from curricula and instruction that situate student reading and related work in areas of deep and broad prior knowledge. However, instruction may have a developmental bias which postpones learning that could contribute to constructively responsive reading until "basics" such as phonics are learned and mastered. Schooling which ignores student prior experience and knowledge and which makes no attempt to build connections between a student's life in the home and community life and school life further misses an opportunity to help children develop critical literacy (Moll, 1992). This effectively cuts developing readers off from the sources that can help fuel constructively responsive reading.

Listening and speaking skills may develop in advance (and in anticipation) of reading and writing. The strengths of students' speaking and listening should be determined and used in relation to developing expertise, such as discussions and detailed knowledge of types of ballet positions, dinosaur diets, and attributes of particular football stars. Precursors to constructively responsive reading may exist in children's related language abilities of speaking, listening, and writing (Gambrell & Almasi, 1996). These can serve as foundations for meaningful learning with instruction that scaffolds from a present competency to an anticipated ability.

Life in the home and life in the community may have a strong and lasting influence on students' language development and reading acquisition. Students within the same school and classroom may operate with different experiences, abilities, and assumptions related to literacy and reading that are formed in diverse cultural settings. These will influence how and how easily a child moves from the world outside the classroom to the world of the classroom (Heath, 1983). They will also influence school learning and achievement. An understanding of different students' literacy experiences in the home, in the community, and outside of school can help teachers anticipate and accommodate differences, and refine curriculum accordingly (Wells, 1990). There is a clear need to work to better understand and engage families and communities in a collaborative effort to educate children (Hannon, 1995). These home and school collaborations should occur on a two-way street. That is, home should not be viewed solely as a place for extending students' skills and strategies learned in school. Rather, schools may also extend, enrich, and make positive use of the knowledge that children construct in their homes and communities. This knowledge can contribute to a curriculum that best fosters constructively responsive reading.

Students need instruction that provides them with increasingly diverse and sophisticated skills and strategies. Reading instruction that targets literal comprehension of text as the goal of successful student learning may be well-intentioned, but short-sighted in outcome. Curriculum and instruction that is comprised only of decontextualized skills and strategies with few (or no) opportunities to learn and practice the sophisticated orchestration of skills and strategies that comprise constructively responsive reading will limit students' development as constructively responsive readers. Given the comprehensive list of strategies and knowledge that constructively responsive readers bring to the reading task, word recognition and literal comprehension are important but not sufficient to move readers to constructively responsive reading. Students will lack the tool kit to understand, interpret, and critically evaluate the texts they read. Successful programs for helping student learn complex reading strategy use are reciprocal teaching (Palincsar & Brown, 1984) and transactional strategies instruction (Pressley, Brown, El-Dinary, & Afflerbach, 1995). Both approaches include detailed modeling and explanation of reading strategies and situating of instruction in students' zones of proximal development.

Palincsar and Brown (1984) taught reading strategies, including summarization, question asking, and comprehension monitoring to learning disabled middle school students. Initially, teachers were responsible for describing and modeling the comprehension strategies, and explaining the "nuts and bolts" of the strategic procedures to students. Teachers provided support, or scaffolding, as students moved from novice status to informed strategy user to increasingly complex and effective strategy user. In this scaffolding routine, the teacher presents valuable comprehension strategies that have direct connection to the model of constructively responsive reading and the macroprocesses described in Van Dijk and Kintsch's (1983) model of discourse comprehension. Applying reciprocal teaching to a constructively responsive reading curriculum, we might imagine teachers modeling the numerous strategies that comprise expert reading. Comprehension strategies related to generating prediction, synthesizing text information, and determining importance could be part of this curriculum. In addition, students could learn how to monitor their comprehension, their progress towards reading goals, and their understanding of author intention.

Transactional strategies instruction is a second program that can help students become constructively responsive readers (Pressley, El-Dinary, Wharton-McDonald, & Brown, 1998). Transactional strategies instruction has similarities with reciprocal teaching in that it requires explicit modeling and explanation of reading strategies and expects that students will take increasing responsibility for modeling, explaining, and using the strategies. However, transactional strategies instruction also provides daily experiences with integrated reading, writing, speaking, and listening strategies. Transactional strategy instruction seeks always to address students' individual needs and interests. Finally, transactional strategies instruction helps students respond cognitively, affectively, and aesthetically to text in different social situations. Students learn to comprehend a short story, as they learn that such interactions with text may have emotional consequences and social opportunities to share their reading experience. Each of these features of transactional strategies instruction aligns well with the reading tasks and contexts that can help students move towards constructively responsive reading.

To be participating members of society, students must control the act of reading, value the act of reading, and know how to use what is learned through reading in many different social, academic, economic, and personal contexts or situations. Students working to solve demanding reading problems can move along the novice-expert continuum towards constructively responsive reading (Bereiter & Scardamalia, 1993). The censorship of texts, subjects, issues, and curricular practices may inhibit students' development as constructively responsive readers. This censorship may be fully intended, as when particular books or curriculum topics are targeted by special interest groups for removal from the school curriculum and libraries. Censorship of ideas and books containing ideas denies access to information that may be puzzling, troubling, demanding, contradictory, and empowering. Yet, these are the very words students and avid readers may use to describe the literacy events that are most crucial to their lives. The path to constructively responsive reading may be blocked by censorship. Avoidance of contentious issues because it denies developing readers access to and familiarity with demanding reading situations, and to the strategy and resource demands needed for them. The absence of controversial issues in curriculum materials denies students experiences with situations in which they must adopt a critical stance towards texts, authors, and critically evaluate their own knowledge and beliefs. Less visible but perhaps more pervasive is the censorship that occurs through curriculum choices. A traditional "basics-first" curriculum may require that students first master phonemic awareness, sound/symbol correspondences and then literal comprehension of text. This traditional approach may prevent children from encountering texts that may well motivate those who have deep and broad prior knowledge which they are quite capable of discussing while unable to read. In either case a result is missed opportunity for students to increase their reading ability by building on existing, related language skills, to use their prior knowledge, to provide materials require and foster constructively responsive reading.

We cannot define basic reading skills as those that allow comprehension of simple text and the answering of predictable comprehension questions. Other basics must help students learn to monitor their construction of meaning, to challenge the primacy of text, and to read for underlying subtexts, such as the author's intention in a dazzling advertisement. A curriculum that neglects any or some of the above concerns may influence students so that they lack engagement with reading and the motivation to read further. Without the incentive to read widely and frequently, students cannot develop into constructively responsive readers. Ultimately, they will be limited in their ability to identify and remember text information, to monitor their progress as readers both within the act of reading and when reflecting on their growth as reader, and to evaluate the accuracy and appropriateness of the texts that they read.

In summary, student reading ability may evolve along the path to constructively responsive reading when conditions support it. Students bring to school considerable knowledge of the world and they often have islands of deep and broad knowledge in particular content areas. Determining these areas and working to make them a part of the school experience will be beneficial. It will provide students with a base of competence to assimilate the basic skills and strategies needed for constructively responsive reading. Teacher and school knowledge of students' home and community life can provide rich opportunities for combining in-school and out-of-school knowledge in classroom activities. When teachers understand the different backgrounds and experiences that students bring to the classroom, accommodation of these differences and taking advantage of them can occur. Students need instruction that clearly demonstrates the nature and value of the skills and strategies that comprise increasingly complex reading. Teacher modeling and explanation can provide this. A curriculum that includes diverse texts and diverse tasks related to the texts will help students gain further reading experience and move towards constructively responsive reading. Censorship of student opportunity to progress as readers can occur intentionally or accidentally, and it is important to closely monitor the types of reading students do to meet the goals of curriculum, and to develop as constructively responsive readers.

## CONCLUSION

In this chapter I propose that becoming a constructively responsive reader is a lifelong task. The skills and strategies needed for constructively responsive reading represent a new conceptualization of what is "basic" for reading success. As readers evolve, they move through stages of reading competency that demand increasingly complex "basics." The situation in which reading takes place is the determinant of the basics necessary for success. The model of constructively responsive reading was developed through the analysis of think-aloud protocol data from talented readers. This data provides considerable detail about what exactly talented readers do when reading a variety of texts, for a variety of purposes, in different contexts. When the model of constructively responsive reader is viewed as a goal for developing readers, the seriousness of the task of teaching and encouraging students' complex and successful reading is evident.

Fortunately, the theory and the means for accomplishing increased student reading ability are available. Careful and detailed modeling and teaching of reading skills and strategies helps students learn. The development of curriculum that honors the knowledge and experiences that students may bring to school from home and community should also help student build on strengths to increase their reading prowess. A curriculum that includes diverse texts, challenging tasks, and varied contexts will provide the real-time reading experiences that all readers need to further develop their abilities. Such curriculum development should be regularly guided by the question, "What is basic for success in this particular reading situation?" Human beings are asked to function and participate in increasingly complex situations, and we need to regularly examine the terms 'basic' and 'functional' to inform our instruction (Verhoeven, 1994). Functional literacy may include the ability to read a tram schedule, dissect an argumentative editorial, understand the subtext of a persuasive advertisement, reconcile conflicting accounts of history, or challenge an account of a science text. Constructively responsive readers will be able to meet the challenge of functioning at any and all of these levels of reading.

## REFERENCES

Afflerbach, P. (1990). The influence of prior knowledge on expert readers' main idea construction strategies. *Reading Research Quarterly, 25,* 31–46.

Anderson, R. C., & Pearson, P. D. (1984). A schema-theoretic view of reading. In P. D. Pearson, M. Kamil, R. Barr, & P. Mosenthal (Eds.) *Handbook of reading research* (Vol. 1, pp. 255–291). White Plains, NY: Longman.

Baker, L., & Brown, A. L. (1984). Metacognitive skills and reading. In P. D. Pearson, M. Kamil, R. Barr, & P. Mosenthal (Eds.) *Handbook of reading research* (Vol. 1, pp. 353–394). White Plains, NY: Longman.

Bereiter, C., & Scardamalia, M. (1993). *Surpassing ourselves: An inquiry into the nature and implications of expertise.* Chicago: Open Court.

Chi, M., Glazer, R., & Farr, M. (1988). *The nature of expertise.* Hillsdale: Erlbaum.

Elley, W. (1992). *How in the world do students read? The IEA study of reading literacy.* Hamburg: Grindeldruck.

Flavell, J. (1977). *Cognitive development.* Englewood Cliffs, NJ: Prentice Hall.

Gambrell, L., & Almasi, J. (1996). *Lively discussions!* Newark, DE: International Reading Association.

Graesser, A., & Bower, G. (1990). *Inferences and text comprehension.* San Diego, CA: Academic Press.

Hannon, P. (1995). *Literacy, home and school.* London: The Falmer Press.

Heath, S. (1983). *Ways with words: Language, life and work in communities and classrooms.* Cambridge, MA: Harvard University Press.

Markman, E. (1979). Realizing that you don't understand: Elementary school children's awareness of inconsistencies. *Child Development, 50,* 643–655.

Moll, L. (1992). Literacy research in community and classrooms: A sociocultural approach. In R. Beach et al. (Eds.), *Multidisciplinary perspectives on literacy research* (pp. 211-244). Urbana, IL: National Conference on Research in English.

Palincsar, A., & Brown, A. L. (1984). Reciprocal teaching of comprehension-fostering and monitoring activities. *Cognition and Instruction, 1,* 117–175.

Pressley, M., & Afflerbach, P. (1995). *Verbal protocols of reading: The nature of constructively responsive reading.* Hillsdale, NJ: Erlbaum Associates.

Pressley, M., Brown, R., El-Dinary, P. B., & Afflerbach, P. (1995). The comprehension instruction that students need: Instruction fostering constructively responsive reading. *Learning Disabilities Research & Practice, 10,* 215–224.

Pressley, M., El-Dinary, P. B., Wharton-McDonald, R., & Brown, R. (1998). Transactional instruction of comprehension strategies in the elementary grades. In D. Schunk & B. Zimmerman (Eds.), *Self-regulated learning: From teaching to self-reflective practice* (pp.42–56). New York, NY: Guilford.

Rosenblatt, L. M. (1978). *The reader, the text, the poem: The transactional theory of the literary work.* Carbondale, IL: Southern Illinois Press.

Strauss, A., & Corbin, J. (1990). *Basics of qualitative research: Grounded theory procedures and techniques.* Newbury Park, CA: Sage.

Van den Broek, P., Fletcher, C., & Risden, K. (1993). Investigations of inferential processes in reading: A theoretical and methodological integration. *Discourse Processes, 16,* 169–180.

Van Dijk, T., & Kintsch, W. (1983). *Strategies of discourse comprehension.* New York: Academic Press.

Verhoeven, L. (1994). Modeling and promoting functional literacy. In L. Verhoeven (Ed.), *Functional literacy: Theoretical issues and educational implications* (pp. 3–34). Amsterdam: Benjamins.

Wells, G. (1990). Talk about text: Where literacy is learned and taught. *Curriculum Inquiry, 20,* 369–405.

# AUTHOR INDEX

Aarnoutse, C.A.J., 99, 100
Aaron, P.G., 132, 133, 135, 136, 293
Aarts, R., 207
Abbott, R.D., 142
Ackerman, P.L., 61
Adams, C., 64
Adams, M.J., 6, 35, 81, 257, 273
Afflerbach, P., 349–362
Ahonen, T., 4
Alegria, J., 29, 113, 163–176
Allington, R.L., 335
Allred, R.A., 308
Almasi, J., 357
Anderson, J.C., 49
Anderson, M., 81, 83
Anderson, R.C., 278, 353
Applebee, A.N., 184
Arnbak, E., 277–290
Atkins, P., 15, 114, 321
Awaida, M., 257, 274

Baddeley, A.D., 49, 53, 148
Badian, N.A., 257
Baker, L., 353
Balke, G., 56
Ball, E.W., 34, 63, 225, 231, 238, 241
Balota, D.A., 3
Baluch, B., 16
Barnes, M., 180
Barnes, M.A., 180, 181, 183
Barnes, W., 5
Baron, J., 34
Bar-Shalom, E.G., 133
Bast, J.W., 49, 51, 95–109
Beck, I., 34, 49, 82
Bedford-Feuell, C., 130, 133
Beech, J.R., 257, 274
Bell, L., 25, 34, 49, 82
Benson, N.J., 6, 300
Bentin, S., 16, 82, 84, 113
Bentler, P.M., 54, 101
Benzing, L., 316
Berch, D., 258
Bereiter, C., 359
Berent, I., 15, 16, 24, 318
Berko, J., 283
Berninger, V.W., 142

Berstein, D., 63
Bertelson, P., 29, 81, 113
Besner, D., 15, 16, 18
Bishop, D.V.M., 64, 76
Blachman, B.A., 4, 34, 63, 225, 226, 231, 238, 241
Blaesser, B., 225, 230, 242
Bleichrodt, N.D., 52
Boder, E., 163
Bonett, D.G., 101
Borden, S.L., 6, 300
Boren, R., 309
Borstrøm, I., 4, 130, 140
Bosman, A.M.T., 307–320, 332
Boudberg, P.A., 30
Bower, G., 353, 354
Bowers, P.G., 148
Bowey, J.A., 76
Bowlby, M., 148
Brackstone, D., 6, 300
Bradley, L.L., 29, 34, 63–65, 81, 92, 147, 157, 225, 229, 238, 241, 243, 309
Brady, S.A., 148
Brame, T., 309
Brittain, M.M., 279
Brooks, L., 35
Brown, A.L., 336, 353, 358
Brown, G.D.A., 316
Brown, R., 358, 359
Browne, M.W., 101
Bruck, M., 130, 137, 321
Bruner, J., 212
Brus, B.T., 54, 99, 100, 295, 298
Bryan, J.H., 75
Bryan, T., 75
Bryant, P.E., 3, 29, 34, 63–65, 81, 92, 147, 157, 174, 225, 229, 238, 241, 243
Butler, B.E., 260
Butler, S.R., 63, 76
Byrne, B., 32, 34, 225, 253

Caesar, F.B., 310
Cahan, S., 82, 113
Cain, K., 134, 177–192
Caramazza, A., 316

Carlisle, J.F., 277, 278, 279
Carroll, J.B., 49
Carter, B., 33, 82, 113
Carver, R.P., 95, 96, 107
Cary, L., 29, 81, 113
Castles, A., 163, 164, 167, 170, 173, 174
Castro, G., 343
Castro, S.L., 113–127
Castro-Caldas, A., 114
Cataldo, S., 3
Catts, H.W., 64, 148
Chall, J.S., 32
Chandler, J., 5
Charniak, E., 178
Chen, M.J., 16, 38
Chi, M., 357
Cipielewski, J., 142
Clark, E.V., 65
Clay, M.M., 5, 211
Cohen Levine, S., 152
Coltheart, M., 15, 34, 114, 163, 164, 167, 170, 173, 258, 316, 321, 322
Conners, F., 36
Content, A., 113, 163–176
Corbin, J., 350
Crain, S., 63, 133
Critchley, M., 129, 131, 132, 141
Crossland, J., 3, 63
Cudeck, R., 101
Cunningham, A.E., 34, 142, 225, 308, 309
Curtis, B., 15, 114, 321
Curtis, S., 76

Dalby, M.A., 135
Damásio, A.R., 114
Damásio, H., 114
Damhuis, R., 52
Daneman, M., 95, 189
Das, J.P., 148, 260
Davidson, M., 322
Davis, C., 34, 322
De Geus, K., 53, 324
De Groot, A.M.B., 307–309, 315, 332
De Jong, P.F., 49–62
DeFrancis, J., 16, 27, 31
DeFries, J.C., 131
Delaney, S., 25
Deltour, J.J., 165
DeLuca, T., 6, 300
Denckla, M.B., 151

Dennis, M., 180
Ding, B., 33
Ditunno, P., 49
Dobrich, W., 211
Doi, L.S., 163
Downey, D.M., 133
Drabman, R.S., 309
Drent, I., 257–276
Drenth, P.J.D., 52
Dreyer, L., 95, 107
Droop, M., 193–208
Dugstad, B.S., 66, 67
Dunn, D., 283, 298
Dunn, L.M., 283
Durrell, D.D., 132

Edwards, P.A., 222
Ehri, L.C., 17, 32, 33, 35, 81, 221, 259, 273, 308, 322, 335
Elbro, C., 3, 4, 6, 64, 129–146, 277–290, 335, 345
El-Dinary, P.B., 358, 359
Elley, W., 337, 355
Ellis, A.W., 6, 34, 82, 163, 165, 226, 253
Ellis, N.C., 3, 316
Emslie, H., 53
Extra, G., 195

Fang, S.P., 24
Farnham-Diggory, S., 309
Farr, M., 357
Farrar, W.T.IV., 316
Fawcett, A.J., 6
Feagans, L., 63, 65
Feldman, L.B., 259
Feng, L., 16
Fielding-Barnsley, R., 34, 225, 253
Fischer, F.W., 33, 113, 278
Flavell, J., 352
Fleisher, L.S., 335
Fletcher, C., 354
Fletcher, J.M., 130, 131, 303, 343
Flores D'Arcais, G.B., 3, 16, 37
Fowler, A.E., 148, 279, 280, 287
Fowler, A.F., 131
Fowler, C.A., 258
Fox, B., 65
Francis, D.J., 131, 303
Freebody, P., 49
French, L., 130, 135
Friedman, R.B., 322

# AUTHOR INDEX

Frith, U., 32, 34, 64, 159, 165, 307, 322
Frost, J., 6, 34, 63, 225, 241, 340
Frost, R., 16, 32, 318
Funnell, E., 322

Galda, L., 212
Gallagher, A.M., 64, 76
Gallimore, R., 212
Gambrell, L.B., 335, 357
Gant, W.N., 335
Garcia, G.E., 222
Garnham, A., 6
Gathercole, S.E., 49, 53, 148
Geiger, S., 130
Gelb, I.J., 29
Gerber, M.M., 309
Gettinger, M., 308
Geva, E., 63, 65
Gilger, J., 4
Gilger, J.W., 131
Gjessing, H., 4
Glazer, R., 357
Gleitman, L.R., 29
Glenn, C.G., 184
Goldenberg, C., 212
Goldinger, S.D., 25, 316, 317
Goodman, I., 5
Goswami, U., 147, 225, 241
Gough, P.B., 32–34, 63, 95–97, 100, 107, 132, 321
Goulandris, N., 148
Graesser, A., 353, 354
Greelman, C.D., 118
Green, P.A., 137
Grønborg, A., 138
Gross, J., 258
Gustafsson, J.E., 49, 56

Haas, K., 309
Hadley, J.A., 322
Haefele-Kalvaitis, J., 180
Hager, M., 211
Hagtvet, B.E., 63–79
Hains, S., 260
Haith, M.M., 137
Hallahan, D.P., 309
Haller, M., 15, 114, 321
Hammer, R., 82, 113
Hamsher, K., 114
Hanley, J.R., 316
Hannon, P., 5, 358

Harris, A.J., 129
Harris, R.J., 193
Harris, T.L., 129
Harward, S.V., 308
Hatcher, P.J., 6, 34, 82, 226, 227, 238, 253
He, H.D., 16
Heath, S., 357
Hemphill, L., 5
Herriman, M.L., 29, 65
Hillinger, M.L., 32, 33, 34
Hodges, R.E., 129
Hoeksma, J.B., 297, 299
Hogaboam, T.W., 35
Høien, T., 63, 131
Holahan, J.M., 130
Holligan, C., 3, 81, 83, 257
Hong, R.Y., 24
Hoosain, R., 22
Hoover, W.A., 63, 95–97, 100, 107
Howell, P., 148
Huey, E.B., 307
Hughes, C., 34, 49, 82
Hulme, C., 6, 34, 82, 174, 226, 253
Hummer, P., 147, 241, 244
Hurley, F.K., 222
Huttenlocher, J., 152

Impey, L., 174
Inhoff, A., 258
Iversen, S., 5

James, J.H., 132, 133
Jansen, H., 159, 227, 228, 238, 241
Jared, D., 260
Jenkins, J.R., 321, 335
Joanette, Y., 113
Johnson, D.M., 308
Johnston, R.S., 3, 81, 83, 84, 90, 91, 93, 257
Jöreskog, K.G., 101
Jorm, A.F., 63
Juel, C., 33, 81, 95, 97, 130, 134, 136, 335

Kang, H., 16
Kaplan, R., 76
Karlsen, B., 4
Karmiloff-Smith, A., 65
Katz, L., 16, 95, 107, 131, 259
Kauffman, J.M., 309
Kawakami, M., 16, 37

Kay, J., 114, 124
Kearney, C.A., 309
Kinnunen, R., 346
Kintsch, W., 353, 358
Kirk, S.J., 67
Klapwijk, M.J.G., 51
Klauer, K.J., 245
Klicpera, Ch., 160
Koda, K., 193
Kolinsky, R., 113
Kreiner, D.S., 321
Kreiner, S., 135, 283
Krom, R.S.H., 53, 311, 324
Kuespert, P., 230, 241–255

Lacerenza, L., 6, 300
Laghi, L., 16
Lamoureux, M., 113
Landerl, K., 147–161, 241
Larsen, J.P., 131
Lau, L.L., 38
Laughon, P., 51
Laurinen, L.I., 211–224
Leck, K.J., 16
Lecours, A.R., 113
Lee, S.Y., 38
Lehtinen, E., 346
Leiwo, M., 4
Leong, C.K., 16, 37, 278
Lepage, Y., 113
Leseman, P., 51
Lesser, R., 114
Levelt, W.J.M., 260
Leybaert, J., 163–176
Liberman, I.Y., 33, 81–84, 113, 131, 148, 278–280, 287
Lie, A., 34
Lillestølen, R., 67
Linortner, R., 147, 241, 244
Lloyd, M., 298
Lobrot, M., 165–167, 169
Lovett, M.W., 6, 300
Lukatela, G., 25
Lundberg, I., 6, 34, 63–67, 131, 225, 229, 230, 241–245, 249, 250, 253, 335, 340, 345
Lyon, G.R., 63, 131, 132, 137, 143
Lyster, S.A., 64
Lyytinen, H., 4

MacLean, M., 3, 63
MacLean, R., 63

MacMillan, N.A., 118
Magnusson, E., 64
Manis, F.R., 35, 163–165, 167, 170, 171, 173, 174, 274
Mann, V., 148
Mann, V.A., 29, 49, 63, 133
Mannhaupt, G., 159, 227, 238, 241
Markman, E., 187, 352
Marmurek, H.H.C., 259, 274
Marsh, G., 32
Marsh, H.W., 32, 63
Marx, H., 129, 130, 159, 227, 228, 238, 241, 243
Mason, J., 5
Massaro, D.W., 35
Mattingly, I.G., 16, 65
May, P., 244
McBride-Chang, C., 163
McCabe, A., 184
McCarthy, J., 67
McClelland, J.L., 15, 32, 316
McCormick, C., 5
McCutchen, D., 21
McDonnell, V., 316
McDougall, S.J.P., 165
McGuinness, D., 6
McNaughton, S., 214, 221
Mishra, R.K., 148
Mitterer, J.O., 163
Moll, L., 357
Møller, O.S., 131
Møller, S., 131
Mommers, M.J.C., 307
Monk, A.F., 165
Morais, J., 29, 33, 81, 93, 113, 114, 163–176, 241
Morgan, S.T., 34, 322
Morrison, F.J., 82
Morrow, L.M., 207, 211, 213
Mousty, P., 163–176
Moyse, S., 130
Murphy, L., 163, 165, 167
Mushinski Fulk, B., 307
Muthén, B.O., 54

Nagy, W., 277, 278
Näslund, J.C., 49, 148, 157, 241, 244
Nauclér, K., 64
Nesdale, A.R., 29, 65, 81
Neuman, S.B., 222
Nicholson, R.I., 6
Nie, H., 33

Nielsen, E.M., 131
Nielsen, I., 130, 134, 283
Nielsen, J.C., 135, 283
Niemi, P., 335–348
Ninio, A., 212
Noel, R.W., 15
Nurss, J., 66
Nutbrown, C., 5

Oakhill, J.V., 6, 133, 143, 177–192
Olofsson, Å., 63–67, 241, 335, 345
Olson, D.R., 63, 65
Olson, R.K., 6, 36, 137, 257, 258, 260, 293, 300, 335, 336, 345, 346
Ormrod, J.E., 308

Paap, K.R., 15
Palincsar, A., 358
Pany, D., 335
Parkin, A.J., 188
Patel, R.K., 76
Patterson, K.E., 15
Pearson, D.P., 353
Pellegrini, A.D., 212
Peng, D.-L., 16, 22
Pennington, B.F., 131, 137, 317
Perfetti, C.A., 15–47, 49, 82, 221, 257, 293, 303, 318
Petersen, C., 163
Petersen, D.K., 4, 130, 134, 140, 283
Petersen, O.P., 34, 63, 225, 241, 340
Peterson, C., 6, 184
Phillips, G., 214, 221
Pignot, E., 113
Pinker, S., 27
Plaut, D.C., 15
Pollatsek, A., 6, 163, 165, 167
Poulsen, A., 135, 283
Power, M.A., 278
Pressley, M., 349, 350, 352, 358, 359

Rack, J.P., 36, 137, 257, 259, 273, 293, 300
Rapp, B., 316
Rashotte, C.A., 49, 51
Rasmussen, I., 6, 335, 345
Raven, J.C., 281, 283
Rayner, K., 3, 6
Read, C., 33, 211, 307
Reimers, P., 241–255
Reitsma, P., 3–12, 35, 81–94, 95–109, 258, 335–337, 345, 346

Resing, W.C.M., 52
Reynell, J., 67
Rinaldo, R., 259, 274
Risden, K., 354
Robbins, C., 221
Roberts, K.T., 308, 335
Rommetveit, R., 67, 68
Rommetveit, S., 67, 68
Rosenblatt, L.M., 353
Roth, E., 225–239
Rourke, B.P., 303
Routh, D.K., 65
Royer, J.M., 133, 134
Rozin, P., 29
Rubert, H., 5
Rubin, H., 278, 279
Rudel, R.G., 151
Rumelhart, D.E., 32, 316
Rutter, M., 131, 293, 298

Saito, H., 16, 37
Salonen, P., 346
Sandven, J., 67
Scanlon, D.M., 29, 49, 257
Scarborough, H.S., 64, 76, 130, 131, 138, 211
Scardamalia, M., 359
Schabmann, A., 160
Scheerer-Neumann, G., 258
Schmidt, R., 148
Schneider, W., 49, 147, 148, 157, 225–239, 241–255
Schneider, W., 36
Schoonen, R., 52
Schreuder, R., 257–276, 321–334
Schroots, J.J.F., 52, 99
Schumer, H., 133
Sears, N.C., 308
Sebastian-Galles, N., 16
Seidenberg, M.S., 15, 321
Seidenberg, P., 63
Seymour, P.H.K., 163
Shankweiler, D.P., 33, 63, 82, 113, 131, 133, 148, 278
Share, D.L., 32, 35, 63, 76
Shaywitz, B.A., 130, 131, 303
Shaywitz, S.E., 130, 131, 303
Shepherd, M.J., 321
Sheppard, J.L., 63
Sheppard, M.J., 63
Shiffrin, R.M., 36
Shimron, J., 16

Short, E.J., 63, 65
Siddiqui, S., 142
Siegel, L.S., 63, 131, 137, 294, 303
Simmons, K., 51
Simon, H.A., 309
Simpson, G.B., 16, 21
Sinatra, G.M., 107, 133, 134
Sinclair, J., 215
Sipay, E.R., 129
Siu, I., 260
Skinkel, R., 165
Skowronek, H., 129, 159, 227, 238, 241
Smeets, H., 297, 300
Smith, J.K., 213
Smith, L., 82
Smith, L.B., 316
Smith, M.C., 18
Smith, S.D., 137
Smith, S.T., 63, 133
Snow, C.E., 5, 51, 65
Snowling, M.J., 6, 64, 137, 148, 174, 257, 300
Snyder, L.S., 133
Søegård, A., 135, 283
Sörbom, D., 101
Spear, L.C., 293
Spearing, D., 257
Spelling, B., 6, 335, 345
Spring, C., 130, 135
Stanovich, K.E., 35, 36, 63, 81, 82, 129, 131, 132, 137, 141, 142, 165, 294, 303, 308, 309, 335
Staphorsius, G., 53, 324
Stein, N.L., 184
Sternberg, R.J., 293
Stevenson, H.W., 38
Sticht, T.G., 132, 133
Stødkilde-Jørgensen, H., 135
Stone, G.O., 317
Stormont-Spurgin, M., 307
Strauss, A., 350
Stuart, M., 34
Stubbs, M., 216
Stuebing, K.K., 131, 303
Sudweeks, R.S., 308
Sulzby, E., 211, 213
Szeszulski, P.A., 274

Tabossi, P., 16
Tallal, P., 76
Tamaoka, K., 16
Tan, L.H., 16, 22, 23, 31, 37

Teale, W.H., 211
Thelen, E., 316
Tønnesen, F.E., 130, 131
Torgesen, J.K., 34, 49, 51, 147, 225, 241, 301, 322
Tornéus, M., 65, 81, 225, 279
Tousman, S., 258
Treiman, R., 6, 34, 258, 307, 322
Tunmer, W.E., 5, 29, 65, 81, 95, 132, 190
Turner, M., 130
Turvey, M.T., 25
Tyler, A., 277
Tzeng, O.J.L., 24

Uhry, J.K., 321

Valdez-Menchacha, M., 5
Van Alphen de Veer, R.J., 52, 99
Van Bergen, J.B.A., 100
Van Bon, W.H.J., 99, 257-276, 331-334
Van Daal, V.H.P., 6, 258, 301, 308, 323, 336
Van de Guchte, C., 84, 99
Van den Bos, K.P., 99, 262
Van den Bosch, K., 257, 258, 260, 262, 274, 332
Van den Broek, P., 354
Van der Leij, A., 49-62, 258, 293-305, 323, 336
Van der Schoot, F.C.J., 99
Van Dijk, T., 353, 358
Van Doorn-van Eijsden, M., 307, 315
Van Leerdam, M., 307-320
Van Orden, G.C., 25, 137, 307-320
Vauras, M., 335-348
Vellutino, F.R., 29, 49, 63, 257, 293
Venezky, R.L., 35
Verhoeven, L., 3-12, 52, 54, 84, 86, 99, 193-208, 263, 318, 361
Vermeer, A., 52, 84, 99
Visé, M., 225, 230, 242
Voeten, M.J.M., 54, 99, 295, 298
Vygotsky, L.S., 211, 220

Wagner, R.K., 49, 51, 56, 58-60, 147, 225, 241
Wall, S., 63, 64
Waters, G., 321
Weatherston, S., 258
Weber, R., 193

Wechsler, D., 67, 165
Weekes, B.S., 16
Weinberger, J., 5
Wells, G., 4, 211, 358
Wentink, H., 257–276
Wesseling, R., 6, 81–94
West, R.F., 36, 142
Wharton-McDonald, R., 359
Wheeldon, L., 260
White, S., 278
White, T.G., 278
Whitehurst, G.J., 5, 222
Wilce, L.S., 259, 273, 335
Wilding, J., 163
Williams, J.P., 34
Willis, C.S., 53
Wilson, R.M., 335
Wimmer, H., 137, 143, 147–161, 165, 241, 244
Wise, B.W., 6, 36, 257, 258, 260, 293, 335, 336, 345, 346
Wolf, M., 148
Wydell, T.N., 16

Yap, R.L., 257, 259, 300, 302
Yopp, H.K., 83, 321
Yuill, N.M., 133, 143, 177, 184, 188, 190
Yule, W., 131
Yung, Y.F., 38

Zaal, J.N., 52
Zhang, C.F., 39
Zhang, S., 16, 17, 20–23, 31, 221
Zhang, W.T., 16
Zhang, Y., 33
Zhou, Y.G., 30

# SUBJECT INDEX

Acquisition of
 language, 27, 194, 206
 lexical representations, 32, 33
 orthographic representations, 35, 322
 morphological skills, 280
 vocabulary, 51, 219, 357
 writing/spelling, 129, 225–228, 237, 242, 253
 grapheme-phoneme correspondences, 81, 90, 173
 phoneme awareness, 81
 second language, 193–207
Adult literacy (problems), 81, 113–126, 129, 132–143, 189, 191, 258
Alliteration detection, 147, 149, 150, 153–157, 225, 229, 243, 247–249, 252
Alphabet, 15–41, 83, 85, 115, 125, 221, 223, 225, 241, 278, 293, 307, 321
Analysis of
 words into syllables, 245,
 words into phonetic segments, 60, 241, 243–245, 249, 251, 252
 words into letters, 308
 initial sound, 244
 word length, 244, 251
 stories, 134
 morphological, 278, 279, 288
 conversations, 222
 contrast between languages, 193, 195
 oral language proficiency, 207
 reading comprehension, 207
 think-aloud protocol data, 349, 350, 352, 353, 361
 *see also* Phonological analysis
Anaphora, 54, 67, 185, 194
Attention (deficit), 136, 159, 230, 303, 350, 353
 visual attention, 215, 228, 232, 233,
At risk for problems, 61, 64, 69, 76, 98, 159, 227–229, 232–238
Articulation, 64, 68–69
Articulation rate, 148, 150, 153–157, 243, 247, 248, 251, 252,
Auditory processing, 114–116

Auditory-visual matching, 303
Auditory feedback, 336
Automaticity, 36, 124, 143, 159, 177, 194, 207, 257, 293, 302,
Automatic phonology, 24, 33, 151
Autonomous lexicon, 33, 36
Awareness
 linguistic, 64, 65, 68, 71, 75, 76, 113, 211, 212, 222
 morphological, 67, 142, 211, 219, 277–289
 syntactic, 67, 68, 142, 219
 grammatical, 280
 semantic, 68, 190
 pragmatic, 211, 219, 221
 *see also* Phonological awareness

Background knowledge, 180, 189, 194
Background of literacy problems, 51, 66, 67, 77, 84, 129, 193, 293, 357
Blending (of phonemes), 58, 82–92, 158, 160, 229, 230, 234, 235, 321
Bottom-up processing, 194, 207, 293, 296
Brain / neural correlates, 66, 114, 125, 131, 135, 141

Causal relationships, 49, 60, 63, 81, 105, 165, 174, 181, 183, 191, 197, 198, 204, 241, 279, 280, *see also* Reciprocal causation
Chinese characters, 30, 278
Cloze
 texts, 66, 67, 196
 oral cloze, 67, 70, 71
 grammatical closure, 67–71, 73, 74
Coherence inference, 182, 183, 196, 198
Cognitive
 abilities, 61, 69, 75, 96, 126, 152, 166, 253, 281, 293–304, 356
 (dys)function, 63, 64, 76, 129, 173, 222, 293–304, 335
 development, 82, 164, 212
 systems/model, 27, 35, 114, 316
 factors/determinants, 51, 77, 353
 processes, 114, 232

371

# SUBJECT INDEX

Comprehension,
  difficulties, 143, 177, 179–191
  jokes, 75
  monitoring, 178, 187–189, 349, 353, 358, 359
  oral language, 63–78, 95, 97, 142, 194–207, 242
  sentences, 21, 63, 114–116, 177
  syntax, 63, 67, 70, 71
  text, 59, 74, 177–191, 351–355, 358, 360
  see also reading comprehension
Computer-based instruction, 257-273, 301, 308, 321–333, 335–346, 349
Connectionist models, 316
Consonant (clusters), 27, 116, 125, 150–153, 196, 231, 245, 258, 271, 301, 322, 324–332
Context, 19-23, 29, 34, 35, 40, 124, 125, 165, 179, 220, 254, 272, 284, 295, 296, 335, 349, 356, 359, 361
Cross-linguistic, 38, 238

Decoding, 22, 27, 32, 35, 40, 74, 130, 131, 137, 139, 143, 280, 285, 288, 294-304, 311, 321, 335–338, 346, 347, 356
Decoding skills, ability, speed, 49–61, 95–108, 131, 137, 143, 165, 173, 193–207, 252, 257–275, 288, 293–304, 322, 327, 332, 343, 350, 355
  acquisition, 49, 51, 60, 61, 131, 293
  errors in oral reading, 34, 122, 152–155, 158, 159, 163, 263, 278, 285, 312, 328–331, 333, 337
Deficits
  decoding, 257, 293, 302, 335
  comprehension, 181
  oral language, 65, 76, 113
  reading, 163–165, 169, 172, 174
  sensory, 66, 125, 131, 141
  verbal, 63, 65, 71
  working memory, 189–191
  see also Phonological deficit
Decontextualized language, 21, 29, 64–68, 71–76, 136, 358
Difficulties in
  blending, 160, 238
  comprehension, 8, 137, 177–191, 338, 356
  decoding, 130–143, 274, 337, 338
  discriminating speech sounds, 4, 85

  inference, 180
  learning, 133
  learning to read, 129, 137–143, 159, 237
  listening, 134, 137
  morphological forms, 148, 285–287
  naming, 159
  phonological processing, 130, 131, 159, 233, 238
  reading, 63, 69, 73–76, 131–143, 147, 149, 160, 173, 293
  reading nonwords, 159
  repeating nonwords, 148
  segmentation, 160, 238
  working memory, 133, 188–190,
Discourse, 96, 134, 165, 194, 353, 358
Discrepancy definitions, 63, 129–143, 300
Dual route hypothesis/model, 3, 15, 316, 321
Dyslexia, 76, 280
  definition of, 63, 129–143, 293–298
  subtypes, 163–175

Elaborative inference, 182
Emotional factors (disturbances), 64, 67, 77, 227, 232, 335, 342, 359
Encoding, 27, 173, 289, 321, 322, 327, 331
Errors in
  semantic matching, 23
  inference, 183
  comprehension, 187
  syntactic, 337
  listening, 113
  naming, 228, 327
  letter discrimination, 117–120
  letter-sound, 121, 125, 336
  repeating sentences, 122, 123, 125
  repeating pseudowords, 150, 153
  voice-key recording, 265–270
Ethnic minority, 205–206
Experience with print, 21, 35–37, 81–83, 93, 125, 134, 142, 174–175, 181, 186, 211, 279, 322, 332, 352, 355–359

Garden variety poor readers, 134, 294–304
Gender differences, 114–126, 311
Genetic aetiology of dyslexia, 4, 130, 131, 293

## SUBJECT INDEX

Grapheme-to-phoneme
  correspondences, 16, 25, 81, 83, 93, 148, 158, 165, 173, 225, 231, 238, 257, 258, 272, 284, 309, 310, 317, 321-325, 336
Grapheme knowledge, 82, 151, 152, 231, 245, 250, 251, 310-315, 322-325
Grammar / grammatical
  anomalous, 116
  class, 277, 282
  closure, 67, 69-71, 73, 74
  form, 18
  knowledge, 75
  morpheme, 150
  structure, 197

Identification of
  letters, 87, 237, 238
  the main idea, 178,
  morphemes, 283, 288
  phonemes, 229, 249, 283
  rhyme, 230, 245,
  first sound, 236, 251
  end sound, 244, 251
Impairments, 135, 156, 163, 174, 293
Individual differences, 50-69, 84-92, 95, 101-108, 131, 138, 147, 153-159, 168, 178-180, 190, 279, 307, 315, 316, 343, 349, 359
Individual growth curves, 304, 343
Inductive reasoning, 241-254
Inference skills, 177-183, 189-191, 194, 351, 353-355
Intelligence, see Cognitive abilities; IQ
Interactive bookreading, 207, 211-222
Interference
  mother tongue, 193
  phonological, 23
  semantic, 23
  span, 53-55, 57
Intervention, 142, 225-238, 241-254, 296-304, 335-346
Irregular words, 32, 42, 66, 163-175, 278
IQ, 50, 66-76, 129-132, 137, 141, 152-156, 165, 190, 244, 281, 293-298, 342, see also Nonverbal intelligence

Language ability, 31, 81, 97, 113-126, 132, 242, 298, 316, 357, 360

Language experience, 279
Learning disabled, 295, 358
Letter knowledge, 49, 51- 53, 56-59, 81, 90-93, 149, 151, 153-155, 225-238, 242, 243, 247, 248, 251
Lexical access, 17-24, 163, 165, 193, 242, 321
  prelexical, 24
  sublexical, 170
Lexical decision, 21, 24, 264-271
Lexical knowledge, 17-24, 96, 120, 124, 173, 194-207, 323-332
Lexical representation, 28-39, 323, 333
Lexicon
  orthographic, 17, 33-36, 173, 257, 278, 322
  phonological, 37, 228
  semantic, 228, 243
Listening
  comprehension, 95-108, 129, 132-139, 141, 177, 194-207, 338, 341-343
  skills, 95-108, 129-143, 177, 197-199, 203, 212, 221, 222, 230, 245, 296, 337, 338, 341-343, 349, 357, 359
Literacy
  acquisition, 81, 124, 147-160, 212, 225, 227, 232, 237, 241, 253, 349, 354
  instruction, 37-41, 51, 64, 77, 81-93, 113, 129, 141, 148-151, 158, 173, 194, 226, 241, 260, 280, 307-318, 336, 349, 356-360
Linguistic knowledge, 28, 42, 63-77, 137, 166, 193-197, 207, 211, 258, 287, 341
Logographic, 27-30
Longitudinal studies, 49-60, 63, 76, 82, 95-108, 134, 143, 147-160, 165, 191, 193-206, 223, 225-238, 241-254, 279, 298-304, 335-346

Matched control groups, 136, 163, 164, 170-175, 179, 186, 257, 259-261, 280, 295, 298, 300, 327, 338, 345
Memory
  phonological, 31, 242-253,
  semantic, 19, 177
  visual, 67, 70
  see also Working memory

# SUBJECT INDEX

Metacognitive skills, 191, 337, 345, 346, 352
Morphology, 18, 27–41, 148, 150, 152
Morphological knowledge, 193–208
see also morphological awareness
Motor skills, 66, 131, 149, 308, 310,

Naming, 20, 22–24, 58–60, 85, 86, 115, 116, 121–125, 152, 159, 214, 259–274, 309, 312, 326–333
Naming speed, 148, 151–158, 243, 332, 333, see also Rapid naming
Nonverbal intelligence, 50–57, 67–69, 152–155, 243–254
Nonword, 15, 34, 53–55, 66, 69, 70, 73–75, 115, 120, 121, 159, 244, 284, see also Pseudoword
Nonword repetition, 53–57, 148–158, 303
Nursery rhymes, 230

Onset (-rime), 148, 158, 211, 258, 259, 264
Oral language, 63–76, 194–207, 245, 278, 280–283, 289, see, also Spoken language
Oral spelling, 309–319
Orthographic depth
transparency, complexity, 16, 24, 32, 83, 125, 158, 173, 196, 257, 258, 272, 278, 310, 321
Orthographic forms, 15–42, 122, 152, 258–271, 282, 324–333
Orthographic knowledge, 15-42, 173, 278, 287, 300, 308–317, 322
Orthography, see Writing systems

Parallel distributed processing, 15, 25, 316
Phoneme deletion, 81–93, 229–236, 243–251
Phonics teaching, 66, 148, 158, 260, 310, 336, 357
Phonological analysis, see Phonological segmentation
Phonological awareness, 29, 33–39, 51–60, 63–69, 71–76, 81–93, 113, 142–148, 153–159, 211, 218, 225–238, 241–254, 285, 294, 356, 360
Phonological deficit, 63, 65, 71, 77, 159, 174, 287, 294, 299–303
Phonological segmentation, 33, 51, 58, 60, 67, 82–92, 113, 157–160, 226, 228–236, 241, 245, 281, 321, 322
Plural formation task, 148–157
Plurals, knowledge of, 197
Precursors, see Predictors
Prerequisite skills, 29, 33, 81, 219
Predictors of
literacy development, 49–61, 81, 92, 97–108, 153–159, 190, 279, 357
reading problems, 63–77, 140, 142, 303
Print exposure, see Experience
Pseudoword, 96, 148, 150–158, 167–172, 193, 228, 233, 243, 257–274, 300–302, 308, 321, 332 see also Nonword

Rapid naming, 53, 56, 59, 159, 228, 233, 243, 247, 248,
Reading acquisition, 29, 32, 36, 49–51, 56, 59, 83, 93, 129, 131, 193, 225, 226, 228, 237, 242, 253, 350, 357
Reading comprehension, 15, 26, 40, 41, 49–59, 95–108, 140, 141, 165–175, 193–208, 279, 280, 283, 285–288, 293, 294, 335, 337–346, 350
Reading disabled, 36, 131, 163, 296–298, 335, 345
Reading instruction, 29, 37–41, 51, 77, 81–84, 91, 93, 98, 113, 149, 151, 158, 159, 173, 195, 226, 260, 280, 336, 356–358
Reciprocal causation, 29, 34, 60, 82, 92, see also Causal relationships
Reciprocal teaching, 358, 359
Remediation, 130, 131, 134, 142, 281, 294, 301, 302, 337
Repetition, see Non-word repetition
Resource limitations, 33, 92, 173, 191, 359
Rhyming, 53–56, 64, 83–92, 147–159, 211, 225–230, 233–238, 243–253
Rime, see Onset

Schooling, 29, 37–40, 65, 82, 91, 113–126, 356, 357
Screening, 227–229, 232, 233, 238
Second / foreign language, 19, 193–207
Self-teaching, 35
Semantic aspects of spelling, 16–40
Semantic familiarity, 311
Semantic information, 21–37, 64–77,

114, 138, 150, 228, 277, 295
Semantic interference, 22–23, 116
Semantic priming, 23
Semantic processing, 23, 31, 37, 41, 64–77, 116, 282
Semantic transparency, 277–289
Sentence reading, 21, 66–74, 96, 99, 107, 108, 114–116, 122, 132–136, 165, 166, 177, 178, 185–188, 193–196, 288, 339
Sentence repetition, 122–126, 181, 197–204, 214
Sentence writing, 245, 337, 340
Serial naming, 58, 59
Sound categorization, 53–57, 60, 225–237, 243
Speech feedback, 301, 326, 335–345
Speech rate, see Articulation rate
Segmentation
  in phonemes, 33, 82–92, 113, 157, 158, 226, 229, 235, 241, 321
  in syllables, 228, 230, 241, 245, 281
Short-term memory, see Word span; Working memory
Sight vocabulary, 40, 174
Spelling difficulties, 147, 149, 237, 311, 338, 340
Spelling errors, 152–155, 158, 278, 284, 286, 309, 312–317, 326–331, 336, 337, 341
Spoken language, 27, 42, 63–77, 81, 135, 141, 211, 245, 279, 281–288
Stages of literacy development, 32–35, 194, 361
Storybooks, 211–222
Structural equation modeling, 54–61, 86–89, 97–106, 197–206
Syllables, 27, 39, 150, 166, 211, 225–238, 241, 258–274, 336, 339
Syntactic knowledge, 63–77, 116, 133, 136, 177, 194–207, 335, 337, 354
Synthesis of phonemes, see Blending

Teaching, see Reading instruction; Training; Remediation
Text comprehension, 74, 108, 133–134, 177–191, 194–207, 339, 341, 349–360
Text reading, 67–74, 132–134, 215, 288, 296, 335
Text structure, 134, 196, 288, 354
Think-aloud protocol, 349–353, 361

Top-down processing, 194, 207, 294–296, 302
Training of
  phonological awareness, 33, 34, 63, 82, 225–238, 241–254
  awareness to make inferences, 190
  morphological awareness, 277–289
  decoding skills, 294–304, 321–333, 335–346
  spelling skills, 307–318, 321–333, 335–346
  reading comprehension, 335–346
  with flash cards, 257–275

Verbal deficit, 63, 65, 71, 113,
Visual attention test, 228–233
Visual dictation training 310–317
Visual perception test, 244
Visual impairments / deficit, 125
Visual discrimination, 149
Visual memory, 67, 70, 308
Visual form of words 16, 18, 29, 42, 193, 221, 298
Visual similarity, 18, 20, 22, 152
Visual-semantic process, 31, 41
Vocabulary
  development of, 56–59, 70–73, 221, 278, 357
  knowledge of, 49–59, 69–74, 86–90, 97, 132–136, 179, 190, 193–207, 244–248, 251–253, 352, 357
  receptive, 52–57, 63–67, 84, 137–142, 196–202, 283–287, 298, 349
  productive, 52–57, 64, 142, 196–203
Vowels, 21, 27, 39, 99, 150, 151, 153, 158, 196, 228, 231, 244, 245, 258, 301, 309, 324, 325
Vowel substitution task, 147, 244, 250–252

Whole language, 66
Whole word, 23, 32, 33, 83, 85, 278, 288, 309–310, 315–317, 322
Word recognition, 17, 58, 85–87, 95, 96, 107, 113, 114, 124, 148–159, 164–175, 177, 179, 190, 194–196, 295, 300, 336–346, 352, 356, 358
Word identification, 15–42, 95, 113, 158, 164, 166, 193, 221, 258, 259, 299, 337, 352
Word frequency, 22, 35, 166, 193, 264–270, 295, 300–302, 324, 344

Word-specific orthography, 35, 173, 322, 323
Word span, 53, 243
Working memory, 19, 51–59, 107, 108, 133–137, 159, 177, 179, 187–191, 193, 228, 241, 246, 288, 303

Writing
  development of skills, 5, 26,
  of texts, 338, 341
  instruction, 37
Writing systems
  alphabetic, 15, 16, 22, 24, 27- 29, 41
  Chinese, 22–40
  Danish, 253, 278
  Dutch, 15, 83–85, 93, 194, 207, 258, 324, 325
  English, 15, 22–40, 83, 165, 258, 278
  Finnish, 221, 336
  French, 15, 28, 165, 173
  German, 16, 24, 147–160, 165, 227, 231, 237, 241, 253
  logographic, 27
  Pin Yin, 38-39
  Portugese, 115–125

# NEUROPSYCHOLOGY AND COGNITION

The purpose of the Neuropsychology and Cognition series is to bring out volumes that promote understanding in topics relating brain and behavior. It is intended for use by both clinicians and research scientists in the fields of neuropsychology, cognitive psychology, psycholinguistics, speech and hearing, as well as education. Examples of topics to be covered in the series would relate to memory, language acquisition and breakdown, reading, attention, developing and aging brain. By addressing the theoretical, empirical, and applied aspects of brain-behavior relationships, this series will try to present the information in the fields of neuropsychology and cognition in a coherent manner.

1. P.G. Aaron: *Dyslexia and Hyperlexia.* 1989
   ISBN 1-55608-079-4; 1994, Pb 0-7923-3155-9
2. R.M. Joshi (ed.): *Written Language Disorders.* 1991     ISBN 0-7923-0902-2
3. A. Caramazza: *Issues in Reading, Writing and Speaking.* A Neuropsychological Perspective. 1991     ISBN 0-7923-0996-0
4. B.F. Pennington (ed.): *Reading Disabilities.* Genetic and Neurological Influences. 1991     ISBN 0-7923-1606-1
5. N.H. Hadley: *Elective Mutism.* A Handbook for Educators, Counsellors and Health Care Professionals. 1994     ISBN 0-7923-2418-8
6. W.C. Watt (ed.): *Writing Systems and Cognition.* Perspectives from Psychology, Physiology, Linguistics, and Semiotics. 1994     ISBN 0-7923-2592-3
7. I. Taylor and D.R. Olson (eds.), *Scripts and Literacy.* Reading and Learning to Read Alphabets, Syllabaries and Characters. 1994     ISBN 0-7923-2912-0
8. V.W. Berninger (ed.): *The Varieties of Orthographic Knowledge.* I: Theoretical and Developmental Issues. 1994     ISBN 0-7923-3080-3
9. C.K. Leong and R.M. Joshi (eds.): *Developmental and Acquired Dyslexia.* Neuropsychological and Neurolinguistic Perspectives. 1995
   ISBN 0-7923-3166-4
10. N. Gregg: *Written Expression Disorders.* 1995     ISBN 0-7923-3355-1
11. V.W. Berninger (ed.): *The Varieties of Orthographic Knowledge.* II: Relationships to Phonology, Reading, and Writing. 1995     ISBN 0-7923-3641-0
    Set (Vols 8 + 11) ISBN 0-7923-3081-1
12. Y. Lebrun (ed.): *From the Brain to the Mouth.* Acquired Dysarthria and Dysfluency in Adults. 1997     ISBN 0-7923-4427-8
13. J. Rispens, T.A. van Yperen and W. Yule (eds.), *Perspectives on the Classification of Specific Developmental Disorders.* 1998
    ISBN 0-7923-4871-0
14. C.K. Leong and K. Tamaoka (eds.), *Cognitive Processing of the Chinese and the Japanese Languages.* 1998     ISBN 0-7923-5479-6
15. P. Reitsma and L. Verhoeven (eds.), *Problems and Interventions in Literacy Development.* 1998     ISBN 0-7923-5557-1

KLUWER ACADEMIC PUBLISHERS – DORDRECHT / BOSTON / LONDON